Women's Health:
Contemporary Advances and Trends

Third Edition

WESTERN®
SCHOOLS

By
Shelton M. Hisley, PhD, RNC, WHNP-BC

24 contact hours will be awarded upon successful completion of this course.
Western Schools is accredited as a provider of continuing nursing education by the
American Nurses Credentialing Center's Commission on Accreditation.

P.O. Box 1930
Brockton, MA 02303
1-800-438-8888

ABOUT THE AUTHOR

Shelton M. Hisley, PhD, RNC, WHNP-BC, Assistant Professor of Nursing and Graduate Clinical Coordinator at the University of North Carolina at Wilmington (retired), is a women's health care nurse practitioner with 35 years of experience in the specialty of women's health. A 1999 American Nurses Foundation Scholar, she has conducted and published nursing research, served on national committees within her specialty, and presently serves on the editorial board for an international women's health nursing journal. Shelton maintains a clinical practice in a women's health clinic at a rural county health department.

> **Shelton Hisley** has disclosed that she has no significant financial or other conflicts of interest pertaining to this course book.

ABOUT THE SUBJECT MATTER REVIEWERS

Rosemary Theroux, RNC, PhD, WHNP, is an associate professor in the Graduate School of Nursing at the University of Massachusetts Worcester. She is a certified women's health nurse practitioner and has practiced in a variety of settings for over 20 years. She has conducted and published research in the area of women's self-care decision-making. She is a reviewer for several nursing journals, including *Nursing for Women's Health,* and serves on the Research Committee for the Association of Women's Health, Obstetric, and Neonatal Nurses. She currently maintains a private collaborative practice in a women's health setting and volunteers at a clinic for the uninsured.

> **Rosemary Theroux** has disclosed that she has no significant financial or other conflicts of interest pertaining to this course book.

Susan Kelly-Weeder, PhD, APRN, BC, FNP, is Assistant Professor of Family and Community Health at Boston College William F. Connell School of Nursing. She is a certified family nurse practitioner who has practiced in a wide variety of clinical venues over the last 15 years. She has had a long-standing interest in the care of infertile women and the prevention of infertility. Her current clinical and research interests are related to reducing risk behaviors in women. She also maintains a clinical practice at the Boston College Primary Health Care Center.

> **Susan Kelly-Weeder** has disclosed that she has no significant financial or other conflicts of interest pertaining to this course book.

Nurse Planner: Amy Bernard, MS, BSN, RN-BC

Copy Editor: Jaime Stockslager Buss, MSPH, ELS

Indexer: Sylvia Coates

Western Schools' courses are designed to provide nursing professionals with the educational information they need to enhance their career development. The information provided within these course materials is the result of research and consultation with prominent nursing and medical authorities and is, to the best of our knowledge, current and accurate. However, the courses and course materials are provided with the understanding that Western Schools is not engaged in offering legal, nursing, medical, or other professional advice.

Western Schools' courses and course materials are not meant to act as a substitute for seeking out professional advice or conducting individual research. When the information provided in the courses and course materials is applied to individual circumstances, all recommendations must be considered in light of the uniqueness pertaining to each situation.

Western Schools' course materials are intended solely for *your* use and *not* for the benefit of providing advice or recommendations to third parties. Western Schools devoids itself of any responsibility for adverse consequences resulting from the failure to seek nursing, medical, or other professional advice. Western Schools further devoids itself of any responsibility for updating or revising any programs or publications presented, published, distributed, or sponsored by Western Schools unless otherwise agreed to as part of an individual purchase contract.

Products (including brand names) mentioned or pictured in Western School's courses are not endorsed by Western Schools, the American Nurses Credentialing Center (ANCC) or any state board.

ISBN: 978-1-57801-257-2

COURSE INSTRUCTIONS
IMPORTANT: Read these instructions *BEFORE* proceeding!

COMPLETING THE FINAL EXAMINATION

Enclosed with your course book you will find a FasTrax® answer sheet. Use this answer sheet to respond to all the final exam questions that appear in this course. If the course has less than 100 questions, leave any remaining answer circles on the FasTrax answer sheet blank.

Be sure to fill in circles completely using **blue or black ink.** The FasTrax grading system will not read pencil. If you make an error, you may use correction fluid (such as White Out) to correct it.

FasTrax answer sheets are preprinted with your name and address and the course title. If you are completing more than one course, be sure to record your answers on the correct corresponding answer sheet.

A PASSING SCORE

The final exam is a multiple choice exam. You must score 70% or better in order to pass this course and receive a certificate of completion. Should you fail to achieve the required score, an additional FasTrax answer sheet will be sent to you so that you may make a second attempt to pass the course. You will be allowed three chances to pass the same course without incurring additional charges. After three failed attempts, your file will be closed.

RECORDING YOUR HOURS

Use the Study Time Log provided in this course book to monitor and record the time it takes to complete this course. Upon completion, tally your total time spent and use this information to respond to the final question of the course evaluation.

COURSE EVALUATIONS

The Course Evaluation provided in this course book is a critical component of the course and must be completed and submitted with your final exam. Responses to evaluation statements should be recorded in the lower right hand corner of the FasTrax answer sheet, in the section marked "Evaluation." Evaluations provide Western Schools with vital feedback regarding courses. Your feedback is important to us; please take a few minutes to complete the evaluation.

To provide additional feedback regarding this course, Western Schools services, or to suggest new course topics, use the space provided on the Important Information form found on the back of the FasTrax instruction sheet included with your course. Return the completed form to Western Schools with your final exam.

SUBMITTING THE COMPLETED FINAL EXAM

For your convenience, Western Schools provides a number of exam grading options. Full instructions and complete grading details are listed on the FasTrax instruction sheet provided with this course. If you are mailing your answer sheet(s) to Western Schools, we recommend you make a copy as a back-up.

EXTENSIONS

You have two (2) years from the date of purchase to complete this course. If you are not able to complete the course within 2 years, a six (6) month extension may be purchased. If you have not completed the course within 30 months from the original enrollment date, your file will be closed and no certificate will be issued.

CHANGE OF ADDRESS?

In the event that your address changes prior to completing this course, please call our customer service department at 1-800-618-1670, so that we may update your file.

WESTERN SCHOOLS GUARANTEES YOUR SATISFACTION

If any continuing education course fails to meet your expectations, or if you are not satisfied for any reason, you may return the course materials for an exchange or a refund (less shipping and handling) within 30 days. Software, video, and audio courses must be returned unopened. Textbooks must not be written in or marked up in any other way.

Thank you for using Western Schools to fulfill your continuing education needs!

WESTERN SCHOOLS
P.O. Box 1930
Brockton, MA 02303
(800) 438-8888
www.westernschools.com

WESTERN SCHOOLS
STUDY TIME LOG

WOMEN'S HEALTH:
CONTEMPORARY ADVANCES AND TRENDS

INSTRUCTIONS: Use this log sheet to document the amount of time you spend completing this course. Include the time it takes you to read the instructions, read the course book, take the final examination, and complete the evaluation.

	Time Spent	
Date	**Hours**	**Minutes**
_____	_____	_____
_____	_____	_____
_____	_____	_____
_____	_____	_____
_____	_____	_____
_____	_____	_____
_____	_____	_____
_____	_____	_____
_____	_____	_____
_____	_____	_____
_____	_____	_____
_____	_____	_____
_____	_____	_____
_____	_____	_____
_____	_____	_____

TOTAL*

Hours	Minutes

* Please use this total study time to answer the final question of the course evaluation.

WESTERN SCHOOLS
COURSE EVALUATION

WOMEN'S HEALTH: CONTEMPORARY ADVANCES AND TRENDS

INSTRUCTIONS: Using the scale below, please respond to the following evaluation statements. All responses should be recorded in the lower right-hand corner of the FasTrax answer sheet, in the section marked "Evaluation." Be sure to fill in each corresponding answer circle completely using blue or black ink. Leave any remaining answer circles blank.

A	B	C	D
Agree Strongly	Agree Somewhat	Disagree Somewhat	Disagree Strongly

OBJECTIVES: After completing this course, I am able to

1. Discuss the influence of trends and forces over time on women's health.
2. Discuss the basic events that occur during the menstrual cycle.
3. Describe normal sexual function.
4. Discuss the process of sexual maturation and various issues during the period of adolescence.
5. Discuss contraceptive methods and counseling.
6. Identify the processes involved in the evaluation and management of infertility.
7. Describe strategies for the prevention and management of the most common sexually transmitted infections.
8. Describe strategies for the management of premenstrual syndrome.
9. Identify major components of health maintenance and good preventive health care for women.
10. Discuss the implications of human papillomavirus and cervical Pap smear screening.
11. Recognize common gynecologic problems and treatments.
12. Describe strategies for promoting breast health.
13. Discuss the special health care needs of women as they enter the menopausal years and beyond.
14. Identify various complementary and alternative therapies to promote women's health across the life span.

COURSE CONTENT

15. The course materials were well-organized and clearly written.
16. The course expanded my knowledge and understanding of the subject matter.
17. This offering met my professional educational needs.
18. The final examination was well-written and at an appropriate level for the content of the course.

ATTESTATION

19. By submitting this answer sheet, I certify that I have read the course materials and personally completed the final examination based on the material presented. Mark "A" for Agree and "B" for Disagree.

continued on next page

COURSE HOURS

20. Please select the response that best reflects the total number of hours that it took to complete this course.

      A. More than 25 hours   C. 21–23 hours

      B. 23–25 hours   D. Fewer than 21 hours

Note: To provide additional feedback regarding this course, Western Schools services, or to suggest new course topics, use the space provided on the Important Information form found on the back of the FasTrax instruction sheet included with your course.

CONTENTS

FIGURES AND TABLES

PRETEST

1. Begin this course by taking the pretest. Circle the answers to the questions on this page, or write the answers on a separate sheet of paper. Do not log answers to the pretest questions on the FasTrax test sheet included with the course.

2. Compare your answers to the PRETEST KEY located in the back of the book. The pretest answer key indicates the course chapter where the content of that question is discussed. Make note of the questions you missed, so that you can focus on those areas as you complete the course.

3. Complete the course by reading each chapter and completing the exam questions at the end of the chapter. Answers to these exam questions should be logged on the FasTrax test sheet included with the course.

1. Infant mortality is higher in the United States than it is in

   a. 2 other developed countries.
   b. 5 other developed countries.
   c. 12 other developed countries.
   d. 21 other developed countries.

2. Estrogen is produced by the

   a. pituitary gland.
   b. hypothalamus.
   c. uterus.
   d. ovaries.

3. Fertile cervical mucus is produced in response to

   a. progesterone.
   b. follicle-stimulating hormone.
   c. estrogen.
   d. gonadotropin-releasing hormone.

4. Dyspareunia is the term for

   a. pain with urination.
   b. pain with intercourse.
   c. muscle spasms of the vaginal opening.
   d. painful menstruation.

5. In women, sexually transmitted infections (STIs)

   a. usually produce some symptoms.
   b. always produce symptoms.
   c. often produce no symptoms.
   d. usually result in vaginal discharge.

6. As a birth control method, the minipill is

   a. less effective than combination pills.
   b. as effective as combination pills.
   c. more effective than combination pills.
   d. the pill of choice for most women.

7. If pregnancy occurs with an intrauterine device in place, there is a high risk of

   a. perforation.
   b. dysmenorrhea.
   c. ectopic pregnancy.
   d. expulsion of the device.

8. Zygote intrafallopian transfer is a process that involves placing

   a. an unfertilized egg into the uterus.
   b. an unfertilized egg into the fallopian tube.
   c. a fertilized egg into the uterus.
   d. a fertilized egg into the fallopian tube.

9. The recording of measurements of basal body temperature can tell a woman

   a. whether ovulation has occurred.

   b. when ovulation will occur.

   c. whether implantation has occurred.

   d. whether she is fertile.

10. One of the most serious long-term consequences of untreated chlamydia infection is

    a. infertility.

    b. increased risk of miscarriage.

    c. chronic vaginal discharge.

    d. abnormal Pap smear findings.

11. Hepatitis B is

    a. an STI.

    b. not considered to be transmitted sexually.

    c. contracted by eating contaminated food.

    d. contracted only through shared needles during intravenous drug use.

12. A good nondairy source of calcium in the diet is

    a. brown rice.

    b. whole grain breads.

    c. tofu.

    d. citrus fruits.

13. An herb that is beneficial for premenstrual syndrome because it has an especially high mineral content is

    a. cramp bark.

    b. wild yam.

    c. nettle.

    d. black cohosh.

14. In addition to a pelvic examination, all women older than age 40 should have a

    a. complete blood cell count.

    b. rectal examination and stool test for blood.

    c. sigmoidoscopy.

    d. check for STIs.

15. The transformation zone of the cervix is the area in which the

    a. cells of the vaginal wall meet the cells of the cervix.

    b. columnar cells of the cervix meet the cells of the uterine lining inside the cervical canal.

    c. columnar cells of the cervix meet the cells of the vaginal wall.

    d. squamous cells of the cervix meet the columnar cervical cells.

16. Fibroids are

    a. precancerous growths of the uterus.

    b. benign growths of the uterus.

    c. misplaced endometrial tissue.

    d. growths that could lead to cancer if not treated.

17. Breast cancer is the second leading cause of cancer deaths in women, exceeded only by

    a. lung cancer.

    b. uterine cancer.

    c. colorectal cancer.

    d. ovarian cancer.

18. Most breast cancer occurs in women with

    a. known risk factors.

    b. no known risk factors, except being female and advancing age.

    c. a family history of breast cancer.

    d. early menarche and late menopause.

19. Menopausal women may experience vaginal dryness due to lack of

    a. estrogen.

    b. progesterone.

    c. testosterone.

    d. luteinizing hormone.

20. Guided imagery

    a. involves the use of equipment to measure physiologic responses.

    b. is considered to be a "quiet listening."

    c. can be used to enhance muscle training of specific muscle groups.

    d. is the purposeful development of mental images while deeply relaxed.

INTRODUCTION

The field of women's health is coming into its own. It is an exciting time for women and for nursing professionals who work with women. Links are forming worldwide, and with a more global perspective, it becomes clear that the health of women is integrally tied to the social, economic, political, and religious forces that shape cultures and societies. For women's health to improve, society must continue to change. Education is one of the keys to this change. With education, women become empowered to make better decisions about their health and the health of their families. Health care providers play an important role in this educational process.

Women's Health: Contemporary Advances and Trends (3rd ed.) is an introduction to the field of women's health for nurses who work with women. The course is intended to assist you in providing nursing care for women of all ages. It is designed for nurses who wish to review, enhance, or expand their knowledge base and level of understanding for women across the life span. Because the focus of this course is contemporary women's health issues, care during pregnancy is not included. Instead, this educational offering is intended to provide information that serves as either a comprehensive review of or an enhancement to your present knowledge base and to assist you in working with various female patient populations.

No doubt, you will find in your reading that there are more questions than answers in many aspects of women's health. This course is intended to expand your understanding of the current controversies and to enhance your ability to knowledgeably approach these issues. It is hoped that the material offered here will be instrumental in equipping you to educate your patients, support them in their decision-making concerning health matters, and assist them in feeling empowered as individuals, as mothers, as family members, and as valued members of our society. Equipped with accurate, up-to-date information, you will be better able to assist your patients as they become aware of health-related choices and make informed decisions.

You will find a "Key Words" section at the beginning of most chapters. These are words that are being introduced in the course, some of which may be unfamiliar. All of their definitions can be found in the glossary. Also, an extensive resource guide appears at the end of the course book to direct you to additional information and resources.

CHAPTER 1

WOMEN'S HEALTH TODAY

CHAPTER OBJECTIVE

After completing this chapter, the reader will be able to discuss the influence of trends and forces over time on women's health.

LEARNING OBJECTIVES

After studying this chapter, the reader will be able to

1. identify the reasons for major improvements in health in the past century.

2. discuss the shift in major causes of illness that has occurred in the United States during the past two decades.

3. identify new developments occurring in women's health care.

4. specify some of the current threats to women's health.

5. recognize ways nurses can provide effective, appropriate care to women in contemporary society.

INTRODUCTION

Women's lives and health are influenced by a multitude of external forces, societal expectations, and personal choices. Today's rapidly changing health care environment provides opportunities for change, growth, and empowerment. On a personal level, most women have the freedom to make choices about various aspects of their daily lives, such as eating habits, social outlets, exercise activities, and relaxation strategies. However, individuals are integrally connected to the many forces that impact society – including social, economic, cultural, religious, and political influences.

The most dramatic change in the last century in the United States, and to some degree worldwide, is that women's voices are finally being heard and heeded. Growing numbers of women are examining and speaking out about issues of universal importance. In contemporary society, women have assumed leadership positions in the political, cultural, religious, and economic arenas. Women of every ethnic group, socioeconomic level, and sexual preference are organizing and making inroads for change and improvement in their local communities and in the larger structure of society.

THE PAST

Examining historical events is sobering yet insightful; tracing women's personal, political, and social progress over the years heightens awareness of the major strides accomplished to date and serves as an important reminder for women to continue to work for change. It is difficult for women of today to recognize that fewer than 100 years have passed since women were granted the right to vote in America. Women's suffragette predecessors won

1

this privilege following a long and courageous struggle. In earlier, sadder times, thousands of women were accused of witchcraft and burned at the stake for practicing healing arts in their communities (Boston Women's Health Book Collective, 2005).

Since the 18th century, there has been a dramatic improvement in the health and life expectancy of Americans. This change is largely attributable to improvements in nutrition and economic status and also to broadscale advances in sanitation practices. Improvements in clean water supplies, sewage disposal, milk pasteurization, and other community sanitation measures have resulted in a dramatically reduced exposure to infectious diseases, historically the greatest causes of morbidity and mortality, especially among women and children (Cudé & Winfrey, 2007; Lowdermilk & Perry, 2007).

Interestingly, improvements in medical care at the time had relatively little impact on these trends. The first antibiotic, developed in the 1930s, was a pivotal discovery that ushered in the era of modern medicine. In the 1960s, the government initiated wide-reaching public health programs, such as Medicaid and Women, Infants, and Children (WIC) Program. The WIC Program was designed to provide essential food items to mothers and children in need. Both of these community health initiatives have resulted in significantly improved health care and nutrition for pregnant women and their children.

In the past three decades, a shift has been occurring in the overall trends of health and disease. Chronic cardiovascular disease and cancer constitute the major causes of morbidity and mortality for men and women. Among the young population, Acquired immune deficiency syndrome (AIDS) remains one of the greatest health threats. Management of these present-day health problems requires a diverse and multifaceted approach that combines modern medicine with consideration of broader issues, such as socioeconomic level, educational background, work conditions, personal environment, and ready access to health care – all

of which influence health-related behaviors and likelihood of recovery. Preventive services, health education, and strategies for health promotion must become universally available.

CURRENT STATUS OF THE HEALTH CARE SYSTEM

In the 21st century, our nation faces serious health issues in spite of all the progress that has been made. The number of uninsured individuals under 65 years of age has continued to climb. Although the proportion of the adult population with a specific source of primary care has increased overall, Hispanic and African-American adults, as well as other subgroups, are less likely to have primary health care providers (Ray, 2007; U.S. Department of Health and Human Services [USDHHS], 2000).

Over 46 million people lacked health insurance at last count in 2006, continuing a rising trend in the number of uninsured in this country. Although the lack of health insurance is clearly a major factor impeding access to care, having health insurance does not guarantee that health care will be accessible or affordable. Significant numbers of privately insured individuals lack a usual source of care or report delays or difficulties in obtaining needed care due to affordability or insurance problems (USDHHS, 2007).

Because of growing scientific evidence concerning the effectiveness of certain preventive services, 82% of employer-sponsored insurance plans now include childhood immunizations and 90% include Pap tests and mammograms. Nonetheless, major gaps still persist in coverage for effective preventive services, such as counseling (USDHHS, 2007).

Health care costs continue to escalate. There is a proliferation of costly technology, which offers great hope for a few, coupled with depleting funds for broad basic health care services for all. The Healthy People 2010 national initiative underscores the magnitude of the problem with the following facts:

- Expenditures for health care exceed $1 trillion per year and are expected to continue to rise.

- Americans spend more than twice as much per person for health care as do people in most other industrial countries.

- Infant mortality is higher in the United States than in 21 other developed countries.

- Ethnic minority groups and those of low income suffer the highest rates of infant mortality.

(USDHHS, 2000)

The population is growing older. In the year 2000, there were 35 million (12.4%) Americans age 65 and over. By the year 2040, this number is expected to more than double to 77.2 million. The aging population brings issues about how to keep individuals as healthy as possible and how to best provide health care services. Prevention, as a strategy for optimizing wellness, takes on added significance (Ruhl, 2006).

In addition, violence, substance abuse, human immunodeficiency virus (HIV) and AIDS, homelessness, and unintended pregnancy have reached epidemic proportions. Most experts agree that there is a need for a fundamental change and restructuring of the health care system. Today, a number of new health reform initiatives on both the state and federal levels are addressing these concerns. Further development and definition of exactly how these initiatives will be implemented continues to constitute a great challenge for the present decade.

PROGRESS IN WOMEN'S HEALTH

Over the past 20 years, unprecedented progress has taken place in the field of women's health in this country. A change in the social context of health care occurred during the 1990s and brought about an increased focus on women's health. In 1991, the Society for the Advancement of Women's Health Research was founded to address the pre-

vention of disease in and violence toward women, women's wellness, and women's access to health care. A year later, Congress authorized the Office of Research on Women's Health, and this action mandated that women routinely be included in health-related research studies. Also at this time, additional funding was allocated for studies related to osteoporosis and heart disease, two major health threats for women (Lowdermilk & Perry, 2007).

In the United States, researchers have long neglected women's health issues, and historically, many studies have routinely excluded women. Consequently, medication dosages and regimens for women with chronic diseases such as cardiovascular disorders are likely to be based on results of studies with men. To address these and other women's health issues, the Association of Women's Health, Obstetric, and Neonatal Nurses (AWHONN; www.awhonn.org) has conducted a number of research-based practice projects to develop evidence-based practice guidelines for such topics as cardiac health, midlife well-being, cyclic pelvic pain and discomfort management, and continence for women. Nurses, whose profession continues to rank high in the public's trust, are in a key position to design, conduct and direct research findings into the provision of safe, effective care for women, infants, and children (Clinical rounds, 2007).

The Women's Health Initiative (WHI), a large-scale investigation designed to study and clarify women's health issues, was initiated in 1997 with an enrollment of more than 16,000 women. The National Heart, Lung, and Blood Institute of the National Institutes of Health halted the study in 2002, when results indicated an increased risk of breast cancer and a lack of overall benefit for the relief of menopausal symptoms with the use of estrogen and progestin (Anderson et al., 2004). However, data continue to emerge from this investigation, and the findings have many far-reaching implications for women and their health care providers.

The Human Genome Project (HGP) is another landmark investigation that carries major implications for all people. Launched in this country in the late 1980s, the 13-year HGP was a major research initiative that produced the first draft of a map identifying the estimated 20,000 to 25,000 genes in human deoxyribonucleic acid (DNA). More than 3 billion sequences of human DNA base pairs were revealed. The base pairs are what are contained in the long, twisted chains that constitute the chemical building blocks for the DNA of the 24 human chromosomes. The DNA provides the detailed instructions about how to manage all the processes within the human body. In 2006, HGP scientists filled in gaps from the first draft and completed the DNA sequence for the last of the 24 human chromosomes. The information (available at http://www.genome.gov/11006929), which provides the basic set of inherited instructions for the development and functioning of every human being, offers an unprecedented understanding of health and disease, life and death.

HEALTHY PEOPLE 2000 AND 2010

A national initiative, Healthy People 2000 was released in 1990 with the purpose of identifying health improvement goals and objectives to be reached by the year 2000 (U.S. Public Health Service [USPHS], 1990). Its health promotion and disease prevention objectives involve government and private organizations. Three overarching goals were identified:

1. to increase the span of healthy life for all Americans

2. to reduce health disparities among Americans

3. to achieve access to preventive health care services for all Americans.

The Healthy People 2010 initiative examines progress made toward achieving the national goals set forth in the original document and presents a comprehensive, nationwide health promotion and disease prevention agenda. Viewed as a guide for improving the health of all people in the United States during the first decade of the 21st century, Healthy People 2010 is committed to a single, overarching purpose: promoting health and preventing illness, disability, and premature death. This national initiative is designed to achieve the following two broad goals:

1. to increase quality and years of healthy life

2. to eliminate health disparities.

These two goals are supported by 467 specific objectives to improve health, organized into 28 focus areas. Ten Leading Health Indicators (LHIs) represent a set of behavioral and systems elements intended to provide an overview of the current health status of Americans. The LHIs provide a baseline assessment of mortality, disability, and morbidity rates along with behavioral factors such as nutritional status, physical activity, and tobacco use. Each LHI contains goals believed to be achievable by the year 2010, provided that behavioral changes, access to health care, and community-based health interventions are implemented (USDHHS, 2000).

Because the Healthy People 2010 initiative offers gender-based objectives, it is possible to compare data for women separately from data for men. For several of the LHIs, such as tobacco, alcohol, and illicit drug use, women are closer to achieving the 2010 target than are men. In the coming years, women are encouraged to increase their physical activity and consumption of fruits and vegetables in an attempt to offset the increasing risk for weight problems among themselves and their children. The underlying premise of the Healthy People 2010 endeavor is that an individual's health is practically inseparable from the health of the larger community. Furthermore, the health of every community in every state and territory determines the overall health status of the nation. It is encouraging that states, communities, and national organizations have rallied behind the priorities, goals, and objectives set in the Healthy People 2010 initiative and have used it to guide their own health planning efforts (USDHHS, 2000).

One of the most valuable lessons learned from the Healthy People 2010 initiative is that dramatic progress can be made in improving the nation's health in a fairly short period of time. The achievements made during the first 10 years are impressive and include reductions in infant mortality; major increases in childhood vaccination rates; decreased numbers of teen parents; reduced alcohol, tobacco, and illicit drug use rates; fewer deaths from coronary artery disease and stroke; and major advances in the diagnosis and treatment of cancer (USDHHS, 2000).

However, other health problems continue to plague our nation. Diabetes and other chronic illnesses constitute a major obstacle to the public's health. Violence and abusive behavior continue to destroy homes in every segment of society. Mental disorders all too often go undiagnosed and untreated. Childhood and adult obesity have risen dramatically during the past two decades. Close to 40% of adults in this country engage in little or no leisure time physical activity. Smoking rates among adolescents have risen over the past 10 years, despite broadscale public awareness campaigns. Also, HIV and AIDS remain serious public health problems and now disproportionately affect women and communities of color (USDHHS, 2000). Other disturbing health disparities also persist in this country. For example, an African-American baby is more than twice as likely to have a low birth weight and two and one half times more likely to die during the first year of life than a European-American baby. The risk of sudden infant death syndrome is more than three times higher in Native American and Native Alaskan babies than in European-American babies. (Additional information about health disparities can be accessed at the Centers for Disease Control and Prevention website, http://www.cdc.gov/)

The national goal to eliminate health disparities stresses that health literacy is essential to help individuals navigate the health system and better manage their own health. Adult literacy is an important predictor of health behavior and touches all aspects of care, including prevention strategies and adherence to prescribed treatment modalities (Kendig, 2006; Wood, Kettinger, & Lessick, 2007). People with low health literacy are more likely to report poor health, have an incomplete understanding of their health problems, and experience increased hospitalizations (Weiss et al., 2005). In the clinical setting, nurses can promote health literacy in a number of ways, such as:

- serving as a patient advocate by enhancing the woman's autonomy and assisting her in voicing her values

- reinforcing risks and benefits of all treatments and procedures and ensuring that full understanding accompanies informed consent

- anticipating that the woman will not be able to "tell" what she cannot read

- using language that the woman can understand

- uusing pictures and stories to illustrate important points

- repeating instructions and precautions

- limiting the amount of information given

- confirming understanding of information by asking the woman to repeat the information in her own words

- demonstrating care, respect, and sensitivity for all women.

(Wood et al., 2007)

Building on the Healthy People 2000 national agenda, the 2010 initiative calls for greater delivery of services and improved outcomes for a wide range of women's health issues. In addition to maternal and child health, the new agenda underscores the need for other services of primary importance to women in areas such as family planning, complications from sexually transmitted diseases, osteoporosis screening and treatment, and reduction of domestic violence (USDHHS, 2000).

CONTEMPORARY CHALLENGES IN PROVIDING HEALTH CARE TO WOMEN

As health care providers, our strategies for promoting wellness in the populations we serve must be adaptable to meet current trends. Much of the general public still adheres to the age-old belief that good health depends primarily on medical intervention and that the requirement for health rests in the early discovery of disease. This long-held notion needs to be replaced by the recognition that disease itself often cannot be treated singularly by medical management; instead, one's state of health and prospect for recovery are greatly influenced by lifestyle choices and health-promoting behaviors.

Health education and ready access to preventive services are of major importance in promoting good health. Another key factor that shapes our physical and mental well-being is how we feel about ourselves. Self-esteem is an attribute deeply influenced by societal factors such as socioeconomic status, cultural influences concerning how women are viewed in our society, and family issues involving childrearing and early education. As health care providers, we must be sensitive to our patients' overall life situations, which no doubt affect their willingness and ability to carry out positive health-related activities.

As nurses in today's health care system, we face a number of profound challenges. We find ourselves fulfilling many roles: educator, skilled listener, care provider, advocate, and resource person, to name a few. For most, the opportunity to serve in these varied yet interrelated roles is what first attracted us to the profession of nursing. Yet we often find ourselves lacking time to accomplish our goals, as the myriad issues surrounding women's health are often complex and personal. In the contemporary women's health care setting, nurses increasingly care for individuals of diverse backgrounds. Thus, cultural competence is an essential component for providing sensitive, appropriate nursing care. Part of this process involves a thoughtful examination of personal feelings and beliefs. Only when we have acknowledged and dealt with our personal biases, prejudices, and attitudes can we honestly create a supportive, empowering environment for our patients as they consider and act on their choices (Cooper, Grywalski, Lamp, Newhouse, & Studlien, 2007).

CONCLUSION

It is evident that the study of women's health, perhaps more than any other health-related area, is all encompassing. As nurses, we are faced with issues that strike at the very root of what it means to be human, issues that stretch our hearts as well as our minds as we seek solutions. The health care of women is a global issue that challenges all of us.

EXAM QUESTIONS

CHAPTER 1
Questions 1-5

Note: Choose the option that BEST answers each question.

1. Historically, the most significant factor in improving the health of the American population was

   a. the development of birth control methods.

   b. the introduction of antibiotics.

   c. the improvement of sanitation measures.

   d. the WIC Program.

2. Today, the major causes of illness and death for American men and women are

   a. pulmonary infections and emphysema.

   b. cardiovascular disease and cancer.

   c. substance abuse and smoking.

   d. domestic abuse and violence.

3. An important change in clinical studies conducted today concerns the

   a. inclusion of women as participants.

   b. use of laboratory animals.

   c. exclusion of older adult participants.

   d. use of computers to collect all data.

4. A major health threat for women is

   a. arthritis.

   b. pancreatic disease.

   c. osteoporosis.

   d. blindness.

5. To provide appropriate, sensitive health care to women, it is important for the nurse to

   a. create an environment that is nonconducive to allowing privacy.

   b. impose personal beliefs on clients.

   c. assume many roles when addressing patients' needs.

   d. use stereotypes during counseling and education sessions.

CHAPTER 2

THE MENSTRUAL CYCLE

CHAPTER OBJECTIVE

After completing this chapter, the reader will be able to discuss the basic events that occur during the menstrual cycle.

LEARNING OBJECTIVES

After studying this chapter, the reader will be able to

1. describe the effects of reproductive hormones on the body.

2. describe a normal menstrual cycle pattern.

3. identify factors that cause disturbances in menstruation.

KEY WORDS

- Corpus luteum
- Endometrium
- Follicle-stimulating hormone (FSH)
- Human chorionic gonadotropin (hCG)
- Hypothalamus
- Leutinizing hormone (LH)
- Menarche
- Mittelschmerz
- Oocyte
- Ovarian follicle
- Pituitary gland

INTRODUCTION

Throughout the history of human civilization, the female menses has been viewed with awe, fear, and reverence. Laws, taboos, and beliefs about menstruation have been an inherent part of the social and religious structure of all societies. Whether viewed positively or negatively, it is evident that the menstrual cycle is a powerful aspect of women's lives, both personally and within the societies in which they live. In modern times in American culture, women sometimes lose touch with this aspect of personal awareness and inner knowledge and expect to function, think, and feel the same every day, regardless of cyclic fluctuations. An understanding of the menstrual cycle and the various hormonal influences that affect physical and mental functioning is useful in fostering an appreciation of the complexity of this monthly event.

A grasp of the fundamentals of the menstrual cycle will help nurses understand and educate patients about many women's health issues, including methods of contraception, premenstrual syndrome, infertility, and various gynecologic problems. The remainder of the course will build on this knowledge.

Note to the reader: Please be aware that this chapter contains much detail, which will serve as a review for some readers and provide new information for others. With a good foundation in the workings of the menstrual cycle, you will be well equipped to answer many of your patients' questions about women's health. For example, a woman might ask you, "Why do I spot at midcycle? Is this normal?" or "My libido is wild around midcycle and nonexistent before my period. Is this normal?" or "Why do I have this discharge? I'm not even sexually active! Do I have an infection?"

Hormones

The word *hormone* describes a group of chemicals that are quite diverse in both their makeup and their effects on the body. What hormones have in common is that they are produced by organs or tissues in the body, secreted internally, and then released into the bloodstream to travel to target organs. A target organ has receptor sites for particular hormones, employing a lock-and-key effect in which the hormone shape fits cozily into the receptor site. This relationship activates the effect of the hormone in the particular target organ.

Traditionally, major target organs have been identified for particular hormones. As research has progressed, however, receptor sites for the known major hormones have been found in unexpected places. For example, estrogen receptors have been found in the brain. Furthermore, study findings have shown that communication is not only two-way but multilevel, with multiple feedback loops connecting numbers of tissues and organs. There is a complex form of intelligence and communication constantly occurring within the body that most women are not aware of unless something goes wrong (Hatcher et al., 2008).

THE MENSTRUAL CYCLE

The menstrual cycle occurs as a coordinated communication among the hypothalamus, the pituitary gland, the ovaries, and the uterus (as shown in Figure 2-1). If any part of the system malfunctions, the normal cycle is interrupted. Because the menstrual cycle is a circle that has no beginning or end, it has become standard to view the first day of menses, or bleeding, as the first day of the cycle. Of course, menstruation is preceded by a series of events that lead to the shedding of the inner lining of the uterus. The endometrial lining has been building up during the previous cycle, in response first to estrogen and later to progesterone. When fertilization of the egg does not occur, the levels of these hormones decline. Without the stimulation and support of hormones, the lining breaks down and is shed as menstrual blood.

Normal Cycle

The term *menarche* denotes the first menstrual flow. Menstrual periods during the first year following menarche are usually irregular, unpredictable, and painless (Chapter 4 will provide more detailed information). Once established, the normal menstrual cycle has the following pattern and characteristics (Lowdermilk & Perry, 2007):

- average 28-day interval, with a normal range of 21 to 35 days
- average 4½ days of flow, with a range of 2 to 8 days
- average 35 ml of blood loss, with a range of 20 to 60 ml.

Please refer to the diagrams and illustrations in this chapter (Figures 2-1, 2-2, and 2-3) as you read the descriptions of the changing hormones and their effects.

Hypothalamus and Pituitary Gland

The hypothalamus, which lies at the base of the brain, performs a variety of important regulatory functions. It is a processing center that receives messages from outside the body by means of higher brain centers and information from inside the body by means of the bloodstream and the central nervous

FIGURE 2-1: MENSTRUAL CYCLE: HYPOTHALAMIC-PITUITARY, OVARIAN, AND ENDOMETRIAL

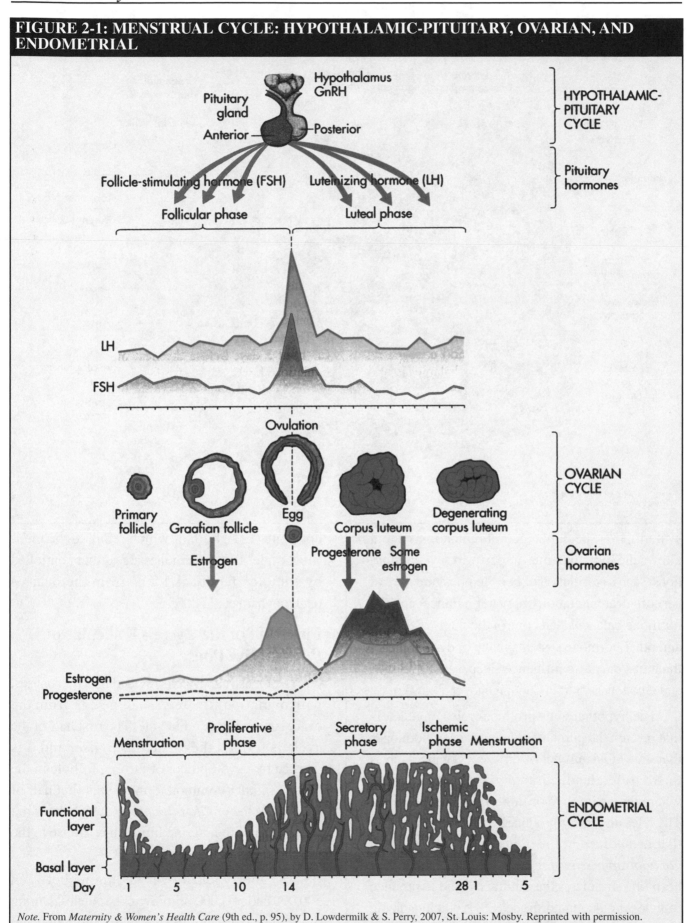

Note. From *Maternity & Women's Health Care* (9th ed., p. 95), by D. Lowdermilk & S. Perry, 2007, St. Louis: Mosby. Reprinted with permission.

FIGURE 2-2: MIDSAGITTAL VIEW OF FEMALE PELVIC ORGANS WITH WOMAN LYING SUPINE

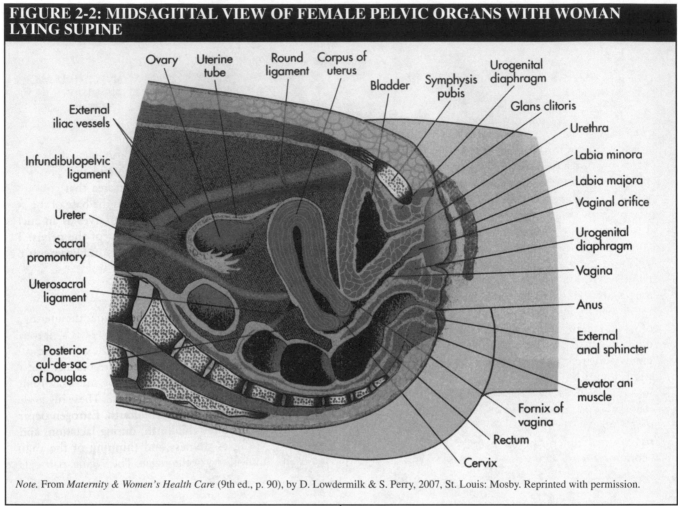

Note. From *Maternity & Women's Health Care* (9th ed., p. 90), by D. Lowdermilk & S. Perry, 2007, St. Louis: Mosby. Reprinted with permission.

system. This specialized communication system allows the hypothalamus to perform several functions, such as regulation of body temperature, fat and carbohydrate metabolism, water balance, and the hormone balances that control the menstrual cycle and other hormone systems in the body. The hypothalamus may also influence sleep, sexual activity, and emotional control (Cunningham et al., 2005).

The hypothalamus produces releasing factors that prompt the pituitary gland to release hormones that travel to a number of different organs, such as the thyroid gland, adrenal glands, and ovaries, where they stimulate or inhibit certain functions. The releasing factor produced by the hypothalamus that is involved in the menstrual cycle is called *gonadotropin-releasing hormone,* or Gn-RH. This hormone stimulates the pituitary gland to produce follicle-stimulating hormone (FSH) and luteinizing

hormone (LH), both of which regulate the menstrual cycle. These hormones are further controlled by complex feedback loops from the ovaries (Cunningham et al., 2005).

First Half of the Cycle – Follicular or Proliferative Phase

The menstrual cycle is divided into two phases, with ovulation (the release of an egg from the ovary) occurring at mid-cycle. The first half of the cycle is termed the *follicular phase,* and it is marked by development of the egg follicle in the ovary. Another common term for this first half of the cycle is the *proliferative phase,* which describes the growth of the uterine lining in response to the steroid hormone estrogen.

At puberty, each ovary contains between 300,000 and 500,000 primitive egg follicles. During the first few days of the cycle, while menstrual

FIGURE 2-3: REGULATION OF THE MENSTRUAL CYCLE

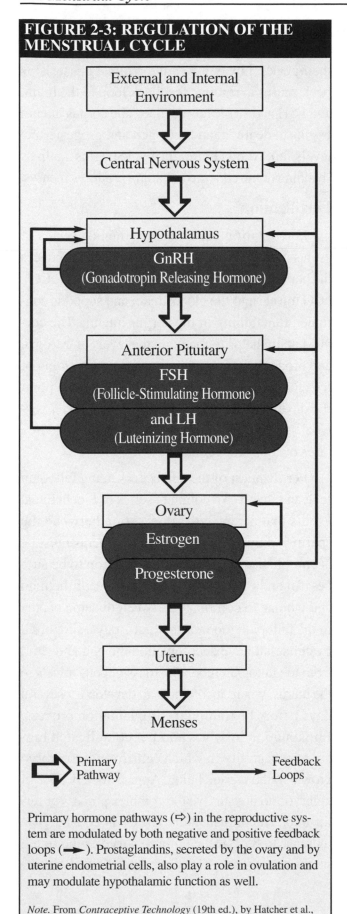

Primary hormone pathways (⇨) in the reproductive system are modulated by both negative and positive feedback loops (➝). Prostaglandins, secreted by the ovary and by uterine endometrial cells, also play a role in ovulation and may modulate hypothalamic function as well.

Note. From *Contraceptive Technology* (19th ed.), by Hatcher et al., 2008. New York: Ardent Media, Inc. Reprinted with permission.

bleeding is occurring, levels of estrogen and progesterone in the blood are very low. In response to these low hormone levels, the hypothalamus is triggered to produce Gn-RH, which acts directly on the anterior pituitary gland and stimulates the release of FSH. FSH travels via the bloodstream to the ovaries and is the primary hormone responsible for stimulating the development of egg follicles within the ovary. The follicle itself is a structure that contains both an egg, or oocyte, and supportive cells to produce estrogen and other hormones. During each menstrual cycle, approximately 1,000 eggs begin to develop, but usually only one becomes dominant (by mechanisms not fully understood) and goes on to be released during ovulation. The other follicles are eventually reabsorbed. As the remaining follicle grows, it produces increasing quantities of estrogen.

Estrogen has a stimulating effect on the lining of the uterus. The cells of the uterine lining multiply, and the lining thickens and produces glycogen, a form of sugar. The cervix also responds to the estrogen by producing a fertile cervical mucus, which is clear, slippery, and stretchy and thus conducive to the transport and survival of sperm.

Ovulation

As the follicle in the ovary continues to develop, it produces increasing levels of estrogen. Once estrogen enters the bloodstream and flows throughout the body, it reaches the brain, where the level is monitored by the pituitary gland. The increasing estrogen level stimulates the pituitary gland to release LH. LH in turn stimulates the ovaries to continue to increase estrogen production. LH also stimulates the ovaries to produce progesterone and androgens. When estrogen production reaches a peak, the pituitary gland is prompted to release a surge of LH. This action represents a critical point in the menstrual cycle. The surge of LH completes the maturation of the dominant egg follicle and triggers ovulation. Ovulation, or the rupture of the mature egg from the ovary, occurs approximately 10 to 12 hours after the LH peak.

When the follicle containing the mature egg (ovum) ruptures and releases the egg from the ovary, a small amount of follicular fluid is also released. Some bleeding may occur as well, which accounts for the reported lower abdominal discomfort often associated with ovulation (termed *mittelschmerz,* or *midpain*). Also, a slight drop in estrogen levels around the time of ovulation may cause some spotting from the uterine lining. The rise in male hormones, including testosterone, just before ovulation may explain the increase in libido that often occurs during this time (Hatcher et al., 2008).

Second Half of the Cycle – Luteal or Secretory Phase

Following ovulation, the remaining cells of the ruptured follicle reorganize. The cell walls take up lipids (fats), giving them a yellow appearance. This structure is called the *corpus luteum* or *yellow body,* and it is the director of the next phase of the cycle.

The corpus luteum secretes some estrogen but mainly produces progesterone. Eighty percent of all the progesterone secreted during the entire menstrual cycle is secreted during the first 8 days after ovulation. The presence of progesterone causes a slight rise in body temperature, and this increase is sustained throughout the second half of the menstrual cycle until progesterone levels fall and menstruation occurs. This temperature change is one of the signs measured in the fertility awareness method of birth control described in Chapter 5. Progesterone stimulates the uterine lining in its final preparations for conception. The velvety, sugary lining provides an endometrial environment suitable for implantation. This phase of the menstrual cycle is known as the *secretory phase* because of the changes that take place in the uterine lining. The mucus-producing glands of the cervix also respond to progesterone by causing the mucus produced to be scant, sticky, and thick and thus inhospitable to sperm (Hatcher et al., 2008).

The next important event in the menstrual cycle occurs as estrogen and progesterone levels reach their peak midway through the luteal phase. This peak causes a negative feedback loop to the brain, and FSH and LH levels decline. The corpus luteum begins to degrade, and estrogen and progesterone levels fall. At this point, the cycle begins again as shedding of the endometrial lining produces menses.

Fertilization

Fertilization can interrupt the last series of events in the luteal phase. A fertilized egg produces the hormone human chorionic gonadotropin (hCG). hCG travels into the bloodstream and supports continued functioning of the corpus luteum. The corpus luteum helps to maintain the levels of estrogen and progesterone necessary to prevent shedding of the uterine lining. The corpus luteum must support the developing embryo for approximately 7 to 9 weeks following conception, when the placenta takes over this function.

Fertilization of the egg occurs in the fallopian tube and involves a complex series of biochemical events that occur in the interaction between the sperm and the egg. Many separate events must be accomplished in order for fertilization to be successful and the genetic contributions of the man and woman to combine. Early cell division occurs in the fallopian tube for the first 2 days, supported by cells that have accompanied the egg and fluid from the fallopian tube. The mass of cells travels to the uterus, where it continues to develop for several days before beginning the implantation process. Implantation involves another complicated biochemical activity in which cells from the embryo grow into the uterine lining. Approximately 50% of embryos do not survive the complex process of fertilization and implantation. The chances of survival increase to 85% if the embryo survives the first 2 weeks of pregnancy (Hatcher et al., 2008).

Other Effects of Menstrual Cycle Hormones

The hormones involved in the menstrual cycle also affect many other body structures and functions.

Cervix

Changes in the cervical mucus caused by hormone stimulation of the mucus-secreting glands in the cervix have already been described. The cervical os (opening) widens during the first half of the cycle, then closes during the second half of the cycle. It is open at its widest point during ovulation.

Breast Tissue

Breast tissue also responds to stimulation by hormones. Increased size, sensitivity, and nodularity are common changes that most often occur during the second half of the cycle.

Vagina

The cells lining the vaginal walls undergo characteristic changes under the influence of first estrogen and then progesterone.

Basal Body Temperature

Shifts in hormone levels affect the temperature-regulating center in the hypothalamus. A small rise in body temperature occurs around ovulation and is sustained throughout the second half of the cycle because of the presence of progesterone.

Senses

The five senses reach a peak in sensitivity at ovulation. Because the appetite center is also affected, women commonly experience an increase in appetite during the second half of the cycle. In addition, brain waves change during the menstrual cycle. Studies have shown that an increased alertness, a sense of well-being, and heightened sexual arousal occur during the first half of the cycle and a decrease in short-term memory and attention occurs during the second half of the cycle (Hatcher et al., 2008).

Fluid Balance

The complex systems involved in regulating the body's salt and water balance are influenced by the vast hormone fluctuations associated with the menstrual cycle, and women often experience an increase in fluid retention during the second half of the cycle (Hatcher et al., 2008).

Other Factors That Affect the Menstrual Cycle

Because the hypothalamus is primarily responsible for initiating and orchestrating the menstrual cycle events, outside influences can have a profound effect on the regularity of the menstrual cycle. The quantity and timing of the hypothalamic hormone releases must follow a specific pattern to properly stimulate the pituitary gland. External influences on the brain, such as physical stress, diet, and excessive exercise (which brings about changes in weight) can influence brain chemistry and impact the menstrual pattern. Emotional stress, medications, certain environmental toxins, and social drugs that affect neurotransmitter function can all profoundly affect the menstrual cycle and result in amenorrhea (absence of menses) or menstrual irregularity (Hatcher et al., 2008).

Ongoing Research

As menstrual cycle research continues, enhanced understanding of various hormones and their functions may have implications for development of additional methods of contraception. One area of investigation concerns the study of ovarian hormones that control specific events in follicular maturation. These agents include inhibin, which suppresses FSH release, and activin, which promotes FSH release. Ongoing research about these and other hormones is key in the continued development and refinement of new birth control agents (Hatcher et al., 2008).

CONCLUSION

The monthly menstrual cycle is the primary bodily event that occurs uniquely in women from menarche to menopause. Hormones are powerful agents that produce both profound and subtle influences on the body's physiologic responses as well as on the way human beings think, feel, and sense. Appropriately educating patients about the events associated with the menstrual cycle requires consideration of many unique personal factors, such as age, education level, and culture. An individualized approach is essential in fostering understanding and helps women to appreciate the normal functioning of their bodies, dispel myths and fears, and empower them to make informed choices.

EXAM QUESTIONS

CHAPTER 2
Questions 6-14

Note: Choose the option that BEST answers each question.

6. Hormones are chemicals produced by organs and tissues that

    a. are excreted through perspiration.

    b. cause a loss of body fat.

    c. travel to target organs in the body.

    d. are influenced by differences in altitude and climate.

7. The length of a normal menstrual flow varies from

    a. 1 to 2 days.

    b. 2 to 8 days.

    c. 8 to 10 days.

    d. 10 to 12 days.

8. The hypothalamus sends messages directly to the

    a. ovary.

    b. uterus.

    c. pituitary gland.

    d. adrenal glands.

9. The hormone primarily responsible for growth and development of the egg follicle is

    a. progesterone.

    b. FSH.

    c. Gn-RH.

    d. testosterone.

10. Estrogen begins to stimulate the uterine lining during the

    a. luteal phase.

    b. menstrual phase.

    c. proliferative phase.

    d. latent phase.

11. Ovulation is triggered by a surge of

    a. estrogen.

    b. FSH.

    c. LH.

    d. progesterone.

12. The primary hormone produced by the corpus luteum during the luteal phase of the menstrual cycle is

    a. progesterone.

    b. LH.

    c. estrogen.

    d. FSH.

13. During the second half of the menstrual cycle, the presence of progesterone causes the basal body temperature to

    a. remain unchanged.

    b. decrease.

    c. increase.

    d. peak and then decrease after 24 hours.

14. Proper functioning of the menstrual cycle can be affected by

    a. sunlight.

    b. sexual intercourse.

    c. stress.

    d. cigarette smoking.

CHAPTER 3

SEXUALITY

CHAPTER OBJECTIVE

After completing this chapter, the reader will be able to describe normal sexual function.

LEARNING OBJECTIVES

After studying this chapter, the reader will be able to

1. indicate some of the influences that can affect sexual response.

2. describe the normal sexual response cycle for men and women.

3. identify common sexual problems experienced by women.

4. recognize the diversity of sexual preference and sexual lifestyles.

KEY WORDS

- Dyspareunia
- Gender identity
- Gender role
- Refractory period
- Sexual dysfunction
- Vaginismus

INTRODUCTION

Understanding the complex tapestry of sexuality is an important component of a women's health provider's knowledge base. It is essential when providing family planning information and guidance or when counseling patients about initiating and sustaining healthy relationships. In addition to the obvious biological functions, sexuality extends to identity roles, relationships, perceptions, and expectations.

Women's sexual response is much more complex than the achievement of an orgasm with intercourse. Sexuality is also integrally tied to self-esteem (Berman, Snyder, Kozier, & Erb, 2008). Sexuality is strongly shaped by cultural influences. Most ethnic groups have established their own practices and values related to their views of such issues as homosexuality, husband-wife roles, nudity, and sexual expression. All are influenced by religious values as well (Hatcher et al., 2008).

When problems with sexual function arise in a relationship, women's health care providers are often among the first professionals to whom the couple turns for help. Thus, it is essential for health professionals to be knowledgeable about and personally comfortable with sexual issues so that they can provide accurate information and appropriate, sensitive counseling in a nonthreatening environment. Historically, sexuality has been closely tied to issues of pregnancy prevention and transmission of infection. In modern times, the threat of human immunodeficiency virus (HIV) has changed sexuality forever and the accompanying fear has prompted a heightened public awareness about transmission of all sexually transmitted infections (STIs) (Hatcher et al., 2008).

PROMOTING WOMEN'S SEXUAL AND REPRODUCTIVE HEALTH

Approaching the Assessment with Sensitivity

The first step in a sexual and reproductive health assessment centers on establishing a trusting relationship in which the woman feels safe asking questions and sharing concerns. For many women, discussion of sexual issues can be an embarrassing experience. Placing educational brochures in waiting areas and examination rooms conveys the message that sexual health promotion is an important issue; it is also helpful to have other resources (e.g., books, information about community resources and self-help groups) on women's sexual health available. Nurses must be aware of their own sexual biases and become educated about the many aspects of sexuality. When assessing women for sexual concerns, nurses must not make assumptions about partner preferences and sexual practices (Martinez, 2007).

When working with very young women, nurses must be mindful of personal beliefs and avoid communicating the viewpoint that adolescent sexual behavior is wrong or shameful. Regardless of her level of active sexual involvement, each young woman needs a reliable source of education and information. In order to feel comfortable expressing concerns about sexuality and sexual behavior, the adolescent must first feel acceptance and a sense of trust in the nurse-patient relationship.

The sexual history elicits information concerning contraceptive use, prior treatment for STIs, pain with intercourse (dyspareunia), spotting or bleeding following intercourse, and coital frequency. Screening for previous, current, and potential sexual abuse should be included in the history. Many assessment forms are available to facilitate this component of the interview. If a male partner has accompanied the woman, he should be asked to leave the room while this aspect of the interview is conducted. The same procedure should be used for partners of lesbians, parents of teens, and adult children of older women (Lowdermilk & Perry, 2007; Yonkers, 2006). All women should be given an opportunity to disclose information regarding current abuse or trauma.

Findings from a research survey indicated that women would feel comfortable discussing sexual matters if their health care providers initiated the discussion (Katz et al., 2007; Lazarus & Brown, 2007). The PLISSIT and BETTER Models have been developed to enhance communication about sexual issues and to assist health care providers in introducing the topic of sexual health to their patients (Annon, 1976; Katz, 2005; Martinez, 2007; Mick, Hughes, & Cohen, 2004). These models are presented in Tables 3-1 and 3-2.

TABLE 3-1: THE PLISSIT MODEL	
P	Obtaining Permission from the patient to initiate sexual discussion
LI	Providing the Limited Information needed to function sexually
SS	Giving Specific Suggestions for the individual to proceed with sexual relations
IT	Providing Intensive Therapy surrounding the issues of sexuality for that patient
(Annon, 1976)	

Although these models may facilitate discussion, it is important for the nurse to first ask permission to discuss sexual issues and also to recognize cues (e.g., body language) that may indicate the woman does not wish to share sexual con-

TABLE 3-2: THE BETTER MODEL	
B	Bring up the topic of sexual health
E	Explain that for many women, sexuality is an important quality-of-life issue and you are open to discussing her concerns
TT	Tell the woman that many resources are available, and you are willing to assist her in finding them
E	Educate the woman regarding sexual side effects of treatments or medical-surgical conditions
R	Record the assessment, treatment, and outcome(s) in the patient's files

Note. From "Using the BETTER Model to Assess Sexuality," by J. Mick, M. Hughes, and M. Cohen, 2004, in *Clinical Journal of Oncology Nursing,* 8(1), 84-86.

cerns. Discussions should take place in a private environment where the woman is fully clothed. All concerns should be acknowledged and validated. If the woman does not wish to discuss her sexual health, the nurse should be respectful and accepting of her decision (Martinez, 2007).

The sexual assessment continues to be important in women ages 50 and older. Because older women may be reluctant to ask questions or voice sexual concerns, direct questioning is often appropriate. The nurse should use an approach that is sensitive to the older woman's level of comfort in discussing the intimate aspects of her life. Using open and reflective questions affirms the woman's right to sexual enjoyment at any age. Many women continue to remain sexually active throughout their lives although the expression of sexuality may change. Some women experience a decrease in sexual interest and desire as they grow older. Often, decreases in sexuality are influenced by culture and attitudes rather than by hormonal events that accompany the natural aging process. For older women, the strength of the relationship and the physical condition of each partner exert the most important influence on the couple's sexual relationship. For many midlife and older women, the lack of an available partner prevents the enjoyment of

sexual intimacy (Lowdermilk & Perry, 2007). An essential component of holistic sexual health care centers on helping all women to understand their bodies' natural functioning throughout the life cycle. This information empowers them to make informed choices about health decisions that impact their lives and their intimate relationships.

A woman who has undergone surgery on her reproductive organs, such as a hysterectomy, may have special needs and concerns. The nurse must listen generously to allow her to express her perception of the experience. For some, the loss of a uterus can convey a loss of femininity. Surgical menopause occurs with bilateral oophorectomy, and the abrupt change in the hormonal milieu that follows may trigger unexpected and frightening changes in the woman's sexual desire and functioning. An exploration of concerns constitutes an important component of the sexual and reproductive health assessment (Katz, 2005).

Nurses must recognize that women who are physically challenged also have sexual desires and needs. An important role for the nurse involves assisting women with disabilities in overcoming myths that they are asexual or incapable of handling intimate relationships (Piotrowski & Snell, 2007). Sexual enjoyment may be difficult, however, due to the effects of the condition. Women with spinal cord injuries are usually unable to experience orgasm, although they can conceive and bear children. A woman who has had a surgical procedure that she perceives to be disfiguring may be reluctant to engage in an intimate relationship due to embarrassment or fear that her partner will be "turned off" by her changed body appearance. Those who experience chronic pain from conditions such as arthritis or osteoporosis may also be too uncomfortable to enjoy sexual relationships. Working with both partners, the nurse can listen to concerns with sensitivity, answer questions, make suggestions, and offer appropriate referrals. Today, rehabilitation nursing recognizes that sexual expression constitutes an important component of daily life, along with eating, dressing, and mobility. As such, nurses must be sensitive to the needs of all women and include the assessment of sexual and reproductive health in all health care settings (Kellogg-Spadt, 2007).

HUMAN SEXUAL PHYSIOLOGY

Sexual arousal and sexual expression differ for every individual as well as for the same individual from one time to another or with different partners. A wide range of intimate expression can be enjoyed. The common denominator is consensual touching – that is, both partners agreeing to and enjoying the experience of sexual intimacy. Sexual intercourse, as it is usually described, is only one of many ways to enjoy this special intimacy (Hatcher et al., 2008).

Women tend to be whole-body oriented for sexual touching and vary greatly in what kind of stimulation produces orgasm. The areas of highest sensitivity for women are the clitoris, the inner surfaces of the labia minora, and the first inch and a half of the vagina. Some women's breasts are very sensitive; others' are not. Anal sex is very stimulating for some women but not for others. It is common to find women who achieve orgasm but not during penile-vaginal contact. Some women have an area of sensitivity termed the *G spot,* which is located along the vaginal wall, halfway between the back of the pubic bone and the cervix. This finding is a normal variation. Orgasm from this area may result in the rhythmic expulsion of fluid from the urethra. The fluid is not urine but is similar to prostatic fluid in men (Hatcher et al., 2008). This variation of orgasm has not been well studied and is not well understood (Boston Women's Health Book Collective, 2005).

There is a wide range of normal sexual response in women. Many women learn that vaginal inter-course should be the route to orgasm. As research on the female sexual response has expanded, this view has, for the most part, been discarded (Boston Women's Health Book Collective, 2005).

Sexual Response Cycle

The sexual response cycle consists of four parts: the excitement phase, the plateau phase, orgasm, and resolution. A brief description of each phase follows.

Excitement Phase

In the excitement phase, pelvic engorgement occurs. Engorgement produces penile erection in men and vaginal lubrication and vasocongestion of the vagina and labia in women. Due to vasocongestion, the vagina lengthens and swells. Men and women experience an increase in muscle tension, heart and respiratory rates, and blood pressure. At this time, the individual's focus of attention becomes increasingly centered on sexual matters.

Plateau Phase

During the plateau phase, engorgement is sustained and the increased muscle tension and respiratory rate persist. The labia minora and vagina appear red and puffy due to vasocongestion. The breasts frequently swell, and the nipples become erect. The clitoris may become sensitive and retract under the clitoral hood. Most women also experience sexual flushing, tachycardia, and hyperventilation. In men, the testicles enlarge and become elevated and the coronal circumference of the penis increases. Both genders experience a generalized muscular tension. This sexual response period may last for minutes to hours.

Orgasm

During orgasm, rhythmic contractions of voluntary and involuntary pelvic muscles occur in both sexes. In men, ejaculation of semen results; in women, a type of ejaculatory fluid may be emitted from the urethra. Women typically require longer to reach orgasm than men. Women also have a shorter refractory period than men. The refractory period is the time during which another erection or orgasm could not occur. Unlike men, women are physiologically capable of moving from plateau to orgasm, back to plateau, and then to orgasm one time or several times. However, they may experience a brief refractory period before they are interested in sexual intercourse again. Women are capable of experiencing multiple orgasms. For young men, the refractory period varies from 5 to 15 minutes; in older men (60+ years), the refractory period may be 18 to 24 hours. However, there is much individual variation between and among the sexes.

Resolution

Resolution is the final stage of the sexual response cycle. The body returns to the preexcitation phase, the muscles relax, and the heart and respiratory rates and blood pressure return to normal levels. Both genders experience a feeling of warmth and relaxation. This physiologic response can occur with or without orgasm.

Sexual Dysfunction

By definition, sexual dysfunction for women is any sexual situation that causes distress for the woman herself. If the woman experiences distress associated with a physical, emotional, or relationship aspect of her sexuality, she may be experiencing a dysfunction (Hicks, 2004).

Because sexual function is interconnected with a multitude of psychologic and emotional concerns, the health care provider's attempts to identify the patient's source of sexual dysfunction must consider a broad range of issues (Hatcher et al., 2008). The issues include:

- fear of
  - pregnancy
  - infertility
  - contracting an infection
  - pain
- type of birth control used

- discrepancies in sexual desire (which may be associated with the increased use of male enhancement drugs, such as sildenafil [Viagra])
- history of or current abuse
- religious and cultural taboos
- medications that cause
  - decreased libido
  - failure to achieve or sustain an erection in men
- trust and control issues in the relationship
- self-esteem and body-image issues
- poor communication between partners

Common Sexual Problems for Women

Low Libido

A lack of sexual interest can be caused by several factors, including those listed earlier. In addition, some birth control methods can decrease libido. Changes in hormone levels associated with increasing age and medications, such as antianxiety agents, antihypertensives, narcotics, and antidepressants, can also have an impact on sexual interest and function (Hatcher et al., 2008; Kellogg-Spadt & McKay, 2006). Women who have symptoms suggestive of a sexual arousal disorder (e.g., difficulty lubricating and feeling erotic genital sensations) have been treated with sildenafil citrate (Viagra) and vardenafil hydrochloride (Levitra), with limited success. These medications are presently approved only for the treatment of male erectile dysfunction, and long-term use in women has not been tested (Hatcher et al., 2008).

Dyspareunia

Dyspareunia, the term used to describe pain with intercourse, may stem from a number of physiologic (e.g., infection), gynecologic (e.g., endometriosis), or other conditions, (e.g., insufficient vaginal lubrication). A history of sexual trauma or abuse and other predominantly psychologic factors may be the underlying source of the problem. Health care providers should first consider dyspareunia to be a physical problem until proven otherwise. A thorough history, physical examination, and appropriate tests should be obtained (Hatcher et al., 2008).

Vaginismus

Defined as spasms of the perineal muscles surrounding the vagina, vaginismus occurs in response to attempted penetration of the vagina. These contractions may be so intense as to preclude insertion of a penis or even a tampon. Rarely, this condition may be the result of a structural problem detected on examination. More often, however, it is related to a fear response, either to a first pelvic examination or to attempted intercourse with the woman's perceived loss of control. In some women, vaginismus results from sexual trauma. One aspect of treatment involves teaching the woman to use her finger or a device to dilate her vagina; counseling and relaxation techniques usually accompany the treatment (Hatcher et al., 2008).

Lack of Orgasm

Lack of orgasm is the most common sexual problem encountered in women. The nature of the problem varies widely; it may occur in women who have never experienced orgasm or in women who have had orgasms in the past but are currently unable to have them. Other women are able to have orgasms but only in certain situations and under certain conditions. Most sex therapists believe that, physiologically, all women have the capacity to become orgasmic. Learning to achieve orgasm can be relatively easy for most women and may involve masturbation, use of a vibrator, or shared intimate contact with the partner. Learning to have an orgasm in every desired situation or with high frequency may be difficult for women and often involves practice, experimentation, and working through emotional and psychologic issues and inhibitions (Hatcher et al., 2008).

It is beyond the scope of this course to provide detailed information concerning the causes and treatment options for sexual problems. Many good sources of information and training in this area are available, and a number of references are included in the "Resources" section of this book.

DIMENSIONS OF SEXUALITY

Understanding Sexual Orientations

Sexuality, an integral and normal dimension of every human being, evokes controversy when it involves sexual orientation or sexual expression at either end of the age spectrum. **Heterosexual** sexual orientation is sexual attraction to or sexual activity with a person of the opposite gender. **Homosexuality** is defined as sexual attraction to or sexual activity with another individual of the same gender. The term *gay* is often used for homosexual males; *lesbian* is used for females. Presently, an estimated 2.3 million women in the United States identify themselves as lesbians (Clark & Marrazzo, 2006; Marrazzo, 2004).

Women may first identify themselves as lesbian during adolescence, young adulthood, or in their later years (Lowdermilk & Perry, 2007). Over the past two decades in the United States, the lesbian community has grown and flourished. Lesbians are numerous in every ethnic group, socioeconomic class, and political persuasion. Although most historical records do not discuss lesbian influence, research has uncovered a lesbian culture dating back to ancient times (Boston Women's Health Book Collective, 2005).

As with all minority groups, discrimination against lesbians remains a very powerful and dominant force in contemporary American society, where present-day culture assumes heterosexuality. This assumption has far-reaching implications for the willingness of individuals and society as a whole to accept and welcome differences. However, a strong lesbian culture has developed that supports and nurtures women who make the choice to love and partner with women as their primary relationships (Youngkin & Davis, 2003).

Sexual Identity

All men and women in American society, regardless of sexual orientation, face the developmental task of finding their identity. The development of a sexual self-concept is a complex process and according to psychologists, has numerous components (Berman et al., 2008):

- biologic gender – one's chromosomal sexual development, male (XY) or female (XX).

- gender identity – sense of being male or female, masculine or feminine. The gender identity may or may not be the same as the biologic gender.

- gender role – how a person expresses his or her sexuality as male or female. This expression may or may not be the same as the biologic gender or the gender identity. The gender role is culturally influenced. In Western society, women have traditionally been viewed as nurturers who assumed the responsibility for child rearing and homemaking; men were the economic providers for the family. Today, gender roles have become more fluid – women are free to pursue a variety of careers without fear of a loss of femininity and men assume responsibility with child rearing and homemaking without fear of a loss of masculinity.

- sexual identity – sexual orientation, preference for a person of the same or opposite sex.

Some of the myriad influences involved in developing identity are described in relation to adolescence in Chapter 4.

Health Issues

Although the health care needs of lesbians mirror those of heterosexual women in most instances, lesbians can experience certain health problems with greater frequency. Thus, it is essential that the nurse be sensitive to and respectful of this particular population and its health-related needs and problems.

Lesbians may choose to give birth and breastfeed. However, women who have never had children are at greater risk for breast cancer due to their lower rates of breastfeeding, and they may also be at increased risk for endometrial and ovarian cancer. It is essential for health care providers to give accurate information to and conduct appropriate cancer and other disease screening for lesbian women. All women deserve to have their health care concerns addressed by compassionate, nonjudgmental health care providers who are knowledgeable about the health care needs of women (Martinez, 2007).

Perhaps the most serious health issue for lesbians is avoidance of needed medical care because of fear of discrimination. Health care providers frequently assume heterosexuality. This assumption may create a climate in which a woman feels pressured to discuss her sexual preferences in order to avoid an inevitable discussion about birth control. As a group, health care providers are often poorly informed about lesbian health issues. While women in general have been neglected in health research for many years, research on the special needs of the lesbian population is even more limited (Boston Women's Health Book Collective, 2005).

The following five topics are common issues pertaining to sexuality that healthcare providers should be equipped to discuss:

1. **Sexually transmitted infections:** All sexually active women, regardless of sexual orientation, should be concerned about STIs. However, transmission of this type of infection from woman to woman is much lower than in heterosexual relationships. Because the organisms that cause some STIs are present in blood and vaginal secretions, sexual activities other than traditional intercourse can result in transmission of organisms from one individual to another, as can intravenous drug use. Viruses such as herpes viruses and human papillomavirus (genital wart virus)

are transmitted by skin-to-skin contact, and they can be transmitted from woman to woman. Safer sex practices are important for lesbians as well as for heterosexual and bisexual women (Boston Women's Health Book Collective, 2005; Clark & Marrazzo, 2006).

2. **Alcoholism and substance abuse:** Traditionally, bars and nightclubs have been gathering places for sexually active, single women. Alcohol abuse among lesbians has been estimated to be significantly higher than among the general population (Youngkin & Davis, 2003). Sexual preference discrimination is a stressor for many lesbians and is compounded by the stresses already faced by heterosexual populations. During the past decade, self-help and treatment opportunities designed especially for lesbian women have grown (Boston Women's Health Book Collective, 2005). Some areas of the country have Alcoholics Anonymous (AA) meetings geared specifically to homosexual men and women (Youngkin & Davis, 2003).

3. **Bisexuality:** Some women choose to partner with either a woman or a man. Their sexual and affectional preferences are directed toward persons of either sex. Furthermore, they may find that their sexual preference changes during different periods of their lives.

4. **Celibacy and abstinence:** The choice not to be sexually active for life (celibacy) or for a certain time (abstinence) is a personal one that is based on many factors, such as upbringing, religious beliefs, goals, and current life situation. The choice may be one of avoidance due to previous emotional or sexual trauma. Or, a woman may view this as a positive lifestyle choice that enables her to focus and expend energy on other activities (Youngkin & Davis, 2003).

5. **Self-stimulation:** Masturbation is a natural part of childhood experimentation, and it can be a healthy way for adult women to learn more about their own sexual responses. It can be a form of erotic play between partners of either sex or a form of sexual pleasure for women who do not have partners (Boston Women's Health Book Collective, 2005).

CONCLUSION

Sexuality is an enlivening and pleasurable part of life. Problems that center around sexuality are common and can be devastating to women and their relationships. A sensitive, well-informed, open, and relaxed health care provider can provide a non-threatening, therapeutic environment for women experiencing sexual difficulties. There is wide sexual diversity among the female population seen in the clinical setting, and health care providers should not routinely assume heterosexuality. Health care providers must be informed about the special requirements and needs of the populations they serve and be sensitive to women's rights to privacy regarding their sexual preference.

EXAM QUESTIONS

CHAPTER 3
Questions 15-22

Note: Choose the option that BEST answers each question.

15. A model that may be used to enhance communication about sexual issues is the

   a. PLISSIT Model.
   b. Health Belief Model.
   c. Health Promotion Model.
   d. McGill Model of Nursing.

16. The female sexual response cycle includes

   a. arousal, plateau, resolution, and excitement.
   b. plateau, orgasm, relaxation, and excitement.
   c. excitement, plateau, orgasm, and resolution.
   d. vasocongestion, arousal, intercourse, and resolution.

17. In the sexual response cycle, the refractory period is

   a. the initial excitement before orgasm occurs.
   b. the period after orgasm in which another orgasm cannot occur.
   c. the period after orgasm when heart and respiratory rates return to resting level.
   d. another term for the plateau period.

18. The resolution phase occurs

   a. only after orgasm.
   b. with or without orgasm.
   c. just before orgasm.
   d. only occasionally.

19. Pain during intercourse is called

   a. cervicitis.
   b. dyspareunia.
   c. endometriosis.
   d. vaginismus.

20. The most common sexual concern for women is

   a. failure to reach resolution.
   b. inability to achieve excitement.
   c. inability to accept penetration.
   d. difficulty having an orgasm.

21. Women who have difficulty having an orgasm are considered to be physiologically

   a. incapable of orgasm.
   b. deficient in the hormone estrogen.
   c. capable of orgasm.
   d. deficient in the hormone progesterone.

22. The most serious issue in medical care for lesbians is

   a. sexual dysfunction.
   b. sexually transmitted infections.
   c. failure to seek medical care for fear of discrimination.
   d. abnormal Pap smear findings.

CHAPTER 4

SPECIAL ISSUES IN HEALTH CARE FOR YOUNG WOMEN

CHAPTER OBJECTIVE

After completing this chapter, the reader will be able to discuss the process of sexual maturation and various issues during the period of adolescence.

LEARNING OBJECTIVES

After studying this chapter, the reader will be able to

1. identify normal changes associated with puberty.

2. specify psychosocial issues in adolescent development.

3. indicate health issues pertinent to the teenage population.

4. identify strategies for effectively educating adolescent patients.

KEY WORDS

- Body image
- Menarche
- Piaget
- Self-esteem
- Sexually transmitted infections (STIs)

INTRODUCTION

Adolescence is a period of life marked by enormous change and tremendous vulnerability. Young people are experimenting, taking risks, and moving further and faster, perhaps, than at any other time during their lives. During this period of rapid emotional and physical growth, however, teenagers lack the judgment and decision-making skills that come with experience. Because of these factors, the teenage population is especially vulnerable to health risks. Accidents, homicide, and suicide are leading causes of death among this age-group (Centers for Disease Control and Prevention [CDC], 2007c; Insurance Institute for Highway Safety, 2006; Menon, Burgis, & Bacon, 2007). The rate of sexually transmitted infections (STIs) occurring in young people has reached epidemic proportions. Unwanted pregnancy rates in teenagers are higher in the United States than in any other developed country (U.S. Census Bureau, 2005). Health care providers face a challenging task: to provide nonjudgmental, nonpatronizing care for young people while challenging them to assume higher degrees of self-responsibility. Promoting self-esteem among this population is key to ensuring the success of all health education efforts.

PUBERTY

Puberty describes a developmental process that occurs over time. It is not a single, isolated event. During puberty, profound changes take place that affect every aspect of the developing young woman. The onset of puberty is widely variable, and studies have shown that it is influenced by heredity, socioeconomic status, nutrition, endocrine function, body weight, percentage of body fat, physical activity, altitude, illness, stress, and abuse or neglect. The maturation of the central nervous system, including the hypothalamus, is a crucial yet poorly understood part of this process. The hypothalamus appears to reach a maturity level that prompts an increased responsiveness to hormones produced in the ovaries. The hypothalamus also initiates an increase in its own hormonal secretion. Activation of the feedback loops between the brain and the ovaries ultimately results in the initiation of the menstrual cycle. Increasing levels of sex hormones produced by the ovaries influence the whole body and result in the development of secondary sex characteristics (Hatcher et al., 2008).

Adolescent Sexual Maturation

The sexual maturation process (or puberty) occurs over a 3 to 5 year period beginning around age 9 with **thelarche,** the appearance of breast tissue. Thelarche is the first signal that ovarian function has begun. Thelarche is followed by the growth of pubic hair. During this time, the "growth spurt," also known as the "period of peak height velocity," occurs. The growth spurt is characterized by increased development of the internal and external genitalia, breast tissue, and axillary and pubic hair.

Menarche, the first menstrual flow, begins approximately 1 year after the peak height velocity (Cunningham et al., 2005). Menarche usually occurs around 13 years of age, although the normal range varies from ages 10 to 16. Following the initiation of menses, hormone cycles take an average of 12 to 18 months to stabilize, as the feedback loops and receptors in the nervous system complete the maturation process. During this time, young women commonly experience cycles in which ovulation does not occur (Hatcher et al., 2008).

Along with the cyclic hormonal changes associated with ovulation, sexual physical changes, known as **secondary sexual characteristics,** occur. Hormones associated with the hypothalamic-pituitary-ovarian axis account for most of the changes that take place in an adolescent's body during this time. Specific changes include growth and development of the vagina, uterus, and fallopian tubes; darkening and growth of the skin on the areolas and external genitals; and widening of the hips (Cunningham et al., 2005).

PERIOD OF ADOLESCENCE

Unlike many traditional cultures, in Western culture, a prolonged period of development is considered to be normal and important in preparing young people to meet the demands of a complex society. The basic psychologic task during this time is to formulate and consolidate an adult identity. Complex forces taking place within the individual and from the outside world combine to make this process one of great depth and magnitude. Identity, or self-concept, consists of many different elements, including cultural, social, gender, sexual, personal, and spiritual influences (Berman et al., 2008).

Recent research suggests that teenagers' brains are not completely developed until late in adolescence. Specifically, the connections between the neurons that affect emotional, physical, and mental abilities are incomplete. This finding might explain why some adolescents seem to be inconsistent in impulse control and judgment and decision-making. Developing autonomy with one's family, developing a sexual life, and establishing and maintaining peer relationships and social responsibility, along with refining value systems, are all part of one's identity formation. The adolescent becomes more future-oriented while he or she grapples with issues of body image, self-esteem, and personal competence. The search for identity and self-expression can include a wide range of behaviors, such as choice of clothing, use of make-up, and experimentation with drugs and alcohol as well as other kinds of risk-taking behavior. In the area of sexuality, experimentation may include masturbation, sexual fantasy, intercourse, and homosexual experiences (Berman et al., 2008).

Changes in Cognition

Piaget (1969), a well-known psychologist who developed theories about how mental functioning matures, characterized the cognitive shift that occurs in adolescence as a movement from concrete to abstract reasoning. Until this developmental milestone is achieved, the young person may have difficulty planning for the future or seeing that behavior can have predictable consequences. Egocentrism tends to characterize the mindset of adolescence and often leads to ideas of invulnerability. For example, this way of thinking may lead young women to believe they can be sexually active without contraception and not get pregnant (Berman et al., 2008).

Caregivers commonly have difficulty realizing that young women who look fully physically mature may have totally different ways of viewing the world. The thought processes involved in thinking through life issues also differs from those of older, more experienced individuals. Thus, caregivers must also make a cognitive shift to understand and reach adolescent patients (Lowdermilk & Perry, 2007).

Self-Esteem

Each person's self-concept is similar to a collage. At the center are the beliefs and images most vital to that person's identity. Many elements combine to create the overall self-concept, and these include body image, role performance and role mas-

tery, and personal identity (Kozier et al., 2007; Lowdermilk & Perry, 2007).

Body Image

Body image refers to how a person perceives the size, appearance, and functioning of his or her body and its parts. It includes an intellectual component and a body sensation component (how one feels and experiences oneself as a physical being, including sensory perceptions such as pain and pleasure). Body image develops throughout childhood, but particularly during adolescence, based on others' attitudes and responses, the individual's own exploration, and cultural and societal values. Personal identity encompasses a person's sense of his or her individuality and uniqueness, beliefs, values, talents, and interests. Role performance and role mastery concern how to act appropriately. Individuals have a basic need to know who they are in relation to others and what society expects of them (Berman et al., 2008).

Indicators of Low Self-Esteem

Health care providers who work with adolescents should be sensitive to expressions of low self-esteem. Knowing the following indicators of low self-esteem can assist the nurse in assessing and counseling young patients:

- avoids eye contact
- exhibits a stooped posture
- demonstrates a hesitant speech pattern
- demonstrates an overly critical attitude regarding self or others
- is frequently apologetic
- is unable to accept positive feedback
- demonstrates an "I don't care" attitude
- is frequently indecisive
- consistently demonstrates a failure to complete or follow through on tasks
- verbalizes expressions of feelings of worthlessness or isolation – "Nobody cares"

- does not seek help when needed

- lacks effective problem-solving skills

- sets unrealistic, vague goals

- exhibits inappropriate attention-seeking behaviors (or the opposite)

- demonstrates or verbalizes a lack of energy or enthusiasm

- maintains poor grooming.

(Berman et al., 2008)

In addition, individuals with low self-esteem generally exhibit illogical and distorted thinking, qualities that then perpetuate and heighten the existing low self-esteem. Common types of illogical thinking include:

- catastrophizing (tending to think the worst)

- minimizing or maximizing (minimize positives and maximize negatives) and thinking in black and white

- over generalizing (thinking that something that happened in one situation will happen in all situations)

- self-referencing (believing that others are very concerned with one's own thoughts, actions, shortcomings, and mistakes)

- filtering (selectively pulling details out of context, usually negative content).

These indicators must be taken seriously. Caregivers must appreciate the limits of their role in any given setting and familiarize themselves with community services available to teenagers in the areas of counseling, mental health screening, peer support, pastoral care, and school services. For health education to be successful, teenagers must develop the basic personal skills required to commit to consistent, positive health behaviors. A young patient who may need long-term counseling should be recognized and appropriately referred. A health care professional's commitment to provide compassionate and sensitive care is essential in fostering a trusting, nonthreatening, therapeutic environment (Berman et al., 2008).

Actions to Promote Positive Self-Esteem

The nurse can help to promote positive self-esteem by:

- assisting in identifying the patient's areas of strength

- helping the patient to define clear, realistic goals, as well as assisting in developing a plan for goal accomplishment

- encouraging a change in language patterns from passive to more active (this helps the patient assume greater responsibility for her own power – for example, the nurse can encourage a change from "I can't" statements to "I choose not to" statements)

- guiding the patient in developing more positive thoughts and images about herself by:
  — modeling positive self-statements
  — providing honest, positive feedback and praise
  — using visualization to envision a goal and its accomplishment
  — eliciting accomplishments that have been achieved (the nurse may suggest that the patient make a list of accomplishments, behaviors, and characteristics about herself that she views to be positive)

- showing physical affection as appropriate

- taking time to interact with the patient (depending on the limits of the health care setting, the nurse should plan for several visits)

- helping the patient to establish a sense of purpose and belonging.

Clearly, these strategies cannot be used in isolation by one health care provider. They must be applied in a coordinated effort with others who play important roles in the patient's life – but only if this is desired by the patient. Educating the family about how to promote self-esteem in the child may be a crucial role for a nurse in developing a successful plan of care (Berman et al., 2008).

HEALTH ISSUES IN ADOLESCENCE

Many health concerns are of particular importance during adolescence. These include accidents, homicide, suicide, eating disorders, STIs, contraception, drug use, undesired sexual activity, and unintended pregnancy. A brief overview of these issues follows.

Traffic Accidents, Homicides, and Suicides

Accidents, homicide, and suicide are among the leading causes of death in adolescents. Suicides are commonly reported as "accidental deaths" among this age-group. Psychological, social, and physiologic stressors are the causes most often attributed to the rising number of adolescent suicides, which occur in rich and impoverished, urban and rural families. Undiagnosed depression and ignored or misunderstood signs of distress may be factors in adolescent suicides. Caucasian males ages 15 to 25 have the highest rate of suicides; however, suicide ranks as the fourth cause of death in women ages 15 to 24. Ten percent of adolescents who attempt suicide make further attempts within 1 year (CDC, 2007c).

Nutritional Deficits and Eating Disorders

Because adolescence is a time when body image and self-esteem are being developed so rapidly and intensely, young women are particularly vulnerable to inadequate nutritional intake. They are also vulnerable to disorders characterized by extreme psychologic and emotional components that can be life-threatening. Pressure from peers and influences from the media are so powerful that nutritional counseling can be a difficult area in which to provide positive guidance to young women. By supporting individuality and encouraging positive, creative expression, the health care

provider can help teenagers find themselves despite many outside pressures and help them to develop the self-esteem needed to safely care for and nourish themselves.

Nutritional Needs

Bone density reaches its peak in adolescent girls after approximately 2 years of normal menstrual periods, or by the end of late adolescence. Regular menses depend on a crucial amount of body adipose tissue. Young women need sufficient protein, vitamins, and minerals to support their development, facilitate the growth spurt, and maintain an adequate immune response. Adolescents gain approximately 25% of their adult height and 50% of their adult weight throughout this period. Some popular birth control methods, such as oral contraceptives and long-acting contraceptive injections, can interfere with the body's utilization and assimilation of vital nutrients. A multivitamin-mineral supplement is a good general recommendation for all teenagers (Hatcher et al., 2008).

Anorexia Nervosa and Bulimia Nervosa

Eating disorders are rooted in issues related to body image development. The core of the problem involves a distortion of body image and a delay in achieving progress toward a healthy, adult body image. Adolescents with severe eating disorders struggle with the developmental task of achieving autonomy. They tend to have unrealistic views of themselves and are dependent upon social opinions and judgments, as evidenced by their heightened preoccupation with food, dieting, and exercise (Gibson & Coupey, 2007; Menon et al., 2007).

Anorexia nervosa is a form of severe and deliberate self-starvation and distortion of body image that, if left untreated, can be fatal. Bulimia nervosa is another distorted eating syndrome that involves binging and then purging, which can be accomplished by laxatives, diuretics, or emetics. When done repeatedly, these behaviors can result in severe tooth decay from regurgitation of stomach acids, damage to the esophagus, rectal bleeding from the overuse of laxatives, and potentially life-threatening electrolyte imbalances. These two illness patterns, which involve severe emotional, psychological, and physical distress, are reaching epidemic proportions in our society and are especially prevalent among teenage and adult white women. Comorbid behaviors such as alcohol and substance abuse, unprotected sexual activity, self-harm and suicide attempts, may be present. Self-mutilation, also known as *self-harm* is the act of deliberate injury to one's own body without suicidal intent. It may involve cutting or scratching the skin with razors, knives, scissors, needles, or broken glass or burning oneself with lighted cigarettes (Aguirre & Smith, 2007). Depression, low self-esteem, and poor body image are psychological factors that most often accompany these eating disorders. (Additional discussion of factors that affect self-esteem and body image can be found in other portions of this text.)

When assessing and counseling women, nurses must be especially attentive to signs of low self-esteem and poor body image as possible indicators of eating disorders. The presence of scars, most often located on the forearms (although the chest, breasts, and thighs are other common sites), non-healing wounds, and a tendency to wear long sleeves or long pants despite warm weather conditions may be indicators of self-harm behavior (Aguirre & Smith, 2007). (Please see the "Resources" section at the back of this book for references to in-depth literature concerning these topics.)

Obesity and Overweight

During adolescence, appetite commonly increases. Also during this time, adipose cells develop rapidly, leading to an increased potential for adipose tissue development and overweight. This growth is influenced by both nutritional and environmental factors. There must be a balance between energy intake and output in the adipose cells to prevent the growth of larger adipose cells,

which can lead to obesity. Overweight and obesity result from a decreased ability to release fat during periods of energy expenditure.

Heredity and environment should be considered key contributing factors in adolescent obesity. For example, a child born to two obese parents has a 75% chance of being obese. However, the influence of heredity must be considered in the context of the adolescent's environment. Psychological, social, and health factors collectively shape the adolescent's environment and its impact on nutritional health (Ogden et al., 2006).

No doubt the psychological factor that exerts the greatest effect on body image and nutritional health is the media. The adolescent is continually bombarded with images of thinness and glamour. However, the media send mixed messages – along with the "thin ideal" are advertisements that focus on eating fast foods and snack foods (Ogden et al., 2006). Television and advertising tend to encourage and condone the pleasures of consuming high-fat, high-carbohydrate foods while using slender, attractive young persons in the commercials. On average, adolescents spend approximately 3 to 4 hours each day watching television, a sedentary activity that can also contribute to the development of overweight and obesity (American College of Obstetricians and Gynecologists [ACOG], 2007; Ogden et al., 2006).

Social factors include the influences of the family and peer group. Family eating behaviors are often initiated at an early age, and in many households, little time is spent on meal preparation and enjoyment. As the dual-income family has become the norm in contemporary society, fast food and "eating on the run" have also become the norm. Eating patterns that contribute to adolescent obesity include the regular consumption of high-calorie, low-nutrient-dense foods; a lack of understanding about nutrition; a lack of structure and sociability in eating patterns; a tendency to eat late in the evening; binge eating when hungry, bored, or depressed; and the habit of eating rapidly. Peer pressure may play a significant role in the development of adolescent obesity. Teenagers tend to congregate and socialize with their peers in areas where food is readily available and consumed, such as fast food restaurants, shopping mall food courts, pizza parlors, and at parties (Ogden et al., 2006).

Depression is one of the most common disorders associated with adolescent obesity. Attempts to fit into the peer group frequently involve unhealthy eating (and drinking) behaviors. At the same time, adolescents are bombarded by media images of overeating by slender, attractive individuals and societal messages that obesity is unattractive and shameful. There is an unspoken message that obese individuals are overindulgent and lack self-control. Unfortunately, these mixed messages negatively impact the adolescent's self-esteem and body image, creating a risk for depression; feelings of social isolation, rejection, and failure; and in some cases, thoughts of suicide (Ogden et al., 2006).

Substance Abuse

Teenagers now use a wider range of substances at younger ages than ever before. During adolescence, experimentation and risk-taking behaviors serve as a means of self-discovery and identity development. Often, the experimentation involves the use of drugs and alcohol. Adolescents give many reasons for trying drugs and alcohol, including to satisfy curiosity, to fit in with peers, to achieve a feeling of well-being while under the influence, and to reduce stress. Young people who are at greatest risk for developing dependency are those with low self-esteem, a family history of substance abuse, or depression and those who do not feel accepted by their peers (ACOG, 2007).

Alcohol and marijuana are the drugs most commonly used by adolescents. On average, alcohol use is initiated at age 12 and marijuana use begins at age 14. Teenage substance abuse has

many profound effects. It is associated with school failure, an increased risk of accidents, violence, suicide, and unplanned and unsafe sexual activity. Tobacco use increases the risk of a number of diseases, including cervical cancer, breast cancer, chronic lung disease, chronic cardiovascular disease, and asthma (Lowdermilk & Perry, 2007).

It is beyond the scope of this course to discuss these areas in detail, but references for further information may be found in the "Resources" section.

Tattooing and Body Piercing

Tattooing and body piercing are other examples of adolescent risk-taking behavior. These practices are associated with other high-risk activities, such as smoking, alcohol use, the use of smokeless tobacco, and riding in a vehicle driven by an individual who has been drinking. The health risks associated with tattooing and body piercing may be infectious or noninfectious (ACOG, 2007; Drifmeyer & Batts, 2007). Infectious health risks include viral, bacterial, and fungal diseases. The most common causative viruses are hepatitis, human immunodeficiency virus, and human papillomavirus (HPV). Bacterial infections may be caused by staphylococcus, streptococcus, pseudomonas, clostridium, and mycobacterium organisms (Drifmeyer & Batts, 2007). These organisms have the potential to cause lifelong infection with adverse effects on various body systems or the progression to other diseases, such as cancer and tuberculosis. Allergic or hypersensitivity reactions are the most common noninfectious responses to tattooing and body piercing. Although these reactions may be temporary, they can lead to the development of more serious lesions that require surgical intervention.

Sexually Transmitted Infections

Many factors have influenced the rising epidemic of STIs among the teenage population. The statistics are sobering. Approximately two-thirds of all STI cases occur among individuals younger than 25 years of age, and one-quarter occur among teenagers (Hatcher et al., 2008). Cervical cancer rates among young women are also troubling. Some of the factors involved in these trends include:

- the asymptomatic nature of many STIs

- multiple sexual partners, which includes serial monogamy (a series of partners with whom the person has a monogamous relationship)

- inconsistent use of barrier methods of birth control

- lack of understanding about STIs.

    STIs are discussed in greater detail in Chapter 7.

Contraception

A large percentage of U.S. teens report having engaged in sexual intercourse prior to age 18. Yet many fail to use contraception. Although the reasons for lack of contraceptive use among this population are varied and complex, several explanations have been offered: misconceptions or ignorance, inability to obtain appropriate contraceptives, inability to plan ahead for engaging in sexual intercourse, belief that contraceptive use will be associated with a promiscuous label, and rebelliousness. Males are less likely to recognize the risk of pregnancy as a result of sexual activity, and they are also less likely to have contraceptive information. The male's attitude often influences the female's likelihood not to use contraception, even if the young woman recognizes the risks involved (Hatcher et al., 2008; Hoyert, Mathews, Menacker, Strobino, & Guyer, 2006).

Approximately one-half of all initial adolescent pregnancies occur within the first 6 months following initiation of intercourse, and 20% occur within the first month alone. In many cases, a prolonged delay occurs between initiation of sexual relations and the first family planning visit. In most states today, adolescent pregnancy is on the decline. Furthermore, adolescents are increasing their use of birth control methods, especially condoms, at first

intercourse, whether or not they have seen a health care provider for contraception. Although this finding indicates that health education efforts are having an important impact, the United States still continues to have one of the highest teenage pregnancy rates in the Western world (Hatcher et al., 2008).

Many factors influence whether an adolescent becomes pregnant. Although unintended pregnancy may truly be "accidental," four broad themes explain other underlying reasons: self-destruction or self-hate; rebellion, anger, hate, or reverse aggressiveness toward parents and authority; lack of responsibility for self and personal behavior; and a plea for attention and help from the parents, the boy involved, or others (National Campaign to Prevent Teen and Unplanned Pregnancy, 2007). Intermingled with these issues are other special concerns pertinent to this age-group, including:

- possible confidentiality issues with parents

- desire to escape from an unpleasant situation

- a means for achieving a goal

- desire to have someone to love

- compliance issues

- age-related health issues.

    Birth control methods will be discussed in detail in Chapter 5.

Undesired Sexual Activity and Rape

Adolescent women are particularly vulnerable to various forms of sexual harassment, coercion, and rape. Peer pressure, feelings of invulnerability, risk-taking behavior, unpredictable situations, dating unfamiliar men, substance abuse, and lack of experience contribute to this vulnerability (ACOG, 2007; Fishwick, Parker, & Campbell, 2005; Moracco et al., 2004).

Rape is generally underreported and underprosecuted. The person committing the rape is often someone known to the individual. Date rape often occurs when a young woman participates in voluntary sexual play but does not consent to sexual intercourse. Young women ages 15 to 24 frequently report that their first sexual experience was nonvoluntary. Adolescent survivors of rape are often reluctant to report the rape for reasons such as guilt, fear of retribution, embarrassment, concern about confidentiality, and lack of access to health care. The young adolescent may also be unwilling to report the assault to authorities because she was involved in risk-taking behaviors, such as underage drug use, drinking, or socializing with older males (Fishwick et al., 2005; Moracco et al., 2004).

Nurses can empower women and their families with factual information and strategies to reduce undesired sexual activity and pregnancies among the teenage population. In the community setting, nurses can advocate for responsible sexual behavior by providing educational programs in schools, churches, clubs, and after-school activities. In the clinical setting, nurses can listen to, counsel, and educate young patients to help prepare them for responsible decision-making. Nurses also have an important role in empowering mothers and fathers of young adults with methods for facilitating open, honest family discussions about sexuality and sexual behavior (Lowdermilk & Perry, 2007).

Sex education must include information about sexual harassment, sexual coercion, and rape. Young women need the tools to recognize and avoid potentially dangerous situations. Self-defense courses are widely available. The nurse should be familiar with community resources as well as the specific state requirements for reporting sexual abuse and violence. Licensed health care providers are commonly mandated by law to report any mention of abuse by a patient, whether or not she wishes to report it herself. The health care system is frequently the first point of contact for a young person who has been raped or coerced into sexual activity (Fishwick et al., 2005).

Rape represents an often life-threatening attack and has a profound psychologic and emotional impact. Physical evidence needs to be gathered according to a very time-specific protocol, especially if the evidence is to be of use in court. Young women especially tend to delay reports of rape or sexual coercion because of confusion, embarrassment, and fear. This situation is very difficult and delicate and must be handled by properly trained health care providers (Lowdermilk & Perry, 2007).

Incest and Family Violence

Incest and violence are widespread in the United States across all socioeconomic, educational, and ethnic levels. It is estimated that approximately 10% of all childhood abuse cases involve sexual abuse and 350,000 or more children in the United States are victims of sexual abuse each year. The actual figures are probably higher due to underreporting. In addition, 15% to 25% of adult women and 12% of adult men experienced incest during childhood. The majority of childhood sexual assaults are perpetrated by a parent, guardian, family member, or maternal significant other, and the abuse peaks from 7 to 12 years of age. Tragically, young women who were raised in families with abusive patterns often later find themselves in situations that resemble those of their upbringing (Hatcher et al., 2008).

Young women with a history of sexual abuse may have great difficulty forming a positive sexual identity. They may also experience emotional and functional sexual problems that can be addressed by providers with special training. It is the responsibility of nurses and other primary health care providers to be attentive to patient cues that may indicate underlying abuse issues that influence current problems. Signs of abuse include expressions of shame, guilt, and anger; unexplained physical complaints; sleep disturbances; school problems; and problems developing relationships (ACOG, 2007; Lowdermilk & Perry, 2007).

Unintended Pregnancy

In this country, approximately one million adolescents, 4 out of every 10 girls, become pregnant each year. The majority of these pregnancies are unintended, and close to 40% are terminated by induced or spontaneous abortion. Adolescents are responsible for close to 500,000 births in the United States each year. The birth rate for Hispanic adolescents is currently the highest, although the rate for African-American adolescents is also higher than that of other groups. Of the girls who become pregnant, one in six experience another pregnancy within 1 year. Most of these young women are unmarried and unprepared for the physical, psychological, and financial responsibilities associated with parenthood (ACOG, 2007; Hoyert et al., 2006).

Health care providers must seriously consider what is missing from not only their health care system but also the whole approach to young people in American culture. Unwanted pregnancy rates are clearly linked to socioeconomic status, which is further associated with deficits in health care access, education, and opportunity. Broad societal efforts involving every aspect of social inequality must be directed toward changing these statistics. Results of international studies show that countries where pregnancy rates are lowest have contraceptive supplies widely available at free or low cost. In addition, sex education is widespread and emphasized in the mass media, and schools are closely linked with adolescent birth control clinics. Although most agree that teenage pregnancy is a major problem in the United States, there is such diversity of opinions and beliefs concerning these issues that there is no agreement on a central approach to the problem (Hatcher et al., 2008).

THE FIRST PELVIC EXAMINATION

The first gynecologic examination serves as an introduction to reproductive health care. This experience can set the stage for the entire future of a woman's relationship with the health care system. The initial and subsequent examinations may be fraught with anxiety related to fear of pain, embarrassment about undressing, feelings of vulnerability about having the body viewed and touched by a stranger, and fear of finding an abnormality. Cultural differences and language barriers may also add to a woman's discomfort and perception of stress.

Health care providers can do much to minimize these concerns and create a positive first experience. Nurses can take many actions to help put the woman at ease:

- Take time to establish a comfortable rapport.

- Remember that 90% of communication is nonverbal.

- Pay attention to your own as well as the patient's nonverbal cues.

- Reassure the patient of confidentiality.

- Take a thorough history.

- Explain in advance exactly what will occur (in the order of occurrence), and make sure that the patient understands everything.

- Be sure that all of the patient's questions and concerns are answered before the examination begins.

- Use illustrations and models. Show a speculum to the patient and allow her to hold it if desired.

- Teach relaxation breathing techniques in advance.

- If desired by the patient, welcome a friend or family member.

- Before proceeding, gain permission to conduct the examination.

- Tell the patient you are going to touch her before you do so.

- When beginning a pelvic examination, touch the patient's thigh before touching her genitalia.

- Offer a mirror to view the cervix if the patient wishes to do so.

- Ensure privacy.

- Let the patient know what you are seeing; reassure her of normalcy.

- Teaching and counseling should be done in the woman's native language, with sensitivity to cultural issues

(Lowdermilk & Perry, 2007).

COUNSELING AND EDUCATING ADOLESCENTS

When working with adolescents and their special issues, health care providers will do well with a considerate and thoughtful approach (Hatcher et al, 2008; Lowdermilk & Perry, 2007). Nurses must be aware that learning about how one's body functions can be fun, an ordeal, or even frightening for some young women. It is important for health care providers who are involved in education to be sensitive to their audience. This includes finding out what information the patient brings to the session, the accuracy and sources of the information, and the level of emotional attachment to the information.

To answer questions appropriately, nurses must first **find out** what the adolescent wants to learn about. At times, health care providers have so much information they wish to share that they fail to determine exactly what the patient's needs are. Nurses should **avoid overwhelming** adolescents with too much information at once.

Many people are visual learners; others learn by listening or writing. Adolescents commonly respond well to **visual aids.** An effective teaching strategy may involve helping the young woman to get a visual picture of exactly what is being described.

Make the session as interactive as possible. Ask questions in a nonthreatening manner and, if appropriate, ask patients to describe their own experiences. The use of hypothetical situations often makes discussions more true to life. It is important to remain relaxed and accepting, create a comfortable environment and, when appropriate, interject humor. These strategies can help to put the patient at ease in what may be perceived as an uncomfortable clinical setting.

When talking to a group, it is often helpful to **create a format for anonymous questions.** Distributing 3½ x 5½ cards and pencils at the beginning of the session usually works best. This strategy allows for more open discussion by creating the privacy to ask "secret" questions.

For effective follow-up, **provide simple reading materials** for patients to take home. If possible, hold a follow-up session or find out if there is any interest in a program that involves peer education. Young people tend to listen to their peers. It is also appropriate to provide resources to guide their further exploration.

Strategies for Promoting Safety

Adolescents are still developing formal thought operations and may not yet have the cognitive abilities to make appropriate decisions regarding safety. At times, their decisions can result in accidents, injuries, and risk-taking behaviors. It is important to provide them with information related to safer sexual practices, substance use and abuse, violence, and suicide prevention.

The risk of motor vehicle accidents is greater for adolescents than for any other age group; each year, more than 5,000 young persons between the ages of 16 and 19 die from injuries related to crashes (Insurance Institute for Highway Safety, 2006). Risk factors include a lack of ability to assess hazardous situations while driving, speeding, driving under the influence of drugs or alcohol, and a low incidence of seat belt use.

Approximately one-third of all homicides in the United States occur among adolescents. Factors related to adolescent violence include a history of abuse and the observation of violent acts at home. Nurses must be aware of various protective factors so that they can provide appropriate health teaching to empower young people with strategies to reduce their risk. Education, religiosity, improved economic conditions, conflict resolution skills and reduced use of drugs and alcohol are areas for education focus and advocacy that can be addressed by health care providers. Also, because access to guns directly impacts the adolescent homicide rate, implementation of gun safety classes represents another appropriate area for intervention (CDC, 2007c).

Suicide, the third leading cause of death among adolescents, must be addressed as well. Nurses should be aware of various risk factors for suicide or suicide attempts, including:

- substance abuse
- previous suicide attempt
- easy access to lethal weapons
- history of sexual or physical abuse
- preoccupation with death
- suicide death of someone known to the teenager.

(ACOG, 2007)

Common symptoms of suicidal ideation include reports of frequent crying, fatigue, insomnia, depression, feelings of isolation, and changes in body weight. Other possible signs include behavior problems, violence, sexual promiscuity, a drop in academic performance, and school absence. Nurses who are aware of any of these symptoms should ask if the adolescent plans to commit suicide and by what means and if there have been any other suicide attempts. Adolescents at low risk for suicide should be promptly referred to a mental health professional; those at high risk for suicide should be immediately evaluated by a mental health professional (CDC, 2007a).

Risk-taking behavior is a normal component of adolescence, in fact, taking healthy risks serves as an avenue for discovering and developing one's identity. Parents should be encouraged to facilitate healthy risk-taking by talking openly and honestly and helping their child to understand the consequences of healthy versus nonhealthy risk-taking behaviors. Unhealthy risk-taking may lead to injuries; the most common injuries among this population are related to motor vehicles, bicycles, firearms, and water. Nurses and parents can provide sensitive, appropriate teaching to adolescents to empower them to take necessary precautions to avoid injury. An important way for parents to foster adolescent safety is to set a good example and be positive role models.

CONCLUSION

A dolescence is a critical time in the lives of young people. Events that occur, choices that are made, and habits that are acquired during this period can have serious and permanent consequences. When working with young patients, it is the health care provider's role to help them establish and practice consistent patterns of behavior that will maintain and enhance their health.

Health care organizations can do much to improve their relationship with the teenage population by employing the following strategies (Hatcher et al., 2008):

- Offer flexible hours.
- Ensure close geographic accessibility.
- Provide transportation schedules.
- Inform patients about free or government-supported services that are available to them.
- Advise young patients of their rights to confidentiality.

Practitioners who assure young patients of their confidentiality find that these young women, many of whom are at high risk for a variety of health problems, are more likely to reveal sensitive information and return for repeat visits.

EXAM QUESTIONS

CHAPTER 4
Questions 23-31

Note: Choose the option that BEST answers each question.

23. The first menstrual period is called

    a. amenorrhea.
    b. dysmenorrhea.
    c. menarche.
    d. menopause.

24. The first evidence of puberty (or sexual maturation) is

    a. the first menstrual period.
    b. the growth of axillary hair.
    c. the growth of pubic hair.
    d. budding of the breasts.

25. After the first menstrual period, cycles are likely to stabilize after

    a. 3 months.
    b. 6 to 12 months.
    c. 12 to 18 months.
    d. 24 months.

26. One developmental milestone that occurs in adolescence is a shift in cognition from

    a. concrete to abstract reasoning.
    b. identification with the mother to a separate sense of self.
    c. concentration on self to focus on others.
    d. abstract to concrete reasoning.

27. Bone density reaches its peak in adolescent girls

    a. when the growth spurt is complete.
    b. when the breasts are fully grown.
    c. after about 2 years of normal menstrual periods.
    d. when menarche occurs.

28. Approximately two-thirds of all STIs occur in individuals

    a. at the time of the first sexual exposure.
    b. younger than age 25.
    c. ages 25 to 35.
    d. ages 40 and older.

29. STIs

    a. always produce symptoms.
    b. usually produce some symptoms in women.
    c. commonly produce no symptoms.
    d. usually result in vaginal discharge.

30. Following the initiation of intercourse, 50% of all adolescent first pregnancies occur in the

    a. first month.
    b. first 3 months.
    c. first 6 months.
    d. first year.

31. Sex education for the adolescent should
include information about

   a. drinking and driving.

   b. ways to enhance self-esteem.

   c. sexual harassment and rape.

   d. strategies to build healthy bones.

CHAPTER 5

BIRTH CONTROL METHODS AND REPRODUCTIVE CHOICES

CHAPTER OBJECTIVE

After completing this chapter, the reader will be able to discuss contraceptive methods and counseling.

LEARNING OBJECTIVES

After studying this chapter, the reader will be able to

1. indicate the mechanisms of action and advantages and disadvantages of various methods of contraception.

2. identify strategies for providing contraceptive education and counseling.

3. specify the options for procedures for pregnancy termination.

KEY WORDS

- Depo-Provera
- Emergency contraceptive pill (ECP)
- Intrauterine device (IUD)
- Medical abortion
- Thromboembolic disease
- Vasectomy

INTRODUCTION

Although they represent vitally important areas of women's health, birth control methods and reproductive choices have traditionally been fraught with controversy. Intertwined with family planning issues are myriad influences, such as women's religious values and constitutional rights, their concept of family, and their entitlement to autonomy, privacy, and respect. Although major advances have been made in the area of contraception, technology has not yet created a perfect birth control method. Historically, societal pressures have had a major impact on reproductive behavior. Due to changing values in today's social climate, there remains a wide range of opinion in the adult community about numerous reproductive issues, such as the appropriate time for the initiation of sexual activity among young people and adolescents' ready access to contraception.

Nurses who work with women of childbearing age must remain knowledgeable about current contraceptive methods and trends so that they can provide accurate information to their patients. Information should be conveyed in a sensitive, nonjudgmental manner that takes into account the many factors that influence a woman's choice of contraception. The woman's age, her health status (and risk of contracting a sexually transmitted disease [STI]), her religion and culture, the perceived impact of an unplanned pregnancy, her desire for future children, her frequency of intercourse and number of sexual partners, her degree of comfort with touching or having her partner touch her body, and the expense and degree of convenience associated with the method all must be considered. Additionally, an important aspect central to effective contraceptive health care is to promote self-esteem in patients, so that the choices they make are safe, personally acceptable, and practiced consistently (Schnare, 2006).

Sterilization is the most common method of contraception in the United States. Considered a permanent method of birth control, sterilization has near-perfect effectiveness. Total abstinence remains the only failure-proof method for preventing unwanted pregnancy and, because of the increased risk of STIs, abstinence is gaining in acceptance, especially among adolescents and young adults. For those who wish to be sexually active, many contraceptive choices are available. One of the crucial issues in decision-making about contraception centers on the prevention of STIs. Unfortunately, the most convenient, longer-acting birth control methods available today offer little, if any, protection against STIs. Since many patients select these methods because they are so "hassle free," patients may find it difficult to accept the idea of adding a barrier method to provide STI protection (Hatcher et al., 2008).

Despite current technology that enables couples to exert considerable control over their fertility, approximately half of all pregnancies in the United States are unintended. However, other industrialized nations report fewer unintended pregnancies, which suggests that, realistically, the United States unintended pregnancy rates could be reduced (Finer & Henshaw, 2006).

UNINTENDED PREGNANCY

Obviously, an important determinant of pregnancy and birth rates is consistent contracep-

tive use. The proportion of all females ages 15 to 44 who practiced contraception (including women who have had sterilization procedures or whose partners have had vasectomies) rose from about 56% in 1982 to 60% in 1988 to 64% in 1995. By 2002, the proportion of women who used a birth control method at first intercourse had risen to 79%. However, 5.2% of all females ages 15 to 44 reported having intercourse without using contraception during the past 3 months (Mosher, Martinez, Chandra, Abma, & Willson, 2004).

In the United States, unintended pregnancy is costly and occurs much too frequently. On a social level, the costs are measured in unintended births, diminished educational achievement, reduced employment opportunities, greater dependency on welfare, and increased potential for child abuse and neglect. Economically, the costs of unintended pregnancies are considerable. The cost of pregnancy care for one woman who did not intend to be pregnant yet was sexually active and used no contraception is estimated to be about $5,000.00 annually in a managed care setting (U.S. Census Bureau, 2007).

Medically, unintended pregnancies are commonly associated with a diminished opportunity to prepare for an optimal pregnancy, an increased potential for maternal and infant illness, and a greater likelihood of induced abortion. The number of elective abortions in the United States has been declining over the past 15 years. Most women who choose to have an elective abortion are Caucasian, younger than 24 years of age, and unmarried (Strauss et al., 2005).

The family planning objectives for the Healthy People 2010 initiative call for the nation to adopt a social norm in which all pregnancies are intended; the United States has set a national goal of decreasing unintended pregnancies to 30% by 2010. Another goal concerns increasing male involvement in pregnancy prevention and family planning efforts (USDHHS, 2000; http://www.healthypeople.gov/). To meet these goals, public education and information about family planning must be expanded. Health care providers can combine efforts with other groups in mass media campaigns on local, regional, and national levels to provide the public with accurate information about the benefits of sexual abstinence and the routine use of contraception.

Various studies and polls have revealed that a disturbing degree of misinformation concerning contraceptive methods exists. The modest health risks of oral contraceptives have often been exaggerated, while the more considerable benefits are frequently underestimated (USDHHS, 2000). A 2000 Gallup survey found that 52% of women were unaware of any noncontraceptive health benefits of oral contraceptives, whereas 41% believed that the pill regimens were associated with serious health risks (Schnare, 2002). Information concerning emergency contraception is not widely available, and the relative effectiveness of various forms of contraception is commonly not well understood. Furthermore, many population groups lack culturally appropriate, accurate information about STI prevention and reproductive health in general.

EFFECTIVENESS OF BIRTH CONTROL METHODS

How effective are birth control methods? What is meant by the term *efficacy*? These are commonly asked questions and, unfortunately, there are no simple answers. Many factors impact the determination of a contraceptive's failure rate. They are described in the discussion that follows.

In general, *efficacy* describes the frequency with which a contraceptive method prevents pregnancy under "perfect use" conditions (Hatcher et al., 2008). Statistically, contraceptive failure rates are affected by a number of influences, such as age, socioeconomic status, educational level, cultural background, and lifestyle choices. Consistency, accuracy, and duration of use of a particular method also affect failure rates. It should be noted that

reports of failure rates often include women who are actually infertile and would be unable to achieve pregnancy regardless of any contraceptive method used. Also, no reliable reporting method has yet been found that adjusts for frequency of intercourse, a major consideration when calculating contraceptive failure. Instead, failure rates are commonly defined as failure with "perfect use" or with "typical use." "Perfect use" of a method indicates correct use of the method every time intercourse takes place. Failure rates for "typical use" are higher, reflecting occasions of incorrect use or failure to use the method at all. These factors all combine to make birth control statistics "best estimates" rather than exact numbers (Hatcher et al., 2008). Thus, when counseling patients about contraceptive choices, effectiveness statistics should be a factor secondary to finding a method that the patient finds acceptable and will use properly and consistently.

REVIEW OF BIRTH CONTROL METHODS

An important nursing role in reproductive health care involves assessment for any current or past problems that may interfere with the use of certain types of contraception. Women with certain chronic health problems, such as diabetes, multiple sclerosis, cancer, pain, or stroke, may be taking medications that are contraindicated with certain contraceptives or are associated with fetal anomalies. Providing individualized counseling and information helps to empower patients to make informed, realistic choices about reproductive planning. Some women have chronic conditions that interfere with fertility and create a sense of powerlessness when pregnancy is desired. Nurses are in a unique position to listen attentively to these women, offer support and information, and make referrals to appropriate resources.

It is beyond the scope of this course to provide all of the details needed to counsel women adequately about each available contraceptive. The health risks of some birth control methods can be more serious than those associated with other methods. Therefore, careful evaluation of the patient's personal and family health history along with her sexual history must be completed by a nurse practitioner, physician's assistant, or physician before any method, however appropriate to the patient's other needs, is prescribed. It is also important to consider the patient's ethnic background because cultural preferences influence birth control decisions. For example, among African-Americans, the use and choice of contraception is usually left up to the females. Males are often reluctant to use condoms because they are believed to diminish sensation and sexual pleasure. Mexican-Americans, a predominantly Catholic population, often use Depo-Provera. Depo-Provera, a long-acting, injectable progesterone, is a method that involves less frequent "sin" than daily forms of birth control, such as oral contraceptives and can be easily concealed from others (St. Hill, Lipson, & Meleis, 2003). Fitting all the pieces together can be challenging for the nurse, and members of a health care team have different roles to play in the ongoing process of evaluation, counseling, and teaching. This section is designed to introduce the basics of each method.

Hatcher and colleagues (2008) note that a perfect birth control method does not yet exist. Contraceptives are imperfect and can fail even with the most diligent user. Methods such as the birth control pill, intrauterine device (IUD), and long-acting hormonal injection offer superior protection against pregnancy in comparison to barrier methods, but they have a greater potential for health risks and side effects. Barrier methods, especially male and female condoms, are superior in their protection against STIs and carry minimal risks and side effects, but they are not as effective in preventing pregnancy. Using a condom along with an appropriate method that provides superior pregnancy protection represents the best option currently available.

Natural Family Planning/Fertility Awareness

This method permits identification of fertile and nonfertile days and generally involves periods of abstinence throughout the cycle. There are several variations within the natural family planning/fertility awareness method of birth control. All are based on daily recording and charting of physiologic changes that occur normally during the menstrual cycle; that is, changes in basal body temperature (BBT) and cervical mucus (Lowdermilk & Perry, 2007).

Basal body temperature

BBT cannot be used to predict ovulation. However, it can indicate when ovulation has occurred. BBT must be taken before arising and at the same time every morning. It is best to use a special BBT thermometer that has the appropriate calibrations for easy reading. Days of menstrual flow, discharge, mucus, illness, nights up late or with less than 6 hours of sleep, and sexual intercourse should also be recorded. Recordings are made for 2 to 6 months so that cyclic patterns can be determined (see Figure 5-1).

Cervical mucus changes

The texture and consistency of cervical mucus change in response to the influence of estrogen (early part of the menstrual cycle) and then progesterone (later half of the menstrual cycle). On a typical fertile day, cervical mucus is abundant; has a thin, egg-white consistency; and is clear and stretchy.

Health care providers should have received special training to enable them to accurately counsel patients about fertility awareness methods; in some states, certification is needed as well. Patient teaching generally involves several sessions, during which the woman develops an awareness and understand-

FIGURE 5-1: BASAL BODY TEMPERATURE METHOD

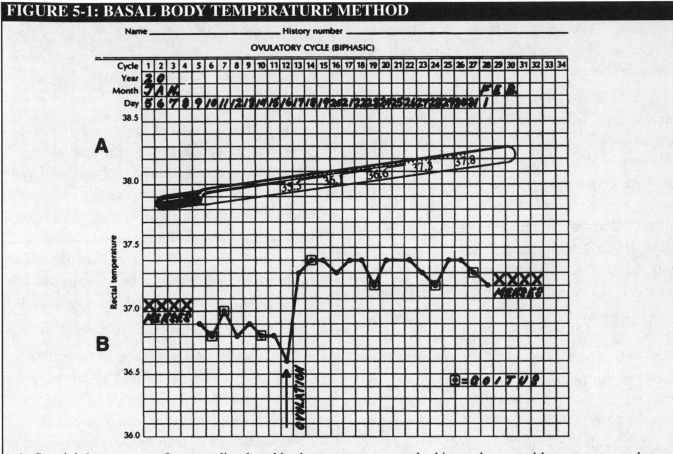

A, Special thermometer for recording basal body temperature, marked in tenths to enable person to read more easily. **B,** Basal temperature record shows drop and sharp rise at time of ovulation. Biphasic curve indicates ovulatory cycle.

Note. From *Maternity & Women's Health Care* (9th ed., p. 95), by D. Lowdermilk & S. Perry, 2007, St. Louis: Mosby. Reprinted with permission.

ing of her fertility signs so that she can accurately chart them. Based on her personal data, individual cyclic patterns are determined and decisions are made concerning abstinence or the use of other forms of contraception during fertile days. A high degree of self and partner commitment is required with this method, along with a personal comfort level in the careful, daily assessment of normal body processes (Lowdermilk & Perry, 2007).

Oral Contraceptive Pills

Oral contraceptive pills (OCPs) contain synthetic forms of estrogen and progestin. Neither is chemically identical to the hormones that the body naturally produces, but each is close enough to exert similar effects. Since the approval of OCPs by the U.S. Food and Drug Administration (FDA) in 1960, much research has been directed at reduc-

ing the effective dose and thereby reducing the risk of serious side effects. Most pills used today are considered low-dose pills. In this country, OCPs are the most commonly used method of reversible birth control (Hatcher et al., 2008). However, none of the hormonal contraceptives offer protection against STIs.

Method of Action and Formulation

The estrogen component of OCPs primarily affects the pituitary gland to inhibit ovulation by preventing the release of follicle-stimulating hormone (FSH). Other effects of the estrogen component are to accelerate transport of the egg, inhibit implantation, and promote premature degeneration of the corpus luteum. The progestin component, when combined with estrogen, inhibits the luteinizing hormone (LH) surge, which is required for ovulation. Progestins also create a thickened cervical mucus, making it more hostile to sperm penetration, and cause atrophy of the endometrium (Rice & Thompson, 2006).

In the United States, OCPs are available in monophasic, biphasic, and triphasic preparations. Monophasic formulas provide fixed doses of estrogen and progestin throughout a 21-day cycle. Biphasic preparations provide a constant amount of estrogen throughout the cycle but provide an increased amount of progestin during the last 11 days. Triphasic formulas, designed to more closely mimic a natural cycle, provide varied levels of estrogen and progestin throughout the cycle. In many women, the worrisome side effect of breakthrough bleeding (bleeding that occurs outside of menstruation) is diminished with triphasic preparations. In all formulations, the first 21 pills contain hormones, and the final 7 pills have no hormone component. For maximal effectiveness, the pill should be taken at approximately the same time each day (Hatcher et al., 2008; Rice & Thompson, 2006).

Current trends in contraceptive hormonal dosing regimens involve shortening or eliminating the hormone-free interval (i.e., the 7 days "off" the pill). The goal of this approach centers on reducing hormone withdrawal bleeding and minimizing hormone withdrawal symptoms. Some women prefer continuous oral contraceptive dosing and studies to date have found no evidence of an increased risk of breast or endometrial cancer with extended oral contraceptive use (Reape & Nelson, 2007; Reiter, 2006; Sulak, 2006; Sulak, Kaunitz, London, Moore, & Nelson, 2007; Wysocki, 2007).

Recent research regarding individual preferences for menstrual frequency have revealed the following trends (Sulak, 2007):

- a general agreement that monthly menstrual cycles may be painful and unpleasant

- an overall willingness to consider menstrual suppression

- a preference among women younger than age 34 years for four cycles per year

- a preference among women older than age 40 years for complete elimination of cycles.

Risk Factors

In general, OCPs pose few serious health risks to most users, and these risks certainly are not as great as pregnancy-related complications. Death, obviously the most serious risk of all, is an extraordinarily low risk for most women. Other major health risks are uncommon, and they are much more likely to occur in women with underlying medical conditions that may be influenced by hormonal contraceptive methods (Hatcher et al., 2008).

Four specific risks warrant consideration:

1. **Cardiovascular risk:** The most serious and well-documented risks of OCPs are the effects on the circulatory system. An increased risk of death caused by cardiovascular disease is found in women older than age 35, especially those who smoke. Also, venous thromboembolic disease constitutes the leading cause of death attributed to oral contraceptives because the estrogens promote blood clotting. Because of this fact, patients in their mid-thirties should be evaluated for cardiovascular risk before OCPs are prescribed. Women ages 35 and older who smoke should not use an estrogen-containing contraceptive. It should also be noted that age increases the risk of other medical conditions, such as high blood pressure and diabetes, both of which place older women at increased risk for complications from OCP use (Hatcher et al., 2008).

2. **Cancer:** OCPs offer protective effects against colorectal, endometrial, and ovarian cancers. At one time, there were concerns about an association between OCPs and breast cancer. However, after more than 50 studies have examined this potential relationship, most experts believe that birth control pills have little, if any, effect on the risk of developing breast cancer. Findings from

the Collaborative Group on Hormonal Factors in Breast Cancer, a long-term epidemiologic analysis with data from over 53,000 women, indicated that women with a family history of breast cancer (mother or sister) did not increase their risk of breast cancer by using OCPs. Likewise, the initiation of birth control pill use at a young age was also not associated with an increased risk of breast cancer. Additionally, OCPs do not increase the risk of developing breast cancer in women with benign breast disease (Hatcher et al., 2008; Shulman & Westhoff, 2006).

3. **Human immunodeficiency virus (HIV):** Oral contraceptives may increase blood flow to the cervical epithelium and alter certain endometrial immune responses. It is unknown whether the use of OCPs actually increases susceptibility to HIV in any way for women or their partners. It is prudent to advise women to combine OCPs with latex or polyurethane condoms unless they are confident their partners are free from HIV and other STIs (Hatcher et al., 2008).

4. **Chlamydial infection:** Epidemiologic and biologic evidence have revealed an increased risk of acquiring chlamydial infection among oral contraceptive users. This finding is probably due to changes in the cervix and an altered endometrial immune response, which increase a woman's vulnerability to upper-tract chlamydial infection. Again, combining OCPs with condoms at every sexual act offers the best protection (Hatcher et al., 2008).

Contraindications

The use of OCPs is contraindicated in women with certain medical conditions. Conditions that are listed in the FDA-approved pill package inserts include (Hatcher et al., 2008):

- thrombophlebitis or thromboembolic disorder (or history of deep vein thrombosis)
- valvular heart disease with thrombogenic complications
- cerebrovascular or coronary artery disease
- diabetes with vascular involvement
- breast cancer
- carcinoma of the endometrium
- other known or suspected estrogen-dependent neoplasia
- undiagnosed abnormal genital bleeding
- major surgery with prolonged immobilization
- benign or malignant liver tumor or impaired liver function
- pregnancy
- cholestatic jaundice of pregnancy or jaundice with prior OCP use
- acute or chronic hepatocellular disease with abnormal liver function, hepatic adenomas, or hepatic carcinomas
- uncontrolled hypertension
- headaches with focal aura
- hypersensitivity to any component of the product.

Benefits

OCPs have many important noncontraceptive benefits. Their use decreases the risk of colorectal, ovarian, and endometrial cancer; benign ovarian cyst formation; and benign breast disease. Because ovulation is inhibited, the risk of ectopic pregnancy and development of functional ovarian cysts is almost eliminated. Endometriosis is suppressed and there is improvement in conditions related to androgen sensitivity and androgen excess, such as polycystic ovary syndrome. With OCP use, menstrual cycle regularity is enhanced, menstrual blood loss and iron deficiency anemia are reduced, and dysmenorrhea is diminished. Also, certain OCP formulations have a positive effect on acne, and some studies have shown a lower risk of postmenopausal hip fractures, increased bone mineral density, and a slight reduction in osteoporosis (Clark & Burkman, 2006; Hatcher et al., 2008).

Effectiveness

Failure rates for OCPs range from 0.1% to 3% during the first year of use. It should be noted that a number of medications can alter the metabolism of oral contraceptives. In general, the lower the dose of the estrogen or progestin component, the greater the risk that a prescribed drug will decrease the pill's effectiveness. Oral contraceptives also may affect the actions of other medications being taken. Women who use OCPs should be educated about the possibility that barbiturates, and such medications as rifampin, isoniazid, and griseofulvin can affect contraceptive effectiveness, and it may be appropriate to suggest a higher dose of estrogen or the use of a back-up method, such as condoms. Also, because they can alter the results of certain laboratory tests, it is important to inform the laboratory that a patient is taking OCPs (Hatcher et al., 2008).

Side Effects

Manufacturers have sought to reduce the hormone levels in OCPs in an attempt to diminish their dangerous and unpleasant side effects. Although the risk of life-threatening side effects is minimal, factors such as age, smoking, and the presence of other diseases compound the risks.

An important focus in patient teaching centers on the warning signs that must be immediately reported to a health care provider. Use of the acronym ACHES can help the nurse and patient to remember these warning sings. ACHES uses the first letter of each sign of cardiovascular, liver, gallbladder, and thromboembolic complications that are side effects of estrogen use and can be life-threatening:

- Abdominal pain (problem with liver or gallbladder)
- Chest pain or shortness of breath (blood clot in lungs or heart)
- Headaches, sudden or persistent (hypertension, cardiovascular accident)
- Eye problems (hypertension, vascular accident)
- Severe leg pain (thromboembolism).

Women should be taught that if they experience any of these signs or symptoms, they must immediately stop taking the OCP and promptly contact a health care provider. All of these symptoms require immediate evaluation.

In addition to the ACHES signs, patients who become depressed or jaundiced, miss two periods (or have other signs of pregnancy), or develop a breast lump should notify their health care providers (Hatcher et al., 2008).

Other side effects, which may be annoying but are not life-threatening, include mood changes, spotting, hair loss, nausea, breast tenderness, weight gain, darkening of the skin, and an increase in headaches. These side effects represent the most common reasons women stop taking OCPs. It is important for nurses to counsel patients about the possibility of side effects, which often subside after a few months of use or after a change in OCP formulation. If women understand that unpleasant symptoms may occur, they are more likely to seek health care provider advice before arbitrarily discontinuing use of OCPs.

Low-dose Progestin-Only Contraceptive Pill – the "Minipill"

The minipill is a variation of the OCP that consists only of a synthetic form of progesterone. Although ovulation can occur, progestins cause cervical mucus thickening and endometrial atrophy. Low-dose progestin-only contraceptive pills are a more appropriate birth control method for certain groups of women. For example, the minipill is commonly prescribed for breast-feeding mothers because estrogen inhibits lactation, whereas progestins do not. Both hormones have been detected in breast milk. The minipill is also prescribed for older women (due to its decreased risk of thrombotic complications), women age 35 and older who smoke, and women with medical conditions such as cardiovascular disease and thromboembolic disease (Hatcher et al., 2008; Rice & Thompson, 2006).

Because it only contains a progestin, the mini-pill has fewer side effects than the combination pill. The major problems associated with this method are amenorrhea and spotting. The minipill is more expensive and slightly less effective than combined OCPs. In lactating women, however, the progestin-only pill is close to 100% effective due to the added contraceptive effect of breast-feeding (Hatcher et al., 2008).

Vaginal Contraceptive Ring

The vaginal contraceptive ring (NuvaRing) is a soft, flexible vaginal ring that slowly releases estrogen and a progestin. The woman places the ring high into the vagina by the fifth day of the menstrual cycle and it is left in place for 3 weeks. The ring is then removed, and during the "off" week, menstruation occurs. A new ring is placed at the end of the 4-week cycle. The efficacy of the NuvaRing® approximates that of combination OCPs and, because liver effects are reduced, the method is associated with a good lipid profile. No pressure trauma occurs to the vaginal mucosa, and NuvaRing® is associated with very regular menses. Unlike the diaphragm, no sizing or fitting is required, although men and women report occasionally having felt the ring during sexual intercourse. If the contraceptive ring comes out of the vagina, it should be washed with plain hand soap and warm water before reinsertion. If the woman has a supply of more than four rings, the rings should be stored in the refrigerator (Hatcher et al., 2008; Rice & Thompson, 2006).

Hormonal Transdermal Contraceptive Patch

The Ortho-Evra transdermal contraceptive patch contains estrogen and a progestin that are delivered in continuous systemic daily doses. One patch is worn at a time, usually on the abdomen, upper outer arm, torso, or buttocks, each week for 3 weeks. This schedule is followed by 1 patch-free week to allow for menstruation. The efficacy

(99%) and incidence of side effects with the Ortho-Evra patch are comparable to those of oral contraceptives (although it also has a risk of local skin irritation), and ovulation suppression is improved. The patch is rapidly reversible and is associated with a high rate of patient compliance. Due to concerns that excessive adipose tissue may be associated with inconsistent levels of hormonal absorption, the transdermal contraceptive patch is not recommended for women who weigh more than 198 lb (Potts & Lobo, 2005).

The pharmacokinetic profile for the Ortho-Evra transdermal contraceptive patch is different from that of an oral contraceptive. The contraceptive patch maintains a steady state of estrogen (ethinyl estradiol) that is approximately 60% higher than in women who use an oral contraceptive containing 35 mg of ethinyl estradiol. In contrast, the peak concentrations for ethinyl estradiol are approximately 25% lower in women using the Ortho-Evra contraceptive patch. The implications of these findings are unknown; clinicians must weigh patient benefits against risks when prescribing any hormonal delivery system for contraception (American College of Obstetricians and Gynecologists [ACOG], 2007).

Depo-Provera and Depo-SubQ Provera 104 Contraceptive Injection

Depot medroxyprogesterone acetate (Depo-Provera [DMPA]) is a long-term, progestin-only contraceptive. It does not contain any estrogen. Its effects last approximately 3 months, and it is injected either intramuscularly (150 mg) or subcutaneously (104 mg). Since its approval in 1992 by the FDA, it has been an increasingly popular birth control method, especially among teenagers. Depo-Provera has been in use worldwide for a number of years. It provides no protection against STIs (Hatcher et al., 2008).

Method of Action and Administration

Depo-Provera (and other progestin-only contraceptives) are believed to prevent pregnancy by:

- inhibiting ovulation

- thickening cervical mucus, thereby impeding sperm permeability

- thickening the endometrium, thereby impeding implantation.

Ideally, Depo-Provera therapy should be initiated during the first 5 days of a normal menstrual cycle to ensure the patient is not pregnant. Medroxyprogesterone 150 mg is injected deep into the deltoid or gluteus maximus muscle every 10 to 12 weeks (the risk of pregnancy increases after 12 weeks). The deltoid muscle may be used if it is of adequate size, and it is the preferred administration site in obese women to ensure that the medication is injected into muscle tissue. The administration site should not be massaged following injection, because this action can reduce the effectiveness of the drug (Hatcher et al., 2008; Rice & Thompson, 2006).

Depo-SubQ Provera 104 was the first subcutaneous hormonal contraceptive product available. It is administered into the anterior thigh or the abdomen. On average, ovulation is restored within 10 months following discontinuation of the medication (both dosages).

Special Considerations

1. **Breast Cancer:** Studies conducted on breast cancer risk and the use of Depo-Provera have revealed inconclusive findings. Early research with animals revealed an increased risk of mammary gland tumors, some of which became malignant. Other international studies found no similar effects in humans, although one New Zealand study found a slightly increased breast cancer risk among women ages 25 to 34 who had used the drug for 6 years or longer. Findings from the study also suggest that Depo-Provera may accelerate the presentation of breast cancer in young women. Ongoing research continues in this area (Hatcher et al., 2008).

2. **Bone Density:** Findings from a 2005 study indicate that adolescents (ages 14 to 18 years) are at increased risk for detrimental effects of Depo-Provera on bone mineral density (BMD). Young women who used Depo-Provera experienced significant losses in BMD in both the hip and spine in comparison to age-matched women not using Depo-Provera, whose BMD increased. Following discontinuation of Depo-Provera, BMD significantly improved (Scholes, LaCroix, Ichikawa, Barlow, & Ott, 2005). These findings suggest that the adverse effect is reversible in adolescents if therapy is discontinued. Recommendations from professional organizations, including the ACOG, Society for Adolescent Medicine, and World Health Organization (WHO), state that for the majority of adolescents, the benefits of Depo-Provera outweigh its potential risks (Arias, Kaunitz, & McClung, 2007). Because of the potential for decreased BMD, it is essential that all women who use Depo-Provera be counseled about the importance of dietary calcium and exercise in promoting good bone health.

Contraindications

Contraindications to the use of Depo-Provera include a current or past history of thromboembolic disorders, a history of depression, undiagnosed vaginal bleeding, missed abortion, known or suspected pregnancy, and carcinoma of the breast (Hatcher et al., 2008).

Warning Signs

Nurses should teach women who use Depo-Provera to contact a health care provider if they experience the following signs (Hatcher et al., 2008):

- repeated, very painful headaches

- heavy bleeding

- depression

- severe, lower abdominal pain (may be a sign of pregnancy)

- pus or prolonged pain or bleeding at the injection site.

Other Symptoms

Women who use Depo-Provera may experience the following symptoms (Hatcher et al., 2008):

- hcadaches
- nervousness
- decreased libido
- breast tenderness
- acne
- hot flashes.

Noncontraceptive Benefits

In addition to providing effective protection against unwanted pregnancy, Depo-Provera has a number of noncontraceptive benefits, including decreased menstrual blood flow and cramping and reduced risk of the following conditions: anemia, endometrial cancer, pelvic infection, ectopic pregnancy, sickle cell crisis, and frequency of grand mal seizures (Burkman, Grimes, Mishell, & Westhoff, 2006; Hatcher et al., 2008).

Effectiveness

The typical effectiveness for the 150 mg intramuscular dose of Depo-Provera is 98% to 99%. The typical effectiveness rate of the subcutaneous 104 mg Depo-Provera injection appears to be greater than 99% (Hatcher et al., 2008).

Side Effects

One of the disadvantages of Depo-Provera use is that any side effects must be endured for the duration of the drug's activity in the body. In addition to the symptoms noted above, two common and particularly disturbing side effects are menstrual irregularities and weight gain:

1. **Disruption of the menstrual cycle:** Menstrual irregularities (e.g., spotting, breakthrough bleeding, amenorrhea) are the most common side effects of Depo-Provera therapy. When first initiated, Depo-Provera is commonly associated with increased bleeding. However, with continued use, most women cease to have periods altogether or have only occasional spotting. Nurses should counsel women that amenorrhea increases over time but is not harmful. Some women experience excessive or irregular bleeding that must be managed with hormone therapy or nonsteroidal anti-inflammatory drugs such as ibuprofen (Hatcher et al., 2008).

2. **Weight gain:** Depo-Provera appears to cause an increase in appetite, and most women do gain some weight, which is not fluid retention. Weight gain is usually about 5 lb the first year. Women who use Depo-Provera should be encouraged to be careful about food choices and to exercise regularly (Brucker, 2005; Hatcher et al., 2008).

Reproductive Effects

Depo-Provera is reversible once the effect of the last injection has worn off. Although Depo-Provera does not cause long-term loss of fertility, ovulation may not occur until 9 to 10 months after the last injection; the delay does not increase with increased duration of use. More than 90% of women become pregnant within 2 years after discontinuation of Depo-Provera. Because ovulation may take up to 2 years to return, women who wish to become pregnant within a year following discontinuation of Depo-Provera may wish to consider another contraceptive option (Hatcher et al., 2008).

Lactation Effects

Depo-Provera does not inhibit lactation; thus, it is considered an appropriate birth control method for lactating women. It is, however, detectable in breast milk (Hatcher et al., 2008).

Subdermal Hormonal Implant

Implanon is a subdermal contraceptive that is effective for 3 years. The single-rod implant, which is inserted on the inner side of the woman's upper arm, contains etonogestrel (ENG), a progestin. It is simpler to insert and remove than the previously available six-capsule levonorgestrel implant (Norplant) (Schulman, 2007). Implanon prevents pregnancy by suppressing ovulation and creating a thickened cervical mucus that hinders sperm penetration. ENG is metabolized by the liver. Thus, hepatic-enzyme inducers, including certain antiepileptic agents, may interfere with the absorption and contraceptive effectiveness of this drug (New Product – Implanon, 2006; Darney & Mishell, 2006).

Advantages

The Implanon contraceptive is a very effective birth control method. It is appropriate for women who desire long-term reversible contraception and who have no objections to the insertion and removal procedures or to palpating the implant when it is in place.

Considerations

Implanon must be removed and replaced every 3 years if continued contraception is desired. Following removal, ovulation occurs within 3 to 6 weeks. The contraceptive efficacy in obese women (> 130% of ideal body weight) has not been studied (Darney & Mishell, 2006).

Effectiveness

The effectiveness rate of Implanon approaches 100%.

Side Effects

Bleeding irregularities are common during the first several months following insertion; amenorrhea becomes more common with increasing duration of use. Other symptoms include emotional lability, weight increase, headaches, depression, dysmenorrhea, and acne (Darney & Mishell, 2006).

Intrauterine Devices

An IUD is a small, plastic device that is inserted into the uterus. Depending on the type, it may contain copper (ParaGard T) or a progestin (Mirena). A tail string affixed to the device extends through the cervix and protrudes into the vagina.

History and Mechanism of Action

Although the exact mechanism of action of an IUD is unclear, it is known that the uterus exhibits a foreign-body response to the presence of the device. White blood cells and other chemicals produce an inflammatory reaction that interferes with sperm transport and survival; the uterine environment is altered as well. The copper-containing IUD, ParaGard, inhibits sperm motility so that sperm rarely reach the fallopian tubes and are unable to fertilize the ovum. The progestin-containing IUD, Mirena, prevents the build-up of the uterine lining, produces thickening of the cervical mucus, and causes changes in the uterotubal fluid that impair sperm migration (Hatcher et al., 2008). Contrary to popular belief, IUDs are not abortifacients and do not increase the risk of ectopic pregnancy. Rather, IUDs are more efficient at preventing uterine pregnancies than ectopic pregnancies. Thus, compared with other methods, a higher percentage of the few pregnancies that do occur are ectopic (Hatcher et al., 2008; Wysocki, Moore, & Ramos, 2007).

The first forms of IUDs, developed centuries ago, were pebbles inserted into the uteruses of camels, so they would not get pregnant during long journeys (Boston Women's Health Book Collective, 2005). The IUD has had an unfortunate history in the United States. First introduced in the 1960s, IUDs rapidly gained popularity because they provided women with a highly effective, carefree, and cost-effective method of birth control. However, the safety of IUDs has always been a controversial issue. The FDA removed several IUDs from the market because of a high incidence of serious side effects. The Dalkon Shield, the most well-known of the recalled IUDs, was linked to 10 maternal deaths resulting from mid-trimester septic abortion. Several other types of IUDs were removed from production as well due to serious side effects, including increased incidence of uterine perforation, bowel strangulation, and a tendency to embed within the uterine wall (Whitaker & Kaunitz, 2007).

Today's IUD manufacturers have corrected the design problems related to the Dalkon Shield and other types, and IUDs are once again safe to use.

The devices are considered an excellent contraceptive choice for women who are not at risk for contracting an STI. The Copper T-380A, or Paragard, is a T-shaped device containing copper, which works as a functional spermicide. It is effective for 10 years. The levonorgestrel-releasing intrauterine system Mirena is another T-shaped device that releases a small amount of the progestin levonorgestrel on a continuous basis. This IUD remains active for 5 years and is believed to prevent pregnancy by exerting effects on the cervical mucus, endometrium, and uterotubal fluid that prevent sperm from fertilizing an ova (Hatcher et al., 2008).

The IUD is inserted in a collapsed position into the uterus and then expand into shape once the inserter is withdrawn. The IUD is wholly contained within the uterus, and the attached plastic string, or "tail," extends through the cervix and into the vagina. Both are impregnated with barium sulfate for radiopacity. The IUD is inserted during menses to ensure that pregnancy has not occurred; it may also be inserted immediately after childbirth or first trimester abortion (Clark & Arias, 2007; Hatcher et al., 2008).

According to the ACOG, appropriate candidates for intrauterine contraception include multiparous women at low risk for STIs, women who desire long-term reversible contraception, and women with certain medical conditions (e.g., diabetes, thromboembolism) for which an IUD may be an optimal method. The Copper T IUD may be used in nulliparous women, lactating women, and women who have a history of pelvic inflammatory disease or ectopic pregnancy. All IUDs are contraindicated in women with acute pelvic inflammatory disease (ACOG, 2007; Centers for Disease Control and Prevention [CDC], 2007a; Hatcher et al., 2008; WHO, 2004; Wysocki, Moore, et al., 2007).

Advantages

The advantages of IUDs include that they:

- are highly effective
- protect against ectopic pregnancy
- are long-lasting
- are convenient
- are well-liked by users
- have a low risk of side effects
- are cost-effective.

(Hatcher et al., 2008)

Disadvantages

Disadvantages of IUDs include:

- longer, heavier, more painful periods
- cannot be inserted or removed by the woman
- expulsion
- perforation
- no protection against STIs
- effectiveness (both types of IUDs have a failure rate of 1% to 2%).

(Hatcher et al., 2008)

Side Effects

Irregular bleeding and spotting may occur for about 3 months following insertion. The progestin-releasing IUD may produce amenorrhea (Rice & Thompson, 2006); the copper-bearing IUD can increase menstrual flow and cramping (Clark & Arias, 2007). Pelvic infections may also occur; the likelihood of occurrence is greatest during the first month following insertion (ACOG, 2005c).

Special Teaching Needs

Nurses should teach women who use IUDs to perform a vaginal "string check" each month to ensure that the IUD remains in place. If the strings are not felt or if they seem to be longer or shorter than they previously were, the woman should return to her health care provider for evaluation. If pregnancy occurs with the IUD in place, the device is usually removed vaginally to decrease the possibility of infection or spontaneous abortion. IUD users should obtain a yearly pelvic examination and Pap smear. All IUD users should be taught the warning signs ("PAINS") that may indicate infection, expulsion, or ectopic pregnancy.

- **P**eriod late (pregnancy)
- **A**bdominal pain or pain with intercourse (infection)
- **I**nfection exposure or vaginal discharge
- **N**ot feeling well, fever, or chills (infection)
- **S**tring missing, shorter, or longer (IUD expelled)

Emergency Postcoital Contraception Pill

Emergency contraception is available to women whose birth control methods fail or who have been the victims of sexual assault. Presently, two forms of emergency postcoital contraception are available: hormonal methods (the emergency contraceptive pill, or ECP) and insertion of a copper-releasing IUD. Emergency contraception is available by prescription, office visit or, in some states, over the counter (Katz, 2006).

Hormonal Method

Often called the "morning after pill," the ECP is not considered to be a method of birth control but is to be used following a contraceptive accident or an incident of unprotected intercourse. The ECP is not an abortifacient. Instead, the high hormone levels in the oral contraceptive pills prevent or delay ovulation, thicken cervical mucus, alter sperm transport to prevent fertilization, and interfere with normal endometrial development. Emergency contraception is ineffective if implantation has already occurred, and it does not harm a developing embryo (Hoskins & Crockett, 2006; Smith, D.M., 2007).

In the United States, two hormonal forms are currently available for emergency contraception: one that uses a combination of estrogen and progestin and one that contains only progestin ("Plan B"). Both must be initiated within 72 hours, although recent studies have demonstrated efficacy of giving ECPs up to 120 hours following unprotected intercourse. However, ECPs are more effective the sooner they are started. Once an existing pregnancy

has been ruled out, certain formulations of birth control pills (combination or progestin only) are prescribed according to a specific protocol. ECPs are given in two doses spaced 12 hours apart. Menses may be slightly delayed; if no menses occurs within 3 weeks, the patient should return for a pregnancy test (Smith, D.M., 2007). Although regular oral contraceptive pills can be taken for emergency contraception, the dose varies with the brand and may require taking a large number of tablets. The risk of pregnancy is reduced by 75% following completion of the emergency contraception dose (Clark & Jordan, 2006; Freeman, 2007; Hatcher et al., 2008; Walker-Jenkins, 2007).

Side Effects

Nausea and vomiting are common side effects, especially following treatment with combined estrogen-progestin ECPs. These effects may be minimized by taking an antiemetic 1 hour before the first ECP dose (Burki, 2005; Hatcher et al., 2008; Lever, 2005). Menstrual changes may include spotting or a change in the amount, duration, and timing of the next menstrual period.

IUD Method

The copper IUD can be inserted within 5 days of unprotected intercourse. Because of the product's cost and the need for insertion by a trained professional, the IUD is used for emergency contraception less frequently than ECPs. The IUD is not recommended for women who have been raped or who are at risk for STIs and pelvic infections (Burki, 2005). Emergency insertion of a copper IUD is significantly more effective than the use of ECPs, reducing the risk of pregnancy following unprotected intercourse by as much as 99% (Hatcher et al., 2008).

The IUD is suitable for women who wish to have the benefit of long-term contraception. Insertion of the IUD within 5 days following intercourse causes an alteration in the endometrium to prevent implantation. Patients should contact their health care provider if no period occurs within 3 weeks following insertion (Lever, 2005).

Side Effects

The side effects for the IUD are the same whether it is being used as an emergency contraception method or as a long-term contraceptive.

Barrier Methods

In contrast to hormonal birth control methods, barrier methods do not alter the physiology of the menstrual cycle. A major advantage of barrier methods is that they offer protection against STIs as well as unwanted pregnancy. Proper and consistent use of barrier methods remains the key to contraceptive effectiveness. With barrier methods, there is a considerable difference in effectiveness between typical use and perfect use. Thus, a crucial role for the nurse lies in patient education concerning the correct use of barrier methods. The teaching approach must be tailored to the patient's age, prior experience, culture, and educational level. It is also essential that adequate time be allowed for discussion, demonstration, and practice.

Condoms

Widespread approval of condom use in the United States is a relatively new occurrence. In fact, the sale of condoms was outlawed by Congress in 1873. In some states, it was a criminal offense for one person to inform another that use of a condom might prevent pregnancy. Similar laws remained in effect in some states until 1975. Today, the condom is the most widely available and popular contraceptive method in the United States (Hatcher et al., 2008).

Male Condoms

Three types of male condoms are currently on the market: those made of natural rubber latex ("rubbers"), those made from the intestinal cecum of lambs ("natural skin," "natural membrane," or "lambskin"), and those made from polyurethane and other synthetic materials. Both latex and polyurethane condoms prevent transmission of bacteria and viruses; the lambskin condom does not offer this protection (Hatcher et al., 2008). The market is currently filled with creative condom variations, including lubricated (usually with a spermicide) and nonlubricated, contoured, ribbed, colored, and flavored.

The polyurethane condom, approved by the FDA for latex-sensitive people, is available for men (Avanti, Trojan Supra, eZ.on) and for women (Reality). Condoms may be used as a primary contraceptive method, as a back-up contraceptive method, or along with another method to provide STI protection. Although condoms containing nonoxynol-9, a spermicide, are available, no clinical evidence supports that these condoms are more effective in preventing pregnancy than condoms without the spermicide. Presently, there is a move away from the use of nonoxynol-9 products due to the potential for adverse effects in some users, and the future availability of spermicidal condoms is unclear (Hatcher et al., 2008). A separate vaginal spermicide may be used as a back-up method preferable to either spermicide-containing condoms or the application of a spermicide to the surface of the condom (Nelson & Le, 2007).

Effectiveness

Typical use of latex condoms shows a failure rate of 15% in the first year; with perfect use, 2% in the first year (Hatcher et al., 2008).

Promoting Proper Use

For proper use of the male condom, these guidelines should be followed:

- Never use oil-based lubricants (e.g., household oils or massage oils) with condoms because they quickly break down the latex. Instead, use water-based lubricants, lubricating jellies, or spermicidal lubricants.

- Use a new condom with every act of intercourse if there is any risk of pregnancy or STIs.

- Before penetration, unroll the condom onto the erect penis, all the way to the base.

- During withdrawal of the penis after ejaculation, hold the rim of the condom against the base of the penis.

- Store condoms in a cool, dry place; never reuse a condom.

(Hatcher et al., 2008)

Female Condom (Reality)

Approved by the FDA in 1993, Reality is a "one size fits all" prelubricated vaginal sheath made of polyurethane. The female condom provides a physical barrier that completely lines the vagina and partially shields the perineum (see Figure 5-2). The soft, loose-fitting sheath contains two flexible polyurethane rings. One ring is placed inside, at the closed end of the sheath. The other ring remains outside the vagina, where it provides protection to the woman's labia and base of the man's penis during intercourse. The sheath is prelubricated on the inside with a silicone-based agent that is not a spermicide (Hatcher et al., 2008).

Advantages

Like the male condom, the female condom barrier method offers protection from pregnancy and STIs, but its use is controlled by the woman. The female condom also offers added protection against herpes and genital warts for both men and women because it covers more of the female external genitalia. In addition, Reality can be safely used if one of the partners has a latex allergy (Hatcher et al., 2008).

Effectiveness

With consistent and correct use, the effectiveness of Reality in preventing pregnancy has been shown to be comparable to other barrier methods. Failure rates during the first year of use range from

FIGURE 5-2: FEMALE CONDOM

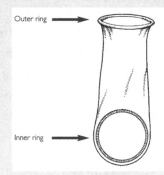

The outer ring covers the area around the opening of the vagina. The inner ring is used for insertion and to hold the sheath in place during intercourse.

Hold the sheath at the closed end; grasp the flexible inner ring and squeeze it with the thumb and middle finger so it becomes long and narrow.

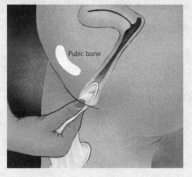

Choose a position that is comfortable for insertion (e.g., squat, raise one leg, sit, or lie down). Gently insert the inner ring into the vagina. Feel the inner ring go up and move into place.

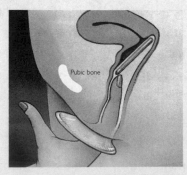

Place the index finger on the inside of the condom, and push the inner ring up as far as it will go. Be sure the sheath is not twisted. The outer ring should remain on the outside of the vagina.

Adapted from "What is FC Female Condom?" (n.d.) by The Female Health Company. Retrieved June 9, 2008 from http://www.femalehealth.com/pdf/PR_Pack_2_whatisfc.pdf

5% (perfect use) to 21% (typical use). The risk of STI transmission and acquisition, especially of cervical, vaginal, and viral infections (e.g., hepatitis B), is reduced (Hatcher et al., 2008).

Promoting Proper Use

The female condom may take some practice to insert and use correctly. Patients should practice insertion before using it for sexual intercourse. One potential problem concerns the outer ring, which can be pushed inside the vagina during sex. The use of additional lubricant usually prevents this problem. Also, the penis can slip to the side of the device during insertion and may have to be guided into the vagina. With some practice, the female condom is hardly noticeable, and its loose-fitting construction allows more comfort and sensitivity for the male partner.

Nurses can provide women with the following tips to promote proper use of the female condom:

- Use the female condom every time sex occurs.
- Use a new condom with each sex act.
- Do not use a male and female condom at the same time.
- Use additional lubricant as needed.
- Use care in handling; be careful of jagged fingernails or rings that could tear the condom.
- Know that the condom can be inserted up to 8 hours prior to intercourse.

(Hatcher et al., 2008)

Disadvantages

Although no prescription is needed, the female condom is often difficult to find. Also, it is more expensive than the male condom (average cost is $2 per condom). Some individuals complain that female condoms generate "noise" during intercourse, but lubricant seems to help alleviate this problem.

Spermicidal Preparations

Spermicidal preparations consist of a formulation (a carrier or base – foam, cream, or gel) and a chemical (usually nonoxynol-9) that kills the sperm. Unfortunately, spermicidal preparations are often used without the addition of another barrier method, and this practice results in a higher failure rate. If using spermicides as a primary method of birth control, patients should be provided with an advance prescription of ECPs. Ideally, spermicides should be used as an adjunct to other barrier methods. Spermicides are readily available without prescription and can be used intermittently with little advance planning (Hatcher et al., 2008).

Spermicidal preparations also include contraceptive films, tablets, sponges, and suppositories. They should be inserted at least 15 minutes before sexual intercourse takes place. Spermicides should be inserted deep into the vagina to facilitate contact with the cervix. The film should be folded in half and then in half again; this action aids insertion. Once inside the vagina, the film melts and adheres to the surface of the cervix. Although douching is never recommended, it should be avoided for 6 hours after intercourse to avoid washing the spermicide away. Douching in and of itself is not a reliable form of birth control (Hatcher et al., 2008).

Following the use of spermicides, some women experience temporary skin irritation involving the vulva or vagina. When this occurs, the product should be discontinued and another contraceptive method should be selected. Spermicides should not be used in women with acute cervicitis because of the potential for further cervical irritation. Spermicides provide little, if any, protection against transmission of STIs. They do not protect against HIV, and frequent use (more than two times per day) may cause tissue irritation that theoretically could increase susceptibility to HIV (Hatcher et al., 2008).

Contraceptive Vaginal Sponge (Today Sponge)

The Today vaginal contraceptive sponge is a small, pillow-shaped polyurethane sponge that is permeated with the spermicide nonoxynol-9 (see Figure 5-3). The sponge has a concave dimple on one side that is intended to fit over the cervix to decrease the chance of dislodgment during intercourse. On the other side of the sponge is a loop to facilitate removal. It comes in one size and is an over-the-counter, nonprescription barrier method.

FIGURE 5-3: CONTRACEPTIVE SPONGE

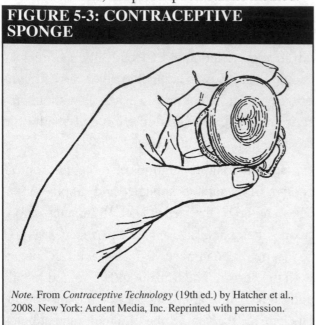

Note. From *Contraceptive Technology* (19th ed.) by Hatcher et al., 2008. New York: Ardent Media, Inc. Reprinted with permission.

The Today Sponge was taken off the market in 1995 due to manufacturer production problems, but is once again available. The sponge should be moistened with tap water prior to use and inserted deep into the vagina. It provides continuous protection for up to 24 hours and should be left in place for at least 6 hours after intercourse. Problems with the sponge include vaginal irritation and difficulty with removal. The sponge's effectiveness rate is 84% to 87%. Because it provides no STI protection, it is recommended that a condom be used along with the sponge. Because of the possible risk of toxic shock syndrome, women should not wear the sponge for longer than 30 hours. Also, it should not be used during menstruation or immediately after abortion or childbirth. It's contraindicated in women with a history of toxic shock syndrome (Bachmann, 2007; Hatcher et al., 2008).

Diaphragm

A soft, dome-shaped device with a firm rim, the diaphragm is inserted up to 6 hours before intercourse and holds spermicidal cream or jelly against the cervix. It must be left in place for 6 hours after the last intercourse. If intercourse occurs more than once, the diaphragm should not be removed; instead, another dose of spermicide should be inserted into the vagina with each intercourse (Hatcher et al., 2008).

Diaphragm purchase requires a prescription. Diaphragms are available in various sizes and styles and must be fitted by a trained health care professional (see Figure 5-4). Women who wish to use a diaphragm should be given an opportunity to practice insertion and removal prior to leaving the health facility. Nurses should teach diaphragm users to wash the device in warm soapy water following removal and allow it to dry thoroughly before storing it in the case in a cool place. The patient should check the diaphragm for holes before each use. The diaphragm should be refitted after a weight gain or loss of 10 lb and after pregnancy and birth. The diaphragm does confer some protection against STIs and cervical dysplasia, a precursor to cancer (Hatcher et al., 2008; Kulczycki, Bosarge, Qu, & Shewchuk, 2007). Women with pelvic relaxation syndrome or a large cystocele are not suitable candidates for the diaphragm.

FIGURE 5-4: TYPES OF DIAPHRAGMS

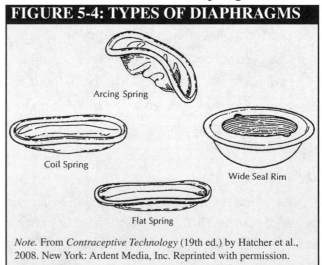

Arcing Spring

Coil Spring

Wide Seal Rim

Flat Spring

Note. From *Contraceptive Technology* (19th ed.) by Hatcher et al., 2008. New York: Ardent Media, Inc. Reprinted with permission.

Effectiveness

With perfect use, the diaphragm has a 6% failure rate. With typical use, 20% of users become pregnant in the first year (Hatcher et al., 2008).

Side Effects

Diaphragms can cause irritation to the lower urinary tract, increasing the patient's susceptibility to bladder infection. Also, they have been shown to alter the normal vaginal flora, which can make a woman more prone to vaginal infections. If used for prolonged periods (> 24 hours) or during menses, the diaphragm may increase a woman's risk of toxic shock syndrome (Hatcher et al., 2008; Kulczycki et al., 2007).

Cervical Caps

Prentif Cavity Rim Cervical Cap

The Prentif Cavity Rim Cervical Cap is a soft, deep rubber cup with a firm round rim. The cap fits firmly around the base of the cervix. The cervical cap may be more difficult to fit than a diaphragm because proper fit depends on the angle of the cervix and uterus (see Figure 5-5) and the device is only available in four sizes in the United States. It offers the advantage of minimal spermicide use (a small amount is placed in the cup), and it can be left in place for up to 48 hours, although prolonged wear may cause cervical irritation. The cap must be left in place for a minimum of 6 hours after the last intercourse. With multiple intercourse, there is no need to insert more spermicidal jelly as with the diaphragm (Hatcher et al., 2008). The Prentif Cavity Rim Cervical Cap is available only by prescription and should be replaced every year.

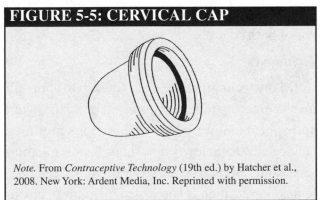

FIGURE 5-5: CERVICAL CAP

Note. From *Contraceptive Technology* (19th ed.) by Hatcher et al., 2008. New York: Ardent Media, Inc. Reprinted with permission.

Lea's Shield

Lea's Shield is a reusable oval device made of silicone rubber with an anterior loop to assist with removal. Similar to the cervical cap, it is inserted vaginally and works by blocking sperm from entering the uterus. Lea's Shield should be used with spermicide. This device contains a central valve that allows passage of cervical secretions and air. Because it comes in only one size, fitting is not required. The device is available by prescription only (Hatcher et al., 2008).

FemCap

The FemCap is a hat-shaped silicone rubber cap with a brim that flares outward. The bowl of the device completely covers the cervix and the rim fits against the vaginal fornices. Spermicide can be placed on the inside and outside of the cap. A strap is located on the convex bowl to aid in removal. The FemCap is available in three sizes and requires a clinician fitting and prescription for purchase. It may be worn for up to 48 hours and should be replaced every 2 years (Hatcher et al., 2008).

Contraindications

Contraindications to use of a cervical cap include history of toxic shock syndrome, known or suspected cervical or uterine malignancy, abnormal Pap smear findings, repeated urinary tract infections (UTIs), or allergy to latex (Hatcher et al., 2008).

Effectiveness

For nulliparous women, the first-year perfect use failure rate is 9%; for parous women, the failure rate is 26%. The typical use failure rate in the first year is 20% for nulliparous women and 40% for parous women (Hatcher et al., 2008).

Side Effects

Women using the cervical cap may be more likely to develop UTIs. Cervical erosion may occur, which can lead to discomfort and spotting. Theoretically, there is an increased risk of toxic shock syndrome, especially if the cap is used during menstruation. A latex allergy may develop with continued use (Hatcher et al., 2008).

Patient Teaching

Women who use cervical caps should be taught to wash the device with soap and water following removal, allow it to air dry, and then store it in a cool place. The cap should be routinely inspected for holes, tears, and cracks (Hatcher et al., 2008).

STERILIZATION

Female Sterilization (Bilateral Tubal Ligation)

Bilateral tubal ligation (BTL) is one of the most popular methods of contraception in the United States and worldwide. In this country, female tubal sterilization accounts for 72% of the sterilization procedures performed. The procedure is considered permanent; reversal has varying success rates depending on the method used, the age of the woman, and the length of the remaining tubes. Overall, sterilization is one of the safest, most economic, and most effective birth control methods available to women who have completed childbearing (Hatcher et al., 2008).

The decision to become sterile is usually not made easily. There are often strong feelings involved. Patients need correct information, a chance to voice their feelings, and a complete discussion of the pros and cons of this procedure and other birth control methods.

Federal sterilization regulations were passed in 1979 to stop sterilization abuse. Today, all states have rigid regulations concerning informed consent for sterilization. Many permit the voluntary sterilization of any mature, rational woman without reference to her marital status. Although the partner's consent is not required by law, every woman should be encouraged to discuss her sterilization plans with her partner, and some health care providers may request the partner's consent. The sterilization of minors and mentally incompetent individuals is restricted by most states and generally requires the approval of court-appointed individuals (Lowdermilk & Perry, 2007).

If federal funds are to be used for the sterilization, the individual must be at least 21 years of age. The informed consent that gives the patient's permission for the sterilization must contain an explanation of the risks of, benefits of, and alternatives to the procedure. Also, a statement that clearly describes the sterilization procedure as a permanent, irreversible method of birth control must be included, along with a statement that mandates a 30-day waiting period between giving consent and undergoing the sterilization procedure. Finally, the informed consent must be in the individual's native language or an interpreter must be provided (Lowdermilk & Perry, 2007).

Counseling for People Considering Sterilization

The decision to undergo permanent female sterilization involves considerable thought and accurate information; this method is reserved for women who have completed their family. During counseling, it is appropriate for the health care provider to direct the woman to consider what her thoughts and reactions would be if something were to happen to her existing family. If the woman believes that she might want to have more children under any circumstances, then she should be encouraged to consider other nonpermanent methods of birth control

Techniques

Many techniques are used for sterilization; all involve interrupting the fallopian tube so the ovum and sperm cannot meet. The various methods include electrocautery, clips, rings, bands, microinserts, and removal of a part of the tube. Usually, female sterilization is conducted by trained personnel using local or general anesthesia in an outpatient setting. A laparoscopy (most common) or suprapubic minilaparotomy is generally performed, and the procedure usually takes less than an hour. Most women resume normal activity within 4 days. BTL can be performed during a cesarean section, following vaginal birth, after abortion, or at a time unrelated to pregnancy or its termination (Hatcher et al., 2008; Lowdermilk & Perry, 2007).

A nonincisional method, called "hysteroscopic tubal ligation," is also available. This procedure is performed in a physician's office or as an outpatient procedure with local anesthesia to the cervix. In 2002, the FDA approved the use of Essure, a sterilization device that is placed via a transcervical approach, which avoids entry into the peritoneal cavity. Microinserts are placed into the openings of the fallopian tubes. During the following months, scar tissue grows into the inserts, causing tubal blockage. A hysterosalpingogram (dye test to evaluate tubal patency) is performed at 3 months to ensure that both tubes have been blocked. Patients are instructed to use an alternate form of contraception until bilateral tubal blockage has been confirmed (ACOG, 2007; Holloway, Moredich, & Aduddell, 2006).

Complications

Recovery is most often uneventful, with mild discomfort at the incision site and mild abdominal and shoulder pain due to the gas used to inflate the abdomen during surgery. More serious complications are rare and include infection, hemorrhage, and anesthesia-related complications. Death is extremely rare. Long-term complications include sterilization failure with resultant pregnancy (with a high rate of ectopic pregnancy) as well as scarring and adhesions, which can result in pelvic pain. For many years, controversy has existed over reports of a post–tubal ligation syndrome characterized by menstrual irregularities and discomforts. No conclusive evidence supporting this syndrome has been found, and further research needs to be conducted on this issue (Hatcher et al., 2008).

Effectiveness

The effectiveness of female sterilization depends on the type of procedure performed and the patient's age (younger women have higher failure rates). Effectiveness rates range from 96.3% to better than 99% with the postpartum procedure (Hatcher et al., 2008).

Male Sterilization (Vasectomy)

Male sterilization, or vasectomy, is more effective, less expensive, and safer than female sterilization. It is technically easier to perform, requires local anesthesia, and is usually done as an outpatient procedure.

The vas deferens is cauterized, clipped, or cut to interrupt the passage of sperm into the seminal fluid. Following vasectomy, the semen no longer contains sperm. Although vasectomy is considered a permanent method of birth control, today's microsurgical reversal techniques result in pregnancy rates of 50% or above and in the return of sperm to the ejaculate in more than 90% of men. Reversal success depends on the microsurgeon's skill, the type of vasectomy performed, the time elapsed since the vasectomy, and the presence of antisperm antibodies, as well as the partner's fertility. Vasectomy is more than 99% effective against pregnancy (Hatcher et al., 2008).

FUTURE BIRTH CONTROL METHODS

New methods of birth control are being researched in both the public and private sectors in an ongoing effort to meet the following goals:

- create female-controlled methods that protect against both pregnancy and STIs, including HIV and acquired immunodeficiency syndrome (AIDS)

- improve hormone-delivery systems to lessen bleeding disruption, a frequent occurrence with progestin-only preparations

- reduce costs of hormonal birth control methods by, for example, advocating for greater third-party reimbursement for all forms of contraception

- continue research on birth control vaccines for both men and women

- create birth control methods that are easier to use, have reduced side effects, and are acceptable in the ethnically and culturally diverse populations served.

(Burkman, 2002; Hatcher et al., 2008).

To this end, many innovative approaches to birth control are currently in various stages of development and refinement. Examples include spermicide/microbicide agents; improved diaphragms, caps, and condoms; hormone receptor blocking agents; redesigned IUDs; immunocontraceptives; and new methods for male contraception and sterility (Hatcher et al., 2008).

Spermicide/Microbicide Agents

Efforts are being focused on the development of an agent that is effective as a spermicide and microbicide. In addition to killing sperm, this product would stop bacterial and viral infections without causing irritation and would ideally enhance one's natural infection defenses and protect against irritation. Under investigation is a systemic microbicide that could be taken prior to exposure or daily or delivered continuously from a vaginal ring or barrier device (Hatcher et al., 2008).

Improved Diaphragms, Cap Devices, and Condoms

Development of improved diaphragm and cap models is underway. One model is an inexpensive, disposable vaginal barrier that could be marketed with a microbicide. Another area of focus involves combining a microbicide with a transparent, disposable, silicone cervical cap. Other research interests include the possibility for self-fitting diaphragms to avoid the need for provider fitting and new female condoms with improved methods for insertion and stabilization in the vagina. Also

being explored is the development of male condoms that can be applied before erection and exert a less-snug fit (Hatcher et al., 2008).

Hormone Receptor Blocking Agents

Efforts are being made in the development of hormone receptor blocking agents. Mifepristone, an antiprogestin that has been studied for use as an emergency contraceptive following unprotected intercourse, may be suitable for low-dose, daily use and also for possible use as a once-a-month regimen. Other work concerns the development of systemic methods that do not disrupt normal hormone cycles. These agents, taken monthly, would provide effective contraception without the side effects related to hormone disruption (Hatcher et al., 2008).

Intrauterine Devices

Work is underway to develop improved versions of existing IUDs that will be associated with reduced expulsion, discomfort, and cramping and will be suitable for women whose uterine depth is too small to accommodate current devices. Another area of investigation concerns an IUD with a non-rigid frame that is anchored by a knot implanted in the myometrium at the uterine fundus (Hatcher et al., 2008).

Immunocontraceptives

Immunocontraceptives are contraceptive vaccines that, in theory, could induce an immune reaction to a reproductive system target to interrupt one or more essential fertility steps. One of the most extensively studied targets is human chorionic gonadotropin (hCG), a hormone that is released by the early embryo and placenta and is necessary for maintaining pregnancy. Another area under investigation concerns a vaccine that targets sperm antigens that could potentially be used by both men and women (Hatcher et al., 2008).

Male Methods

Development of systemic contraceptive methods for men is challenging, in part, due to male fertility physiology: sperm are continuously produced, mature, and develop over an interval of weeks. Other issues concern factors such as adverse effects, side effects, acceptability, and affordability. Approaches under investigation include agents that block hormonal support for testicular cell function by stopping pituitary LH and FSH; interference with seminiferous tubule function to stop sperm production; and disruption of the maturation, function, and transport of sperm after they are produced. Other areas of focus concern non-hormonal agents, such as a cottonseed oil derivative and anti-cancer drugs that reduce sperm without causing systemic toxicity (Hatcher et al., 2008).

Efforts are also being made to improve sterilization methods for men. A device to provide a nonsurgical vasectomy is under investigation. Ultrasound pulses are used to cause localized heat sufficient to seal the vas deferens, while the overlying skin is shielded from the heat (Hatcher et al., 2008).

SUGGESTIONS FOR PROVIDING CONTRACEPTIVE EDUCATION AND COUNSELING TO YOUNG ADULTS

When educating and counseling young adults about contraceptive use, it is helpful to follow certain guidelines:

Begin a counseling session by **assessing** the patient's current knowledge of, level of prior experience with, and misconceptions about birth control methods. Peers serve as the primary source of knowledge about sex and contraception for most young patients. Ask questions to determine what it is that a patient wants to know.

Explore with patients their individual needs, prior experiences, lifestyle factors, frequency of intercourse, situations in which intercourse usually occurs, confidentiality issues, number of partners,

cultural and religious beliefs, and motivating factors. Accurately present the advantages and disadvantages (including health risks) associated with each contraceptive method.

Present questions and situations for patients to consider. Help patients think through how they might react to various situations. It may be appropriate to include role-playing as a teaching method. For example, ask adolescents to consider the logistics of "hiding" a contraceptive method from their parents — where are they going to keep it? If OCPs are selected, will they remember to consistently take one every day? Other areas for exploration include the frequency of intercourse and appropriateness of the contraceptive method chosen.

Follow-up with patients to evaluate the effectiveness and comfort of use with the method. Be sure to have the patient contact you if she experiences any side effects and is considering not using her method or if she finds that she is not being consistent (Rice & Thompson, 2006).

Promote self-responsibility; **encourage** decision-making skills. Encourage patients' partners to be involved. Be nonjudgmental, especially in working with young patients. Health care providers who impose personal attitudes and judgments on their patients are unable to provide effective and appropriate counseling; those who are honest, open, and comfortable with their own sexuality are most likely to gain the trust of young patients and establish a therapeutic environment.

Case Study

Laurie, a 15-year-old, presents to the contraception clinic with her girlfriend for a "routine check-up." During the health history, Laurie tells the nurse that she doubts she can get pregnant because she has been having occasional unprotected sex with different boyfriends for the past 6 months and has never gotten pregnant. Yet she feels that she should probably get "the pill," just in case.

1. What are the major teaching needs for Laurie?

    First, the nurse explores Laurie's level of understanding about menstruation, conception and contraception. Laurie states again that she wishes to use "the pill."

2. The nurse determines that this will be Laurie's first gynecological examination. What are some teaching needs and strategies?

    The nurse explains what will take place during the examination. Showing Laurie a speculum and other equipment helps to facilitate understanding and decrease anxiety. The nurse may also ask Laurie if she would like for her friend to be present with her in the examining room. Exploring Laurie's home situation may provide some insights into the appropriateness of the contraceptive method that Laurie wishes to use, for example, whether she will need to hide the pills from her parents and whether she will be able to incorporate taking the pills into her daily routine so that they are taken consistently.

3. In addition to specific instructions about the prescribed oral contraceptive, what other information should the nurse emphasize?

    The nurse should teach Laurie (and her friend) about safer sex practices, emphasize that oral contraceptives offer no protection against STIs, and discuss the importance of using condoms consistently.

PREGNANCY TERMINATION

Pregnancy termination can be spontaneous (miscarriage) or induced (abortion). Termination of an unwanted pregnancy has been legal in the United States since 1973. Procedures performed after the first trimester are subject to individual state law.

Abortion is an emotionally charged subject for most people. The issues involved are deeply personal ones and must be accorded due respect. Nurses must examine their own values and beliefs carefully and come to their own conclusions. All health care providers must be able to present accurate information and provide nonjudgmental counseling and supportive care for patients who choose pregnancy termination.

Historical Perspective

Throughout history, women in all cultures have used abortion as a solution to unwanted pregnancy. Before the late 1800s, abortion was not addressed in U.S. law, but by 1880, every state had passed some kind of abortion law. During the 100 or so years during which pregnancy termination was not legislated, abortion remained an option mostly for economically privileged women, deemed necessary by the medical establishment for the woman's physical or psychologic health. Abortion was socially acceptable because the decision to terminate the pregnancy was made by the physician, not the woman. Abortion law reform came gradually on a state-by-state basis until 1973, when the Supreme Court ruled on the test case, *Roe v. Wade.* The ruling states that during the first 3 months of pregnancy, the decision to abort can be made by the woman and her physician without interference of the state. After the first trimester, states could impose their own regulations. This ruling resulted in an immediate decrease in maternal mortality from illegal abortion. Abortion-related morbidity also greatly decreased (Hatcher et al., 2008).

Preabortion Counseling

Many areas need to be addressed when a woman learns she has an unintended pregnancy. Crucial to the decision-making process is a nonjudgmental person with whom to explore feelings. Each woman has different needs.

The woman must be helped to deal with her feelings. Accidental pregnancy often triggers a reassessment of a woman's entire life goals. Most often, the woman feels overwhelmed. She may need time to process her feelings before she is ready to receive more information. More than one visit may be necessary.

There should be a thorough discussion of options, which include continuing the pregnancy to term and raising the infant, continuing the pregnancy to term and placing the infant for legal adoption, and terminating the pregnancy (with information about the different kinds of abortion procedures appropriate for the woman's situation). The discussion with the patient should also determine her wishes as to what counseling should be offered to her partner or what information given to her parents (if she is a dependent adolescent). Some states require parental notification or consent before a minor can obtain an abortion. Also, in some states, pregnancy in women younger than a certain age is considered child abuse and must be reported. Nurses must be aware of their state laws in this regard and patient confidentiality is essential (ACOG, 2007).

Pregnancy confirmation paperwork should be completed to obtain financial aid for the woman, as needed, for the procedure. Some women delay seeking pregnancy confirmation because of irregular menses, denial, lack of knowledge about normal cycles, lack of access to abortion services, lack of knowledge about options, and concerns about the cost (Lowdermilk & Perry, 2007).

The woman should be prepared for the abortion. Information provided should include details about the abortion procedure itself, discomforts, medication options, safety, risks, potential complications, and self-care after the procedure. During counseling, the nurse should identify misinformation and gaps in knowledge, verify the woman's understanding, and review the medical record to ensure a signed informed consent has been obtained. The woman needs to understand that, ultimately, the decision for pregnancy termination must be hers and for her own reasons.

Abortion Procedures

Abortion procedures performed during the first trimester are technically easier and safer than pregnancy termination during the second trimester. Abortion may be performed by surgical techniques, including dilatation and curettage (D&C), minisuction, or vacuum curettage. Procedures conducted under local anesthesia have a lower complication rate and are more cost-effective than those performed in a hospital for first and early second trimester abortions. The major risks associated with surgical abortion include perforation of the uterus, cervical lacerations, anesthetic reactions, hemorrhage, and infection (Hatcher et al., 2008).

Medical methods for early pregnancy termination are also available and involve use of mifepristone (Mifeprex, originally called RU-486), an abortifacient, and methotrexate, an antimetabolite used to treat certain types of cancer. Both medications may be followed by vaginal administration of misoprostol (Cytotec), a prostaglandin analogue that promotes expulsion of the pregnancy. Some women believe "medical abortion" a more "natural" method that more closely resembles a miscarriage. Also, medical abortion generally avoids an invasive surgical procedure. However, women often must wait, sometimes for as long as several weeks, for the abortion to occur. The medical abortion is less predictable and may involve substantial cramping (Hatcher et al., 2008).

Initial screening is important to rule out problems, such as bleeding disorders and cardiac problems that might warrant an in-hospital procedure. A physical examination and appropriate screening tests (e.g., complete blood count, blood typing and Rh, gonococcal smear, serologic test for syphilis, urinalysis, and Pap smear) are obtained. Counseling is provided, and informed consent documents are signed and placed in the patient's chart. The type of termination procedure depends on the length of the pregnancy (Hatcher et al., 2008).

Vacuum Aspiration With or Without Curettage

Vacuum aspiration with or without curettage is the most common method used for first trimester and early second trimester abortion. Very early abortions (menstrual extraction or endometrial aspiration) may be performed with a small, flexible, plastic cannula without cervical dilatation or anesthesia. For pregnancy termination at 10 to 12 weeks gestation or more, a sterile piece of dried seaweed (*Laminaria japonica*) or, in some cases a synthetic dilator is inserted into the cervix 4 to 24 hours before the abortion procedure. The laminaria absorbs moisture from body fluids and expands, acting as a mechanical cervical dilator. Upon removal, the cervix has usually dilated two to three times its original diameter and further instrumental dilation is unnecessary. Some providers offer prophylactic antibiotic therapy. Following the 2 to 3 minute procedure, the woman is escorted to an aftercare room, where her vital signs and bleeding are monitored for 15 to 30 minutes, self-care instructions are given, and a 2-week follow-up visit is scheduled. Patients who are Rh-negative receive an injection of immune anti-D globulin (RhoGAM) to prevent blood incompatibility problems in future pregnancies (Hatcher et al., 2008).

Second trimester abortion (i.e., at 13 weeks and later) is associated with increased costs and an increased possibility of complications. Methods used include dilatation and evacuation (D&E), induction of uterine contractions, and major operations.

Dilatation and Evacuation

D&E, the predominant abortion method used beyond the first trimester, may be performed at up to 20 weeks' gestation. This method combines dilatation, suction, curettage, and possibly the use of forceps. Repeated insertions of *Laminaria japonica* are essential to prepare the cervix adequately and greatly decrease the risk of uterine perforation. After the procedure, the woman rests in a recovery area for 1 to 3 hours to ensure that no excessive cramping or bleeding occurs. The aspirated uterine contents are inspected to ascertain that all fetal parts and adequate placental tissue have been aspirated (Hatcher et al., 2008).

Induction of Uterine Contractions

Induction of uterine contractions for abortion most commonly involves the administration of prostaglandins by suppository, cervical gel, or intrauterine injection. Uterine contractions are stimulated to expel the fetus and placenta. Repeated doses may be necessary, and the procedure is usually done in the hospital with medications to ease the discomfort of labor and delivery. Infrequently used techniques involve an intrauterine instillation of hypertonic sodium chloride, hypertonic glucose, or urea to induce contractions. Laminaria and oxytocin may be used to facilitate the process. Complications include infection, failure to abort, excessive bleeding, and the need for surgical removal of retained tissue. Hysterotomy and hysterectomy are rarely used because of the increased morbidity and mortality associated with these methods (Hatcher et al., 2008).

Medical/Chemical Abortion
Mifepristone and Misoprostol

Approved by the FDA in 2000, mifepristone (Mifeprex) is an oral antiprogestational agent. It blocks the action of progesterone on the uterine lining and creates an environment in the uterus that is not conducive to sustained implantation. It also causes cervical softening. Misoprostol, similar to prostaglandin, induces uterine contractions and expulsion of the pregnancy. It is usually given 36 to 48 hours after the mifepristone and may be administered orally or vaginally. More than 50% of abortions occur within 4 hours following the misoprostol. A surgical procedure (D&C) may be required for an incomplete or failed abortion. Side effects of the medications include cramping, abdominal pain, nausea and vomiting, diarrhea, fever, and chills. Failed and incomplete abortion, hemorrhage, and infection are the complications of this pregnancy termination method (Hatcher et al., 2008).

Methotrexate and Misoprostol

Methotrexate is a drug that stops rapidly growing cells. It is used in chemotherapy as well as in the treatment of other conditions. When used in combination with misoprostol, it is 94% to 96% successful in terminating early pregnancy through 7 weeks' gestation dated from the last menstrual period. Methotrexate may be administered orally or by intramuscular injection. Three to seven days later, the patient self-inserts misoprostol vaginal tablets. The misoprostol induces uterine contractions to expel the products of conception. A repeated dose of misoprostol may be necessary, and surgical intervention (D&C) may be required for an incomplete or failed abortion (occurs in 5% of women). Side effects associated with the medications include cramping, abdominal pain, nausea and vomiting, diarrhea, fever, and chills. The woman returns for a follow-up visit 3 to 7 days after the initial misoprostol administration. If complete abortion is not confirmed at this time, she may be offered an additional dose of misoprostol or a vacuum aspiration. Failed and incomplete abortion, hemorrhage, and infection are the complications of this pregnancy termination method (Hatcher et al., 2008).

Aftercare for Abortion

Immediate aftercare for a patient who has undergone an abortion procedure consists of monitoring vital signs and assessing for evidence of bleeding as well as administering Rho(D) immune globulin to women who are Rh D negative.

Abortion Complications

Complications can occur with any type of pregnancy termination, including miscarriage. Recovery for first and early second trimester abortion procedures is most often uneventful. However, possible complications include:

- missed procedure (this is more common in early pregnancy termination when the embryo is very small and may be missed)

- retained tissue and intrauterine blood clots

- infection

- excessive bleeding

- perforation of the cervix or uterus at the time of the procedure

- tearing of the cervix

- allergic reactions to the drugs or anesthetic agent.

(Hatcher et al., 2008)

Offices and clinics where abortion procedures are performed are required to have an emergency cart readily available and trained personnel on staff who are familiar with emergency procedures.

Counseling and Self-Care After an Abortion Procedure

Some women experience a heightened sense of perinatal loss following an elective abortion. Unfortunately, the loss is often "hidden" because friends and other support persons may not know about the pregnancy or may not feel comfortable discussing the experience with the woman (Bennett, Litz, Lee, & Maguen, 2005). Research shows that the most important factor affecting a woman's reaction to her abortion is the level of support provided by those who are important to her. Abortion can be an extremely difficult and emotionally draining process for many women. However, major psychiatric problems following abortion are rare. Nurses can be sensitive to these issues, listen generously to their patients, and provide caring, supportive interventions, such as referrals to local support groups when appropriate (Lowdermilk & Perry, 2007).

Most women experience some bleeding and cramping during the 2 weeks following an abortion procedure. Pregnancy symptoms should subside gradually, although some symptoms such as nausea generally disappear shortly after the procedure. Nurses can counsel women that it is also normal to experience emotional ups and downs during this period.

Following an abortion, all women should be given these instructions on self-care:

- Watch for signs of infection, including fever, chills, foul-smelling vaginal discharge, continuous severe abdominal pain or cramping, severe backache, and heavy bleeding.

- Take your temperature daily (call the physician if your temperature is higher than 38° C [100° F]).

- Do not use tampons until after the 2-week follow-up visit.

- Do not put anything in the vagina until after the next check-up: no douching, no baths, no intercourse.

- Avoid lifting and heavy exercise.

- Drink lots of fluids and eat well to aid the body's recovery.

- Take the full course of any medications prescribed, even if no symptoms are experienced.

(Hatcher et al., 2008)

CONCLUSION

Choosing an appropriate birth control method can be challenging for both the patient and her health care provider. Reproductive planning is a process that requires careful consideration of each woman's individual needs. Prevention of STIs should always constitute an added consideration. Women who experience an unwanted pregnancy need factual, objective information about their options. If they choose pregnancy termination, they must be informed about the procedures available to

them and guided through the process with respect and sensitivity.

EXAM QUESTIONS

CHAPTER 5
Questions 32-44

Note: Choose the option that BEST answers each question.

32. The only method of birth control that is 100% effective is

    a. an IUD.
    b. abstinence.
    c. sterilization.
    d. Depo-Provera.

33. The most common reason women stop taking their birth control pills is

    a. misunderstanding of the instructions.
    b. fear of STIs.
    c. side effects.
    d. confidentiality issues with parents.

34. Both the transdermal patch and the vaginal ring should be kept in place for

    a. 3 weeks.
    b. 4 weeks.
    c. 6 weeks.
    d. 1 year.

35. Depo-Provera has no effect on

    a. the menstrual cycle.
    b. mood.
    c. immunity to STIs.
    d. BMD.

36. Depo-Provera should not be given to women who have a history of

    a. problems with oral contraceptives.
    b. depression.
    c. menstrual irregularities.
    d. STIs.

37. The Implanon subdermal hormonal implant must be replaced every

    a. 4 years.
    b. 3 years.
    c. 2 years.
    d. 1 year.

38. For the highest level of effectiveness, an emergency contraceptive pill should be taken

    a. between 2 and 36 hours after intercourse.
    b. within 72 hours after intercourse.
    c. when the first menstrual period is missed.
    d. any time after intercourse.

39. With an IUD, the greatest danger of infection occurs during the

    a. first month after insertion.
    b. first 6 months after insertion.
    c. first year after insertion.
    d. menstrual period.

40. One of the main advantages of the female condom is that it

    a. is less expensive than the male condom.

    b. is controlled by the woman.

    c. does not interfere with the spontaneity of sex.

    d. can be reused.

41. A woman comes to your facility for counseling to choose a birth control method. You should begin to work with her by first

    a. describing all the different methods on the market.

    b. finding out what she already knows about birth control methods.

    c. listing the pros and cons of each method.

    d. asking her if she had unprotected sex.

42. First trimester and early second trimester surgical abortions can be performed more safely by using

    a. general anesthesia.

    b. an intravenous sedative.

    c. local anesthesia.

    d. no anesthesia.

43. For surgical abortion procedures, *Laminaria japonica* is used to

    a. dilate the cervix before the procedure.

    b. prevent excessive bleeding.

    c. dilate the cervix at the time of the procedure.

    d. empty the contents of the uterus.

44. During a chemical abortion, the insertion of prostaglandin tablets into the vagina is for the purpose of

    a. preventing the embryo from attaching to the uterine wall.

    b. stopping the growth of rapidly dividing cells.

    c. preventing bleeding.

    d. inducing uterine contractions.

CHAPTER 6

INFERTILITY

CHAPTER OBJECTIVE

After completing this chapter, the reader will be able to identify the processes involved in the evaluation and management of infertility.

LEARNING OBJECTIVES

After studying this chapter, the reader will be able to

1. define the term *infertility*.

2. indicate the factors involved in male and female infertility.

3. identify various testing methods used during an infertility assessment.

4. specify the various procedures available for assisted reproduction.

5. identify resources for infertile couples and some of the psychosocial issues associated with infertility.

KEY WORDS

- Assisted hatching
- Assisted reproductive technologies (ARTs)
- Basal body temperature (BBT) charting
- Diethylstilbestrol (DES)
- Endometrial biopsy
- Gamete intrafallopian transfer (GIFT)

- Intracytoplasmic sperm injection (ICSI)
- Micromanipulation
- Ovarian hyperstimulation
- Pelvic inflammatory disease (PID)
- Postcoital test (PCT)
- Semen evaluation
- Spinnbarkeit
- Tubal embryo transfer (TET)
- Zygote intrafallopian transfer (ZIFT)

INTRODUCTION

Infertility is defined as an inability to conceive after 1 year with appropriately timed sexual intercourse without the use of contraception. Today, infertility affects approximately 10% to15% of reproductive-age couples, and the risk increases for women after 35 years of age. After age 35, close to one-third of women who desire a child are unable to conceive (American Society for Reproductive Medicine [ASRM], n.d.). For those who have difficulty or are unable to conceive, infertility can be devastating (RESOLVE, 2006).

Approximately 4.5 million women in the United States reported infertility in 1982; this figure rose to 4.8 million in 1988 and 6.2 million in 1995. These increases are no doubt related to many factors. Delayed childbearing by baby boomers, decreased popularity of permanent sterilization as a birth control method, and an advancement of the age limit beyond 35 years as a criterion to qualify for infertility treatment are believed to have played roles, as many couples now postpone first pregnancy attempts until later in life (Hatcher et al., 2008).

The financial and psychological costs of infertility can be enormous. Diagnosis and treatment of infertility require extensive physical, emotional, and economic resources over an extended period of time. Often, men and women perceive infertility differently. Women may experience more stress from the various tests and treatments.

DEFINITIONS

It is helpful to review some of the relevant terms associated with infertility:

- **Primary infertility:** The diagnosis when the couple has never conceived

- **Secondary infertility:** The term used for couples who have previously conceived but have not conceived now despite at least 12 months of unprotected intercourse

- **Pregnancy wastage:** The woman is able to conceive but is unable to carry the fetus to a viable age

- **Subfertility:** The couple has difficulty in conceiving jointly because both partners may have reduced fertility.

(Hatcher et al., 2008)

PROBABILITY OF CONCEPTION

In general, couples should be referred for infertility evaluation if they have been unable to conceive after 1 year of regular, unprotected intercourse. For women older than age 35, or for couples whose history predisposes them to infertility, referral for infertility evaluation may be appropriate after only 6 months of unprotected

intercourse. At 25 years of age, the age at which men and women are most fertile, conception usually occurs in 5.3 months. The average 20- to 30-year-old American couple has intercourse one to three times a week, and this frequency should be sufficient to achieve a pregnancy if all other factors are satisfactory. In approximately 20% of cases, conception occurs in the first month of unprotected intercourse (Hatcher et al., 2008).

REQUIREMENTS FOR FERTILITY

The following factors are necessary for fertility in men and women.

For the Male Partner

- Normal reproductive structures for the manufacture and maturation of sperm

- Normal count, motility, and morphologic characteristics of sperm

- Adequate sexual drive

- Ability to maintain an erection and achieve normal ejaculation within the vaginal vault

(Hatcher et al., 2008)

For the Female Partner

- Adequate sexual drive

- Normal reproductive anatomy

- Cervical mucus conducive to sperm survival and transport

- Ovulatory cycles

- Functional fallopian tubes

- Uterus that develops an environment favorable to implantation

- Normal hormone balance

- Normal immunologic response to sperm

- Adequate nutritional status to maintain a pregnancy

(Hatcher et al., 2008)

RISK FACTORS FOR INFERTILITY

Infertility may be attributed to problem sources in either partner, reduced fertility in both partners, or unknown factors. Sometimes, minor problems in each partner combine to prevent fertility in the couple. Among couples who have an identifiable cause of infertility, 40% are related to male factors, 40% are related to female factors, and 20% are related to both male and female factors. Approximately 20% of couples have no identifiable cause of infertility; they are classified as having "unexplained infertility" (Hatcher et al., 2008).

Eight major risk factors have particular importance with regard to infertility: age, sexually transmitted infections (STIs), lifestyle patterns, environmental pollution, medications, surgery, radiation, and intrauterine exposure to diethylstilbestrol (DES).

Age

Probably the single most important factor in female fertility is age. A woman's decision to delay childbearing may result in an inability to conceive due to declining fertility. Approximately one in seven women ages 30 to 34, one in five women ages 35 to 39, and one in four women ages 40 to 44 experience infertility. There are a number of reasons for the age-related decline in fertility. A decrease in egg quality, an increase in spontaneous abortions, an increase in diseases of the reproductive tract (especially endometriosis), and a reduced frequency of intercourse are all associated with advancing age in women. Oocyte abnormalities are believed to be the primary reason for age-associated infertility. By age 42, approximately 90% of a woman's eggs have chromosomal abnormalities (Forbus, 2005).

Male age as an infertility factor has been studied less often. The risk of sperm chromosomal abnormalities increases as men age. Also, with increasing age, frequency of intercourse tends to decline and sexual function problems related to medications or surgery are more likely to emerge. However, there is no cessation of sperm production analogous to cessation of ovulation during female menopause (Hatcher et al., 2008).

Sexually Transmitted Infections

STIs constitute one of the most important risk factors in infertility for both men and women. The incidence of pelvic inflammatory disease (PID) has risen over the past 20 years and now exceeds one million reported cases per year. PID can cause permanent damage to the ovaries and fallopian tubes. Because many STIs are asymptomatic, scarring and tubal adhesions may remain unrecognized until the woman attempts pregnancy. Findings from various studies have shown that approximately one-half of women who are diagnosed with infertility related to tubal factors have no history suggestive of PID. Exposure to STIs also increases the risk of cervical dysplasia and cervical cancer, conditions that commonly require interventions that can adversely affect a woman's reproductive ability (Hatcher et al., 2008).

Lifestyle

Research to examine the relationship between lifestyle habits and fertility is difficult to design because individual lifestyle factors are usually not isolated. The use of alcohol, social drugs, caffeine, and cigarettes have all been found to have a negative effect on fertility. Alcohol consumption can cause erectile problems (impotence). Men who smoke have decreased sperm motility, decreased sperm count, alterations in sperm morphology and nicotine present in the seminal fluid. The heavy use of marijuana, alcohol, and cocaine is associated with a decreased sperm count and depressed testosterone levels. Heroin, methadone, selective serotonin reuptake inhibitors, and barbiturates decrease libido. In women, smoking is associated with decreased fertility and an increased rate of spontaneous abortions and ectopic pregnancies. Tobacco use is also an important risk factor for cervical cancer. Menopause occurs earlier in women who smoke, a fact that underscores the relationship between smoking and hormonal function. Other lifestyle activities that may affect male fertility include those that expose the scrotum to high temperatures (e.g., hot tubs, prolonged bike riding, and wearing tight clothing), which can decrease sperm production and cause abnormal sperm morphology (Muthusami & Chinnaswamy, 2005; Sheweita, Tilmisany, & Al-Sawaf, 2005).

Environmental Pollution

Toxic trace metals (e.g., mercury and cadmium), textile dyes, dry cleaning fluid, lead, pesticides, radiation, and many chemicals commonly found in the workplace and home can have a negative impact on fertility as well as on fetal growth and development. Often, exposure to these substances occurs years before infertility is diagnosed (Hatcher et al., 2008).

Medications

A number of medications, such as narcotics, tranquilizers, antidepressants, and antihypertensives, can cause impotence or affect sperm count (or both). Barbiturates and narcotics may inhibit ovulation and affect menstrual cycle function. Various other drugs are associated with miscarriage, and birth defects. Chemotherapy may permanently impair fertility (Lowdermilk & Perry, 2007).

Surgery

Removal of or damage to reproductive structures, nerve damage in the genital area, and adhesions from pelvic surgery can directly or indirectly cause infertility.

Radiation

Used to kill cancer cells, radiation therapy involves the delivery of high-energy ionizing radiation. Radiation that treats cancer is given in doses much greater than the amount given for reg-

ular X-rays. In cancer treatment, radiation emissions damage the deoxyribonucleic acid of tumor cells, which prevents cell division and growth. Rapidly growing cells are especially sensitive to radiation effects. Radiation therapy is designed to destroy cancer cells while limiting the amount of normal tissue exposed to and injured by the rays. Depending on the site, dose, and duration of exposure, however, radiation can lead to structural damage of the reproductive organs and cause an increase in chromosomal aberrations (Krychman & Goldrich, 2007).

Exposure to Diethylstilbestrol

DES is a synthetic estrogen that was once given to women early in pregnancy to prevent miscarriage. It was taken off the market because of its multiple effects on the offspring of women who took it. Prenatal exposure to DES can impair fertility in both women (abnormal uteruses and tubes) and men (reduced sperm counts and epididymal cysts). In female fetuses, DES exposure is associated with hypoplasia (underdevelopment) of the uterine cavity, T-shaped uterus, intrauterine adhesions, and cervical stenosis. Also, intrauterine DES exposure has been shown to be linked to ectopic pregnancy, pregnancy loss, and preterm birth (Cunningham et al., 2005; Lauver, Nelles, & Hanson, 2005).

INITIAL ASSESSMENT OF AN INFERTILE COUPLE

Consider the circumstances that prompt a woman or a couple to seek infertility evaluation. Often, months or even years have been invested in attempts to conceive before the couple seeks professional help. No doubt the emotional impact of the entire process has had profound implications for their self-esteem, their sexual interaction, and their relationship altogether. At this point, they are faced with possible solutions and no guarantees. Their treatment may range from education and lifestyle changes to complex hormone manipulation or surgery. The process of infertility evaluation and treatment is often lengthy and costly, taxing the personal, financial, and coping resources of the couple. Inherent in the work-up is an intense scrutiny of what is usually the most private and intimate aspect of a couple's relationship.

Nurses have a special role when working with infertile couples. They serve as educators to ensure that couples are provided with culturally sensitive, reliable, and understandable information and sources for further assistance. Nurses are also caregivers who provide couples with emotional support, ensure as much privacy as possible, accurately answer questions, respond to concerns, and lend an attentive and compassionate ear by allowing the couple time to express their feelings. Nurses also function as patient advocates who respect and affirm couples' decisions not to proceed with further intervention but instead to choose alternatives, such as adoption. Providing an overview of what to expect during the initial and subsequent visits empowers the couple to make an informed decision about their level of commitment to the evaluation and possible treatment and affords them some sense of control over their situation (Lowdermilk & Perry, 2007).

The initial infertility evaluation begins with a complete history and physical examination for each partner. Many tests will be recommended, which commonly include charting cyclic temperature fluctuations, semen analysis, and hormone testing. Depending on the findings, more invasive diagnostic procedures for both partners may follow. Findings from this level of testing will diagnose the infertility problem in approximately 60% of infertile couples. Referral to a specialty center is appropriate if pregnancy has not been achieved within 1 year after developing a plan, or within 6 months if the woman is older than age 35 (Brown, 2004).

The history and physical examination, crucial components in the diagnostic workup, should include the following details:

- *For women:*
  - Menstrual history
  - Pregnancy history
  - Evidence of any weight gain, hirsutism, or acne
  - Diet
  - Exercise practices
  - Environmental exposures
  - Exposure to DES
  - Substance use or abuse
  - Medical conditions (e.g., infections, exposure to tuberculosis, chronic illness)
  - Sexual history (e.g., birth control methods, number of partners, STI exposure, and treatment)
  - Surgeries, especially those involving the reproductive system
  - Psychosocial and cultural histories.

- *For men:*
  - Evidence of exposure to environmental toxins (e.g., heavy metals, agent orange)
  - Current or history of infection (e.g., mumps, urinary tract infection, STIs)
  - History of trauma to the scrotal area
  - Lifestyle (e.g., substance abuse) and cultural issues
  - Surgeries
  - History of undescended testes, hernia, other abnormalities of the reproductive system, or intrauterine exposure to DES.

(Hatcher et al., 2008)

Education is an essential element in infertility management. The couple benefits from a basic understanding of the normal menstrual cycle, so that they can learn how to optimize their fertility. They also need information concerning planned tests and procedures: why and when specific tests will be performed, what preparation is required, what discomfort to expect, and what the usual length of recovery is (American College of Obstetricians and Gynecologists [ACOG], 2007; Hatcher et al., 2008).

Tests and Procedures

A complete workup is usually conducted, even if abnormalities are found on a particular test. Crucial tests should be repeated after corrective suggestions have been initiated, allowing enough time in between for the interventions to have an effect. For example, because the process of sperm maturation takes approximately 10 weeks, desirable changes would not be apparent for several months (Hatcher et al., 2008).

Evaluation of the Man

Evaluation of the man can include semen analysis, a postcoital test (PCT), sperm penetration assay, hormone tests, and surgical diagnostic interventions. Each of these tests is briefly described here.

Semen Analysis

Normal sperm production is a continuous process. It takes approximately 2.5 to 3 months for an immature spermatocyte to reach maturity. During a male infertility workup, a semen analysis to assess the quality and quantity of sperm is the first test performed. Because variations in the sperm count of healthy men may occur, abnormal results should be rechecked. If the results of the semen analysis fall within the fertile range, no additional evaluation of the sperm is required (Hatcher et al., 2008).

The level of sophistication in testing different factors involved in male fertility has improved dramatically in recent years with the advent of computer-assisted analysis. Semen analysis includes evaluation of such factors as volume, pH, sperm count, consistency of seminal fluid, morphologic characteristics, and motility of sperm and signs of infection, inflammation, or agglutination (Hatcher et al., 2008).

Postcoital Test

The PCT, also called the *Sims-Huhner test,* is one method used to assess the number of sperm present in cervical mucus within several hours after intercourse. This test also provides information concerning the adequacy of coital technique, adequacy of cervical mucus, and ability of the sperm to penetrate the cervical mucus (ACOG, 2007; Hatcher et al., 2008).

The PCT needs to be timed carefully with the immediate preovulatory phase. The woman's basal body temperature (BBT) should not yet show an increase (indicative that ovulation has already occurred). Following 2 to 4 days of abstinence, sexual intercourse should have taken place at home either the night before or morning of the planned evaluation. A sample of mucus from the exocervix and endocervix is obtained with a small syringe during a pelvic examination. Microscopic evaluation of the cervical mucus specimen reveals the type of mucus present and the number and motility of sperm. A normal sperm count is a minimum of 5 to 10 motile sperm per high-power field. Mucus conducive to sperm penetration should be present. If the mucus is favorable and the semen analysis reveals normal findings, additional specialized testing is needed to determine the presence of sperm-mucus incompatibilities or sperm capacitation problems (Hatcher et al., 2008; Lowdermilk & Perry, 2007).

Sperm Penetration Assay/Ovum Penetration Test

Successful fertilization involves a complex series of biochemical reactions that occur when the sperm interacts with the egg. The sperm penetration assay (also called the hamster zona-free ovum test or hamster test) checks the ability of the sperm to penetrate the egg. Sperm are mixed with specially prepared hamster eggs in a laboratory; the number of sperm that penetrate the egg (termed the "sperm capacitation index") is measured. The latest testing methods assess different aspects of this process and include analysis of the ability of sperm to shed their protein coating and release the enzymes needed to penetrate the egg (Hatcher et al., 2008).

Other Tests

Because hormonal imbalances such as low testosterone levels can cause abnormal sperm production, hormone assays may be included in the male workup. Serum hormone analyses may include testosterone, estradiol, follicle stimulating hormone (FSH), and luteinizing hormone (LH) levels. In addition, the male may also be assessed for hypopituitarism, nutritional deficiencies, debilitating or chronic disease, trauma, exposure to environmental hazards (e.g., radiation, toxic substances), and obstructions of the epididymis and vas deferens. Referral to a urologist may be indicated (Hatcher et al., 2008).

Surgical Interventions

Surgical interventions may be performed to evaluate for the presence of tubal obstructions. Radiographic studies, which involve the use of contrast dye injected into the vas deferens or ejaculatory duct, may also be indicated. A testicular biopsy may be recommended to confirm evidence of the development of structures needed to support normal sperm maturation (Hatcher et al., 2008).

Evaluation of the Woman

Evaluation of the woman includes documentation of ovulation, determination of fallopian tube patency, and testing for the presence of cervical or uterine factors.

Charting of Fertility Signs

Approximately 15% to 20% of couples' infertility can be attributed to ovulation problems. The most basic and least expensive tests involve charting the events that occur during the menstrual cycle (e.g., changes in BBT and cervical mucus) (Hatcher et al., 2008; Lowdermilk & Perry, 2007).

1. **BBT charting:** Charting BBT consists of documenting the subtle changes that occur during a normal ovulatory cycle. The temperature-regulating centers in the hypothalamus are controlled in part by progesterone levels. After ovulation, when progesterone levels increase dramatically, BBT rises approximately $0.28°$ C $(0.5°$ F). This rise in temperature indicates that ovulation has already occurred; thus, it cannot be used to predict ovulation. BBT normally stays elevated for a minimum of 11 days. Large deviations from this pattern may indicate other cycle abnormalities. Several months of charting are usually needed to establish the presence of a cyclic ovulatory pattern.

2. **Cervical mucus charting:** Noting changes in the consistency of cervical mucus provides another time-tested method to indicate ovulation. The increase in estrogen levels that occurs around midcycle causes the cervical mucus to change from a thick, tacky, opaque mucus to a clear, stretchy, slippery mucus with a thinner consistency. The thin, watery mucus that occurs prior to ovulation resembles egg whites. The stretchable quality of cervical mucus is termed *spinnbarkeit*. Cervical mucus does not break when stretched between the thumb and forefinger and, if examined under a microscope, an organized fern-like pattern is present. This physiologic response occurs due to the action of glycoproteins (molecules made of sugars and protein) in the mucus that line up to create a pathway for sperm passage through the cervical canal. The glycoproteins also provide nutrients for the sperm. Some women lack this type of "favorable" mucus because of infection, hormonal imbalance, or injury to the endocervical glands, which produce the mucus.

   Several over-the-counter testing kits are available to assist a woman in identifying the presence of fertile-type mucus. These kits assess for an electrical change that occurs in the cervical mucus and in saliva from hormone-induced biochemical changes. As is the case with BBT, cervical mucus assessment is not an accurate predictor of ovulation.

Predicting Ovulation

An over-the-counter kit that measures the levels of LH in urine is available. The LH surge precedes ovulation by 24 to 28 hours. This test both predicts and verifies ovulation and can be used to time intercourse.

Home-Based Fertility Screening

An over-the counter testing kit (Fertell) that provides assessment of key elements of both male and female fertility has recently become available. The male fertility test measures the concentration of motile sperm in ejaculate. The female test measures the concentration of FSH in the first voided urine on day 3 of the menstrual cycle. A dipstick similar to that used in at-home pregnancy testing kits is used. The male fertility test should be performed 2 days after the last ejaculation; semen samples collected into condoms cannot be used. Nurses should ensure that couples understand the test is intended as a screening tool only; any couple who has been actively attempting to conceive for 12 months or longer (6 months or longer if the woman is over 35 years old) should consult a fertility specialist regardless of test results (Moore, 2007).

Hormone Tests

Various hormone tests (e.g., progesterone, estrogen, prolactin, FSH, LH) can be used to evaluate a woman's fertility. Specific blood tests can be performed to assess the functioning of the thyroid and adrenal glands as well as to measure the levels of the hypothalamic, pituitary, and ovarian hormones. Some of the most common hormonal assays are described here (Cunningham et al., 2005; Hatcher et al., 2008):

1. **Serum progesterone levels:** Progesterone is measured in the middle of the second half of the cycle (the luteal phase). Adequate levels of this hormone are an indication that ovulation has occurred and that the corpus luteum has fully formed and is functioning adequately to produce the progesterone needed to provide a receptive environment for implantation. If ovulation does not occur, serum progesterone levels fall below normal range. When deficient, exogenous progesterone may be administered (orally, vaginally, intramuscularly) as an adjunct to infertility treatment (Cedars, 2007).

2. **Serum estrogen levels:** Serum estrogen levels are obtained to measure the levels of estrogen produced by the granulosa cells of the ovary during the first half of the cycle. Estrogen is needed for adequate maturation of the ovarian follicle before ovulation can occur.

3. **Serum prolactin levels:** Elevated prolactin levels may prevent ovulation and menstruation. A number of drugs, including phenothiazine, opiates, diazepam, reserpine, methyldopa, and tricyclic antidepressants can affect the secretion of prolactin. These agents are believed to inhibit the release of prolactin-inhibiting factor from the hypothalamus. Emotional stress has also been shown to inhibit the release of prolactin-inhibiting factor, which causes the release of excess prolactin. In addition, physical stressors such as surgery, trauma, and cranial lesions can produce this response. Benign pituitary adenoma, a lesion diagnosed through radiographic techniques or computed tomography scanning, is another common cause of hyperprolactinemia.

Procedures

Several different procedures can be used to evaluate a woman's fertility. These include endometrial biopsy, ultrasound techniques, hysterosalpingogram (HSG), hysteroscopy, and laparoscopy (Cunningham et al., 2005; Hatcher et al., 2008):

1. **Endometrial biopsy:** The thickness and glandular structure of the endometrial lining of the uterus undergo dramatic cyclic changes in response to estrogen and, later, to progesterone. Endometrial lining samples can be correlated with serum progesterone levels to determine

whether the uterine environment is conducive to implantation.

2. **Ultrasound techniques:** Transvaginal ultrasound can be used to identify pelvic abnormalities (e.g., fibroids, ovarian or tubal cysts, some uterine anomalies) as well as to evaluate the growth and development of the ovarian follicle and the corpus luteum. Color flow Doppler to investigate uterine blood flow is also a valuable tool in infertility assessment.

3. **Hysterosalpingogram:** The HSG is used to evaluate tubal patency and gather information about the internal anatomy of the uterus and fallopian tubes. A contrast dye is injected into the uterine cavity, allowing these structures to be visualized (see Figure 6-1). In some cases, this test can be used to open a blockage in the fallopian tube. It is performed during the first half (follicular phase) of the menstrual cycle to avoid interrupting an early pregnancy. Moderate to severe cramping may occur. All patients should be warned about the possibility of pain during the test, and many providers prescribe a nonsteroidal anti-inflammatory drug, such as ibuprofen, to be given 30 minutes prior to the procedure.

FIGURE 6-1: HYSTEROSALPINGOGRAPHY

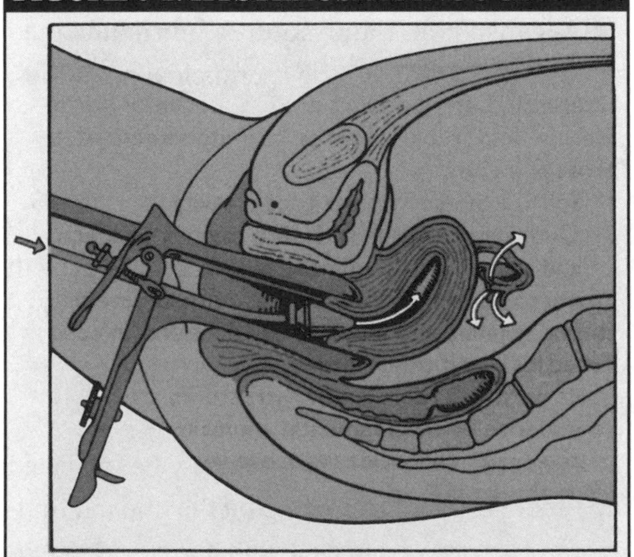

Note. From *Maternity & Women's Health Care* (9th ed., p. 242), by D. Lowdermilk & S. Perry, 2007, St. Louis, Mosby. Reprinted with permission.

4. **Hysteroscopy:** A hysteroscope is a fiber-optic instrument that is placed into the uterus to allow evaluation of the endometrial cavity. Often used in conjunction with laparoscopy, hysteroscopy can also be done in a physician's office and does not require general anesthesia.

5. **Laparoscopy:** In laparoscopy, a laparoscope is inserted through a small incision in a woman's umbilicus, allowing direct visualization of pelvic structures and the opportunity for surgical removal of adhesions and other lesions, such as those associated with endometriosis (see Figure 6-2). Because carbon dioxide gas is instilled into the abdomen to enhance visibility of the organs, the woman may experience postoperative cramping and referred shoulder pain, which can be relieved with a mild analgesic.

FIGURE 6-2: LAPAROSCOPY

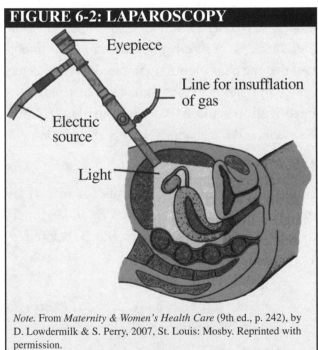

Eyepiece

Line for insufflation of gas

Electric source

Light

Note. From *Maternity & Women's Health Care* (9th ed., p. 242), by D. Lowdermilk & S. Perry, 2007, St. Louis: Mosby. Reprinted with permission.

COUNSELING, REFERRALS, AND TREATMENT

If testing reveals structural abnormalities of the reproductive system, referral for evaluation and possible surgical repair is indicated. A number of strategies and interventions are available to assist the health care provider in working with the infertile couple.

Timing of Intercourse

The simplest intervention involves counseling the couple about the events of the menstrual cycle and strategies to maximize their chances for conception. Infrequent sexual intercourse is a common cause of infertility; it is recommended that couples have intercourse every other day around the time of ovulation. Less frequent coitus may miss ovulation, while more frequent intercourse decreases sperm count (Hatcher et al., 2008; Lowdermilk & Perry, 2007).

The timing of intercourse before ovulation occurs is crucial. Sperm can survive for more than 72 hours in the female genital tract. The ovum has a shorter life span of only 12 hours if unfertilized. The actual time an egg is capable of fertilization is thought to be only a few hours. Thus, sperm must be present before or shortly after ovulation. It is important that the careful timing of intercourse be determined in relation to the woman's menstrual cycle. Fertilization is more likely to take place if intercourse precedes ovulation (Hatcher et al., 2008).

Lifestyle Changes

Other simple interventions for infertility involve general changes in lifestyle. For women, the following recommendations may be helpful:

- changing
  — the diet
  — exercise patterns to prevent exercise-induced amenorrhea (lack of menses)
- establishing adequate weight for a regular menstrual cycle to occur
- avoiding the use of cigarettes, alcohol, social drugs, and caffeine
- reducing exposure to chemicals
- using only water-soluble lubricants during intercourse.

(Hatcher et al., 2008; Lowdermilk & Perry, 2007)

For men, keeping cool – that is, avoiding daily hot tubs, saunas, and tight-fitting clothes, which increase scrotal temperature – may help.

Sexual Intercourse Strategies

Positioning

During intercourse, positions that maximize the exposure of sperm to the cervix enhance the chances of conception. A woman whose uterus tilts forward accomplishes prolonged contact of the sperm with her cervix by lying on her back with her hips elevated. Remaining in this position for at least 20 minutes following intercourse allows sperm to pool around the cervix (Hatcher et al., 2008).

Use of Condoms

Some women develop antisperm antibodies as an immunologic reaction to sperm. Using condoms during sexual intercourse for 6 to 12 months reduces antisperm antibody production in most women who have elevated antisperm antibody titers. Once the serum reaction has subsided, condoms are used at all times except during the expected time of ovulation. Approximately one-third of couples with antisperm antibodies are able to conceive after taking these measures (Hatcher et al., 2008; Lowdermilk and Perry, 2007).

Use of Non-Water-Soluble Lubricants

Because non-water-soluble lubricants may contain spermicide or have spermicidal properties, they should be avoided.

Douching

Douching should be avoided because this practice can alter the vaginal pH and allow the growth of pathogens; it also counteracts efforts to achieve pregnancy.

Hormonal Interventions

Intervention with hormones may be indicated for either partner. Depending on the clinical findings, women may be treated with hormones including LH, FSH, estrogen, progesterone, and hCG;

men may be treated with testosterone, tamoxifen, and clomiphene.

Surgical Interventions

Uterine fibroid tumors (leiomyomas) can result in implantation failure by creating a chronic inflammatory response in the uterus. Surgical removal (myomectomy) may be indicated. Ovarian tumors and scar tissue adhesions caused by chronic infections can be excised. Reconstructive surgery for uterine anomalies might improve a woman's chance for conceiving and carrying a pregnancy to viability (Lowdermilk & Perry, 2007).

Pharmacologic Methods

Certain medications can be used in varying combinations to stimulate ovulation and, depending on the extent of intervention involved, the development of multiple ovarian follicles. During treatment with these drugs, sexual intercourse is carefully timed around ovulation. Certain fertility protocols increase the likelihood of multiple gestation.

Several medications are commonly used in the pharmacologic management of infertility. These include clomiphene citrate (Clomid, Milophene, Serophene); menotropins (Pergonal, Humegon, Repronex); follitropins (Follistim); follitropin alpha (Gonal-F); and urofollitropin (Fertinex).

1. **Clomiphene citrate:** Clomiphene citrate (Clomid) was first introduced in the late 1950s. This drug is used to induce ovulation by acting directly on the hypothalamus. It is useful for women who fail to ovulate because of a problem at the hypothalamic or pituitary level. When given early in the menstrual cycle, clomiphene citrate suppresses the amount of natural estrogen and "fools" the pituitary gland into producing more FSH and LH, which cause maturation of a follicle and ovulation. With this medication, about 70% of women will ovulate,

and approximately 40% of those will become pregnant without any further assistance.

Women taking clomiphene citrate should be monitored with daily urine LH tests and examined with ultrasound when the LH surge occurs. Clomiphene citrate may cause blurred vision, ovarian cysts, pelvic discomfort, hot flashes, insomnia, and irritability. Multiple pregnancy can also occur; about 6% of women who receive this medication produce twins (Hatcher et al., 2008; Lowdermilk & Perry, 2007).

2. **Menotropins:** Menotropins, or human menopausal gonadotropins, are a mixture of FSH and LH in a 1:1 ratio. These agents are marketed under several names, including Pergonal, Humegon, and Repronex. Naturally occurring FSH and LH are extracted from the urine of postmenopausal women, purified, and freeze-dried into a powder. Urofollitropin (Fertinex) is further purified and contains only FSH. When given via injection to premenopausal women according to a specific timing protocol, these medications stimulate the ovarian follicles. They are given with human chorionic gonadotropin (hCG) to stimulate ovulation (Lowdermilk & Perry, 2007).

3. **Follitropins:** Follitropins are newer and purer forms of purified FSH that have more predictable bioeffects. Marketed under the names Follistim, Gonal-F, and Fertinex, these drugs contain recombinant FSH produced through genetic engineering. They exert a direct effect on the ovarian follicles. Because recombinant FSH is free from contaminants by proteins, it may be administered subcutaneously using a small needle or intramuscularly (Lowdermilk & Perry, 2007).

As with all medications, complications and side effects can occur with the use of fertility drugs. Problems are usually related to ovarian hyperstimulation, with the possibility of increased ovulation, multiple gestation, and preterm delivery.

Hyperstimulation is a serious complication that can result from ovulation induction. It is characterized by marked ovarian enlargement, ascites with or without pain, and pleural effusion. When hyperstimulation is detected, hCG is not given and ovulation does not occur. The patient undergoes a rest period and postponement of infertility treatment until the following cycle. These symptoms usually resolve spontaneously with rest and pelvic rest (no intercourse), but hospitalization occasionally is required for observation and fluid management (Lowdermilk & Perry, 2007).

Medications used for the treatment of infertility are extremely potent and require daily monitoring with ovarian ultrasonography along with monitoring of serum estrogen (estradiol, E2) levels to prevent ovarian hyperstimulation. The prevalence of multiple pregnancy with these medications is greater than 25% (Lowdermilk & Perry, 2007).

Nonpharmacologic Therapies

Therapeutic Insemination

Therapeutic insemination, previously termed *artificial insemination,* may be accomplished using the partner's semen or using the semen of a donor. This technique involves the instillation of sperm at the cervical os or into the uterus (intrauterine insemination) by mechanical means. Use of the partner's sperm is indicated in a number of conditions, such as in unexplained infertility, low sperm count, and ejaculatory dysfunction. Donor sperm are used for situations, such as an absence of sperm or the presence of certain chromosomal disorders. Single or lesbian women who wish to become pregnant may also choose therapeutic insemination with donor sperm. To ensure that the sperm do not carry any diseases, guidelines for the preparation, storage, and screening of sperm have been established by the American Fertility Society. Its current recommendation is that donated sperm be frozen and quarantined for 6 months to ensure that it is disease-free. Also, the donor should be retested

before the sperm is released for use (Lowdermilk & Perry, 2007).

Intrauterine Insemination

Intrauterine insemination (IUI) bypasses problems with cervical issues such as stenosis (narrowing) or unfavorable cervical mucus by the instillation of a small amount of specially prepared sperm directly into the uterus (Lowdermilk & Perry, 2007).

Emotional Impact of Infertility

Infertility is recognized as a major life stressor for both partners. Self-esteem and relationships with the spouse, friends, and family are all affected. Couples commonly need assistance in sorting through success and failure related to their infertility treatment. A common myth is that if the woman just relaxes, pregnancy will occur. In actuality, an identifiable physiologic explanation exists in 90% of all cases of infertility. It is important for the nurse to help couples recognize the significance of their infertility as a loss, even if treatment proves to be successful. Encouraging couples to openly express and discuss their feelings is an important component of infertility counseling, and referrals to support groups or for mental health counseling may be appropriate (Lowdermilk & Perry, 2007; RESOLVE, 2006).

ASSISTED REPRODUCTIVE TECHNOLOGIES

On July 25, 1978, an event occurred that changed the course of human society forever: the birth of Louise Brown, the first test-tube baby conceived through in vitro fertilization (IVF). Reproductive technology has been advancing at a rapid rate ever since this major breakthrough on the fertility frontier. Current issues in fertility now include ethical concerns as well as the latest treatment innovations. It is essential that nurses sort through their own feelings and value systems so that they can provide sensitive, nonjudgmental care to their patients who are dealing with infertility.

Approximately one-third of infertile couples are appropriate candidates for assisted reproductive technologies (ARTs). Which procedures are selected depends on the circumstances of the couple – that is, the cause of the infertility, the woman's age, the financial circumstances, and individual lifestyle choices, beliefs, and values. Despite major advances in these methods, ARTs actually account for less then 1% of all U.S. births (Van Voorhis, 2006) and less than 3% of infertility treatment (ASRM, n.d.).

Typical Cycle

In general, ARTs involve a number of steps that are initially similar and usually begin with ovarian stimulation. The ovaries are medically prompted to produce multiple eggs, which are retrieved in one of the ART procedures. Vaginal ultrasound and hormonal assays are used to provide frequent monitoring and assessment of the developing egg follicles. Once the eggs reach the appropriate maturity, an injection of hCG is given to stimulate final egg maturation and to control the ovulation induction. The egg retrieval procedure is scheduled for the next day (Lowdermilk & Perry, 2007).

Egg retrievals are performed almost exclusively by vaginal approach with the aid of ultrasound guidance. A needle is advanced through the back of the woman's vagina into the ovaries, and the eggs are aspirated from the ovaries. The procedure takes about 30 minutes and is performed as an outpatient procedure using intravenous sedation and a local cervical block. Risks include infection, bleeding and, rarely, injury to the bowel or bladder. The woman usually returns home after 2 hours and is advised to engage in limited activity for 24 hours. Progesterone may be used to prepare the uterine lining for implantation. Once the eggs have been retrieved, they are either incubated or placed with sperm for fertilization, depending on the ART procedure to be used (Lowdermilk & Perry, 2007).

Oocyte Donation and Cryopreservation; Embryo Donation

Oocyte donation provides an alternative for women who have had their ovaries removed, who have a genetic defect, or who are unable to achieve pregnancy with their own oocytes. Donor ova from healthy women under the age of 35 are used. The eggs are fertilized in a laboratory with the recipient's partner's sperm. The recipient woman undergoes hormonal stimulation to prepare her uterus for pregnancy. The embryos are then transferred. Pregnancy rates range from 5% to 20%. On occasion, couples decide they do not wish to keep their frozen embryos and release them for adoption by other infertile couples. Organizations such as the Embryo Adoption Awareness Campaign (www.embryoadoption.org/) offer a network of fertility specialists who provide embryo adoption and embryo donor programs (Krychman & Goldrich, 2007; Lowdermilk & Perry, 2007).

Available Procedures

In Vitro Fertilization/Embryo Transfer

In vitro means "in glass" and refers to a natural process that is performed outside the body. It is from this literal translation that the term *test-tube baby* arises. With IVF/embryo transfer (IVF/ET), an egg (oocyte) is taken from the female (partner or donor), incubated, and then placed in culture medium with sperm from the male (partner or donor). Conditions are carefully controlled. After fertilization, the embryo is allowed to grow for 1 to 3 days. The single egg cell, containing the genetic contributions from the male and the female, begins to divide. Transfer of the growing embryo into the uterus is usually performed at the 2- to 12-cell stage in a procedure similar to IUI. Because IVF bypasses the fallopian tubes, women with blocked or absent fallopian tubes, pelvic adhesions, or a history of multiple tubal pregnancies are appropriate candidates for IVF. One cycle of IVF/ET costs approximately $12,400; on average, women who undergo three IVF cycles have a good chance of achieving pregnancy (ASRM, n.d.; Lowdermilk & Perry, 2007).

Gamete Intrafallopian Transfer

Gamete intrafallopian transfer (GIFT) uses unfertilized oocytes aspirated from a woman's ovary during a laparoscopy. The oocytes are immediately combined with prepared sperm and placed in the fallopian tube (see Figure 6-3). This technique most closely resembles the natural fertilization process because conception takes place in the fallopian tube. The fertilized egg then travels through the fallopian tube to the uterus for implantation. The disadvantage of this procedure is the uncertainty of whether fertilization will occur. A lack of tubal patency in the area below the placement site can result in a tubal (ectopic) pregnancy. Less than 1% of all ARTs use this technique (Lowdermilk & Perry, 2007; Van Voorhis, 2006).

FIGURE 6-3: GAMETE INTRAFALLOPIAN TRANSFER

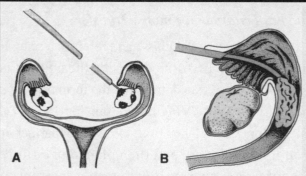

A, Through laparoscopy, a ripe follicle is located and fluid containing the egg is removed. **B,** The sperm and egg are placed separately in the uterine tube, where fertilization occurs.

Note. From *Maternity & Women's Health Care* (9th ed., p. 249), by D. Lowdermilk & S. Perry, 2007, St. Louis: Mosby. Reprinted with permission.

Zygote Intrafallopian Transfer and Tubal Embryo Transfer

Zygote intrafallopian transfer (ZIFT) and tubal embryo transfer (TET) are modifications of the GIFT and IVF procedures in which fertilization is determined before the egg is transferred to the fal-

lopian tube. ZIFT involves the placement of zygotes; TET involves the placement of embryos. Initially, these procedures were believed to be associated with higher pregnancy rates because the conceptus is placed in the fallopian tube, where the environment is more conducive to normal embryo development and implantation. However, because laboratory culture techniques have advanced in recent years, IVF success rates are now similar to those achieved with the GIFT procedure. Additionally, IVF is less invasive and less costly. ZIFT accounts for less than 1% of all ART procedures; IVF techniques are most often used (Lowdermilk & Perry, 2007; Van Voorhis, 2006).

Intracytoplasmic Sperm Injection

Intracytoplasmic sperm injection (ICSI) is a micromanipulation procedure in which a single sperm is injected directly into an egg, bypassing the outer coverings of the egg. If the egg is fertilized, the embryo is inserted into the uterus. ICSI is used for men with very low sperm numbers or absent sperm motility (Van Voorhis, 2006).

Assisted Embryo Hatching

Assisted embryo hatching is another micromanipulation procedure that can be used as an adjunct therapy in IVF. It is indicated in women whose normal hatching process may be diminished because of a hardening of the outer covering of the egg. A small opening is made in the zona pellucida (outer covering) of the embryo to allow the embryo to escape ("hatch") and interact with the endometrium for implantation. This technique is considered experimental (Lowdermilk & Perry, 2007).

Complications

Risks are associated with laparoscopy and general anesthesia. Otherwise, there are few risks associated with IVF/ET, GIFT, and ZIFT. Techniques that utilize transvaginal needle aspiration are performed under local or intravenous analgesia. Congenital anomalies do not occur more frequently among embryos conceived using ARTs than among naturally conceived embryos. Multiple gestations occur more often and are associated with increased risks for the mother and her fetuses (Wright, Schieve, Reynolds, Jeng, & Kissin, 2004). There is no increase in maternal or perinatal complications with therapeutic donor insemination.

Adjunct Support

Genetic counseling about individual risks for a specific condition in the offspring and amniocentesis may be indicated with ARTs, just as in naturally occurring pregnancies. Indications for these interventions depend on family history and the age of the couple.

Success Rates

The success rates for ARTs have improved steadily since these procedures were introduced in the late 1970s. In most instances, more than one attempt is necessary before conception occurs. However, this is also true with normally fertile couples, who have only an 18% to 25% chance of achieving pregnancy within any given month. Success rates for pregnancy and for live births vary from center to center. The couples' physical condition and ages, as well as whether the embryos are fresh or frozen and from donor or nondonor eggs, are factors that affect the likelihood of success. The Centers for Disease Control and Prevention keep detailed yearly statistics concerning all aspects of ART, including success rates with the different techniques. Their web site is listed in the bibliography. The ASRM sets standards and guidelines for ART procedures. When choosing an ART center, patients should become knowledgeable about differences in protocols and criteria for accepting patients as well as how the center reports its success rates (Lowdermilk & Perry, 2007).

Costs

ARTs are very expensive. Couples can quickly spend up to $30,000, depending on the procedures and the number of cycles required to achieve a successful pregnancy. Most health insurance providers pay for only a limited portion of fertility evaluation and treatment. Government funding for couples of low income is limited and varies from state to state. Income level is tied to access in the treatment of infertility perhaps more than in any other area of women's health (Lowdermilk & Perry, 2007).

ADDITIONAL OPTIONS

For individuals and couples for whom ARTs are unsuccessful or undesirable, surrogacy, use of a gestational carrier, or adoption may be the best option. Surrogate mothers contract to carry pregnancies for women who are unable to carry a pregnancy due to an absent or anomalous uterus or medical condition that would be life-threatening during pregnancy. A gestational carrier contracts to carry a pregnancy that is not genetically her own offspring. Surrogacy and the use of gestational carriers involve legal and ethical considerations. Financial resources, personal values, and religious beliefs are factors that may prohibit these options from being viable alternatives to a traditional pregnancy. Individuals and couples who are considering these options should be advised to see an attorney to ensure that their rights, the surrogate's or carrier's rights, and the rights of the child are protected (Lowdermilk & Perry, 2007; Van Voohis, 2006).

Many infertile couples choose adoption. This process can also be lengthy and frustrating, although the number of possibilities for adoption has expanded in recent years. Open adoption, which involves cooperation between adoptive and birth parents, represents one option. In addition to licensed adoption agencies, sources for possible adoption connections include clergy, attorneys, independent adoption agencies, and friends. Children from other countries and those with special needs can often be adopted with shorter waiting periods (ASRM, n.d.).

Remaining childless is another option for fertile and infertile individuals and couples. Many advantages, such as opportunity for career fulfillment, travel, and continued education, may make a child-free lifestyle the right choice for many men and women. Nurses who work with people who are exploring these alternative options should provide education, empowerment, and advocacy along with guidance to appropriate community and national resources (Piotrowski & Snell, 2007).

PSYCHOLOGICAL AND EMOTIONAL ASPECTS

Infertility is an extremely complex, deep, and multifaceted area of health care. Many factors can add to the couple's stress, such as:

- the age of the couple and their perception of "pressure" to achieve pregnancy

- previous pregnancies in this or other relationships in one or both spouses

- differences in the desire to achieve a pregnancy between members of the couple

- pressures from extended family

- religious beliefs

- financial resources

- career choices.

Normal reactions to the diagnosis of infertility include those that have been identified for other grieving processes: surprise, denial, anger, isolation, guilt, grief and, finally, resolution. Depression and prolonged stress are common, and they may have a profound impact on the life of the individual and the health of the relationship. Stress itself has unknown but possibly profound effects on fertility (Lowdermilk & Perry, 2007; RESOLVE, 2006).

CONCLUSION

The health care team is challenged to accomplish the infertility evaluation and treatment in a thorough, timely, and sensitive fashion. Members of the health care team may need to set the stage and tone for intimate discussions involving details of sexuality and other private aspects of the couple's life together. Difficult ethical decisions also require discussion in an honest, forthright, and nonjudgmental manner. Couples may benefit from information concerning adoption and fostering as well as referrals to infertility networks and support groups. It is important that members of the health care team practice self-reflection and remain in touch with their personal beliefs and biases, so that they can truly assist couples in making their own informed choices.

EXAM QUESTIONS

CHAPTER 6
Questions 45-52

Note: Choose the option that BEST answers each question.

45. *Secondary infertility* is the term applied when a couple who has previously conceived has not conceived now despite unprotected intercourse for at least

    a. 6 months.
    b. 1 year.
    c. 18 months.
    d. 2 years.

46. Couples who are 25 years of age generally achieve conception within how many months of unprotected intercourse?

    a. 2 months
    b. 3 months
    c. 5 months
    d. 12 months

47. Women are asked to chart their basal body temperature (BBT) and cervical mucus characteristics for evidence of

    a. ovulation.
    b. STIs that could interfere with fertility.
    c. blockage of the fallopian tubes.
    d. changes in the lining of the uterus.

48. A hysterosalpingogram (HSG) is a diagnostic test used to determine

    a. hormone insufficiencies.
    b. abnormalities of ovulation.
    c. patency of the fallopian tubes.
    d. presence of cysts on the ovaries.

49. IVF is most appropriate for

    a. all infertile women.
    b. women who do not ovulate regularly.
    c. women who have a blockage of the fallopian tubes.
    d. women who want to know the sex of their child.

50. GIFT is a procedure that involves placing

    a. unfertilized oocytes and sperm into the uterus.
    b. unfertilized oocytes and sperm into the fallopian tube.
    c. an embryo into the uterus.
    d. unfertilized oocytes and sperm into culture medium.

51. An appropriate referral for infertile couples would be to suggest

    a. national and local infertility support groups.
    b. anger management seminars.
    c. substance abuse programs.
    d. parenting classes.

52. Couples who experience infertility often have reactions of

    a. relief.
    b. envy.
    c. guilt.
    d. happiness.

CHAPTER 7

SEXUALLY TRANSMITTED INFECTIONS

CHAPTER OBJECTIVE

After completing this chapter, the reader will be able to describe strategies for the prevention and management of the most common sexually transmitted infections (STIs).

LEARNING OBJECTIVES

After studying this chapter, the reader will be able to

1. specify health education, disease prevention, and self-care for sexually active patients.

2. recognize safer sex practices.

3. identify signs and symptoms, modes of transmission, and treatment options for the most common STIs.

KEY WORDS

- Pelvic inflammatory disease (PID)
- Safer sex
- Sexually transmitted infection (STI)

INTRODUCTION

STIs, also called *sexually transmitted diseases* (STDs), include more than 25 infectious organisms that cause reproductive tract infections that are primarily transmitted by close, intimate contact. In recent years, the incidence of many STIs has increased. While some are more life-threatening than others, each takes its toll – both physically and emotionally. Individuals younger than 25 years of age continue to account for the majority of people affected, and it is estimated that more than 19 million Americans become infected with STIs every year (Centers for Disease Control and Prevention [CDC], Workowski & Berman, 2006). It is urgent that young people be helped to understand the seriousness of sexual activity and the consequences of risky behaviors.

Serious long-term effects of STIs can include blockage of the fallopian tubes that leads to infertility, a high risk of ectopic pregnancy, chronic pelvic pain, an increased risk of liver cancer and serious liver disease, and death. In general, women suffer more long-term reproductive consequences from STIs than do men, and women are more likely than men to acquire an infection from any single sexual encounter. Because of the asymptomatic nature of many STIs, especially in women, treatment is often delayed. This factor increases the likelihood of more serious long-term consequences (Adler, 2007; Johnson-Mallard & Lengacher, 2007).

It is beyond the scope of this course to provide complete treatment protocols for each disease because protocols are constantly being revised. The CDC regularly publishes recommendations and updates. The most current information can be accessed on-line at *http://cdc.gov/.*

PATIENT EDUCATION

When educating patients about STIs, health care providers should include basic information along with sexual decision-making skills. These skills include:

- communication skills needed to negotiate in a relationship

- knowledge of how to operate from an internal value system rather than under peer pressure.

(Berman et al., 2008)

Safer sex options for physical intimacy are described in Table 7-1. It is also helpful to teach patients these facts:

- Condoms still offer the best protection.

- Spermicide is less effective than condoms and may cause or exacerbate tiny abrasions on the vulva and in the vagina. Therefore, patients should check for reddened or sore areas before using these products.

- Sexual contact should be avoided if the person or partner has any sore areas or lesions.

Health care professionals should recognize that women who use nonbarrier contraceptive methods usually do so for the freedom involved. Thus, it may be more difficult to influence them to practice safer sex (Hatcher et al., 2008). The care provider should:

TABLE 7-1: SAFER SEX OPTIONS FOR PHYSICAL INTIMACY

Safe
- Sexual fantasies
- Massage
- Hugging
- Body rubbing
- Dry kissing
- Masturbation without contact with partner's semen or vaginal secretions
- Erotic conversation, books, movies, videos or DVDs
- Erotic bathing or showering
- Eroticizing feet, fingers, buttocks, abdomen, ears, or other body parts
- All sexual activities, when both partners are monogamous, trustworthy, and known by testing to be free from human immunodeficiency virus (HIV)

Possibly Safe
- Wet kissing with no broken skin, cracked lips, or damaged mouth tissue
- Hand-to-genital touching or mutual masturbation
- Vaginal or anal intercourse using latex or plastic condom correctly with adequate lubrication
- Oral sex on a man using a latex or plastic condom
- Oral sex on a woman using a latex or plastic barrier, such as a female condom, dental dam, or modified male condom (especially if she does not have a vaginal infection with discharge and is not menstruating)
- All sexual activities, when both partners agree to a monogamous relationship and trust each other

Unsafe in the Absence of HIV Testing and Trust and Monogamy
- Blood contact of any kind, including menstrual blood
- Any vaginal or anal intercourse without a latex or plastic condom
- Oral sex on a woman without a latex or plastic barrier, such as a female condom, dental dam, or modified male condom (especially if she has a vaginal infection with discharge or is menstruating)
- Semen in the mouth
- Oral-anal contact
- Sharing sex toys or douching equipment
- Any sex (fisting, rough vaginal or anal intercourse, rape) that causes tissue damage or bleeding

(Hatcher et al., 2008)

- inform patients that oral contraceptives cause changes in the cervix and the immune system that may make women who use them more susceptible to HIV infection

- encourage the concomitant use of barrier methods and oral contraceptives for new or non-monogamous relationships

- inquire about substance use (Women who smoke have a higher rate of cervical cancer. Women who drink heavily or practice binge drinking may not remember details of sexual encounters that took place during drinking. A history of injected drug use increases the risk of infection with hepatitis and HIV [Ravin, 2007]).

Partners should routinely be included in discussions concerning matters of contraception and reproductive health. Focus on these issues:

- Work to dispel views that talking about infection and safer sex or asking about a partner's sexual history means that the patient does not trust her partner. It is easy to have an STI and never know it.

- Encourage delaying intercourse; discuss other ways to enjoy sexual intimacy and ways to make these forms of intimacy safer.

- Confirm knowledge about proper condom use by both partners.

- Teach patients to do genital self-examination on a regular basis.

- Teach patients not to share personal care items, such as toothbrushes and razors.

Health care professionals should be aware of special circumstances if treatment is needed for an existing STI.

- Both the patient and her partner(s) need to be treated (except for herpes simplex virus).

- The complete course of antibiotic therapy prescribed should be taken, even if symptoms resolve.

- To prevent reinfection, the couple should abstain from sexual intercourse until both partners have completed treatment.

- The patient should be encouraged to return after treatment is completed to assess whether the infection has been cured.

(Hatcher et al., 2008; Lowdermilk & Perry, 2007)

The reportability of some STIs (e.g., chlamydia, gonorrhea) is state-specific.

HUMAN IMMUNODEFICIENCY VIRUS AND ACQUIRED IMMUNODEFICIENCY SYNDROME

The acquired immunodeficiency syndrome (AIDS) epidemic has in some way touched everyone's life, and health care providers have been affected profoundly. Still, many people in the United States are somewhat ignorant of the fact that AIDS affects men, women, and children and has reached epidemic proportions in many areas. Because HIV infection can be asymptomatic for years, a number of female patients who are infected are unaware that they carry HIV. Women who are infected with HIV have special gynecologic health needs that must be watched and addressed (Hatcher et al., 2008; Lowdermilk & Perry, 2007).

Much progress has been made in understanding the nature of HIV and AIDS. New antiviral medications are being continually introduced. These drugs offer the hope of allowing the disease to be managed as a chronic illness for longer and longer periods. Vaccines are being researched that may eventually prevent the spread of the virus.

It is discouraging that more and more young people, especially women, are contracting HIV. In the United States, women ages 15 to 44 years represent one of the fastest growing segments of the epidemic. Women are more likely than men to acquire HIV at any one contact. Consider the following trends in the U.S. HIV epidemic (CDC, 2005; Hatcher et al., 2008):

- Women infected with HIV are young. Approximately 21% are 20 to 29 years old when their AIDS is reported. This fact suggests that many women became infected during their teen years. Through the year 2000, 80% of women with AIDS and 86% of women with HIV were 13 to 44 years old. Among AIDS cases reported in 2000, 24% of those age 25 and older were women. Of the estimated 120,000 to 160,000 HIV-infected women in the United States, 80% are of childbearing age (CDC, 2005).

- In 1992, women accounted for just under 14% of people over age 13 years living with AIDS; this number rose to 20% in 1998. Today, women are the fastest-growing population of individuals with HIV infection and AIDS. An estimated that 27% of new infections occur in women.

- Women of color are disproportionately represented in reported AIDS cases (Black women – 50%; Hispanic women – 15%; Caucasian women – 32%), especially in urban areas of the Northeast and the rural South.

- There has been a decline in the perinatal transmission of HIV, a trend related to the increased use of effective antiviral therapy as well as U.S. Public Health Service guidelines concerning HIV counseling and testing for all pregnant women.

AIDS is the leading cause of death among young women in most of the world. Most of these women contracted the disease by exposure to infected men. The ratio of infected men and women worldwide approaches 1:1. Both sexual activity and intravenous drug use play a major role in current transmission statistics.

Factors That Place Women at Risk for HIV Infection

Certain lifestyle behaviors place a woman at risk for contracting HIV. When obtaining the patient history, the nurse should routinely ask about symptoms that may be associated with HIV. Although the infection can be asymptomatic, women often describe flu-like discomforts, such as fever, headache, night sweats, malaise, muscle aches, nausea, diarrhea, weight loss, sore throat, rash, and swollen lymph nodes. Nurses should also be aware of factors that place women at risk for contracting HIV infection:

- current or past drug use, especially intravenous drug use

- history of prostitution

- frequent sexual intercourse with multiple partners

- sexual intercourse under the influence of drugs

- sexual intercourse with men who also have sex with men

- residence in an area with a high prevalence of HIV infection (e.g., rural South and Northeastern United States)

- history of transfusions of blood or blood products before 1985.

(CDC, 2005; Hatcher et al., 2008; Lowdermilk & Perry, 2007)

Counseling for HIV Testing

Confidential counseling before and after HIV testing is a component of standard nursing practice today. The CDC (2006) recommends routine HIV screening of adults, adolescents, and pregnant women in health care settings in the United States. According to the recommendations, separate written consent should not be required for HIV testing; general consent for medical care should be considered sufficient to encompass consent for HIV testing. "Opt-out screening" is a component of the recommendations. With opt-out screening, an HIV test is performed after notifying the patient that the test will be done, and consent is inferred unless the patient declines. The CDC recommends routine HIV screening for all women ages 13 to 64 years, regardless of risk, with rescreening at least annually for those at risk. The American College of

Obstetricians and Gynecologists (ACOG) supports routine screening for women ages 19 to 64 years and recommends screening for patients at high risk, including adolescents who are, or ever have been, sexually active (ACOG, 2007).

Before the test, the nurse must assess the patient's level of understanding to ensure that the patient is aware of the legal, emotional, and medical implications of a positive or negative HIV test. Pregnancy is not encouraged for women who are HIV-positive; contraceptive counseling should be offered to HIV-positive women who do not desire pregnancy. Posttest counseling involves telling the patient her test results, explaining the meaning of the results, and reinforcing infection prevention measures. Women should be advised to be retested if they have been exposed in the past 6 months. All pretest and posttest counseling should be documented (CDC, Workowski, & Berman, 2006; Lowdermilk & Perry, 2007).

If the HIV test results are placed in the patient's chart, they are then available to everyone who accesses the chart. The woman must be advised of this before testing. Health care facilities should have policies in place to safeguard patient information from inadvertent or inappropriate breaches of confidentiality. Federal regulations set forth in the Health Insurance Portability and Accountability Act (HIPAA) also provide specific rules for what information may be shared with other practitioners and agencies with and without an individual's permission. Results of HIV testing may need to be recorded and stored in a certain way. Nurses should become familiar with the legal requirements that exist in their particular clinical settings (ACOG, 2007).

Testing

HIV infection is usually diagnosed with the use of HIV-1 and HIV-2 antibody tests. Antibody testing is first performed with a sensitive screening test such as the enzyme immunoassay (EIA), which detects serum antibodies to HIV. Reactive screening tests are then confirmed by an additional test, such as an immunofluorescence assay, enzyme-linked immunosorbent assay (ELISA), or Western blot test. If a positive antibody test is confirmed by a supplemental test, the woman is infected with HIV and is capable of infecting others. These diagnostic tests are very reliable; false-positives and false-negatives are rare. In general, seroconversion for HIV in adolescents and adults occurs 6 to 12 weeks after transmission of the virus; HIV antibodies are detectable in at least 95% of patients within 3 months after infection (Lowdermilk & Perry, 2007).

Two methods of rapid testing for HIV are also available. The OraQuick Rapid HIV Antibody Tests which provide test results within 20 minutes, can be performed with a blood sample obtained by fingerstick or venipuncture or with an oral fluid sample. The accuracy rate associated with these tests is 99%; if the results are reactive, further testing is done (CDC, 2007a; U.S. Food and Drug Administration [FDA], 2004).

Management

No cure is available for HIV at this time. The use of antiretroviral agents has been shown to be effective in maintaining the health of HIV-positive women and in reducing perinatal transmission of the virus. A number of opportunistic infections often accompany HIV infection.

Discussion of the medical care of HIV-positive women is beyond the scope of this course. The CDC offers information via its AIDS hotline (1-800-342-2437) and website (see the "Resources" at the back of this course book for current information and recommendations).

Special Health Issues for Women Who Are Seropositive for HIV

In addition to the symptoms experienced by men, women who are seropositive for HIV often experience a number of gynecologic problems. They may have special psychosocial issues as well, which have an impact on their health.

Gynecologic Issues

- **Contraception:** Intrauterine devices (IUDs) are not ideal choices for contraception due to the immunosuppresive nature of the HIV infection; also, the increased bleeding associated with some IUDs may increase the risk of HIV transmission. Latex condoms should be part of any contraceptive plan. Because women infected with HIV are often at high risk for unplanned pregnancies, effective contraception, including the concepts of abstinence and sterilization, should always be discussed (ACOG, 2007; Hatcher et al., 2008).

- **Infection:** Recurrent vaginal yeast infections are common and may require prophylactic therapy (ACOG, 2007; Hatcher et al., 2008).

- **Cervical disease:** For women who are seropositive for HIV, cervical disease can be much more aggressive and progress rapidly, requiring prompt treatment and careful monitoring (Lowdermilk & Perry, 2007).

- **Pelvic inflammatory disease (PID):** PID is more common in HIV-infected women. If PID develops, hospitalization and aggressive intravenous antibiotic treatment are necessary (ACOG, 2007; Lowdermilk & Perry, 2007).

- **Herpes:** The lesions of herpes may appear more frequently, produce more intense pain, and take longer to heal. Acyclovir as suppressive therapy may help control outbreaks (ACOG, 2007; Hatcher et al., 2008).

- **Pregnancy:** The risk of transmission of HIV from mother to offspring is in the range of 13% to 45% but averages 20% to 30%. Transmission can occur in utero, during birth, or through breastfeeding. Infants are all seropositive at birth because of maternal antibodies in the neonate's blood. An accurate test can be performed when the infant is 15 to 18 months old (CDC, 2007a; Lowdermilk & Perry, 2007).

Psychosocial Issues

Women who are seropositive for HIV are likely to be caregivers themselves, attending to the needs of their children and spouse. It may be difficult for these women to take care of themselves. They may have trouble keeping appointments, getting adequate rest, and complying with medication regimens. Oftentimes, other family members are also infected. These women commonly have many other more immediate issues, such as housing and financial problems (Lowdermilk & Perry, 2007).

Risk to Health Care Providers

The three routes of transmission of HIV are direct sexual contact, perinatal transmission from an HIV-infected mother to her fetus or newborn, and direct inoculation with contaminated blood products, needles, or syringes. All health care workers who may come in contact with contaminated blood products, needles, or syringes in any acute care, long-term care, or home care settings are at risk for occupational exposure to HIV. To address this risk, the CDC developed standard precautions, a set of principles to be used in the care of all patients at all times. Please refer to the CDC website for a complete description. In more than 6,000 reported cases of a single needlestick or percutaneous exposure, the rate of HIV infection was about 0.3% (Hatcher et al., 2008).

CHLAMYDIA

Chlamydia infection is the most common, fastest-spreading STI in the United States and the leading cause of preventable infertility and ectopic pregnancy. An estimated 3 million new cases occur each year. This trend primarily reflects increased screening, recognition of asymptomatic infection (mostly in women), and improved reporting capacity, rather than a true increase in disease incidence. The reported rate of chlamydia infection for women substantially exceeds the rate for men, primarily due to increased detection of asymptomatic infection in women through screening. It is estimated that 1 in 10 adolescent girls tested for chlamydia is infected. Teenage girls tend to have the highest rates of chlamydial infection; it is widespread geographically and highly prevalent among economically disadvantaged young women (CDC, Workowski, & Berman, 2006; Ravin, 2007).

Symptoms

Caused by the organism *Chlamydia trachomatis,* chlamydia is commonly asymptomatic, especially in women. Approximately 70% of women with chlamydia infection report no symptoms. However, if present, symptoms include spotting or postcoital bleeding, mucoid or purulent cervical discharge, and dysuria. Women using birth control pills may also experience breakthrough bleeding. *Chlamydia* is the organism most often responsible for PID. Also, infection of the cervix causes inflammation, which produces microscopic ulcerations that can increase a woman's risk of contracting HIV (Hatcher et al., 2008; Lowdermilk & Perry, 2007).

Testing

A large percentage of chlamydia infections are detected through broadscale screening programs. Testing can be done using nucleic acid amplification tests (NAATs) on either urine specimens (first few drops of the stream) or swabs from the endocervix or vagina (CDC, Workowski, & Berman, 2006; Nelson, 2007).

Treatment

Oral antibiotics (e.g., azithromycin; doxycycline) are the treatment of choice for chlamydia infection. Please refer to the specific CDC guidelines for protocols (CDC, Workowski, & Berman, 2006; Nelson, 2007).

Long-Term Complications

Because most (75%) women infected with chlamydia have no symptoms, diagnosis and treatment are often delayed. Untreated, chlamydia can cause severe, costly reproductive damage and other health problems. Up to 40% of women with untreated chlamydia develop PID and, of these, 20% become infertile, 18% experience chronic pelvic pain, and 9% have a life-threatening tubal pregnancy. Infected mothers can pass chlamydia to their infants during childbirth. In neonates, chlamydia is the most common infectious cause of ophthalmia neonatorum (CDC, Workowski, & Berman, 2006).

GONORRHEA

Gonorrhea, probably the oldest communicable disease in the United States, is caused by the bacterium *Neisseria gonorrhoeae.* According to the CDC, gonorrhea rates have declined since the early 1970s, when government screening programs began. However, an estimated 600,000 men and women still contract gonorrhea each year. The incidence of drug-resistant cases of gonorrhea continues to rise in the United States. Gonorrhea is almost exclusively transmitted by sexual contact (CDC, Workowski, & Berman, 2006).

Symptoms

Men with gonorrhea usually experience pain with urination and penile discharge. Women are often asymptomatic, but when symptoms are present, they are commonly less specific than the symptoms in men. Some women report vaginal discharge, abnormal menses, low backache, and pain with urination.

Testing

Gonorrhea is most often detected through government screening programs. Diagnosis may be performed by testing endocervical, vaginal, or urine specimens. Cultures, nucleic acid hybridization tests, and NAATs are the available testing methods. In clinical settings that use cultures with selected media for gonorrhea testing, Thayer-Martin cultures are recommended. Sampling sites include the endocervix, rectum and, when indicated, the pharynx. Women who are suspected of having gonorrhea should also have a chlamydia culture and a serologic test for syphilis, because coinfection is common (ACOG, 2007; CDC, n.d.; Lowdermilk & Perry, 2007; Nelson, 2007).

Treatment

A number of different drug regimens are available, and cure is usually rapid with appropriate antibiotic therapy. Often, a one-time intramuscular injection of an antibiotic is administered. Other treatment regimens involve oral medications given as one dose or administered over the course of several days. Treatment covering possible concomitant chlamydial infection has become the standard of care (CDC, n.d.; Nelson, 2007).

Long-Term Complications

In up to 40% of untreated women with cervical gonorrhea, PID develops and can progress to a systemic infection. Because gonorrhea can infect the pharynx, patients with gonorrhea who have oral sex should be evaluated and treated for pharyngeal gonorrhea as necessary. Like chlamydia, gonorrhea can be transmitted from a mother to her infant during childbirth, causing an eye infection in the newborn (Hatcher et al., 2008).

TRICHOMONIASIS

Trichomoniasis is a vaginal infection that is caused by the protozoan *Trichomonas vaginalis.*

Symptoms

Although trichomoniasis may be asymptomatic, it often produces a profuse, bubbly, gray, green or yellow discharge with a foul odor. The discharge can cause inflammation of the vulva or vagina. Painful urination and painful intercourse are often present (CDC, 2005; Nelson, 2007).

Testing

Microscopic evaluation is used to confirm trichomoniasis. The trichomonad parasites have a characteristic tail, which can be seen moving under microscopic examination. The pH of the vaginal discharge is usually higher (more alkaline) than normal. Several other FDA-approved methods for testing for trichomoniasis in women are available. These include the OSOM Trichomonas Rapid Test, which uses immunochromatographic capillary flow dipstick technology to identify infections in 10 minutes and Affirm VPIII Microbial Identification Test, which uses a nucleic acid probe test to detect *T. vaginalis, Gardnerella vaginalis,* and *Candida albicans* in 45 minutes (CDC, n.d.; Nelson, 2007).

Treatment

Metronidazole (Flagyl) is the drug of choice for trichomoniasis and is associated with a 95% cure rate. Tinidazole 2 g is an alternative first-line therapy and also recommended for treating resistant *T. vaginalis* infection. Partners should also be treated because men often harbor the trichomonads in the urethra or prostate (CDC, 2005; Nelson, 2007).

PELVIC INFLAMMATORY DISEASE

PID is an acute infection of the uterus and fallopian tubes which, left untreated or unresolved, results in scarring, adhesions, or blockage of the fallopian tubes. A number of different organisms are usually involved, but the most common causative agents are *Chlamydia trachomatis* (> 50%) and *Neisseria gonorrhoeae.* Severe infection can cause abscesses on the ovaries or fallopian tubes and inflammation of the lining of the pelvic cavity. Because PID can be caused by many organisms and encompasses a wide spectrum of pathologic processes, the infection may be acute, subacute, or chronic. More than one million cases of PID occur annually in the United States, and the two greatest consequences of acute PID are infertility and tubal pregnancy due to scarring of the fallopian tubes (Lowdermilk & Perry, 2007).

Risk Factors

An increased incidence of PID is associated with multiple sexual partners, lower age at first intercourse, and lower economic status. Adolescents have the highest incidence of any age-group, and 70% of all cases of PID occur in women under 25 years old. Because they are at higher risk for an STI, women who use IUDs are also at increased risk for PID if they have more than one sexual partner or if their partner has other sexual partners (Hatcher et al., 2008; Lowdermilk & Perry, 2007).

Symptoms

PID can range from being almost completely asymptomatic to causing severe pain, extreme uterine tenderness, ovarian tenderness, abnormal bleeding, nausea, and vomiting. The infected individual can experience extreme tenderness when the cervix is moved on examination. Fever and chills may also be present (Hatcher et al., 2008; Lowdermilk & Perry, 2007).

Treatment

PID can be treated on an outpatient basis, but hospitalization may be necessary, depending on the individual case. For patients treated on an outpatient basis, reexamination within 72 hours is a crucial part of therapy. Combination drug therapy is advised because the full spectrum of organisms involved is often unknown. The CDC provides specific guidelines for PID treatment as well as for treatment of all STIs (Hatcher et al., 2008; Lowdermilk & Perry, 2007).

HUMAN PAPILLOMAVIRUS

Human papillomavirus (HPV), which causes genital warts, also called condylomata acuminata, is a deoxyribonucleic acid (DNA) virus transmitted by skin-to-skin contact. More than 100 viral types have been identified; of these, more than 30 types can infect the genital area. Approximately one-half of HPV genital infections occur in young women and men between the ages of 15 and 24 years. The majority of HPV infections are asymptomatic, unrecognized, or subclinical. Genital HPV infection can cause warty growths in the vagina or on the vulva, perineum, or anal area. These growths can be single or multiple, soft, and fleshy, and they are usually painless. Other strains of HPV infect the cervix and remain unnoticed until findings from a routine Pap smear reveal the presence of the virus. Certain viral types are associated with the growth of abnormal cervical cells, which can lead to cancer of the cervix (Cates, 1999; CDC, 2005; Mayeaux, 2007; Schmidt, 2007).

Prevention and Testing

Strategies for HPV prevention include sexual abstinence, long-term monogamy, and prophylactic vaccination. A vaccine against HPV types 6, 11, 16, and 18 became available in 2006 and is recommended for all females ages 9 to 26 years (Advisory Committee on Immunization Practices, 2006; ACOG, 2005a).

Although testing is available based on HPV-DNA in cells scraped from the cervix, routine screening is not recommended except in specific circumstances following an abnormal Pap test (CDC, 2005; Nelson, 2007). HPV and cervical cytology are discussed in greater detail in Chapter 10.

Treatment

For treatment of external genital warts, several topical chemicals are available. These include trichloroacetic acid (TCA) and podophyllin (provider administered) and podofilox 0.5% (Condylox) and imiquimod (Aldara), both of which are patient administered. Cryotherapy (freezing), carbon dioxide laser surgery, electrosurgery, and surgical removal are other treatment options, depending on severity and resistance to treatment (CDC, Workowski, & Berman, 2006; Lowdermilk & Perry, 2007).

HERPES SIMPLEX VIRUS I AND II

Herpes simplex virus type 1 (HSV-1) is usually transmitted during childhood via nonsexual contact. It is most commonly associated with cold sores or fever blisters on the mouth or face. Genital HSV-1 may result from oral-genital sexual contact with a person with an oral HSV-1 infection. Genital HSV-1 is unlikely to recur and treatment may only be needed in individuals with initial symptoms (Xu et al., 2006). Herpes simplex virus II (HSV-2) is usually transmitted sexually and is associated with genital lesions, although depending on sexual practices, both types are not exclusively associated with the respective sites. HSV-2 occurs more frequently in women (23%) than in men (11%), which undoubtedly results from the greater likelihood of male-to-female transmission. HSV infection rates are significantly higher among African-Americans (46%) than among Caucasians (18%). HSV infection is not a reportable disease, but it is estimated that 50 million Americans are infected with genital herpes (CDC, n.d.; Winer & Richwald, 2007).

Symptoms

Most individuals have no or only minimal signs and symptoms of HSV-1 or HSV-2 infection. If symptoms occur during the first HSV-2 outbreak, they usually appear within 2 weeks after exposure and can be quite pronounced. The infected individual experiences flu-like symptoms, with malaise, muscle aches, and headache accompanied by painful urination and multiple blister-like lesions, which can be extremely tender and last 2 to 3 weeks. Before the actual outbreak, there may be a period of prodromal symptoms characterized by skin sensitivity and nerve pain in the area where the lesion appears; this is followed by a reddening of the skin. The lesions form pustules and ulcers that dry up, crust over, and then heal without scarring. Women may also experience itching, inguinal tenderness, and vulvar edema and may complain of a heavy watery to purulent vaginal discharge (CDC, Workowski, & Berman, 2006; Gardner, 2006).

Recurrent outbreaks are typically less severe than the primary infection and usually involve local symptoms, with less severe lesions lasting 5 to 7 days. The prodromal characteristic genital tingling is common. The virus goes into a latent stage in the nerves at the base of the spine and may reactivate when the patient's immune system is weakened. The lesions may occur along any skin surface supplied by that nerve distribution, including the vulva, vagina, cervix, urethral meatus, and buttocks. Transmission of the virus is most likely during times when an active outbreak is occurring, and patients should abstain from sexual contact during this time. However, herpes is contagious if the infected individual is producing and releasing ("shedding") virus. Although viral shedding occurs most often during an outbreak, individuals may also shed virus between outbreaks. In some instances, women with "chronic yeast infections" may be experiencing herpes outbreaks that are undiagnosed because the typical herpetic lesions are not present (Gardner, 2006).

In pregnancy, HSV-2 infection can have devastating effects on both the mother and her fetus. Primary infection during the first trimester has been associated with a higher miscarriage rate. Late in the second trimester or in the third trimester, HSV-2 infection increases the risk of preterm labor and intrauterine growth restriction of the fetus. The woman also has a much greater risk of transmitting the infection to the neonate. The most severe complication of HSV is neonatal herpes, and risk of neonatal infection is highest among women whose primary infection occurs near term. There is a 60% neonatal mortality rate associated with neonates who contract HSV infection; of those who survive, approximately 50% suffer from serious neurologic damage. Cesarean delivery does not completely eliminate the risk of HSV infection transmission to the neonate (Gardner, 2006).

Testing

Most often, a diagnosis of HSV is suspected according to the history and physical exam. HSV can be confirmed by obtaining a viral culture from exudate swabbed from the vesicular (blister) lesion. Testing for the presence of HSV-2 antibodies in capillary blood or serum (i.e., HSV glycoprotein G-specific antibodies, IgG by Immunoblot [HerpeSelect]) is also available for office use. However, screening of the general population is not indicated (CDC, n.d.; Nelson, 2007).

Treatment

The goal of therapy is to hasten healing and reduce symptoms. Three antiviral medications are available: acyclovir (Zovirax), valacyclovir (Valtrex), and famciclovir (Famvir). These oral agents may be used for primary or recurrent episodes or as daily suppressive therapy. They do not eradicate the infection and do not alter subsequent risk, frequency, or recurrences once the medication has been stopped. Acyclovir may be also given intravenously for 5 to 7 days in people with severe disease (CDC, Workowski, & Berman, 2006; Nelson, 2007).

Some women with herpes have found that certain comfort measures and dietary changes help decrease their symptoms and the frequency and severity of outbreaks. Comfort measures include taking warm sitz baths with baking soda or oatmeal; the use of cotton underwear; the application of cool, wet, black tea bags or tea tree oil to lesions; the use of a hair dryer (set on cool) to enhance drying of the lesions; and the application of compresses containing peppermint oil and clove oil to the lesions. Oral analgesics such as aspirin or ibuprofen may be used to help relieve pain. Dietary measures include a diet rich in vitamin C, B-complex vitamins, zinc, and calcium and daily use of kelp powder and sunflower seed oil as well as the amino acid l-lysine, which is believed to suppress the herpes simplex virus (Gardner, 2006; Lowdermilk & Perry, 2007; Stonehouse & Studdiford, 2007).

Patient Education

Providing counseling and patient education are essential components of holistic care for women with herpes infections. It is important to offer information about the etiology, signs, symptoms, mode of transmission, treatment options, and the possibility of suppression therapy to prevent partner transmission. Women should be informed about the times when transmission is most likely and should be advised to avoid sexual contact from the onset of prodromal symptoms until the complete healing of lesions. Some experts recommend the consistent use of condoms for all individuals with genital herpes. It is helpful to teach women about potential precipitating factors in the reactivation of the latent herpes virus. These "triggers" may include stress, menstruation, febrile illnesses, chronic illnesses, and ultraviolet light. Keeping a personal diary may be useful in helping women to identify specific precipitating events for their herpetic outbreaks. Nurses can also suggest lifestyle modifications such as stress reduction and relaxation strategies, and avoidance of excessive heat, sun, and hot baths (Lowdermilk & Perry, 2007).

SYPHILIS

One of the oldest known STIs, syphilis is caused by the spirochete *Treponema pallidum.* The incidence of syphilis is highest among young adult African Americans who live in urban areas and in southern states. The rise in cases of syphilis since 1990 is thought to be related to illicit drug use and the exchange of sex for drugs and money. Syphilis is believed to be transmitted through microscopic abrasions that can occur during sexual intercourse. It may also be transmitted by kissing, biting, and oral-genital sex. If left untreated, syphilis can cause severe systemic disease and death (CDC, Workowski, & Berman, 2006; Lowdermilk & Perry, 2007).

Symptoms

Syphilis is a complex disease, and it is beyond the scope of this course to describe each stage in detail. Instead, each clinical stage is summarized in the descriptions below.

Primary Stage

In the primary stage, a painless ulcer (chancre) appears at the site of exposure; it resolves on its own without treatment (see Figure7-1). The ulcer may go unnoticed; if not, it usually appears 1 week to 3 months after the initial exposure.

FIGURE 7-1: SYPHILIS

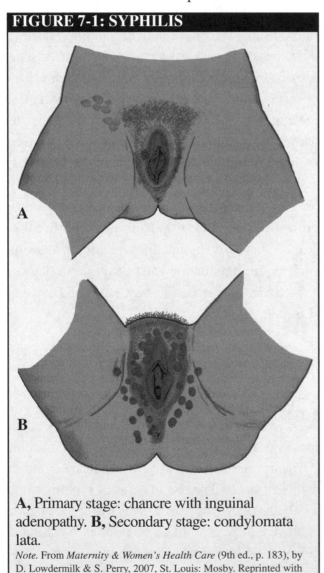

A, Primary stage: chancre with inguinal adenopathy. **B,** Secondary stage: condylomata lata.

Note. From *Maternity & Women's Health Care* (9th ed., p. 183), by D. Lowdermilk & S. Perry, 2007, St. Louis: Mosby. Reprinted with permission.

Secondary Stage

Secondary syphilis occurs 6 weeks to 6 months after the appearance of the chancre. This stage is characterized by a generalized malaise; skin rash; mucus patches; the appearance of moist, flat warts (condylomata lata) in the genital and anal areas; swollen lymph nodes; and hair loss. If left untreated, these symptoms resolve within 2 to 10 weeks. Approximately one-third of infected individuals develop tertiary syphilis (CDC, Workowski, & Berman, 2006).

Latent Stage

If left untreated, the disease enters a latent phase, which generally is not associated with symptoms.

Tertiary Stage

In the tertiary stage, systemic symptoms appear anywhere from 1 to 2 years after the onset of infection to as long as 30 or 40 years later. Approximately 20% to 30% of untreated individuals with syphilis develop tertiary syphilis. Neurologic symptoms, destruction of bone tissue, and cardiovascular disease characterize this stage (CDC, Workowski, & Berman, 2006).

Testing

Tests for detecting syphilis vary with the stage of the disease. In primary and secondary syphilis, the material obtained from the lesion can be tested with either a dark-field microscope or a fluorescent antibody test. Blood testing is also diagnostic, although up to one-third of individuals with early primary syphilis have nonreactive serologic tests. Presumptive diagnosis is possible with nontreponemal tests (VDRL and RPR) and treponemal tests (e.g., FTA-ABS and TP-PA). Latent syphilis can be detected only by using a blood test. All persons who have syphilis should be tested for HIV infection (ACOG, 2007; CDC, Workowski, & Berman, 2006; Workowski & Berman, 2006).

Treatment

Penicillin is the treatment of choice for syphilis; the specific regimen and duration depend on the length of infection. Doxycycline and tetracycline may be used as alternative treatments for people who are allergic to penicillin (CDC, Workowski, & Berman, 2006).

Long-Term Complications

If left untreated, syphilis can develop into systemic infection with serious neurologic and cardiac problems.

HEPATITIS B VIRUS

Heterosexual intercourse is the predominant mode of transmission, but hepatitis B virus (HBV) can also be spread through blood-to-blood contact, which can occur by sharing of razors, toothbrushes, and manicure tools, as well as through contaminated instruments used for dental procedures, tattooing, and body piercing. Vertical transmission occurs when a pregnant woman passes the virus to her fetus. The highest incidence occurs among people ages 20 to 40 years. HBV is 50 to 100 times more contagious than HIV. It causes liver disease and can be fatal. Each year, approximately 6,000 Americans die from HBV infection and its complications (Holloway & D'Acunto, 2006).

Symptoms

Most HBV infections are asymptomatic. However, if symptoms do occur, they may include nausea, vomiting, malaise, headache, fever, dark urine, jaundice, joint pain, and skin eruptions (CDC, Workowski, & Berman, 2006).

Testing

People at high risk for contracting HBV should be screened on a regular basis. Populations at risk include women born in Haiti or sub-Saharan Africa and those of Asian, Pacific Island, or Alaskan-Eskimo descent. Women who have a history of acute or chronic liver disease, those who work or receive treatment in a dialysis unit, those with multiple sexual partners, and those with a history of intravenous drug use are also considered to be at increased risk for contracting HBV.

According to recommendations from the U.S. Preventive Services Task Force (USPSTF) (2007), all women should be screened for HBV at the first prenatal visit, regardless of whether they have previously been tested and screening should be repeated later in pregnancy for women with high-risk behaviors. No routine screening is recommended for the general population.

Testing for HBV is complex. A number of different markers are identified in a blood test, some of which indicate active infection, chronic carrier state, or past infection. About 5% to 10% of adults who contract HBV become chronically infected (American Academy of Pediatrics [AAP] & ACOG, 2007; CDC, Workowski, & Berman, 2006; USPSTF, 2007).

Prevention

Two products are available for HBV prevention: hepatitis B immune globulin (HBIG), which provides temporary protection, and hepatitis B vaccine. Current (2006) CDC recommendations include vaccination of individuals with multiple sex partners in the past 6 months, intravenous drug users, hemophiliacs, residents of long-term care or correctional facilities, persons seeking STI treatment, prostitutes, others at high risk for STIs, health care workers who have a risk of exposure, and anyone planning travel to China, Asia, or Africa. Hepatitis B vaccine is given in a series of three doses over a 6-month period, with the first two doses given at least 1 month apart (CDC, Workowski, & Berman, 2006; Holloway & D'Acunto, 2006; Lowdermilk & Perry, 2007).

Treatment

There is no specific therapy for HBV; treatment is supportive. Recovery is usually spontaneous in 3 to 16 weeks (CDC, Workowski, & Berman, 2006).

Long-Term Complications

Long-term complications of HBV include chronic active hepatitis, cirrhosis, liver cancer, liver failure, and death (CDC, Workowski, & Berman, 2006).

HEPATITIS C VIRUS

Largely unknown to the American public, hepatitis C virus (HCV) has become an important health concern in the United States. Approximately 2 million people in this country are chronically infected with HCV. Previously known as *non-A, non-B hepatitis,* up to 85% of individuals infected with HCV progress to chronic viral hepatitis (CDC, Workowski, & Berman, 2006).

Transmission

HCV is primarily spread through blood-to-blood contact and less efficiently through semen, saliva, and urine. As with HBV, transmission of HCV can potentially occur through blood contact with shared needles, razors, and toothbrushes. Breastfeeding does not transmit HCV infection unless the woman's nipples are cracked or bleeding. The most common risk factor for pregnant women is a history of injecting intravenous drugs (CDC, Workowski, & Berman, 2006; Holloway & D'Acunto, 2006; Lowdermilk & Perry, 2007; Nelson, 2007). Transmission of the virus through breast milk has not been reported (CDC, Workowski, & Berman, 2006; Holloway & D'Acunto, 2006).

Risk Factors

Persons at risk for HCV include those with STIs, such as HBV and HIV, and those with multiple sex partners, a history of blood transfusions, or a history of intravenous drug use (CDC, Workowski, & Berman, 2006).

Symptoms

Infection with the HCV is often asymptomatic, or initial symptoms may be mild (e.g., malaise) and easily mistaken for a cold or flu. Symptoms may be brief, intermittent, or unnoticed. More prominent symptoms appear as the disease progresses and include fatigue, muscle weakness, abdominal pain, nausea, loss of appetite, arthralgia, weight loss, jaundice, and dark-colored urine in the later stages of the infection (CDC, Workowski, & Berman, 2006).

Testing

A serum EIA can be used to detect HCV antibodies (HCV IgG). If the EIA is positive, a recombinant immunoblot assay (RIBA) is required for confirmation. Routine testing is recommended for women who have a history of intravenous drug injection; those who received a blood transfusion prior to July 1992; health care, emergency, medical, and public safety workers; and women with chronic liver disease (CDC, Workowski, & Berman, 2006; Holloway & D'Acunto, 2006). In its *Guide to Clinical Preventive Services, 2007,* the USPSTF recommends against routine screening for HCV in asymptomatic adults who are not at increased risk for infection and found insufficient evidence to recommend for or against routine screening for HCV infection in adults at high risk for infection (USPSTF, 2007).

Prevention and Treatment

No vaccine for HCV is available; prophylaxis with immune globulin is not effective in preventing HCV after exposure. The goal of hepatitis C therapy is to eliminate the virus and prevent complications. Combination therapy with pegylated interferon and ribavirin is the treatment of choice for people with chronic hepatitis C.

Long-Term Complications

Most people infected with HCV are silent carriers, and HCV represents nearly 50% of cases of chronic viral hepatitis. The disease usually takes the form of cirrhosis and causes irreversible and progressive destruction of the liver. HCV infection is the most common indication for liver transplantation. However, recurrence after transplantation is common. Liver cancer (hepatocellular carcinoma) is another potential long-term complication of HCV (Holloway & D'Acunto, 2006).

Self-Care

Holistic nursing care for individuals with chronic infection includes education and counseling about strategies to optimize health, reduce the transmission of infection, and communicate concerns with intimate sexual partners. Referrals to resources, including professional counselors and peer support groups, may be useful. To reduce the possibility of transmission of HBV or HBC, individuals should be advised to maintain a high level of personal hygiene and take measures such as washing hands after toileting; carefully disposing of tampons, pads, and bandages; avoiding sharing razor blades, toothbrushes, needles, and manicure implements; having male partner use a latex condom if unvaccinated (HBV); and wiping up blood spills immediately with soap and water. Dietary measures may include a low-protein, low-fat diet with avoidance of protein or amino acid supplements; use of an antioxidant formula vitamin supplement; and avoidance of alcohol and tobacco (Holloway & D'Acunto, 2006; Lowdermilk & Perry, 2007).

LESS COMMON SEXUALLY TRANSMITTED INFECTIONS

Although they occur less commonly, chancroid, lymphogranuloma venereum (LGV), granuloma inguinale, and vulvar ulcers are other STIs that may be seen in the clinical setting:

1. **Chancroid:** Chancroid is caused by the organism *Haemophilus ducreyi*. It causes painful inguinal adenopathy and is treated with antibiotics (CDC, Workowski, & Berman, 2006).

2. **Lymphogranuloma venereum:** LGV is caused by *Chlamydia trachomatis*. It also produces inguinal adenopathy; a self-limited genital ulcer or papule may also occur at the site of inoculation. It is treated with antibiotics (CDC, Workowski, & Berman, 2006).

3. **Granuloma inguinale:** Granuloma inguinale is caused by *Calymmatobacterium granulomatis*. It is rarely seen in the United States. It causes ulcerative symptoms and is treated with antibiotics (Hatcher et al., 2008).

4. **Vulvar ulcers:** Tuberculosis can cause vulvar ulcers. A tuberculin test with injection of purified protein derivative and chest X-ray films are used for diagnosis. Tuberculosis should be suspected in high-risk populations (Hatcher et al., 2008).

CONCLUSION

STIs are a major public health problem today. Reports from new cases represent only a percentage of those actually affected. Each year, STIs cost our nation millions of dollars, place tremendous demands on health care facilities, and create untold human suffering. Women and children bear the major burdens associated with STIs: sterility, ectopic pregnancy, fetal and infant deaths, birth defects, and mental retardation. Cancer of the cervix has been linked to the herpes II virus. Education, prevention, and contraceptive services must be widely available, and health care providers must be knowledgeable and ready to provide up-to-date, accurate information in a sensitive, nonjudgmental manner.

CHAPTER 7
Questions 53-60

Note: Choose the option that BEST answers each question.

53. Self-care measures to reduce the transmission of STIs include

    a. use of barrier methods.

    b. mutual masturbation.

    c. douching immediately after sexual intercourse.

    d. withdrawal of the penis before ejaculation.

54. Strategies for safer sex that avoid contact with bodily fluids include

    a. careful anal intercourse.

    b. erotic massage.

    c. oral genital stimulation.

    d. consensual sharing of sex toys.

55. Factors that place women at increased risk for HIV infection include

    a. history of an ectopic pregnancy.

    b. history of premenstrual syndrome.

    c. history of a seizure disorder.

    d. history of prostitution.

56. The most common STI that often produces no signs or symptoms in women is

    a. syphilis.

    b. herpes.

    c. chlamydia.

    d. chancroid.

57. Infection with chlamydia is one of the most common causes of

    a. menstrual period abnormalities.

    b. PID.

    c. dysmenorrhea.

    d. vaginal discharge.

58. One of the two agents most commonly responsible for PID is

    a. HPV.

    b. *Trichomonas vaginalis*.

    c. *Neisseria gonorrhoeae*.

    d. HBV.

59. The first sign of syphilis is a sore that is

    a. blistery and filled with clear fluid.

    b. painful.

    c. itchy.

    d. painless.

60. A common therapy for various STIs is

    a. radiotherapy.

    b. antibiotics.

    c. beta blockers.

    d. phototherapy.

CHAPTER 8

PREMENSTRUAL SYNDROME

CHAPTER OBJECTIVE

After completing this chapter, the reader will be able to describe strategies for the management of premenstrual syndrome (PMS).

LEARNING OBJECTIVES

After studying this chapter, the reader will be able to

1. recognize how views of PMS held by the medical community have evolved.

2. indicate possible causes of PMS.

3. identify self-help and other management options for PMS.

KEY WORDS

* Premenstrual syndrome (PMS)
* Premenstrual tension
* Premenstrual dysphoric disorder (PMDD)

INTRODUCTION

Premenstrual syndrome (PMS), or premenstrual tension, is defined as the presence of emotional and physical symptoms and behavioral changes that occur during the second half, or luteal phase, of the menstrual cycle and cease at or within a few days after the onset of menses. The timing of the symptoms in relation to the menstrual cycle, rather than the symptoms themselves, is what is unique in this disorder. Diagnosis depends on the determination that the symptoms experienced occur in this cyclic pattern, are not caused by any underlying physical or mental condition, and greatly disrupt one or more areas of the woman's life. Since 1987, PMS has been recognized as a mental disorder. More than 150 symptoms, which can affect almost every organ system in various combinations and intensity, have been identified (American Psychiatric Association [APA], 2000; Dickerson, 2007; Polaneczky, 2007).

PMS has an interesting history. Until recent times, much of the medical profession believed that the symptoms of PMS were inherent in a woman's nature or based entirely on emotion, with no source of physiologic imbalance. PMS-related research was infrequently conducted until the last few decades. As the Women's Movement grew in strength and awareness about women's health issues increased, views began to shift. At the same time, a growing body of medical information identified various physiologic imbalances and proposed theories to explain the cause of PMS. Over time, PMS has come to be viewed as a complex constellation of hormonal imbalances that can affect a woman's physical, emotional, and mental health (Dickerson, 2007).

PREVALENCE

Sources vary in estimates of the number of women who experience symptoms of PMS. It has been estimated that as much as 85% of childbearing-age women experience various emotional and physical changes during the premenstrual period, although the vast degree of patients with these symptoms do not actually have PMS (American College of Obstetricians and Gynecologists [ACOG], 2000, 2007). Of the women with premenstrual symptoms, approximately 20% to 40% regard the emotional and physical changes as difficult, although only 5% to 10% report a significant degree of impact on their work or lifestyle (ACOG, 2007; Arrowsmith, 2007).

SYMPTOMS

The constellation of PMS symptoms described by women include:

- irritability
- anxiety
- mood swings
- depression
- hostility
- headaches
- dizziness
- fainting
- shakiness
- bloating
- weight gain
- sugar cravings
- constipation
- diarrhea
- backache
- asthma
- breast tenderness
- breast swelling
- joint pain
- sore throat
- cramps
- nausea
- insomnia
- water retention
- fatigue
- increased appetite
- cold sweats
- hot flashes
- lack of coordination
- easy bruising
- palpitations
- hives
- joint swelling
- hay fever
- migraine.

Clinical criteria from the National Institute of Mental Health for the diagnosis of PMS include a marked change in the intensity of symptoms between the follicular and late luteal phases, along with documentation of the symptoms for at least two consecutive cycles (Dickerson, 2007). Other definitions have been developed for research purposes. These include symptom intensity as a criterion for diagnosis. According to the ACOG (2000), at least one of the affective or somatic symptoms associated with PMS must be present (and appropriately timed with the menstrual cycle) to meet the diagnostic criteria. According to Speroff and Fritz (2004), the simplest definition of PMS is a commonsense one: "The cyclic appearance of one or more of a large constellation of symptoms just prior to menses, occurring to such a degree that lifestyle or work is affected, followed by a period of time entirely free of symptoms" (p. 247).

PMS symptoms commonly occur in clusters, with women reporting as many as 10 symptoms at one time. Women who experience severe symptoms may be prone to extremes of behavior, increasing the likelihood of accidents, alcohol abuse, and suicide attempts. Among other women, symptoms may be annoying but mild (Dickerson, 2007).

Premenstrual dysphoric disorder (PMDD) is a diagnostic term for the most severe form of PMS, as defined by the APA's *Diagnostic and Statistical Manual of Mental Disorders,* 4th Edition, Text Revision (DSM-IV-TR). It is estimated that 5% to 8% of women have PMDD (Polaneczky, 2007). Thus, PMDD pertains to women with PMS who have more severe and disabling emotional symptomatology. It is helpful to view PMS and PMDD as a spectrum that begins with mild emotional and physical symptoms that are cyclic but not debilitating and proceeds through PMS to PMDD (Dickerson, 2007). Symptoms that are most commonly reported with PMDD include abdominal bloating, anxiety, tension, breast tenderness, crying episodes, depression, fatigue and a lack of energy, irritability, difficulty concentrating, appetite changes, thirst, and swelling of the extremities (Speroff & Fritz, 2004).

When evaluating a woman for PMS and PMDD symptoms, the health care provider must take very seriously any report of suicidal thoughts or other indications of extreme mood change. A woman with these symptoms needs appropriate medications, close follow-up, and referrals to a qualified mental health professional. Once she is stable, lifestyle and dietary changes can be initiated that will become an important part of her long-term health maintenance (Dickerson, 2007).

Women who come to be evaluated for any of the above symptoms should be given a complete physical examination and work-up to rule out illnesses that may be the source of symptoms. Eliciting a thorough history is crucial to accurately formulating a diagnosis of PMS or PMDD. Particular attention must be paid to the cyclic timing of symptoms. For most women with PMS,

symptoms develop from 2 to 12 days prior to the onset of menstruation and resolve within 24 hours following the onset of menses. Women who have symptoms that primarily occur during the menstrual flow or during the first 2 weeks of the menstrual cycle do not have PMS as defined in the literature (Dickerson, 2007; Speroff & Fritz, 2004).

RISK FACTORS

All age-groups are affected. However, women who are in their twenties and thirties most frequently report symptoms. Premenstrual disorders occur *only* in ovulatory women and *only* during the luteal phase of the menstrual cycle and resolve within 4 days of the onset of menses. Thus, PMS and PMDD do not occur before puberty, after menopause, or during pregnancy. Also, the occurrence of premenstrual disorders is not dependent on the presence of monthly menses; women who have had a hysterectomy without bilateral salpingo-oophorectomy can still have cyclic PMS symptoms (Andolsek & Rapkin, 2006; Lowdermilk & Perry, 2007).

CAUSES OF PREMENSTRUAL DISORDERS

Medical researchers have not yet determined the exact cause of premenstrual disorders, but some believe that the normal fluctuation of estrogen and progesterone during the menstrual cycle plays an important role in many cases. However, the etiology is believed to be multifactorial. A multitude of biologic, psychosocial, and sociocultural factors likely contribute to PMS and PMDD (Speroff & Fritz, 2004; Taylor, Schuiling, & Sharp, 2005).

DIAGNOSIS

Four steps are generally recommended in the evaluation of PMS:

1. a complete medical history
2. a physical examination
3. laboratory tests (as appropriate to rule out other disorders)
4. a 2- to 3-month record of the woman's symptoms.

(Speroff & Fritz, 2004)

The purpose of these steps is to determine:

- whether the symptoms correspond to the cyclic pattern of PMS
- whether there are any possible underlying physical, mental, or emotional conditions, such as psychiatric disorders (e.g., depressive disorders and anxiety); pain disorders, including dysmenorrhea and endometriosis; and hypothyroidism or other endocrine disorders that may lead to cyclic mastalgia
- to what degree the symptoms interfere with the woman's quality of life.

(Speroff & Fritz, 2004)

The nurse should encourage the patient to keep a daily record of her symptom types, timing, and severity. A standardized form called the Daily Record of Severity of Problems is available on the Internet from the Madison Institute of Medicine at (www.pmdd.factsforhealth.org/have/dailyrecord.asp) and can be used to facilitate the diagnosis (Andolsek & Rapkin, 2006).

According to the ACOG (2000), to meet the diagnostic criteria for PMS, at least one of the following symptoms must be present, occur during the luteal phase of the menstrual cycle, and resolve within 4 days of the onset of menses:

Affective Symptoms
- Angry outbursts
- Irritability
- Mild psychological discomfort

- Confusion
- Poor concentration
- Depression
- Sleep disturbances
- Social withdrawal

Somatic Symptoms
- Abdominal bloating
- Headache
- Aches and pains
- Swelling of the extremities
- Breast tenderness
- Weight gain
- Change in appetite

Also, the symptoms must not represent an exacerbation of another disorder, and the symptoms should be bothersome but not necessarily debilitating.

The diagnostic criteria for PMDD includes four major symptom categories and seven additional symptoms. To meet the criteria, the woman must report that her symptoms interfere with her usual activities; the symptoms must not represent an exacerbation of another disorder; and the criteria must be confirmed by prospective daily ratings for at least two cycles (APA, 2000; Dickerson, 2007). At least 5 of the following 11 symptoms must be present:

Major Symptom Categories (at least one must be present)
- Anger or irritability
- Anxiety, edginess, or nervousness
- Depressed mood
- Moodiness

Other Additional Symptoms – (at least five must be present)
- Appetite changes or cravings
- Decreased interest in usual activities
- Difficulty concentrating
- Fatigue
- Feeling overwhelmed or out of control
- Insomnia or hypersomnia
- Physical symptoms (listed in PMS diagnostic criteria)

MANAGEMENT

Once the diagnosis of PMS has been made, the first step in treatment is to validate the woman's experience and reassure her that her symptoms are real and have a physiologic base. This simple validation can be a great source of relief and healing for women who have concerns about their sanity. Many women find measurable relief from their symptoms by making lifestyle changes that include increased physical activity, aerobic exercise, stress reduction, and relaxation techniques such as yoga and meditation. Dietary alterations may include the use of vitamins, minerals, or herbal supplements. In women with mild PMS, these interventions often bring significant relief of symptoms. However, women with severe PMS or PMDD commonly require pharmacologic intervention (Dickerson, 2007).

Strategies for Health Promotion

Most women with mild to moderate symptoms of PMS respond well to simple health promotion strategies. Education is a central component of the management of PMS. Nurses can teach women about self-help modalities that often result in significant improvement of their symptoms. This area of health promotion is one in which women have reason to feel very encouraged. Health care providers must guide and support women about long-term changes that promote a healthy lifestyle and often help to decrease their premenstrual discomfort (Dickerson, 2007; Lowdermilk & Perry, 2007).

Assisting patients in making dietary changes can be a very challenging and rewarding endeavor. Long-standing habits and those associated with cultural preferences need to be addressed. Women need reassurance and encouragement while making these changes. Health care providers are of greatest assistance when they can recommend appropriate community resources, support groups, and educational programs.

When counseling and assisting patients with PMS, there are six major areas of focus:

1. foods to avoid or include
2. exercise
3. vitamins, minerals, and other nutrients
4. herbs
5. relaxation techniques, including massage, yoga, meditation, and biofeedback
6. Asian medicine.

(Dickerson, 2007; Polaneczky, 2007)

Detrimental and Beneficial Foods for Premenstrual Disorders

Women should be aware of foods that can worsen PMS symptoms and those that can help to lessen symptoms. Foods that tend to worsen PMS symptoms include:

- foods high in
  - refined sugars (should consume less than 5 tbsp/day)
  - animal fat, including dairy products (should only consume up to 3 oz/day)
  - salt (should consume less than 3 grams/day and beware of the "hidden" sodium in most packaged and processed foods.)
- foods that are processed and full of chemicals
- caffeinated beverages, which may increase feelings of irritability
- alcoholic beverages (should consume less than 1 oz/day).

(Lowdermilk & Perry, 2007)

This list includes such foods as cola drinks, alcohol, chocolate, candy, ice cream, hamburgers, hot dogs, hard cheese, beef, pork, and pizza. In many cases, women with PMS develop intense cravings for one or more of these foods.

Foods that help to reduce PMS symptoms tend to be whole foods and vegetable-based foods that are rich in complex carbohydrates and fiber. These include:

- foods made from whole grains (e.g., breads, pasta, pancake mix, and crackers)

- nuts and seeds

- fresh fruits and vegetables

- oils, especially safflower, sesame, olive, corn, and flax

- seaweeds

- seafood and skinless natural poultry (no hormones or growth factors)

- legumes, including soy products such as tofu

- decreasing the intake of salt and sugar approximately 7 to 10 days prior to the expected menses may help to reduce fluid retention.

In addition, women should be encouraged to increase their water intake 7 to 10 days prior to their expected menses. Water may serve as a natural diuretic; other "natural" diuretics (e.g., asparagus, cranberry juice, peaches, parsley, and watermelon) may be beneficial in reducing edema and related discomforts. Consuming small, frequent meals may help to decrease feelings of irritability related to hypoglycemia (Lowdermilk & Perry, 2007).

Exercise

Exercise is another key component of PMS self-help. Results of numerous investigations have proven its merit in alleviating premenstrual disorder symptoms. Regular aerobic exercise three or four times per week, especially during the luteal phase, has many physiologic and psychologic benefits. Nurses can encourage women to engage in a monthly program of exercise that varies in intensity and the type of exercise according to PMS symptoms. Those who participate in regular exercise seem to have less premenstrual anxiety than do nonathletic women. Aerobic exercise is thought to increase endorphin levels to offset symptoms of depression and elevate the mood (Lowdermilk & Perry, 2007).

Vitamins, Minerals, and Other Nutrients

Diet is always the first and best source of nutrients. Vitamins and minerals as they are naturally found in food tend to be better absorbed. Essential nutrients can be lost in cooking and preparation. In addition to recommending specific types of healthy foods, health care providers should guide patients in how to prepare them to maintain their nutritional value. For example:

- steaming vegetables instead of boiling them in water preserves many of the more delicate nutrients, such as vitamin C

- including raw foods at each meal is a great way to maximize nutritional value and add fiber to the diet

- eating a wide variety of fruits and vegetables ensures more nutrient balance

- eating seasonal fruits and vegetables, organically grown if possible, provides the best chance for patients to ingest foods that have not been stored for long periods or irradiated, both of which diminish the nutritional value of these foods

- substituting whole grains and whole grain breads, pasta, and pancake mixes for the same products made with white flour gives these foods much more nutritional value

- encouraging the use of vegetable oils, especially for patients from cultures that commonly use lard as part of the cuisine.

A positive, enthusiastic, and reassuring approach with specific suggestions can help to empower women as they become actively involved with their PMS care program.

Certain nutrients, including beta carotene, B complex vitamins, vitamin E, calcium, magnesium, zinc, and essential fatty acids, have been purported to be useful for the management of PMS.

- **Beta carotene:** Beta carotene is useful in improving the condition of the skin.

- **B complex vitamins:** The B complex vitamins include choline and inositol, which help the liver break down fatty foods and hormones and also calm the nervous system. Soybeans, wheat germ, bran, and corn are high in these nutrients.

- **Vitamin E:** Vitamin E may help to improve cystic breast symptoms; it is also believed to protect cells from the harmful effects of chemicals. Sources of this vitamin include sunflower, corn, sesame, and walnut oils; nuts and seeds; broccoli; and corn. Women must be cautioned that vitamin E affects blood clotting, and daily vitamin E supplementation in excess of 400 IU is associated with increased mortality (Natural Standard, n.d.).

- **Calcium:** Adequate calcium intake helps to reduce menstrual cramps and balances nervous system function. Sources of calcium include tofu, broccoli, sesame seeds, greens, and yogurt. Supplements of 1,200 mg/day may be advised (ACOG, 2007; Lowdermilk & Perry, 2007).

- Magnesium: Menstrual cramps are also improved with adequate magnesium intake. Magnesium is involved in glucose metabolism and helps to stabilize mood. This mineral also enhances the absorption of calcium. Sources of magnesium include legumes, dark leafy greens, carrots, corn, nuts and seeds, and whole grains. Supplements of 300 to 400 mg/day may be advised (ACOG, 2007; Lowdermilk & Perry, 2007).

- **Zinc:** Zinc, a trace mineral, functions along with vitamins C and A to promote healthy skin. Sources of zinc include pumpkin seeds, legumes, and whole grains.

- **Essential fatty acids:** Essential fatty acids are a type of oil that the body cannot make and must be obtained from food. Sources of these nutrients include flaxseed oil and evening primrose or borage oil (often taken in supplement form). Essential fatty acids are also found in certain types of fish. Evening primrose oil may decrease premenstrual mood symptoms, breast pain, and fluid retention, although there are no high-quality studies to support this claim. Women who wish to use evening primrose oil should be warned that it is associated with stomach distress, nausea and headaches in some individuals (Lowdermilk & Perry, 2007).

However, according to the Natural Standard (n.d.), calcium is the only dietary supplement with good evidence for PMS treatment.

Herbs

Throughout history, women have used a number of safe herbal medicines to help alleviate PMS symptoms. Herbal preparations can be taken as teas or tinctures. Certain herbs, such as nettle and alfalfa, are very high in vitamins and minerals; others, such as burdock root, dandelion root, and milk thistle, support healthy liver function (Lowdermilk & Perry, 2007; Sego, 2007).

Helpful herbs include red raspberry leaf, which tones the uterus; cramp bark and wild yam, which relieve uterine cramps; and hormone-balancing herbs, such as chaste tree fruit, black cohosh root, and licorice. The leaf of the common dandelion is a safe and effective diuretic (Lowdermilk & Perry, 2007).

Relaxation Techniques, Massage, Yoga, Meditation, and Biofeedback

Relaxation techniques, massage, yoga, meditation, biofeedback, acupuncture, hypnosis, and chiropractic therapy may have a beneficial effect on PMS (Andolsek & Rapkin, 2006; Lowdermilk & Perry, 2007).

Asian Medicine

The healing approach in Asian medicine has much to offer for women who suffer from PMS symptoms. The Asian perspective views PMS as an energy imbalance, a blockage and stagnation of vital energy, or *chi,* which normally flows through the body and enlivens it. When this energy is blocked in the pelvic region, it can manifest in many of the symptoms previously described. The Asian healing approaches seek to rebalance body energies, allowing the hormonal and nervous systems to return to a balanced function (Lowdermilk & Perry, 2007).

The Nurses Role

Nurses can empower women with strategies for positive lifestyle changes that will enhance their sense of well-being and hopefully help to diminish their PMS symptoms. Explaining the relationship between cyclic estrogen fluctuation and changes in serotonin levels may provide insights about serotonin, one of the natural brain chemicals that assists an individual in coping with normal life stresses. The various management strategies described help to maintain balance in the body's serotonin levels. Counseling and stress reduction techniques may also be beneficial (Lowdermilk & Perry, 2007).

Pharmacologic Interventions

If the nonpharmacologic approaches do not provide significant symptom relief in 1 to 2 months, medication is often initiated. The two main pharmacologic treatment strategies involve: 1) targeting the central nervous system processes that are believed to contribute to premenstrual mood symptoms; and 2) eliminating the hormonal cyclicity by suppressing ovulation. The U.S. Food and Drug Administration (FDA) has approved pharmacologic treatments only for PMDD; their use for PMS, which may be effective for some women with severe symptoms, must be considered "off label." Presently, the use of natural progesterone is believed to be no more effective than a placebo for the treatment of premenstrual disorders (Andolsek & Rapkin, 2006; Polaneczky, 2007).

For treatment of somatic symptoms, medications may include nonsteroidal anti-inflammatory drugs, diuretics, and combination (estrogen/progestin) oral contraceptives. For women with affective-predominant symptoms, the FDA has approved certain selective serotonin reuptake inhibitors (SSRIs), followed by other SSRIs or serotonin/norepinephrine reuptake inhibitors. These medications include fluoxetine (Prozac or Sarafem), sertraline (Zoloft), paroxetine (Paxil), and citalopram (Celexa), which have been shown to decrease pre-

menstrual symptoms such as depression. Nurses should be aware that the use of antidepressants in the treatment of PMDD is different from their typical use in treating other mood and depressive disorders. When used for PMDD, these medications are taken in lower doses and with less frequency. Providing this information is important in helping women to understand their diagnosis and the rationale for pharmacologic treatment. It is also important to explain to patients that other mood and depressive disorders will not respond in the same way to the prescribed medications (ACOG, 2007; Andolsek & Rapkin, 2006; Dickerson, 2007; Lowdermilk & Perry, 2007; Polaneczky, 2007).

Patients should be counseled about the possibility of side effects that can accompany the use of these medications, including headaches, sleep disturbances, gastrointestinal irritability, tremors, sweating, anxiety, dizziness, weight gain, dry mouth, and decreased libido (Khouzam, 2007). Use of any of the central nervous system agents for treatment of PMS or PMDD does not contraindicate the use of any hormonal or nonhormonal contraceptive method to prevent pregnancy. One oral contraceptive, drospirenone (Yaz) has been approved by the FDA for the treatment of symptoms of PMDD (ACOG, 2007; Andolsek & Rapkin, 2006; Dickerson, 2007; Lowdermilk & Perry, 2007; Polaneczky, 2007).

CASE STUDY

L.V. is a single, 27-year-old, white female who has come to the women's health clinic with numerous complaints consistent with PMS, including weight gain, breast swelling and tenderness, and feelings of depression and low self-esteem. L.V. has never been pregnant. She has a menstrual period every 30 to 31 days that lasts approximately 6 days. Presently, L.V. is not sexually active. She has a diaphragm for contraception when needed.

Questions

1. What additional information is needed to help confirm the diagnosis of PMS?

2. What self-care strategies can the nurse offer to L.V.?

3. What other resources are appropriate?

Discussion

It is important to ascertain the timing and duration of L.V.'s symptoms in order to establish that they are consistent with PMS. The symptoms should occur during the luteal phase of the menstrual cycle and resolve within 4 days after the onset of menses. It may be helpful to ask L.V. to record her symptoms on a daily basis to establish the timing and repetitiveness of her symptoms although, according to her history, she is a regular, cyclic menstruator and her symptoms consistently precede menstruation and resolve within a few days following the onset of menstruation.

The nurse can counsel L.V. to wear a supportive bra and take prescribed medications to minimize breast tenderness. Increased premenstrual body weight occurs due to fluid retention related to cyclic hormonal influences. Self-care strategies include limiting the intake of salt- and sodium-containing foods approximately 7 to 10 days before the expected menses to decrease fluid retention. She should also be advised to take diuretics as prescribed to facilitate fluid excretion and encouraged to increase her water intake and consume natural diuretic foods, such as cranberry juice, watermelon, peaches, asparagus, and parsley, to encourage fluid excretion.

The nurse can employ therapeutic communication techniques to help validate L.V.'s feelings of depression and low self-esteem. Suggesting that L.V. limit her caffeine intake and eat small, frequent meals to decrease irritability aggravated by caffeine and hypoglycemia are other strategies. Exercise and relaxation techniques, especially during the luteal phase, may be useful in helping to decrease anxiety and improve feelings of well-

being. The nurse can also refer L.V. to community resources such as women's support groups, which encourage the sharing of feelings and experiences and offer and reinforce strategies for self-care.

CONCLUSION

PMS in some form is common among the large majority of reproductive-age women in this country. A woman's stressful lifestyle, coupled with inconsistent diet or exercise patterns and a lack of rest and play time, are believed to be major factors. Premenstrual disorders as an entity can be viewed as a spectrum ranging from the cyclic appearance of mild emotional and physical symptoms to the cyclic presence of severe, disabling symptoms that interfere with the individual's usual activities. The cyclic nature of the appearance and disappearance of symptoms that coincides with menses is a common thread of this condition.

For most women, making simple changes can reduce PMS symptoms and dramatically improve quality of life. Education and counseling about health-promoting behaviors constitute major tools in the management of PMS. Various pharmacological agents are also used when necessary. Nurses are instrumental in the management of premenstrual disorders by offering ongoing education and support. These interventions empower women to adopt strategies to help them exert control over their lives and, hopefully, to enjoy improvement in their symptoms.

EXAM QUESTIONS

CHAPTER 8
Questions 61-65

Note: Choose the option that BEST answers each question.

61. In the past, PMS was thought to be associated with

    a. insanity.

    b. pregnancy.

    c. tobacco use.

    d. women's emotional make-up.

62. Although the exact cause of PMS is unknown, one theory proposes that PMS is related to

    a. excessive magnesium.

    b. early menopause.

    c. fluctuations of estrogen and progesterone.

    d. low levels of insulin.

63. When counseling women about self-help strategies for PMS, health care providers should suggest

    a. increasing caffeine intake several days before the onset of menses.

    b. reducing the amount of physical activity.

    c. using relaxation and stress-relief techniques such as meditation.

    d. increasing sugar intake to satisfy the natural craving.

64. Adequate calcium intake helps to reduce

    a. menstrual flow.

    b. menstrual cramps.

    c. acne.

    d. dry skin.

65. Supplementation with vitamin E may be useful in alleviating

    a. high blood pressure associated with PMS.

    b. premenstrual fluid retention and weight gain.

    c. symptoms associated with cystic breasts.

    d. mood swings during the second half of the menstrual cycle.

CHAPTER 9

PREVENTIVE HEALTH CARE

CHAPTER OBJECTIVE

After completing this chapter, the reader will be able to identify major components of health maintenance and good preventive health care for women.

LEARNING OBJECTIVES

After studying this chapter, the reader will be able to

1. specify components of a good health history.
2. identify common components of a well-woman examination.
3. identify individual factors that influence choice and frequency of tests and evaluation.

KEY WORDS

- Bimanual examination
- Body mass index (BMI)
- Breast self-examination (BSE)
- Clinical breast examination (CBE)
- Integrated medical therapies

INTRODUCTION

An annual examination provides an opportunity to develop and nurture the ongoing relation-ship that health care providers share with their patients. The yearly visit also serves as an ideal time to teach and reinforce health-promotion strategies. Most practitioners advise that annual exams be initiated whenever a woman becomes sexually active or, in the absence of sexual activity, by age 20. Depending on the setting, nurses' roles are varied and include assessing vital signs, taking the health history, providing personalized counseling and teaching, assisting with office procedures, and making referrals. It is wise never to assume that other health care providers are fully aware of all diagnoses, therapies, and medications prescribed for a patient. Not infrequently, errors and inconsistencies in care occur because one provider is uninformed about what others are doing. The responsibility of keeping each provider fully informed should be shared between providers and their patients.

HEALTH HISTORY

History-taking may be viewed as an art. Obtaining a thorough history is essential to providing optimal care. Major components of history-taking are a nonjudgmental attitude and guided listening, a skill that can be practiced by:

- allowing the woman to tell what she wants to be known about why she came in for evaluation
- eliciting from the woman what needs to be known to plan her care.

To elicit the chief complaint, allow the patient to tell her story without interruption. Being heard often marks the beginning of the healing process for the woman. When conducting the patient interview, the recorded history should include at least the following components:

- **General health history** – review of systems, immunization status, illnesses, hospitalizations, and surgeries.

- **Personal data** – woman's age, employment status, and living arrangements. When appropriate, cultural values and beliefs are explored. The communication practices of women in different cultural groups influences the expression of ideas, perceptions, and decision-making (Wood, Kettinger, & Lessick, 2007). Spirituality is also included in this component of the health history. In order for the nurse to provide holistic care that encompasses all aspects of the woman's physical and psychosocial health, an understanding of the role spirituality plays in her life is essential (Shay-Zapien, 2007). Presently, the Joint Commission on Accreditation of Health Care Organizations (2007) requires an assessment of the patient's religious, spiritual, and cultural beliefs upon every hospital admission. Obtaining this information during the health interview in any clinical setting demonstrates the nurse's sensitivity to the woman's values and beliefs and enhances the delivery of individualized care:

- **Menstrual history** – Typical cycle, including quantity, duration, and problems.

- **Pregnancy history** – Each pregnancy, with details regarding miscarriages, abortions, ectopic pregnancies, and any complications.

- **Gynecologic history** – Infections, sexually transmitted infections (STIs), surgeries, diagnostic procedures, and history of Pap smear findings.

- **Sexual history** – Current and past partner history, STI testing and results, and sexual function.

- **Contraceptive history** – past and current use of birth control methods and reasons the woman stopped using a particular method (e.g., side effects, problems).

- **Medications** – Past and current.

- **Allergies** – To prescription/nonprescription medications, herbal supplements, latex, food sources, adhesives, seasonal (note if medication is required), and note symptoms that occur following exposure.

- **Family history** – Genetic diseases, serious illnesses, cause of death in family members, pregnancy problems, and use of medications (e.g., diethylstilbestrol) during pregnancy.

- **Lifestyle history** – Current and past use of alcohol, cigarettes, and social drugs; diet and exercise habits and patterns; living situation; partner habits; occupation and other possible hazards and exposures; and travel.

- **Personal safety history** – Current or history of abuse or trauma. (Asking specific questions to screen for abuse, such as "Have you ever been emotionally or physically abused by your partner or someone important to you?" and "Within the last year, have you been hit, slapped, kicked, or otherwise physically hurt by someone?" Also assess for community or other violence using questions such as "Do you feel safe at home?" and "Do you feel safe in your neighborhood?"

- **Psychiatric history** – Emotional and psychological problems, illness, and weight issues.

- **Vision for personal health in the future** – Asking the female patient of any age how she envisions her health and fitness levels in the future is an important component of health promotion. This information assists the nurse in developing an individualized plan for health education that incorporates strategies to help the woman maintain or achieve health and fitness in the years to come.

(American College of Obstetricians and Gynecologists [ACOG], 2007; Lowdermilk & Perry, 2007; Ruhl, 2006; Seidel, Ball, Dains, & Benedict, 2006)

The above-listed information should be updated each year during the annual health examination.

Therapeutic communication techniques that can enhance patient sharing during the health history interview include information seeking, facilitation, reflection, clarification, empathic responses, and interpretation. *Information seeking* is an attempt to make clear that which is not meaningful or that which is vague. By using phrases such as " I'm not sure that I follow" or "Have I heard you correctly?" the nurse avoids making assumptions that understanding has occurred and the patient is able to articulate her thoughts, feelings, and ideas more clearly. *Facilitation* incorporates the use of a word or posture that encourages the woman to continue. For example, the nurse may lean forward, make eye contact, or provide verbal cues such as "please continue" or "yes, go on." *Reflection* involves repeating a word or phrase that the woman has used to encourage her to continue. *Clarification* involves asking the woman what she means by a word or phrase that she has used. *Empathic responses* such as "That must have been very stressful!" acknowledge and validate the woman's feelings. *Interpretation* involves describing what the patient is believed to have said – the nurse puts into words the information inferred from the woman's descriptions or explanations of events, symptoms, or other matters (Lowdermilk & Perry, 2007; Seidel et al., 2006).

Schedule for Health Maintenance and Preventive Screening

Health maintenance and screening is an essential component of well-woman care. Information obtained during the history can be used as a guide for appropriate testing and patient education. Recommendations for immunizations and laboratory and diagnostic tests have been developed by diverse professional and community agencies. Guidelines for addressing high-priority services through preventive screening are pre-

sented in Table 9-1. These guidelines represent a compilation of recommendations from the ACOG (2007), the U.S. Preventive Services Task Force (USPSTF, 2007), and the Institute for Clinical Systems Improvement (2007). The health maintenance examination (Michigan Quality Improvement Consortium, 2006a, 2006b) is one of the essential components of health maintenance. Ideally, preventive screening should begin during adolescence and continue throughout life. Conducting risk assessment and providing strategies for health promotion are essential components of screening throughout the life cycle. According to the guidelines, adolescents and young adults ages 18 to 49 years should have one health maintenance examination every 1 to 5 years, based on their risk status. Adults ages 50 to 64 years should have one health maintenance examination every 1 to 3 years based on their risk status, and adults ages 65 and older should have one health maintenance examination at least every 2 years, regardless of their risk status.

THE PHYSICAL EXAMINATION

An annual health examination should include the components of a general physical examination, with evaluation of the thyroid gland, heart, lungs, extremities, and reflexes. A gynecologically oriented HME should also include the following components:

1. Complete pelvic examination, including:
    *   inspection of the:
        *   external genitalia for evidence of infection, abnormal coloration, growths, irritation, or discharge
        *   vagina for evidence of inflammation or discharge
        *   cervix for lesions, discharge, and signs of irritation
    *   a Pap smear with a sampling of the outer and inner portions of the cervix

TABLE 9-1: PREVENTIVE SCREENING RECOMMENDATIONS

Service	19–39 Years	40–64 Years	65+ Years
Aspirin prophylaxis	Discuss with postmenopausal women, men over age 40, and younger individuals at increased risk for coronary heart disease		
Breast cancer screening		Annual mammogram for women with risk factors; every 1 to 2 years for women 40 to 64 years of age with no risk factors	Annual mammogram for women with risk factors; every 1 to 2 years for women 65 and older with no risk factors
Cervical cancer screening	First Pap Smear at age 21 or 3 years after first sexual intercourse, whichever is earlier. Yearly screening to age 30; then every 2 to 3 years after three consecutive normal results	Every 2 to 3 years after three consecutive normal results	Pap Smear with new sexual partner
Chlamydia and gonorrhea screening	All sexually active females, including asymptomatic women ages 25 years and younger		
Colon cancer screening		Beginning at age 50, fecal occult blood testing (guaiac-based test cards from three consecutive stool samples) or flexible sigmoidoscopy every 5 years or double-contrast barium enema every 5 years or colonoscopy every 10 years (ACOG, 2007). According to the latest screening guidelines from the American College of Gastroenterology, African American women should be screened for colorectal cancer every 10 years, beginning at age 45.	
Hypertension screening	Blood pressure screening every 2 years if less than 120/80 mm Hg; annual blood pressure screening if 120 to 139/80 to 89 mm Hg		
Influenza vaccine**	Annually between October and March for individuals ages 50 and above, those with chronic illnesses, members of the health care team, and others at high risk		
Pneumococcal vaccine**	Immunize individuals at high risk once; reimmunize once after 5 years if at risk for losing immunity		Immunize at age 65 if not done previously; reimmunize once if first vaccination received greater than 5 years ago and before age 65
Problem drinking screening	Screen for problem drinking among all adults and provide brief counseling		
Tobacco cessation counseling	Assess all adults for tobacco use and provide ongoing cessation services for those who smoke or are at risk for smoking relapse		
Total cholesterol and high-density lipoprotein cholesterol screening	Serum total cholesterol in all adults over age 20	Fasting fractionated lipid screening for men over age 34 and for women over age 44 every 5 years	
Vision screening			Asymptomatic elderly adults

** For the schedule of additional recommended immunizations, see Table 9-2.

(ACOG, 2007; USPSTF, 2007; Institute for Clinical Systems Improvement, 2007)

A Pap smear is a microscopic examination of cells taken from the cervical area by various techniques. It is the most reliable method used to screen patients for preinvasive cervical cancer. The USPSTF and the American Cancer Society (ACS) recommend that Pap tests begin approximately 3 years after a woman becomes sexually active but not later than age 21. Yearly screening is recommended to age 30 with conventional Pap tests; every 2 years with liquid-based Pap tests. After age 30 and three negative Pap tests, screening may be performed every 2 to 3 years, in consultation with a health care provider. Women ages 65 to 70 who have had no abnormal tests in the previous 10 years may choose to stop Pap screenings (ACS, 2006; USPSTF, 2007). Women in high-risk categories including those exposed to DES in utero, those with a history of abnormal Pap tests, and those at high risk for STIs should have more frequent Pa2p tests. Pap tests will be discussed in detail in Chapter 10.

- a bimanual examination, determining the size, shape, position, and consistency of the uterus and ovaries (see Figure 9-1)

2. The ACS recommends colon cancer screening of all adults beginning at age 40. The ACOG and the USPSTF recommend colon cancer screening beginning at age 50. For women, this involves:

- a rectovaginal examination to check for masses as well as to palpate the uterus and pelvic structures for masses not detectable with bimanual examination

- annual fecal occult blood testing beginning at age 50, which involves a stool sample to check for blood in the stool (One method consists of a "take-home-mail-back" kit with specific dietary instructions and tools for sampling the stool. According to recommen-

FIGURE 9-1: BIMANUAL PALPATION OF THE UTERUS

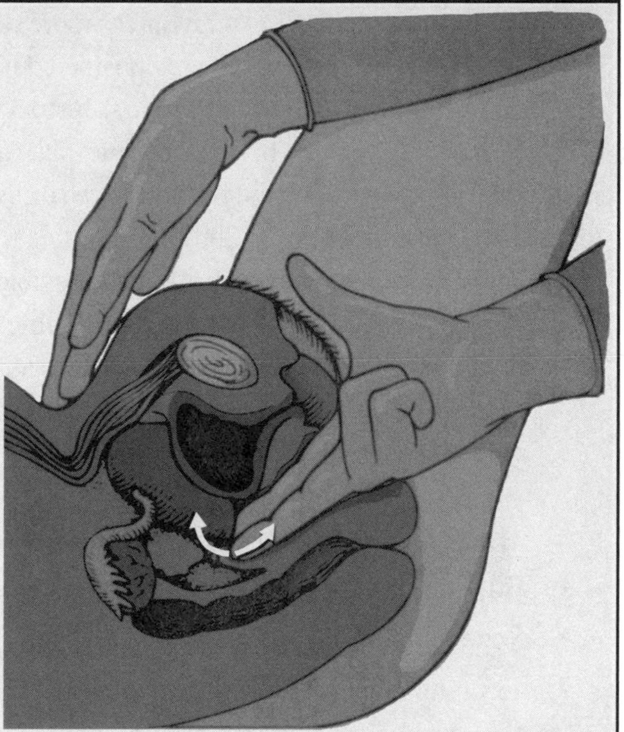

Note. From *Maternity & Women's Health Care* (9th ed., p. 118), by D. Lowdermilk & S. Perry, 2007, St. Louis, Mosby.

dations from the ACOG and USPSTF, a single stool sample for fecal occult blood testing or fecal immunochemical testing obtained by digital rectal examination is not adequate for the detection of colorectal cancer. Fecal occult blood testing requires three consecutive samples of stool collected by the patient at home and returned for analysis [ACOG, 2007; USPSTF, 2007]).

(ACOG, 2007; ACS, 2006; USPSTF, 2007)

Other colon health recommendations include:

- a flexible sigmoidoscopy every 5 years (the USPSTF [2007] states there is no direct evidence with which to determine the optimal interval for tests other than the fecal occult blood test) *or*

- a double-contrast barium enema (The USPSTF [2007] states there is no direct evidence with which to determine the optimal interval for tests other than the fecal occult blood test) *or*

- a colonoscopy every 10 years, with special attention paid to individuals at *high risk* for colon cancer (Persons with one or more of the following risk factors are considered to be at high risk: significant family history; personal history of breast, endometrial, or ovarian cancer; polyps; or ulcerative colitis [Lowdermilk & Perry, 2007]. According to recommendations from the ACOG, flexible sigmoidoscopy, colonscopy, and double-contrast barium enema performed at specified intervals can increase the ability to detect asymptomatic lesions and are recommended for patients beginning at age 50 years [ACOG, 2007]).

3. Screening for breast cancer, including:
   - yearly clinical breast examination (CBE).
   - teaching of and performing monthly breast self-examination (BSE). According to recommendations from the USPSTF (2007), insufficient evidence was found to recommend for or against teaching or performing routine BSE. According to ACOG guidelines (2007), despite a lack of definitive data for or against BSE, BSE has the potential to detect palpable breast cancer and can be recommended.
   - mammography, ultrasound, or magnetic resonance imaging.

Breast health will be discussed in detail in Chapter 12.

4. Screening for STIs as needed. Women ages 25 and younger should be screened for chlamydia and gonorrhea (ACOG, 2007; USPSTF, 2007).

5. Immunizations (see Table 9-2 for immunization guidelines). When counseling women who plan international travel, additional immunizations may be needed (Rice, 2007). Internet sources for travel health information that

TABLE 9-2: RECOMMENDED VACCINES FOR WOMEN

For women who do not have immunity:

Ages 19–49 Years	Ages 50–64 Years	65+ Years
Tetanus, diphtheria, pertussis (Td/Tdap): Initial 3-dose series, then a 1-dose booster every 10 years **Human papillomavirus (HPV):** a 3-dose series for women 26 years of age and younger **Measles, mumps, rubella (MMR):** 1 or 2 doses **Varicella (chickenpox):** 2 doses	**TD/Tdap:** Initial 3-dose series, then a 1-dose booster every 10 years **Herpes zoster:** 1 dose for women ages 60 years and older **Influenza:** 1 dose every year **Varicella (chickenpox):** 2 doses	**TD/Tdap:** Initial 3-dose series, then a 1-dose booster every 10 years **Herpes zoster:** 1 dose for women ages 60 years and older **Influenza:** 1 dose every year **Pneumococcal (polysaccharide):** 1 dose **Varicella (chickenpox):** 2 doses

For women with conditions that place them at risk:

Influenza: 1 dose every year **Pneumococcal (polysaccharide):** 1 or 2 doses **Hepatitis A:** 2 doses **Hepatitis B:** 3 doses **Meningococcal:** 1 or more doses	**MMR:** 1 dose **Varicella (chickenpox):** 2 doses, for women ages 60 years and younger **Pneumococcal (polysaccharide):** 1 or 2 doses **Hepatitis A:** 2 doses **Hepatitis B:** 3 doses **Meningococcal:** 1 or more doses	**Hepatitis A:** 2 doses **Hepatitis B:** 3 doses **Meningococcal:** 1 or more doses

(Miller & Wysocki, 2007)

includes areas of current outbreaks and areas where specific diseases are endemic are provided in the "Resources" at the back of the course book.

6. Screening all postmenopausal women age 65 years and older for osteoporosis through measurement of bone density. (Osteoporosis will be discussed in detail in Chapter 13.)

7. Screenings for other health conditions, including:
   - serum cholesterol level to screen for heart disease in all adults over the age of 20 at least once every 5 years.
   - tests to evaluate possible thyroid disease; diabetes; tuberculosis; possible occupational exposure to body fluids, toxic chemicals, and radiation; and parasites in patients who travel to high-risk areas – all of which would be indicated on the basis of examination findings and history.

(ACOG, 2007; Lowdermilk & Perry, 2007)

Obesity: An Essential Topic for Health Education

Obesity is a global epidemic and a chronic health problem that shows no regard for national boundaries and personal demographics. Persons of both genders and all ages, racial and ethnic groups, and socioeconomic strata can be victims of this "equal opportunity" disease (Dennis, 2007). Dubbed "globesity," obesity is now replacing the more traditional health concerns of undernutrition and infectious diseases as one of the most powerful and influential contributors to a myriad of health problems (World Health Organization [WHO], 2006).

In the United States, obesity is a leading cause of morbidity and mortality. Approximately 60% of adult women are classified as overweight and 30% are obese (Ogden et al., 2006). Biologic, genetic, environmental, and behavioral influences all contribute to the rising rate of obesity. Culture also plays a role, as do social influences such as time constraints, the cost of healthful foods, and a lack of

nutritional knowledge (Faucher, 2007). Because women are at greater risk for being overweight or obese and are at risk for gaining weight as they age, it is important for health care professionals to understand the consequences of obesity and to incorporate health promotion strategies for women across the lifespan (Dennis, 2007).

Body Mass Index

The designations of overweight and obesity are based on body mass index (BMI), which is a method of evaluating the appropriateness of weight for height. BMI is calculated using the formula:

$$BMI = \frac{Weight}{Height^2}$$

where weight is recorded in kilograms and height is in meters. For example, the calculated BMI for a woman who weighs 52 kg and is 1.58 m tall is:

$$BMI = \frac{52}{1.58^2} = 20.8$$

Persons with a BMI less than 18.5 are underweight; those with a BMI between 18.5 and 24.9 are normal; those with a BMI between 25 and 29.9 are overweight. Persons with a BMI between 30 and 34.9 are classified at Level 1 obesity; those with a BMI between 35 and 39.9 are classified at Level 2 obesity. Extreme obesity, or Level 3 obesity, includes persons with a BMI of 40 or above (Dennis, 2007; Faucher, 2007).

Routinely screening patients for obesity and, when indicated, providing counseling and behavioral interventions is an important component of health promotion (Appel & Bannon, 2007; USPSTF, 2003, 2007). Although weight loss strategies such as dietary approaches (e.g., Atkins diet) and structured weight loss programs (e.g., Weight Watchers) result in successful weight loss and lead to health benefits in the short term, the challenge lies in maintaining the initial weight loss over the long term. For women, group-based programs may be a better strategy for weight loss maintenance than individual counseling. Care providers can facilitate weight-loss and weight-loss maintenance efforts by organizing peer-lead support groups for their patients who are attempting to lose weight. Therapy groups that are directed by participants provide a means of social support and enhance psychological well-being, important elements that improve the likelihood of weight loss maintenance (Faucher, 2007). Nurses can be proactive in implementing these and other interventions that have the potential to contribute to improved health outcomes for all populations of women (Morin, 2007).

Individualized Nutrition With MyPyramid

In an effort to motivate Americans to eat better, avoid obesity, and get more active, the U.S. Department of Agriculture (USDA) has developed a new food guide based on individual factors, including age, gender, and activity level. It is based on the guiding principles of overall health, up-to-date research, total diet, usefulness, realism, flexibility, practicality, and evolution (see Figure 9-2). Using the name "MyPyramid," the innovative approach focuses the patient on developing an individualized plan for improving diet and lifestyle.

FIGURE 9-2: MYPYRAMID

(U.S. Department of Agriculture, 2005)

MyPyramid incorporates recommendations from the *2005 Dietary Guidelines for Americans,* which was released by the USDA and U.S. Department of Health and Human Services (USD-HHS) in January 2005 (USDHHS & USDA, 2005).

Published every 5 years, the dietary guidelines provide authoritative advice for people ages 2 and older about how good dietary habits can promote health and reduce the risk of major chronic diseases. This document can be accessed at www.health.gov/dietaryguidelines/dga2005/document/default.htm. MyPyramid was developed to communicate the messages of the dietary guidelines to make Americans aware of the important health benefits of simple and modest improvements in nutrition, physical activity, and lifestyle behavior.

Deliberately simple, the MyPyramid symbol is intended to encourage consumers to make healthier food choices and to be physically active every day. The pyramid is color-coded to provide a visual view of the types and amounts of foods that should be eaten. Physical activity is a new element in the symbol, which also illustrates personalization (provides the consumer with a personalized recommendation of the kinds and amounts of foods to eat each day), gradual improvement, variety, moderation, and proportionality.

During discussions focused on weight maintenance and loss, nurses can encourage women who have Internet access to visit http://mypyramid.gov/ to view and interact with MyPyramid. At the website, individuals are able to key in their age, gender, and physical activity level to obtain a personalized recommendation on their daily calorie level based on the *Dietary Guidelines for Americans, 2005.* People are also able to obtain general food guidance and suggestions for making wise choices from each food group. Health care professionals can obtain educational materials from the MyPyramid website to facilitate teaching and to distribute to individuals who do not have access to the Internet.

Health Promotion During Times of Transition

Major changes in women's lives require mobilization of personal resources and often strain their coping abilities. Even changes that are viewed to be positive, such as new careers, childbirth, and marriage, are stressors, nonetheless, and they often occur at a time when women need extra emotional and physical support. Menarche and menopause represent two major passages for women. These events are marked by considerable shifts in hormone levels and in self-perception. Special attention to health maintenance during these major transitions can help women move through the stressful periods with a diminished likelihood of experiencing illness or emotional distress. Often during these times, healthy diets and routine exercise are pushed aside and the woman's support systems may be neglected. With sensitivity and compassion, nurses can help women remain focused on health-promoting behaviors and stay attentive to their personal needs.

Women are more likely than men to seek preventive health care, including mental health care. This observation suggests that women do recognize their problems and are more likely to value the process of collaborating with others. In general, an inability to manage stress threatens a woman's personal integrity and her mental well-being. How well a woman manages stress often depends on the woman's perceived intensity of the stressor, level of self-esteem, and ability to mobilize effective coping skills as well as the quality of her supportive relationships and other available resources (Ruhl, 2006)

Women who become "engaged" in mutually supportive relationships tend to experience a sense of power, self-value, and the opportunity to affirm and clarify their emotions and thoughts. Most often, mental health problems emerge when women are not involved in meaningful relationships, when they lack confidence and when they fail to recognize and value their own self-worth. Over time, an inability to deal with stress may well lead to major mental disorders. To provide appropriate care, it is important to address women's problems from a relational perspective, because understanding their personal response to stress and identifying their

support systems are essential elements in developing an effective treatment plan.

Health education that provides anticipatory guidance for easing the stress of transitions may incorporate the following strategies:

- **Diet:** Specific dietary suggestions for stressful times emphasize the intake of fresh fruits and vegetables, tips for creating healthy snacks, diet supplementation with vitamins and minerals, and herbal preparations to help the body cope with stress.

- **Exercise:** Regular exercise is one of the best stress reducers and often can be implemented free of charge. The American Heart Association (AHA, 2007a) recommendations include 30 to 60 minutes of moderate to vigorous activity on most days of the week. Daily exercise throughout life helps with weight management, builds healthy bones, reduces feelings of depression and anxiety, improves mood, and promotes a sense of well-being (AHA, 2007a; Lowdermilk & Perry, 2007).

- **Massage therapy and other complementary methods.**

- **Support groups and other resources.**
(Lowdermilk & Perry, 2007).

INTEGRATED MEDICAL THERAPIES

When health care providers consider health care, they most often think of Western medicine because it is currently the predominant form of health care in the United States. Such was not always the case. Other forms of healing, such as herbal medicine and homeopathic medicine, were once widely available and broadly accepted. As political and other forces shaped the course of health care in America, these other forms of medicine decreased in popularity and lost credibility in many professional circles.

In the past two decades, however, there has been a resurgence of interest in forms of health care other than the Western medical model. This change has resulted, in part, from the failure of Western medicine to identify causes or provide cures for many chronic health conditions. Today's international explosion in the exchange of information has produced a better-informed society.

Health care providers are learning about health care systems from all over the world that have been effective in maintaining and restoring health. In China, where herbal medicine and acupuncture have been practiced for several thousand years, it was common for the practitioner to be paid for assisting the individual in maintaining good health. If illness occurred, the practitioner's payment ceased. Many alternative forms of healing utilize a whole-systems approach to understanding and describing how the body and mind interact and function. These therapies have much to offer in the areas of health promotion and maintenance, as well in the treatment of specific ailments (Dossey, Keegan, & Guzzetta, 2005; Lowdermilk & Perry, 2007; Weil, 2004).

The following list includes several non-Western medical systems of healing that are beneficial in the area of health promotion. Integrated health modalities include:

- herbal medicine
- homeopathy
- Asian medicine and acupuncture
- Ayurvedic medicine
- massage techniques
- color therapy
- water therapy
- energy-healing techniques
- therapeutic touch
- healing with sound
- nutritional medicine

- osteopathic and chiropractic manipulation
- living foods
- macrobiotic diet
- psychic healing
- traditional native healing practices from around the world.

Along with the heightened public awareness of alternative health care systems and practices come challenges in selecting appropriate therapies for health maintenance and promotion. Consumers often must sift through considerable amounts of information as they attempt to make informed choices concerning their health practices. To address this problem, many organizations now self-regulate, and governmental licensing programs and requirements for providers such as acupuncturists, naturopaths, and chiropractors have been established. Actual regulations vary from state to state.

Another area of concern involves casual consumer use and abuse of widely accepted and available remedies. Herbs and vitamins are very powerful substances that must be used knowledgeably and with caution. Although these substances may be of invaluable benefit, they must be respected and viewed as medicine. Today, many Western and non-Western health care providers embrace a philosophy of care that integrates Western medical theory and practice with other "nontraditional" methods to promote health maintenance and healing.

In today's health care climate, more and more women look to their care providers for reliable information about integrated medical therapies. It is beyond the scope of this course to provide detailed information about all of the alternative approaches to care. However, overviews of many of the alternative and complementary therapies are provided in Chapter 14. For additional resources, please refer to the "Resource" and recommended reading list located at the end of the course.

CONCLUSION

There is much that women can do to maintain the quality of their health throughout the life cycle. One major strategy is regular HMEs. These routine examinations should be thorough and accomplished with attention to the individual needs of each woman, including age-appropriate health screening. Ultimately, it is the responsibility of each woman to engage in self-care behaviors that enhance, foster, and promote well-being. Many healing traditions and modalities are beneficial in enhancing and promoting health across the lifespan.

EXAM QUESTIONS

CHAPTER 9
Questions 66-68

Note: Choose the option that BEST answers each question.

66. A health history should elicit information concerning a woman's

    a. educational achievements.

    b. vacation plans.

    c. lifestyle.

    d. views on abortion.

67. To determine appropriate tests, screening methods, and interventions such as immunizations, the healthcare provider should consider the woman's

    a. social support systems.

    b. religious affiliation.

    c. visual acuity.

    d. age.

68. Well-woman examinations typically include

    a. an intravenous pyelogram.

    b. a hysterosalpingogram.

    c. a bimanual examination.

    d. laparoscopy.

CHAPTER 10

HUMAN PAPILLOMAVIRUS AND ABNORMAL CERVICAL PAP SMEAR FINDINGS

CHAPTER OBJECTIVE

After completing this chapter, the reader will be able to discuss implications of human papillomavirus (HPV) and cervical Pap smear screening.

LEARNING OBJECTIVES

After studying this chapter, the reader will be able to

1. identify some of the myths and facts about HPV.

2. describe normal cervical cytology.

3. identify risk factors for cervical cancer.

4. recognize the problems with Pap smear accuracy.

5. specify technologic advances in Pap smear screening and evaluation.

6. discuss patient education and counseling regarding Pap testing and HPV.

7. describe treatments for abnormal conditions identified with the use of Pap smears.

KEY WORDS

- Colposcopy
- Columnar epithelium
- Cryosurgery
- Endocervical canal
- Human papillomavirus
- Squamocolumnar junction
- Squamous epithelium
- Transformation zone

INTRODUCTION

Human papillomavirus (HPV), a nonenveloped, double-stranded deoxyribonucleic acid (DNA) virus, is the most common sexually transmitted infection (STI) in the United States. Approximately 20 million people are currently infected and it is estimated that at least 80% of sexually active American women will have been exposed to HPV by the time they reach age 50. Approximately 6.2 million Americans acquire new genital HPV infections each year. Most people with HPV are asymptomatic and have subclinical or unrecognized infections (Centers for Disease Control and Prevention [CDC], n.d.; Schmidt, 2007; Wysocki, Reiter, & Berman, 2007).

HPV infection is known to be the primary cause of cervical cancer. It is also thought to be linked to cancers of the vulva, vagina, anus, penis, and oropharynx. Although the virus has been described since the beginning of recorded history, only within the past 25 years has an understanding of HPV evolved and its link to cervical and other cancers been clearly established. The past decade has brought advances in cervical screening technologies with liquid-based Pap tests and HPV testing. Most recently, an HPV vaccine has become available. It is indicated for the prevention of cervical cancer, genital warts, and dysplastic or precancerous cervical lesions caused by several of the HPV types (Moore & Seybold, 2007; National Association of Nurse Practitioners in Women's Health [NPWH], 2007; Wysocki, Reiter et al., 2007).

This chapter, which focuses on the abnormal Pap smear and its association with HPV, has been included in this women's health course because of the enormity of the problem and its far-reaching implications for women and their families.

HUMAN PAPILLOMAVIRUS

Cervical cancer, rarely found among women in celibate religious orders, has long been associated with sexual activity. Due to the rising epidemic of the sexually transmitted HPV infection, the average age of women with abnormal Pap smear findings is declining steadily. HPV is most prevalent among the younger population of women, although it does occur with some frequency in older women as well (Wysocki, Reiter et al., 2007).

HPVs are a family of more than 100 virus types. Manifestations of HPV infection range from common warts, plantar warts, skin cancers, anal and genital warts, and recurrent respiratory papillomatosis (a rare benign infection of type HPV 6 or 11, it passes from mothers to infants during childbirth) to head and neck cancers, genital cancers, and cervical cancer (Hellwig, 2006; Moore & Seybold, 2007; Schmidt, 2007). Young men and women between the ages of 15 and 24 account for approximately one-half of all new HPV infections (Cates, 1999).

Of the more than 100 known types of HPV, about 40 strains are thought to be capable of infecting the genital tract. HPV types 6 and 11 have been identified as low-risk – these are the types most likely to be associated with condylomata acuminata (genital warts), benign cervical changes, and low-grade cervical intraepithelial lesions. Important associations have been identified between HPV type 16 and squamous cell carcinoma and between type 18 and cervical adenocarcinoma. Many other HPV types are considered to be high risk (e.g., types 31, 33, 35, 39, 45, 51); one or more of these types is detected in nearly every patient with cervical cancer (Moore & Seybold, 2007). HPV is the primary cause of cervical neoplasia, and persistent infection with high-risk types of HPV constitutes the most significant risk factor for cervical cancer (American Cancer Society [ACS], 2006; Moore & Seybold, 2007).

With most HPV infections, there are no symptoms and a woman may learn that she has been exposed to the virus only after undergoing a routine Pap smear. Reflex HPV DNA testing (Digene HPV test) is performed on a sample of cervical cells collected during a pelvic exam in the same way they are obtained for a Pap smear; the HPV test can often be done on the same sample collected for the Pap (Gupton, 2007). In women with HPV infection, abnormal findings on Pap screening are common. Only about 1% of people infected with HPV, develop external genital warts, while approximately 10% develop cervical lesions. When present, HPV lesions are most commonly seen in the posterior part of the vaginal introitus. Lesions may also occur on the buttocks, vulva, vagina, anus, and cervix. It is possible to be infected with several different genotypes of HPV; some may be associated with a low risk for the development of cervical cancer, whereas others are associated with a high risk (Lowdermilk & Perry, 2007; Moore & Seybold, 2007).

Four different types of genital warts have been identified:

1. **Condylomata acuminata:** These are soft; moist; pink, red, or gray lesions that can occur singularly or in multiples; they often cluster to form a cauliflower shape. They occur on moist surfaces.

2. **Smooth papular warts:** These small papules are dome-shaped and are usually skin-colored. They tend to occur on hair-bearing or non-hair-bearing skin but do not occur on mucosal tissue.

3. **Keratotic genital warts:** These lesions have a thick layer and often look like common warts. They also tend to develop on hair-bearing or on non-hair-bearing skin as opposed to mucosa and other nonskin tissues.

4. **Flat warts:** As the name implies, these warts are generally flat or slightly raised with flat tops and can occur on moist or dry areas.

(Wysocki, Reiter et al., 2007)

HPV is an elusive virus. Its clinical course varies and is characterized by spontaneous regressions and recurrences. For most women, HPV infection resolves without intervention. In fact, 70% of infections clear in 1 year and 91% of infected women do not have detectable levels of cervical HPV infection after 2 years. At this time, it is unknown whether the virus is truly absent or is simply reduced to undetectable levels. For the other 10% of women, persistent infection with certain types of HPV constitutes a major risk factor for cervical cancer (Dunne & Markowitz, 2006; Frazer et al., 2006; Schmidt, 2007).

Latent Infection

Latent HPV infection in women can only be detected by sophisticated DNA hybridization tests that analyze cells obtained from the cervix. The HPV test is not recommended as a primary screen for STIs in women due to its poor specificity and the lack of an effective treatment for latent HPV infection (Lowdermilk & Perry, 2007).

Subclinical Infection

Subclinical infection can be detected with the application of acetic acid and inspection under magnification (colposcopy) for presence of acetowhite areas on the genitals, vagina, and cervix. Current (2006) CDC guidelines do not recommend the routine use of this method for screening to detect subclinical HPV infection because it is not a highly specific diagnostic test (CDC, 2005; Wysocki, Reiter et al., 2007).

The triggers that activate the virus and cause abnormal cell growth, as well as why some lesions heal on their own and others become precancerous, are not known. Cervical infections are caused by a group of about 15 oncogenic (cancer-causing) types of HPV. Persistent infection with these viruses can lead to a precancerous condition. While the vast majority of cervical HPV infections (including those caused by the oncogenic types) heal through the body's natural immune response, some of them persist and can eventually progress to invasive cervical cancer. The strains most strongly associated with cervical cancer are types 16, 18, 31, and 45, and a few others to a lesser degree. However, in most women with high-risk types of cervical HPV, cervical cancer does not develop (Castle, Solomon, Schiffman, & Wheeler, 2005; NPWH, 2007).

Presently, researchers continue to investigate factors that may promote the development of cervical cancer. The role of smoking and the progression of HPV-induced lesions into cancer has recently become more clear. In several studies, a dose-response relationship with the amount of tobacco consumed was noted. Other potential factors that link HPV with cervical cancer include long-term oral contraceptive use, young age, nutritional deficiency, other genital tract infections, and immunodeficiency, such as human immunodeficiency virus (HIV) infection. For women with healthy immune systems, it may take decades for cervical cancer to develop from an initial exposure to high-risk viral types (Moore & Seybold, 2007; NPWH, 2007; Wysocki, Reiter et al., 2007).

Myths and Misconceptions

There are many myths and misconceptions about genital HPV. Inaccurate information can create unnecessary anxiety and lead to doubt about a partner's faithfulness. Overwhelming fear can also cause a woman to avoid a simple Pap smear that could save her life. To provide accurate counseling and education for women, it is helpful to consider some of the common HPV myths and misconceptions:

Myth: I'm the only one with HPV.

Fact: According to recent statistics, 75% to 90% of sexually active Americans will be infected with genital HPV at some point in their lives. Because genital HPV usually produces no symptoms or illness, a person who has been infected may never know about it.

Myth: Only people who have casual sex get HPV.

Fact: It is true that the greater the number of sexual partners a woman has, the higher her risk of exposure. HPV can be transmitted via vaginal, anal, or oral intercourse as well as by skin-to-skin contact during sex play (Mahoney, Cox, & Kimmel, 2006). During the course of their lives, most women do have more than one partner or they become sexually intimate with a partner who has already had other partners. This behavior pattern is not consistent with casual sex. STIs can be passed along as readily in a loving, long-term relationship as in a casual sexual encounter.

Myth: An HPV diagnosis means one partner has not been monogamous.

Fact: The virus can remain in the body for months or years without symptoms. An HPV diagnosis means only that the infection was contracted at some point in the person's life. Most people infected with HPV never know they have it.

Myth: Genital warts lead to cervical cancer.

Fact: Approximately 1% to 2% of HPV-infected women exhibit HPV lesions in the form of fleshy growths on the external genital area. In most cases, these growths do not lead to or predispose a woman to the development of cervical cancer. As discussed earlier, there are many different viral types of HPV, and the types that cause genital warts are not generally the same as those that predispose a woman to cervical cancer.

Myth: An abnormal Pap smear finding means a woman is at high risk for cervical cancer.

Fact: An abnormal Pap smear can result from infection, local irritation, a low-risk HPV type, or a high risk HPV type. Depending on the degree of abnormality, further evaluation or a follow-up Pap smear obtained 3 months later may be recommended. Reflex HPV DNA testing may obviate the need for repeated Pap smears: if no high-risk HPV types are identified, the Pap smear may be repeated in 1 year. Only one in four cases of cervical lesions left untreated progresses to cancer, and treatment is almost always successful in preventing cancer if the cells are discovered early. Clearly, it is of major importance that women be encouraged to undergo routine Pap testing according to the recommendations of their health care provider. (American Society for Colposcopy and Cervical Pathology [ASCCP], n.d.).

Prevention

There are no easy answers in the area of prevention, considering the long-term and often asymptomatic nature of HPV infection. Limiting the number of sexual partners is one of the keys to HPV prevention. Health practices that enhance the strength of the immune system – such as refraining from smoking; limiting the use of alcohol; eating a healthful, high-nutrient diet; and avoiding chemical and environmental exposures – help the body fight any current HPV infections and also help prevent recurrences after initial infection. Other preventive strategies include abstinence from all sexual activity and prophylactic vaccination (American College of Obstetricians and Gynecologists [ACOG], 2005a).

A vaccine (Gardasil) against HPV types 6, 11, 16, and 18 became available in 2006. Gardasil is the first HPV vaccine in the United States. The quadrivalent recombinant (nonlive virus) vaccine is recommended for females ages 9 to 26 years. Vaccination consists of three intramuscular injections given over 6 months, with the second dose to be given 2 months after the first dose and the third dose given 6 months after the first dose. The vaccine is supplied in prefilled syringes for single use and in single-use vials; the vials must be stored under refrigeration and protected from light (Moore & Seybold, 2007; Wysocki, Reiter et al., 2007).

Ideally, vaccination should be initiated before the patient becomes sexually active although sexually active females can also benefit from vaccination. If the patient has already been infected with one or more of the four strains covered by the vaccine, the vaccine helps to protect her from the remaining strains (Snow, 2007). Because 90% of genital warts are caused by one of the four HPV types in the quadrivalent vaccine, it is believed to produce an effective immune response against these lesions (Moore & Seybold, 2007). Vaccines for other HPV types continue to be investigated (CDC et al., 2006).

Although latex male condoms provide effective protection against many STIs, they are less effective against HPV and herpes because these viruses spread through skin-to-skin contact. The female is protected from getting HPV only if her partner has lesions on the penis in areas fully covered by the condom. Lesions located on the base of the penis and scrotum will not be covered by the condom and expose the partner's vulva. The male will not be protected by condom use when the female partner's lesions are located on the vulva. Also, condom use is only partially protective for the male when HPV lesions are on the cervix or in the vagina because the vaginal discharge can bathe the base of the penis and the scrotum with HPV infected cells. Female condoms cover more of the female introital epithelium at risk for HPV and thus may provide more of a protective barrier for both partners. However, the female condom may be more easily dislodged (ASCCP, 2007).

Typing

Reflex HPV DNA testing (Digene HPV test) for various HPV types is now available through some laboratories that evaluate Pap smears. These tests can distinguish between more benign strains of the virus and those that have been found to be more aggressive in promoting cervical disease and cervical cancer (Coutlée et al., 2006). These tests are expensive; however, as they become more available and cost-effective, they hold promise in helping clinicians plan follow-up care and treatment for women with HPV-related abnormal Pap smear findings. Information about viral type can potentially save patients needless worry and invasive procedures, along with the accompanying financial burden.

Treatment

Although no treatment has been developed for latent HPV infection, several therapies are available to manage external genital warts and clearly identifiable subclinical HPV lesions on the genitalia, cervix, and vagina. The goal of all treatments is to destroy visible lesions and reduce patient symptoms, not the eradication of HPV (CDC et al., 2006). Eradication of the virus is not considered to be conclusive even after there is no visible evidence of wart tissue because of the high incidence of recurrence (Lowdermilk & Perry, 2007).

HPV therapies include the topical, provider-applied substances podophyllin and trichloroacetic acid/bichloroacetic acid as well as topical patient-applied medications, such as podofilox solution or gel and imiquimod cream. Imiquimod, podophyllin, and podofilox should not be used during pregnancy. No one treatment is ideal for all warts. Surgical therapies used to eliminate the lesions include cryosurgery with liquid nitrogen or cryoprobe, manual excision, electrosurgical excision, and laser vaporization. Injection of interferon is another treatment that is usually reserved for recurrent lesions that are unresponsive to standard treatments (CDC et al., 2006; Lowdermilk & Perry, 2007).

The Cervix and the Cervical Transformation Zone

To understand normal and abnormal Pap smear findings, nurses should be knowledgeable about cervical cytology and the normal cellular changes that take place throughout a woman's life. The following discussion briefly describes the major cervical cellular changes.

The surface of the cervix and the canal that leads into the uterus (the endocervical canal) are made up of two types of cells:

- **Squamous epithelium** covers the vagina and the outside surface of the cervix. It is smooth and pink in appearance (Cunningham et al., 2005).

- **Columnar epithelium** is located in the endocervical canal; in young women, it can also be noted on the outer surface of the cervix around the external cervical opening (os). This glandular tissue has a rough texture and is dark pink. Women who take oral contraceptives often have columnar epithelial cells on the outer surface of the cervix due to the hormonal effects of the pills (Cunningham et al., 2005; Lowdermilk & Perry, 2007).

The area in which the squamous epithelium and the columnar epithelium come together on the cervix is called the *squamocolumnar junction* or the *transformation zone* (see Figure 10-1). This is a site in which there is much cell growth and replacement. The squamous type of cell replaces the columnar type of cell in a constant cycle of cell turnover, which is influenced by the female hormones. The term for this process is *squamous metaplasia*. Metaplasia, which is a normal process of cell turnover, occurs most rapidly during adolescence and pregnancy (Lowdermilk & Perry, 2007).

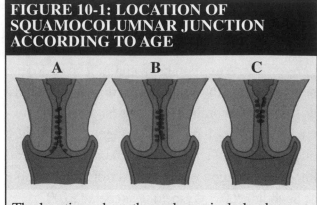

FIGURE 10-1: LOCATION OF SQUAMOCOLUMNAR JUNCTION ACCORDING TO AGE

The location where the endocervical glands meet the squamous epithelium becomes progressively higher with age. **A,** Puberty. **B,** Reproductive years. **C,** Postmenopausal.

Note. From *Maternity & Women's Health Care* (9th ed., p. 295), by D. Lowdermilk & S. Perry, 2007, St. Louis: Mosby. Reprinted with permission.

Cervical cancer usually develops in this area of rapid cell division. Immature cells undergoing the transformation from squamous to columnar tissue are especially vulnerable to events that can change their genetic material. These changes, or mutations, may result in premalignant changes or cancer (Wysocki et al., 2007).

Abnormalities on Pap smear results may be related to a number of causes, such as a mild injury to or irritation of the cervix from intercourse or tampon use or a bacterial or yeast infection. After appropriate treatment, a repeat of the Pap smear (recommended intervals range from 6 weeks to 3 months) most often results in a normal test result. Cervical cell mutations that can lead to cervical cancer may be caused by infection with certain strains of HPV in combination with other cancer-promoting cofactors (Lowdermilk & Perry, 2007).

CERVICAL CANCER

Although an in-depth discussion of cervical cancer is beyond the scope of this course, relevant background information will enhance discussion and understanding of the disease, Pap smear screening, and HPV and its relationship to cervical cancer.

Cervical Cancer and Pap Smear Screening

Before the 1940s, when the Pap smear was developed by Dr. George N. Papanicolaou and Herbert Traut, cervical cancer was the most common cause of cancer death in women in the United States. The incidence of invasive cancer has decreased by 50% over the last 30 years. However, approximately 9,710 American women are still diagnosed with invasive cervical cancer each year (Saraiya et al., 2007), and approximately 3,700 women die from their disease (Gray, 2007; NPWH, 2007).

The incidence of preinvasive cancer has increased, however, and more women in their twenties and thirties are being diagnosed with preinvasive cervical lesions (ACS, 2006). In the United States, approximately 82% of women have had a Pap smear within the past 3 years. Cervical cancer now ranks eleventh among the most common cancers in women (CDC, 2005). Worldwide, this is not the case. According to the Guttmacher Review, 80% to 85% of the 22,500 global deaths from cervical cancer this year will occur in developing countries where Pap smears are unavailable (Schmidt, 2007).

In the United States, the incidence of cervical cancer is highest among Hispanic women and lowest among Native-American women. The highest mortality occurs in African-American women (ACS, 2006). Factors that influence cervical screening behaviors for these populations include lack of a health promotion/disease prevention perspective, lack of knowledge about Pap smears, lack of information about availability of Pap smear screening, financial barriers, and failure of health care providers to recommend screening (Giarratano, Bustamante-Forest, & Carter, 2005; Lowdermilk & Perry, 2007; Wysocki, Reiter et al., 2007).

Risk Factors

Although the exact mechanism of cervical cancer progression is unknown, a number of key contributing factors have been identified. Risk factors are understood to include certain behaviors or elements of the personal history that may increase an individual's vulnerability to a particular disease. It is important that nurses remain up-to-date about disease risk factors so they can appropriately identify and screen individuals at risk and accurately counsel and educate their patients. A number of risk factors have been identified as having an association with cervical cancer:

- smoking (doubles the risk)
- early onset of sexual activity (before age 16)
- multiple sexual partners (three or more in a lifetime)
- an uncircumcised sexual partner and/or one who has had
  - multiple partners
  - genital warts
- age younger than 25 years
- a history of herpes simplex virus, chlamydia, or vulvar warts
- a history of abnormal Pap smear findings
- lower socioeconomic status
- exposure to diethylstilbestrol (DES) during fetal development
- possible nutritional deficiencies, especially of folic acid, a B vitamin important for normal cell growth
- immunosuppression
- use of oral contraceptives for 2 years or longer
- alcoholism.

(ACS, 2006; Lowdermilk & Perry, 2007; Moore & Seybold, 2007; Wysocki, Reiter et al., 2007)

Some of these may also predispose women to susceptibility to infection by HPV.

Older Women and Cervical Cancer

Cervical cancer has often been perceived by the public to be a young woman's disease, but most cases of cervical cancer and related deaths occur in women older than age 50. Up to two-thirds of older women with cervical cancer have not received adequate Pap screening prior to their cancer diagnosis. Thus, all women with a cervix should continue to have Pap test screenings according to standard guidelines and their care provider's recommendations (Gupta, 2007).

Presently, the ACS suggests that cervical cancer screening may be stopped in women ages 70 years and older if they have had three or more recent, consecutive, negative test findings and no abnormal test findings in the previous 10 years (Smith, Cokkinides, & Eyre, 2006). The U.S. Preventive Services Task Force (USPSTF) recommends screening cessation in women older than 65 years with negative test results who are not otherwise considered to be at high risk for cancer (USPSTF, 2007). The ACOG has determined that there is inconclusive evidence to establish an upper age limit for cervical cancer screening. All expert groups are in agreement that screening can be discontinued in women who have had a hysterectomy if the surgery was done for benign reasons and there is no past history of high-grade cervical lesions (Murphy & Schwarz, 2007).

Reflex HPV DNA testing has been advocated for screening for women ages 30 and older by the ACOG, ACS, ASCCP, and other professional organizations. If the test for high-risk (cancer-causing) HPV types is negative, a longer (3-year) interval for Pap screening can be developed. HPV testing with the Digene HPV test is performed at the same time as the Pap test (ACOG, 2007; www.thehpvtest.com).

CERVICAL PAP SMEARS

Methods for Obtaining a Cervical Pap Smear

The Pap smear is obtained before any digital examination of the vagina is made or endocervical bacteriologic specimens are taken. The examiner may use a cotton swab to remove excess cervical discharge before the cytologic specimen is collected. The tissue sample should include both squamous cells and columnar cells. Various sampling devices (cytobrush, cervex-brush, spatula or broom) may be used. If the two-sample method of obtaining cells is used, the ectocervix (outer area) is first sampled with the spatula. This is done first to minimize obscuring the cells with blood. The endocervix (inner area) is then sampled with the brush placed into the cervical os (Bickley & Szilagyi, 2007). Broom devices are inserted and rotated 360 degrees for a total of five times. These devices obtain endocervical and ectocervical samples at the same time. If the woman has had a hysterectomy, the vaginal cuff is sampled. The vaginal wall is usually not sampled unless the woman is nearing menopause. In this case, a second sample may be obtained to evaluate the hormonal effects on vaginal tissue. If the one-slide technique is used, the cytobrush sample is gently rolled on the glass slide in the opposite direction from which it was obtained. The slide is then sprayed with preservative within 5 seconds to prevent drying of the specimen (Lowdermilk & Perry, 2007).

Problems With Screening and Initial Solutions

Problems

Two major problems continue to accompany Pap smear screening. The first concerns the large number of women who still fail to obtain regular Pap smears due to a lack of awareness or motivation, fear, and cost or access to care problems. A second problem with Pap smear screening concerns the overall accuracy of the test. Because the Pap smear is a relatively simple and low-cost test, health care providers and patients view it as an integral part of routine gynecologic care. Unfortunately, more than six decades of reliance on this tool have elevated the status of the Pap smear in the public perception from that of a general screening procedure to a foolproof diagnostic test.

The Pap test was never expected to have a 100% accuracy rate (Gupton, 2007; Lowdermilk & Perry, 2007; Wysocki, Reiker et al., 2007).

The Pap test is designed to serve as the primary screening tool for cervical disease. In the traditional Pap test, the sample cells are smeared onto a slide and "fixed" with a preservative. The slide is sent to a pathology laboratory, where it is viewed under a microscope, and a cytologist interprets the cellular changes present. This screening test was never meant to be explicitly diagnostic. Instead, the findings of abnormal, undetermined, or atypical Pap smears are followed up with a repeat Pap test or with other methods of diagnosis. Because early-stage cervical cancer usually progresses slowly, women should have a Pap smear performed regularly to ensure a higher accuracy rate over the course of the multiple tests. In addition, it has been estimated that with conventional Pap screening, up to 50% of women with negative results have abnormalities that are not detected (Wysocki, Reiter et al., 2007).

Many issues contribute to the low sensitivity of Pap tests and to the problems associated with cervical screening in general. Of primary importance is sample adequacy. Cervical cells may be obscured by the presence of blood, debris, or other cells; they must be obtained in sufficient numbers to allow an accurate cytologic examination. Other screening issues include methods of slide preparation and interpretation as well as patient compliance in obtaining regular Pap tests and the appropriate follow-up for unsatisfactory or abnormal results (ACOG, 2003; Wysocki, Reiter et al., 2007).

Initial Solutions

A number of solutions have been proposed to address the problems associated with conventional Pap smear screening.

Initial solutions for Pap smear inaccuracy begin with the patient. Ideally, Pap smears should be collected at midcycle, with no intercourse, douching, or use of vaginal medications for 24 to 48 hours prior to the test. Any localized vaginal infection, such as a yeast infection, can interfere with the results due to the presence of inflammation. Over-the-counter creams, gels, foams, or suppositories used 24 to 48 hours before the Pap smear is obtained will also impair the collection of a good sample (Lowdermilk & Perry, 2007).

The next crucial step involves the sample collection. The quality of the smear depends on how well the health care provider has collected and preserved the sample. It has been estimated that up to two-thirds of false-negative Pap smear findings can be accounted for by sampling errors. In addition, there are problems with the conventional methods of obtaining the Pap smear. Approximately 300,000 cells are collected onto the collection tool, but only 50,000 to 200,000 of these cells actually get transferred onto the slide. Cells that show abnormalities could easily be lost in the transfer process. Data from a recent (2005) literature search indicate that regardless of the collection medium of slide or liquid, the best collection devices are the cytobrush followed by the extended-tip spatula, especially if the transformation zone is not visible (Lowdermilk & Perry, 2007; Martin-Hirsch, Jarvis, Kitchener, & Lilford, 2000).

The last step concerns the reading by the cytologist. The slide that reveals a positive finding may have only a few abnormal cells among hundreds of thousands of normal cells. Thus, it is not surprising that some abnormal cells could be overlooked (Lowdermilk & Perry, 2007; Wysocki, Reiter et al., 2007).

Current Developments

In response to the need for more accuracy in Pap smear screening, improved sampling and screening technologies are becoming more widely available. These technologies are designed to improve the quality of the test sample and reduce the false-negative rate. It is estimated that approximately two-thirds of false-negative Pap tests are related to sampling errors, while the remaining one third are related to laboratory detection errors (Martin-Hirsch et al., 2000; Wysocki, Reiter et al., 2007).

Advances in the collection and preparation of cervical cells primarily address sampling errors. The ThinPrep Pap Test and SurePath are newer alternatives to the conventional Pap smear. These thin-layer, liquid-based systems involve suspension of the cervical cell sample in an alcohol-based preservative solution. With this method, almost all of the sample cells are transferred to the liquid preservative, and blood, mucous, and inflammatory cells are filtered out or lysed. In the laboratory, the cells are deposited onto the slide by an automatic device; the slide is then stained and screened in the traditional manner. It has been estimated that with this technique, between 50,000 and 70,000 diagnostic cells are available for screening, as compared to the old process in which 4,000 to 300,000 cells are "smeared" onto a slide, where they often overlap or are obscured by noncervical material. The ThinPrep liquid-based sample can also be used for testing for HPV, *Chlamydia trachomatis,* and *Neisseria gonorrhea* after preparation of the Pap (Gupton, 2007).

In the United States, 10% of all negative Pap samples are rescreened to minimize detection error. False-negative readings can result from human fatigue and error. Computerized screening systems are used to assist with the cellular analysis of the Pap test. Negative tests are reviewed and those at risk for abnormalities are selected for rescreening by cytologists. It should be noted, however, that the computerized screening systems are designed to assist in the identification of potentially abnormal cells. They do not compensate for specimens that are inadequately prepared, poorly sampled, or misinterpreted by cytologists (ACOG, 2003; Wysocki, Reiter et al., 2007).

Other cervical screening technologies include cervicography and speculoscopy. They are briefly described below. It should be noted that according to the USPSTF (2007), there is insufficient evidence to recommend for or against the routine use of these new technologies.

Cervicography is a patented process whereby a diluted acetic acid (vinegar) solution is applied to the woman's cervix. After several minutes, a specially designed camera is used to take two standardized photographs ("cervigrams") of the area. The photographs are then mailed to a laboratory, where they are interpreted by trained colposcopists. If changes consistent with dysplasia (abnormal tissue development) are found, the patient is referred for colposcopy and directed biopsies (Lowdermilk & Perry, 2007).

Speculoscopy involves using a light source and magnifier attached to the speculum to examine the cervix after the application of a dilute solution of acetic acid. The cervix is then viewed under a blue-white speculight, and if any whitened lesions or unusual areas are found, the patient is referred for colposcopy. Thus, speculoscopy is not considered to be an alternative to colposcopy but rather a screening adjunct (Lowdermilk & Perry, 2007).

Providing Education and Counseling About Pap Test Results

Informing women of Pap test results is an essential role for the nurse. Legal action may be taken for false-negative errors that result in a delayed detection of advanced disease. The clinical setting must provide timely patient notification of abnormal Pap test results and have a system in place to ensure that this happens. All patients should be counseled about the limits of Pap smear accuracy and the following information should also be included:

- The Pap test is the single most reliable method to detect preinvasive cancer of the cervix.

- No guarantee exists, however, that a particular Pap smear will identify abnormal cells that may be present.

- New enhanced-screening techniques are now available in many facilities.
- Rescreening adds to the cost of the Pap smear and may or may not be covered by insurance, whether funded by private, state, or federal sources.

(ACOG, 2003; Gupton, 2007; Lowdermilk & Perry, 2007)

After receiving this information, all women should be given the option to have their negative Pap smear finding rescreened as a protective measure.

Cervical Cancer Screening Guidelines: The Bethesda System

The Bethesda System, the classification of abnormal Pap result terminology most commonly used today, was developed in 1988 under sponsorship of the National Institutes of Health. This system has replaced the older Papanicolaou system and the World Health Organization system.

Terminology for cervical cancer screening used with the Bethesda System includes:

- *Atypical glandular cells (AGC)* – a cytologic abnormality of the glandular cells that line the endocervix or uterus
- *Atypical squamous cells of undetermined significance (ASC-US)* – the most minor form of cytologic abnormality detected by the Pap test
- *Cervical intraepithelial neoplasia* (CIN) – cervical cancer precursor (confirmed by biopsy), divided into low-grade (CIN 1) and high-grade (CIN 2 and 3)
- *High-grade squamous intraepithelial lesion (HSIL)* – encompasses HPV, moderate and severe dysplasia, carcinoma in situ, and CIN 2 and 3
- *Low-grade squamous intraepithelial lesion (LSIL)* – encompasses HPV, mild dysplasia, and CIN 1
- *Squamous intraepithelial lesion (SIL)* – cytologic abnormalities identified on the Pap test, classified as low-grade (LSIL) or high-grade (HSIL).

(ACOG, 2007; Wysocki, Reiter et al., 2007)

The Bethesda System for reporting Pap smear results has undergone several major changes in approach and terminology in attempts to standardize reporting systems worldwide and provide more information about what was actually identified in the sample. Developed by major medical groups, including the ACOG, ACS, Association of Reproductive Health Professionals, and ASCCP, the original guidelines have undergone review a number of times in the past several years in response to emerging data on the role of HPV in cervical cancer. The latest (2007) ASCCP consensus guidelines reflect evidence-based advances in the understanding of the natural history of HPV, its influence on the development of cervical dysplasia and cancer, and the role of Pap tests with a liquid-based sample (ACOG, 2007; Wright et al., 2007; Wysocki, Reiter et al., 2007).

It is beyond the scope of this course to include a detailed discussion of the Pap smear grading system. Please refer to the references located in the bibliography section of this book to access more specific information.

Further Evaluation

Depending on the result of the Pap test, further evaluation, treatment, or both may be advised. Reflex HPV DNA testing is an option for the management of an ASCUS Pap test result. Reflex HPV DNA testing is done to determine whether HPV is present and if referral for colposcopy is indicated. Women of all ages with ASCUS Pap test results should be tested for HPV. The liquid-based Pap samples can be immediately tested for HPV if there is an ASCUS result. Women with an ASCUS Pap result who test positive for HPV should be referred for a colposcopic examination (ACOG, 2007; Wysocki, Reiter et al., 2007).

Colposcopy

The colposcope is essentially a low-powered binocular microscope with a powerful light source that is mounted to allow visualization of the vagina and cervix during a pelvic examination. This instrument allows for a close-up view of the cervix and surrounding tissue for evaluation. The area to be examined is typically painted with an acetic acid (vinegar) solution. Acetic acid has a dehydrating effect on HPV lesions. Abnormal areas turn white (acetowhite) and become more prominent in response to the acetic acid, allowing for improved visualization. Some examiners also apply iodine (Schiller's or Lugol's solution) to the cervix and vagina as part of the evaluation.

In addition to learning colposcopic technique, colposcopy training involves learning to identify other specific features characteristic of abnormal cell growth, such as blood vessel patterns, and interpreting these findings. Biopsies are performed on any suspicious areas, and the biopsy samples are evaluated. A biopsy is the removal of cervical tissue for study. Several techniques may be used to perform the biopsy. Endocervical curettage (scraping of the endocervical cells) is an effective diagnostic tool in about 90% of cases. A sample of tissue is taken from the endocervical canal to be sent to the pathologist for evaluation. Examination of this sample will determine whether HPV lesions are found inside the endocervical canal; this information is an important determinant in what type of treatment will be recommended (Lowdermilk & Perry, 2007).

Patient Preparation for Colposcopy

Colposcopy is often a source of anxiety for patients because they are unfamiliar with the procedure and concerned about what will be discovered. The procedure should be thoroughly explained prior to the examination. Many practitioners advise the woman to take a mild pain reliever, such as ibuprofen, 30 minutes to 1 hour before the procedure begins because she may experience mild to moderate cramping when the biopsy and endocervical samples are obtained. The patient should also be encouraged to bring a support person with her (Lowdermilk & Perry, 2007).

Treatment for Abnormal Pap Test Results

There are a number of ways to treat the lesions identified in a colposcopic examination; treatment depends on the location and severity of the lesions. Four interventional techniques are described:

1. **Cryosurgery:** Cryosurgery is performed in an office setting. This technique freezes the top layer of cervical cells and causes a destruction of the abnormal tissue. Prior to cryosurgery, patients should be educated about the procedure and advised that discomfort may occur. Cramping can usually be controlled with ibuprofen taken before the procedure. Vasovagal reactions may also occur during cryosurgery. The woman is told to expect a foul-smelling, watery, vaginal discharge (related to sloughing of the necrotic tissue) for 2 to 4 weeks after the procedure. Patients should be advised to postpone intercourse for 2 weeks until their follow-up examination (Lowdermilk & Perry, 2007; Youngkin & Davis, 2003).

   One of the complications observed with this procedure concerns the migration of the transformation zone (squamocolumnar junction). Following cryosurgery, the transformation zone migrates upward into the cervical canal. This relocation can create the need for a more invasive procedure in the future if lesions recur that are not visible with the colposcope (because they are located inside the endocervical canal). Although rare, cryosurgery can also cause scarring of the cervix and lead to stenosis of the cervical opening, making future Pap testing difficult (Lowdermilk & Perry, 2007; Youngkin & Davis, 2003).

2. **Laser ablation:** This technique involves using a laser mounted on a colposcope to vaporize the transformation zone, which contains the abnormal cells. The advantages of laser treat-

ment are rapid healing (3 to 4 weeks), minimal scarring, and no retraction of the transformation zone. Women may experience less vaginal discharge than with cryosurgery but more discomfort immediately after the procedure (Lowdermilk & Perry, 2007; Youngkin & Davis, 2003).

3. **Conization; cold knife cone; laser conization:** If the lesion found on colposcopy extends into the endocervical canal and cannot be fully seen, a cone biopsy is performed to ensure that the entire lesion is removed. A cone-like section of the cervix is removed for evaluation. Cold knife conization involves use of a scalpel without electrosurgical current; laser conization employs use of a laser for the excision of tissue (Lowdermilk & Perry, 2007; Youngkin & Davis, 2003).

4. **Loop electrosurgical excision procedure (LEEP):** With LEEP, the cervix is anesthetized with a local anesthetic, and a fine wire loop electrode is used to simultaneously remove and cauterize a portion of the cervix. The advantage of this and other excisional techniques (e.g., conization) over the ablative therapies (e.g., cryosurgery, laser vaporization) is that the tissue is removed, not destroyed. Thus, the tissue is available for evaluation by a pathologist. Following the procedure, healing is rapid and only a mild discharge occurs. Possible complications include bleeding, cervical stenosis, infertility, and loss of cervical mucus (ACOG, 2005b).

Follow-up Pap smears after these procedures are advised every 3 to 4 months for a year. Protocols for the second year vary from every 3 to 4 months to every 6 months (Lowdermilk & Perry, 2007; Youngkin & Davis, 2003).

Guidelines during Pregnancy

Management of abnormal Pap smear results during pregnancy presents some difficulties. Considerations include the duration of the pregnancy, the woman's desire to maintain the pregnancy, and the degree of cellular abnormality. Colposcopy is used for diagnosis. Usually with low-grade lesions, a rescreening by Pap smear or colposcopy (or both) is advised every 2 to 3 months. Cervical biopsies are safe and should be done for suspected high-grade disease or cancer. Endocervical sampling should not be done. Unless invasive cancer is identified, treatment is postponed until after the pregnancy has ended (ACOG, 2002).

Treatment Specific to Cervical Cancer

Treatment for cervical cancer depends on the stage of the cancer – that is, whether it is localized or has spread to surrounding tissues or distant organs. A high-grade, preinvasive lesion (e.g., carcinoma in situ [CIS]) is removed to prevent progression to invasive disease. A conization procedure is usually recommended, although hysterectomy may also be advised, depending on the individual situation (ACOG, 2002; Lowdermilk & Perry, 2007).

For invasive cancer, radiation can be used alone or in combination with some form of surgery. Surgery options range from conization of the cervix to radical hysterectomy, in which the cervix, uterus, upper portion of the vagina, and lymph nodes in the area are removed. Two forms of radiation are used: radioactive implants placed directly at the cancerous site and external radiation. The former option destroys less healthy tissue and is associated with fewer side effects. Implants usually require a hospital stay of 2 to 3 days. External radiation is an outpatient procedure, delivered for 5 days a week for several weeks. It can be used in combination with internal radiation therapy. Depending on the lesion, external radiation may be initially given to treat the regional pelvic nodes and shrink the tumor. Side effects include diarrhea, nausea, vomiting, bladder irritation, loss of appetite, fatigue, premature menopause, and the long-term effect of destruction of the ovaries. Cervical cancer, when detected at an early stage, has a high rate of cure (ACOG, 2002; Lowdermilk & Perry, 2007).

CASE STUDY

*E*mma is a 32-year-old gravida 3, para 3 (i.e., three pregnancies and three births) Hispanic woman who arrives at the women's health clinic in a small, rural community. She presents for a gynecologic examination and states that this is her first examination in 3 years. Emma's past medical history is unremarkable and she has no complaints. Emma has recently married and engages in normal sexual activity with her husband. She is considering having another child. Her Pap test reveals a high-grade SIL and, following colposcopy, her physician recommends cryosurgery.

Questions

1. What are the immediate patient teaching needs for Emma?

2. What specific information should be given about the scheduled cryosurgery?

3. What other information should the nurse provide?

Discussion

The nurse explains that cervical dysplasia is considered a "preinvasive" condition. Several methods of treatment are available for women who wish to continue childbearing. The treatment is aimed toward eradicating the abnormal cells, while trying to preserve the structure of the cervix. All treatment methods have comparable rates for success treating the preinvasive lesions.

The nurse explains that cryosurgery is a standard treatment for high-grade SIL in the United States. The doctor performs the procedure in the clinic treatment room. A freezing technique will be used to freeze the abnormal cells, which will then slough. New, healthy cells will replace the sloughed tissue. She can expect to experience a profuse, watery discharge for up to 4 weeks following the procedure. To prevent infection, she should avoid tampons and refrain from intercourse until her follow-up visit in 2 weeks. She is unlikely to experience discomfort, but

she may take an over-the-counter analgesic, such as ibuprofen, if needed. She may experience vaginal spotting as the new tissue regenerates.

Emma should have a support person accompany her on the day of the scheduled procedure. She should telephone the clinic if she experiences fever, abdominal pain or, heavy bleeding following the cryosurgery. Emma should also be advised that cervical stenosis is a rare, but possible, complication of the procedure. The nurse should ensure that Emma understands that follow-up Pap tests and colposcopy examinations will be necessary for an indefinite period of time.

CONCLUSION

The prevalence of HPV and its link to cervical cancer has changed the way health care providers approach health care for women. Providers now recognize that most women are at risk for becoming infected with HPV and thus must be educated and counseled appropriately. The major cofactors and risk factors now known to influence cervical cancer risk can be changed by personal behavior choices. Although this information is essential for all women, it holds special implications for young women who are just beginning sexual activity. In addition, women of all ages need education about the benefits and limitations of Pap smear screening and encouragement to have Pap smears performed at regular intervals. It is also essential that nurses give accurate and up-to-date information about HPV infection and the possibility of prevention through vaccination. Nurses must continue to provide compassionate and sensitive care to women struggling with a new diagnosis of HPV or those dealing with ongoing life issues that have resulted from exposure.

EXAM QUESTIONS

CHAPTER 10
Questions 69-84

Note: Choose the option that BEST answers each question.

69. A definite link has been confirmed between cervical cancer and infection with

    a. herpes simplex virus.

    b. anaerobic bacteria.

    c. HIV.

    d. HPV.

70. The viral types of HPV that have been identified as low-risk are

    a. HPV types 6 and 11.

    b. HPV types 16 and 18.

    c. HPV types 31 and 33.

    d. HPV types 45 and 51.

71. The most important health intervention for a patient who just received the results of her Pap smear, which are abnormal and indicate infection with HPV, is to

    a. advise her to adhere to a vegetarian diet.

    b. advise her that her infection with HPV will only last for 1 to 2 weeks.

    c. advise her to quit smoking.

    d. advise her to use oral contraceptives as her method of birth control.

72. The HPV vaccine Gardasil

    a. is administered orally.

    b. is indicated for women between the ages of 35 and 50.

    c. is administered in two doses.

    d. protects against four HPV types.

73. The squamocolumnar junction of the cervix

    a. surrounds the vaginal introitus.

    b. is the area where the squamous epithelium and the columnar epithelium come together.

    c. is shed during menstruation.

    d. is devoid of cellular growth and replacement.

74. Risk factors for cervical cancer include

    a. a history of infection with the varicella virus.

    b. age older than 25 years.

    c. a history of three or more sexual partners.

    d. onset of sexual activity after age 24.

75. The Pap smear sample should include

    a. squamous cells and columnar cells.

    b. squamous cells only.

    c. columnar cells only.

    d. mast cells.

76. Accuracy of Pap test results may be enhanced by instructing the patient to prepare for the test by

    a. douching 24 hours before the appointment.

    b. using lubricants with intercourse.

    c. avoiding intercourse for 48 hours.

    d. scheduling the appointment to occur during menstruation.

77. Most cells that are lost during the Pap smear sampling process are lost

    a. during shipping of the slide to the laboratory.

    b. in the process of transferring the sample to the slide.

    c. in the process of applying the fixative to the slide.

    d. during processing by the laboratory.

78. Compared to the conventional Pap smear sampling technique, an advantage of the ThinPrep Pap test is that it

    a. uses new sampling tools to take a cell sample from the cervix.

    b. involves suspension of the cervical cell sample in a saline solution.

    c. increases the number of diagnostic cells available for screening.

    d. allows for computer reading of the Pap slides.

79. The ThinPrep liquid-based system can also be used to test for

    a. *Chlamydia trachomatis.*

    b. HIV.

    c. syphilis.

    d. bacterial vaginosis.

80. Cervicography is a technique that

    a. involves the application of normal saline solution to the cervix and a magnifier to view the cervix.

    b. uses a computer to scan the cervix.

    c. takes a sample of abnormal areas seen on the cervix.

    d. involves the application of acetic acid to the cervix followed by a cervigram.

81. An abnormal Pap smear finding is

    a. always associated with HPV.

    b. not always related to viral infection.

    c. always associated with an STI.

    d. always associated with a history of multiple sexual partners.

82. During counseling about the limits of Pap smear accuracy, patients should be advised that

    a. the cost of rescreening is always covered by health insurance.

    b. the Pap smear is guaranteed to identify all abnormal cells that are present.

    c. new enhanced screening techniques are available in all health facilities.

    d. the Pap test is the single most reliable method to detect preinvasive cancer of the cervix.

83. If an abnormal Pap smear result requires further evaluation, a procedure that allows for close-up visualization of the vagina and cervix is

    a. cryosurgery.

    b. colposcopy.

    c. hysteroscopy.

    d. cervicography.

84. A method of treatment for an abnormal Pap test result is

    a. cervicography.

    b. conization.

    c. SurePath.

    d. laparoscopy.

CHAPTER 11

COMMON GYNECOLOGIC DISORDERS

CHAPTER OBJECTIVE

After completing this chapter, the reader will be able to recognize common gynecologic problems and treatments.

LEARNING OBJECTIVES

After studying this chapter, the reader will be able to

1. identify diagnostic and therapeutic modalities for common gynecologic disorders.

2. describe health maintenance and prevention practices related to gynecologic problems.

KEY WORDS

- Amenorrhea
- Dysmenorrhea
- Endometriosis
- Leiomyoma
- Toxic shock syndrome (TSS)

INTRODUCTION

It is important to keep in mind that the body functions as a whole system. Although a gynecologic problem may appear to be confined to the pelvic area, it could actually result from a host of other influences, activities, and imbalances. For example, amenorrhea may be related to excessive exercise, eating disorders, obesity, weight loss, chronic illness, or endocrine disorders that can adversely influence the menstrual cycle (American College of Obstetricians and Gynecologists [ACOG], 2007).

Many gynecologic problems encountered today remain poorly understood by practitioners of Western medicine, who often are unable to offer safe, effective therapy. Women may exhibit pronounced emotional responses to certain gynecologic disorders that can profoundly affect their quality of life and ability to function. Health care providers must always remain sensitive to these broader dimensions of gynecologic care.

It is beyond the scope of this course to consider each topic in great detail. Please refer to the "Resources" and "Bibliography" located in the back of the course book for sources of more in-depth information on each topic. Abnormal Pap smear findings constitute one of the more common gynecologic disorders seen in women; this subject is discussed in detail in Chapter 10.

MENSTRUAL DISORDERS

Four menstrual disorders are commonly encountered by health care practitioners as they care for women: amenorrhea, irregular bleeding, dysmenorrhea, and premenstrual syndrome (PMS). The first three of these four conditions are briefly discussed here. Please refer to Chapter 8 for a detailed discussion of PMS.

Amenorrhea

The normal menstrual cycle depends on the integrated functioning of the hypothalamus, pituitary gland, ovaries, uterus, cervix, and vagina. Lack of menstruation, or amenorrhea, may result from abnormalities of the structure or function of any of these organs.

Amenorrhea may be classified as primary or secondary. Evaluation for amenorrhea should begin when the following circumstances are present.

Primary

- Lack of secondary sex characteristics by age 14
- Lack of menarche (the initial menstrual period) by age 15
- Lack of menses within 3 years after breast development (thelarche) or the appearance of pubic or axillary hair (pubarche or adrenarche) (ACOG, 2007)

The etiology of primary amenorrhea includes:

- pregnancy
- breast-feeding (lactation)
- missed abortion
- eating disorders (e.g., anorexia nervosa, bulimia)
- obesity
- hyperthyroidism
- hypoglycemia
- cystic fibrosis
- Crohn's disease
- genetic abnormalities
- vaginal or cervical absence
- polycystic ovary syndrome (PCOS).
(Wolfe, 2006)

Secondary

- Absence of menses for at least 3 months in a woman who has had regular monthly menses; lack of menses for at least 6 to 12 months in a woman who normally experiences irregular menses (absence for a shorter period is termed "delayed menses" [ACOG, 2007; Hatcher et al., 2008])

The etiology of secondary amenorrhea includes:

- pregnancy
- breast-feeding (lactation)
- premature ovarian failure (menopause before age 40)
- hormonal contraceptive effects
- postpill amenorrhea
- pituitary gland dysfunction, especially hyperprolactinemia
- polycystic ovary syndrome
- endocrine disorders (e.g., Cushing's syndrome, Cushing's disease, thyroid dysfunction)
- emotional or physical stress
- weight loss
- eating disorders (e.g., anorexia nervosa)
- obesity
- frequent strenuous exercise
- chronic illness (e.g., colitis, kidney failure, cystic fibrosis)
- cancer chemotherapy
- ovarian cysts or tumors.
(ACOG, 2007)

The first step when evaluating a woman for amenorrhea is to test for pregnancy. After pregnancy has been ruled out, there is a long list of potential causes for both primary and secondary amenorrhea. Along with a physical examination, an extensive medical workup may be indicated. A careful review of the patient's health history can often provide clues to the cause of amenorrhea, which may be related to a hormonal imbalance or pituitary gland tumor (Hatcher et al., 2008; Lowdermilk & Perry, 2007).

Irregular Bleeding

A host of possible diagnoses are associated with bleeding disorders. While many factors influence the menstrual pattern, one of the first considerations is the patient's age. In adolescence, approximately 20 hormonal cycles occur before ovulation takes place regularly. Bleeding that is irregular in both timing and amount tends to be the rule rather than the exception in early adolescence. Similarly, older women often experience an increased variation in their menstrual intervals and quantity of flow during the 5 years preceding menopause (Lowdermilk & Perry, 2007; Speroff & Fritz, 2005).

Common Age-Related Causes of Irregular Uterine Bleeding

- Adolescence: persistent anovulation (failure to ovulate), which may be caused by contraception, pregnancy, polycystic ovary syndrome, coagulopathies

- Midlife ages 30 to 50: pregnancy, structural lesions (e.g., leiomyomata, polyps), and anovulation, including that caused by polycystic ovary syndrome, hormone therapy, and endometrial hyperplasia (overgrowth of the endometrial lining)

- Menopausal: hormone therapy, endometrial atrophy, leiomyomata, endometrial hyperplasia, malignancy (ACOG, 2007)

Similar to amenorrhea, causes of irregular bleeding range from simple to complex. Evaluation of this problem requires a careful and thorough history and workup, including physical examination, laboratory tests, and possible ultrasound examination to rule out uterine tumors or polyps.

Dysmenorrhea

Dysmenorrhea, defined as pain that occurs during or shortly before menstruation, is one of the most common gynecologic problems in women of all ages. The pain is usually most intense in the suprapubic region or in the lower abdomen.

Dysmenorrhea may be classified as primary or secondary (Lowdermilk & Perry, 2007).

- **Primary:** Primary dysmenorrhea usually begins in 1 to 3 years following menarche, and no apparent pathology is involved.

- **Secondary:** Secondary dysmenorrhea is related to illness or disease, such as endometriosis or fibroid tumors.

The pain during menses is caused by myometrial contractions induced by prostaglandins. Prostaglandins, substances found in various tissues throughout the body, control local functions such as vasodilation and vasoconstriction. Although the uterine muscle of both normal and dysmenorrheic women is sensitive to prostaglandins, the major differentiating factor is the amount of prostaglandins present (Speroff & Fritz, 2005). The pain usually begins at the onset of menstrual flow and persists for 8 to 48 hours. During menstruation, the highest levels of prostaglandins are released during the first 48 hours, which coincides with the greatest intensity of pain. Dietary factors and stress have been shown to influence prostaglandin levels (ACOG, 2004a; Lowdermilk & Perry, 2007).

Prior to the discovery of prostaglandins, painful periods were largely ignored and often considered to be primarily of psychologic origin. Today, dysmenorrhea is recognized as a physiologic problem that responds well to various interventions. Prostaglandin inhibitors such as ibuprofen and other nonsteroidal anti-inflammatory drugs (NSAIDs) are very effective in controlling dysmenorrhea. Women who desire contraception may wish to use oral contraceptive pills, which are associated with decreased prostaglandin synthesis (Speroff & Fritz, 2005).

Throughout the ages, women have used herbal remedies such as cramp bark, wild yam, black haw, ginger, and raspberry leaf to ease menstrual cramps. However, it is important to counsel patients that herbal preparations may be toxic, they may interact with other medications, and only preparations obtained from reputable companies should be used. Other strategies for alleviating menstrual pain include the application of heat or cold, massage, meditation, and progressive relaxation. Some women find exercise to be beneficial. Physical activity improves blood flow to the pelvic region, prompts the release of endogenous opiates, suppresses the release of prostaglandins and reduces pelvic congestion. Dietary measures include using natural diuretics (e.g., peaches, parsley, cranberry juice) to reduce edema and decreasing meat intake to minimize the symptoms of dysmenorrhea. Essential fatty acids, such as evening primrose oil, borage, and black currant oil, may decrease dysmenorrhea, breast tenderness, and fluid retention (Collins Sharp, Taylor, Thomas, Killeen, & Dawood, 2002; Lowdermilk & Perry, 2007).

VAGINAL INFECTIONS

The vaginal environment is an ecosystem that maintains a fairly constant or steady state as it interacts with the environment outside the vagina. A number of organisms normally reside in the vagina, and these include various species of bacteria and yeast. At any one time, 5 to 10 different types of microorganisms are usually present in the vaginal flora. *Lactobacillus,* the dominant bacterial species, is important in maintaining balance in the vagina by producing by-products such as lactic acid and hydrogen peroxide. These by-products help the vagina sustain a fairly constant acidic pH of less than 4.5, which prevents the overgrowth of less desirable vaginal microorganisms. When the complex balance of microorganisms is upset, the potentially pathogenic minor bacteria can proliferate to a concentration that causes symptoms (Hatcher et al., 2008; Lowdermilk & Perry, 2007).

Mechanisms

Vaginal infections primarily occur through two mechanisms:

1. Imbalance and overgrowth of organisms that normally inhabit the vagina proliferate and cause symptoms once the normal balance has been altered.

2. Introduction of organisms from outside the vagina, usually from intimate sexual contact.

(Hatcher et al., 2008; Lowdermilk & Perry, 2007)

Causes of an Altered Vaginal Environment

Several events or factors can cause the normal vaginal environment to be altered and vulnerable to infection. These include:

- stress
- douching
- use of feminine hygiene products
- use of harsh soaps for washing or as laundry detergent
- dietary changes, such as increased consumption of sugar or caffeine
- sexual intercourse
- use of barrier contraceptive methods, such as condoms and diaphragms
- spermicides
- wearing of synthetic underwear or tight-fitting pants
- illness
- chronic metabolic diseases, such as diabetes
- immunosuppression or illness that weakens the immune system
- certain medications
- pregnancy.

(Hatcher et al., 2008; Lowdermilk & Perry, 2007)

Health Education

Many women do not realize that a vaginal discharge is normal. Due to hormonal influences, the discharge, termed *leukorrhea,* changes throughout the menstrual cycle. During the early cycle phase, vaginal discharge is clear, thin, and stretchy in response to estrogen; later, it becomes thicker and tacky due to effects from progesterone, the dominant hormone during the second half of the menstrual cycle. Normal discharge varies in quantity from woman to woman and often from cycle to cycle (Lowdermilk & Perry, 2007).

Nurses can help patients explore ways to maintain a balanced vaginal environment through alterations in lifestyle and choice of birth control method. The possibility of exposure to a sexually transmitted infection (STI) should be discussed with any woman who comes in for evaluation of vaginal symptoms, even when the primary diagnosis is related to an imbalance in normal flora (ACOG, 2007; Lowdermilk & Perry, 2007).

Douching, which has a drying effect on the vagina and disrupts the normal vaginal flora, can increase the amount of vaginal discharge. Douching has been shown to contribute to serious infection of the upper reproductive tract (e.g., pelvic inflammatory disease [PID]) and should be discouraged (Lowdermilk & Perry, 2007).

Common Infections

Several infections and conditions that involve the vaginal environment are commonly encountered in women with gynecologic disorders. These include bacterial vaginosis (BV), candidiasis, STIs, cervicitis, and PID. Other conditions include vaginal carcinoma (primary, which is rare, or secondary, which results from the spread of cancer to the vagina from another site); cancer may also be associated with in utero exposure to diethylstilbestrol (DES) and toxic shock syndrome (TSS). With the exception of STIs, cervicitis, and PID, each is discussed briefly below. Please refer to Chapter 7 for a discussion on STIs and PID. Cervicitis may be accompanied by a purulent cervical discharge, a symptom of gonorrhea or chlamydia infection (Hatcher et al., 2008; Lowdermilk & Perry, 2007). Both of these infections are discussed in Chapter 7.

Bacterial Vaginosis (BV)

BV, formerly called *nonspecific vaginitis, Haemophilus vaginitis,* and *Gardnerella,* is the most common vaginal infection. Although it is a sexually associated condition, it is not usually considered a specific STI (Hatcher et al., 2008).

Causes: BV occurs due to a lack of hydrogen peroxide–producing lactobacilli (which normally maintain a low vaginal pH) and a dramatic overgrowth of the vaginal resident bacterium *Gardnerella vaginalis* and anaerobic bacteria (often *Mycoplasma hominis; Mobiluncus*). Anaerobic bacteria live in a low-oxygen environment (ACOG, 2007).

Signs and symptoms: BV is characterized by a thin, milky discharge with a fishy amine odor; the odor is commonly worse after intercourse and menses. It may also be present without clinical signs or symptoms (Hatcher et al., 2008).

Diagnosis: The diagnosis is made on the basis of a positive finding on the *whiff* test (the characteristic amine odor is produced when a sample of the discharge is combined with a 10% solution of potassium hydroxide). Microscopic examination of the vaginal fluid reveals the presence of clue cells, sloughed vaginal epithelial cells with bacteria clinging to their edges. Lactobacillus species are rarely seen, and the pH of the vagina is above the typical 4.5 (Lowdermilk & Perry, 2007).

Treatment: When BV is found during a routine examination of an asymptomatic woman, it is not usually treated unless she will be undergoing an invasive surgical procedure. Abortion, hysterectomy, or insertion of an intrauterine device are procedures that increase the risk of pelvic infection in the presence of BV. BV has also been shown to be associated with pregnancy complications, such as preterm birth and infection following Cesarean birth (Hatcher et al., 2008).

In women with symptoms, the standard treatment is metronidazole (Flagyl), given either orally (500 mg twice a day for 7 days) or vaginally (metronidazole gel [Metro-Gel] 0.75% gel, 5 g intravaginally for 5 days). Flagyl should not be used in women who have a history of seizures. No alcohol should be ingested 24 hours before or after taking this medication, because the combination of metronidazole and alcohol causes abdominal discomfort, nausea, vomiting, and headache. Also, because the most common side effect of Flagyl is nausea, it is recommended that the drug be taken with food. This medication crosses the placental barrier and enters fetal circulation rapidly. G.D. Searle & Company, the pharmaceutical manufacturer, cautions against the use of Flagyl during the first trimester of pregnancy and the product packaging carries this warning. Also, Flagyl is contraindicated if the woman is breast-feeding. Clindamycin given orally (300 mg twice a day for 7 days) or in a vaginal cream (5 g intravaginally for 7 days) is also used to treat BV. Tinidazole (Tindamax) tablets have recently been approved for the treatment of BV in nonpregnant, adult women. The recommended dose is 2 g once daily for 2 days, or 1 g once daily for 5 days. The medication should be taken with food. Treatment of male partners has no effect on the recurrence rate in female partners and thus is not indicated (ACOG, 2007; Centers for Disease Control and Prevention [CDC], Workowski, Berman, 2006; Hatcher et al., 2008; Lowdermilk & Perry, 2007).

Candidiasis

Causes: Commonly known as a *yeast infection,* candidiasis is generally caused by *Candida albicans.* Other related yeast species, however, can be causative agents (non-*C. albicans*) as well.

Signs and symptoms: Candidiasis classically produces a characteristic itching (pruritis) and irritation of the vulva and often a thick, white, cottage cheese–like vaginal discharge that can have a sour odor. The discharge may be found on the vaginal walls, cervix, and labia. Often, the vulva and labia folds are red and swollen. In some women, the symptoms are more subtle (Hatcher et al., 2008; Lowdermilk & Perry, 2007).

Diagnosis: A diagnosis can be made on the basis of microscopic examination of vaginal discharge. A saline and potassium hydroxide wet smear reveals budding yeast or pseudohyphae. The pH of the vagina is usually unaltered, although it may be slightly more acidic than normal.

Treatment: Many over-the-counter treatments, such as miconazole (Monistat) and clotramazole (Gyne-Lotrimin) are available for candidiasis. These products are usually fungistats that inhibit the organisms from reproducing, so the woman's immune system can suppress the yeast. Although these medications are available without prescription, women should be advised to avoid self-treatment without first undergoing a clinical evaluation to confirm the diagnosis of vulvovaginal candidiasis (ACOG, 2007). Boric acid, 600 mg in size 0 gelatin capsules inserted into the vagina each night for 14 days, has been reported to be effective against resistant infections. Vaginal suppositories containing acidophilic bacteria as well as long-term (6 months) daily ingestion of dairy products or powders, capsules, or tablets that contain *Lactobacillus acidophilus* are other strategies that anecdotally have been associated with prevention and relief of symptoms (Goodman, Herman, Murdaugh, Moneyham, & Phillips, 2007), although the evidence supporting this intervention is conflicting. Nurses can counsel women to take sitz baths and add Aveeno powder to a bath to help relieve symptoms. Not wearing underpants to bed may be helpful in preventing recurrence (Lowdermilk & Perry, 2007).

Stronger antifungal prescription medications are also available in creams or suppositories, along with a one-time oral dose of the antifungal fluconazole (Diflucan). Fluconazole is associated with side effects such as nausea, vomiting, diarrhea, abdominal pain, and headache but is well tolerated by most women. Oral antifungals and boric acid suppositories should not be used during pregnancy; topical antifungals have limited systemic absorption and are considered safe to use. Patients who experience recurrent yeast infections should be evaluated for diabetes and infection with human immunodeficiency virus (HIV) (Hatcher et al., 2008; Lowdermilk & Perry, 2007).

Vaginal Carcinoma

Vaginal carcinomas can be primary, secondary, or related to in-utero DES exposure. Extremely rare, vaginal carcinomas account for only 1% to 2% of gynecologic malignancies. Most lesions are squamous cell carcinomas and most are secondary carcinomas of the vagina. Vaginal cancer is typically asymptomatic. Patients with a history of cervical or vulvar cancer are at a higher risk for this type of cancer. For these women, Pap testing should include a vaginal wall cell sample (Cunningham et al., 2005).

DES is a nonsteroidal synthetic estrogen that was used between 1940 and 1971 to prevent miscarriage in high-risk pregnant women. It was taken off the market when study results revealed that DES was linked to abnormalities in both male and female offspring of women who received this drug during pregnancy. Clear cell adenocarcinoma of the vagina, formerly a rare disease, was seen in young women who were exposed to DES in utero (Cunningham et al., 2005).

Structural alterations along with changes in the tissue of the vagina and cervix are often seen in women exposed prenatally to DES, and DES exposure has also been linked to infertility. Women who have been exposed to DES should have their first Pap smear at the onset of menstruation. A baseline colposcopy should be obtained at first intercourse. Pap smears should be performed every 6 to 12 months until the age of 30 and then annually thereafter (Cunningham et al., 2005).

Toxic Shock Syndrome (TSS)

TSS is a potentially lethal disorder that affects many body systems. Although it is not well understood, TSS is believed to be associated with tampon use during menses; however, nonmenstrual TSS risk is increased for women who use vaginal barrier contraceptives (e.g., vaginal sponge, cervical cap, and diaphragm). The incidence of TSS peaked in the late 1970s and 1980s, most likely because of the widespread availability of superabsorbent tampons. Today, the overall rate of TSS is 1 to 3 per 100,000 per year and only 55% of current cases are associated with menstruation (Hatcher et al., 2008).

Causes: TSS is caused almost exclusively by toxins produced by some strains of colonized *Staphylococcus aureus* bacteria. Although the exact mechanism of cause is not known, several conditions are believed to contribute to the development of the disorder:

- alterations in normal vaginal flora
- mechanical blockage of menstrual flow
- contamination of tampons by the bacteria *S. aureus*
- absorption of bacteria-resistant cervical fluids
- superabsorbent or synthetic materials of which some tampons are composed
- damaged cervical or vaginal tissue.

(Lowdermilk & Perry, 2007; Youngkin & Davis, 2003)

Signs and symptoms: Signs and symptoms include acute illness with high fever (38.8° C [102° F] or higher), hypotension, tachycardia, dizziness, abdominal pain, diarrhea, and nausea. The skin gets a characteristic sunburn-red appearance, or a rash may develop. TSS may also produce flulike symptoms of malaise, sore throat, and aching muscles. This condition can be life-threatening, and coma or death may result (Lowdermilk & Perry, 2007; Youngkin & Davis, 2003).

Diagnosis: The diagnosis of TSS is made on the basis of physical examination findings and symptoms, along with results of a complete blood count, which often shows an elevated white blood cell count indicative of an acute infectious process (Youngkin & Davis, 2003).

Treatment: Treatment for TSS involves immediate hospitalization with fluid replacement and aggressive antibiotic therapy (Youngkin & Davis, 2003).

Health teaching: Women should be taught to avoid use of superabsorbent tampons, change tampons frequently (at least every 6 hours), and alternate sanitary pads with tampons, especially during the night. A woman who develops symptoms suggestive of TSS should remove the tampon and seek medical attention immediately (Youngkin & Davis, 2003).

URINARY TRACT INFECTIONS

Urinary tract infections (UTIs) occur more commonly in women than in men because of the shorter route from the external environment to the bladder in women, along with the close proximity of the urethra to the vagina and anal area. Normally, the flow of urine keeps bacteria flushed from the tract, and the entire urinary system remains sterile. The bladder wall has antibacterial properties, and urine is usually acidic, which inhibits growth of bacteria. Infection of the lower urinary tract can extend upward to include the bladder, ureters, or kidneys. Thus the infection can become increasingly serious as it extends upward (Lowdermilk & Perry, 2007; Sadovsky, 2007).

Causes

Up to 90% of uncomplicated UTIs are due to the bacterium *Escherichia coli,* a common inhabitant of the intestine that causes infection when introduced into the urinary tract. Other common culprits are *Enterococcus faecalis, Staphylococcus saprophyticus, Klebsiella pneumoniae,* and *Proteus*

mirabilis (Sadovsky, 2007). Because STIs can cause symptoms of UTI, testing for chlamydia and gonorrhea should be conducted if the woman is at risk (Lowdermilk & Perry, 2007; Youngkin & Davis, 2003).

Risk Factors

Extremes of age, altered immunity, diabetes, obstructions, pregnancy, sexual activity, and diaphragm use represent the major risk factors for UTI. Irritation of the urethra during sexual activity can cause bacteria to migrate upward into the urinary tract. Spermicides can alter the vaginal pH and decrease levels of normal protective bacteria, which allow more bacteria to grow in the vagina. In turn, the bacteria can migrate to the bladder (Lowdermilk & Perry, 2007).

Signs and Symptoms

Common signs and symptoms include dysuria (pain with urination), urinary frequency and urgency, discomfort in the area above the pubic bone, and cloudy, foul-smelling urine. If the infection has ascended to the kidneys, the lower back region where the vertebrae and ribs meet can be tender or extremely painful, and fever may be present (Lowdermilk & Perry, 2007).

Diagnosis

Diagnosis varies according to the location and extent of the infection. For uncomplicated infection of the lower urinary tract, the diagnosis is made on the basis of symptoms and urinalysis, including microscopic examination of a clean-catch urine sample for the presence of white or red blood cells and bacteria. Complicated cases require a urine culture and sensitivity. Some providers use leukocyte esterase or nitrite urine dipstick screening tests to detect bacteriuria in women with suspected uncomplicated UTI (ACOG, 2007; Lowdermilk & Perry, 2007).

Treatment

For uncomplicated lower UTIs in nonpregnant women, antibiotic therapy given in a 3-day course is effective and may be initiated based on clinical evidence before urine culture results are available. Several medications are commonly used, including trimethoprim/sulfamethoxazole (Bactrim, Septra), amoxicillin (Amoxil, Trimox), ampicillin (Omnipen), nitrofurantoin (Macrodantin), and ciproflaxin (Cipro) (Lowdermilk & Perry, 2007).

Prevention and Health Teaching

Many UTIs can be prevented or diminished by increasing womens' awareness of the causes and by teaching them to implement these simple health-promotion measures:

- Void frequently (every 2 to 4 hours); do not ignore the urge to urinate because holding urine lengthens the time bacteria are in the bladder and allows them to multiply.

- Empty the bladder before and after intercourse.

- Drink plenty of water (6 to 8 glasses per day). However, patients should be advised not to drink lots of water while taking an antibiotic for a UTI because this may dilute the urinary concentration of the antimicrobial (Sadovsky, 2007).

- Drink liquids before and after intercourse.

- Avoid harsh soaps, powders, and sprays; avoid bath oils and bubble baths if tub baths are taken.

- Avoid tight-fitting underwear and pants.

- Use cotton underwear.

- Take vitamin C regularly to inhibit bacterial growth.

- Drink cranberry juice or take cranberry capsules, which prevent bacteria from adhering to the bladder wall. *Note:* There is conflicting evidence regarding the effectiveness of cranberry juice in the prevention of UTIs (Jepson, Mihaljevic, & Craig, 2004; Raz, Chazan, & Dan, 2004).

- Wipe the urethral meatus and perineum from front to back after voiding.

- Take the full course of any antibiotics prescribed.

ENDOMETRIOSIS

Endometriosis, a benign disorder of the reproductive tract, is characterized by the presence and growth of endometrial tissue (tissue that lines the uterus) in sites outside of the uterus. Women ages 30 to 40 are most likely to develop endometriosis, which is found in 20% to 40% of infertile women and in up to 33% of women with chronic pelvic pain (Guo & Wang, 2006; Speroff & Fritz, 2005; Woodson, 2007). Endometrial lesions have been found on the ovaries, fallopian tubes, lining of the inside of the pelvic cavity, cervix, bladder, bowel, liver, and lungs. The misplaced endometrial tissue responds to cyclic hormonal stimulation during the secretory and proliferative stages of the menstrual cycle, where it grows and thickens in a similar fashion to the endometrial tissue lining the uterus. However, during the ischemic and menstrual phases of the cycle, the misplaced endometrial tissue breaks down and bleeds into the surrounding tissue, causing inflammation. The blood becomes trapped in the surrounding tissues, causing the development of blood-containing cysts. The recurrence of inflammation in the areas outside of the uterus eventually results in scarring, fibrosis, and the development of adhesions, scar tissue that binds the organs together causing increased abdominal pain and a risk of infertility (Lowdermilk & Perry, 2007).

Causes

The etiology of endometriosis is unknown. One of the most widely accepted theories is "retrograde menstruation": during menstruation, endometrial tissue is transported through the fallopian tubes into the peritoneal cavity, where it implants on the ovaries and other structures. Although retrograde menstruation occurs in most women, it is unknown why some develop endometriosis. The level of functioning of the immune system is thought to be a factor in the development of endometriosis, although the exact mechanism is not known (Lowdermilk & Perry, 2007; Speroff & Fritz, 2005).

Signs and Symptoms

Signs and symptoms of endometriosis vary from woman to woman, and the severity of symptoms may increase over time. The major symptoms include pain during menses (dysmenorrhea), pain with intercourse (dyspareunia), pelvic pain and heaviness not associated with menstruation, abnormal menstrual bleeding, and infertility. Bowel symptoms such as diarrhea, pain with defecation, and constipation may also occur (Lowdermilk & Perry, 2007; Ninia, 2007). Abnormal bleeding (hypermenorrhea, menorrhagia and pain during exercise (related to adhesions) have also been reported (Lemaire, 2004).

Diagnosis

Laparoscopy confirms the diagnosis, although endometriosis is generally suspected based on the woman's symptoms and physical examination. A vaginal ultrasound may also be performed to provide imaging of the displaced endometrial tissue or cyst. Interestingly, symptoms of the disease do not always correspond to the actual volume of lesions that are found on laparoscopy. Some women with extensive endometrial implants, or endometriomas, have mild symptoms, whereas other women with severe symptoms have fewer lesions (Lowdermilk & Perry, 2007).

Treatment

Because endometriosis can persist during the entire reproductive life of a woman, her treatment plan should be individualized and holistic. When determining the appropriate therapy, many factors in the woman's life must be taken into account, such as her desire to bear children, the size of her current family, and general lifestyle patterns. Although there are no ideal treatments for endometriosis, the treatment plan is based on the severity of symptoms and the woman's or the couple's goals.

Drug Therapy

The aim of treatment is to suppress the production of endogenous estrogen and the subsequent growth of endometrial tissue. To accomplish endogenous estrogen suppression, two main classes of drugs are used: gonadotropin-releasing hormone (GnRH) agonists and androgen derivatives. GnRH agonists, such as leuprolide (Lupron) and nafarelin (Synarel) act by suppressing the secretion of pituitary gonadotropins, causing anovulation and amenorrhea with a subsequent shrinkage of the endometrial tissue. The patient experiences significant pain relief and an interruption in the further development of endometrial lesions. Common side effects are similar to those associated with natural menopause and include hot flashes and vaginal dryness (Lowdermilk & Perry, 2007).

Danazol (Danocrine), a testosterone derivative, causes anovulation by suppressing the secretion of follicle-stimulating hormone (FSH) and luteinizing hormone (LH). This medication was widely used in the treatment of endometriosis during the 1970s and 1980s. Because it is an androgenic synthetic steroid, masculinizing side effects, such as decreased breast size, weight gain, edema, oily skin, acne, hirsutism, and deepening of the voice, are common. Other side effects associated with danazol include hot flashes, vaginal dryness, insomnia, and decreased libido (Lowdermilk & Perry, 2007).

Medroxyprogesterone (Depo-Provera) is an injectable medication used to reduce the growth of endometrial tissue, but this agent is also associated with undesired side effects, including weight gain and depression. Newer pharmacological modalities utilize aromatase inhibitors, including anastrozole (Arimidex), exemestane (Aromasin) and letrozole (Femara), chemicals that block the conversion of androgens to estrogen and suppress the production of estrogen from the abnormal endometrial tissue, thereby decreasing tissue growth (Lowdermilk & Perry, 2007).

Women who have early disease and wish to postpone pregnancy may be treated with continuous oral contraceptives. The pain associated with tissue inflammation may be managed with NSAIDs such as ibuprofen to inhibit the synthesis of prostaglandin and reduce inflammation (Lowdermilk & Perry, 2007).

Surgery

Laparoscopic surgery remains the only method to accurately diagnose and determine the severity of the lesions of endometriosis. During laparoscopy, the endometrial lesions can be removed or destroyed by using thermal cautery or laser vaporization. For women who do not wish to preserve their fertility, the only definitive cure is total abdominal hysterectomy with bilateral salpingo-oophorectomy (TAH with BSO). Regardless of treatment (other than the surgical TAH with BSO), up to 40% of women with endometriosis experience recurrence (Grow & Hsu, 2006; Lowdermilk & Perry, 2007).

Providing Counseling and Support

Counseling and support are essential components of care for women with endometriosis. Nurses who work with patients with this chronic disease must provide factual information about treatment options, including the risks and benefits of each. Referral to support groups may be helpful and women and couples may wish to contact national organizations such as Resolve (www.resolve.org), an organization for infertile couples, or the Endometriosis Association (www.endometriosisassn.org).

FIBROIDS (LEIOMYOMAS)

Uterine fibroids, or leiomyomas, are the most common tumors of the pelvis. They arise from the multiplication of smooth muscle cells of the uterus. Although the exact cause is unknown, the growth of leiomyomas is dependent on estrogen. They are almost always benign or noncancerous (Cunningham et al., 2005).

Leiomyomas can be located in different places in and around the uterus. The most common fibroids form within the uterine wall. Leiomyomas may also protrude into the uterine cavity, bulge outward through the uterine wall and into the pelvic cavity, or grow on a stalk (called a *pedicle*) that can become twisted and cause pain (see Figure 11-1). Fibroids are more common in African-American women than in Caucasian or Hispanic women; approximately one in three African-American women develops them. Stimulated by estrogen and progesterone, fibroids occur more frequently with increasing age and regress after menopause (Cook & Walker, 2004; Lowdermilk & Perry, 2007).

Causes

Leiomyomas arise from a single neoplastic smooth muscle cell in the uterus, grow slowly, and diminish rapidly after menopause. It is unclear what factors prompt the initial neoplastic transformation (Cunningham et al., 2005).

Signs and Symptoms

In the majority of women, fibroids do not cause any symptoms. Instead, they are most often discovered on a routine bimanual pelvic examination. When women do experience signs and symptoms, the following three complaints tend to be most common:

1. **Abnormal bleeding:** Increased flow and duration of menses are the most common symptoms.

FIGURE 11-1: TYPES OF LEIOMYOMAS

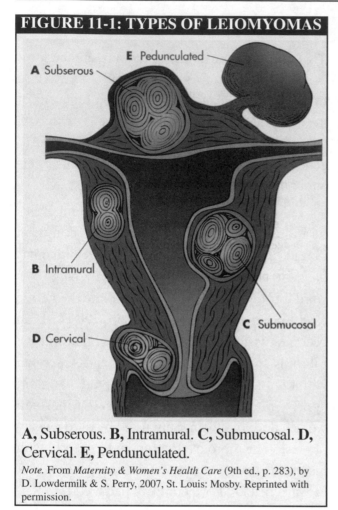

A, Subserous. **B,** Intramural. **C,** Submucosal. **D,** Cervical. **E,** Pendunculated.

Note. From *Maternity & Women's Health Care* (9th ed., p. 283), by D. Lowdermilk & S. Perry, 2007, St. Louis: Mosby. Reprinted with permission.

2. **Pelvic Pressure:** Depending on the location of the leiomyoma, pressure may be experienced in the bladder and rectal regions. Bladder pressure produces urinary frequency or incontinence, while rectal pressure may cause constipation and feelings of heaviness.

3. **Dysmenorrhea:** Although women with fibroids may experience heavier cramping with menses, dysmenorrhea is not a typical complaint. If chronic pain is present, the possibility of a coexisting problem should be investigated. Acute pain could indicate twisting of a fibroid that is on a stalk.

(Lowdermilk & Perry, 2007)

Diagnosis

On examination, the uterus is nontender and may feel enlarged, irregularly shaped, or both. Pregnancy should always be suspected. A sonogram can confirm presence of the leiomyoma and provide baseline measurements. Hysteroscopy, a procedure in which an instrument is used to view the uterine cavity, or laparoscopy, which can differentiate ovarian masses from uterine masses, may be used to aid in the diagnosis (Lowdermilk & Perry, 2007).

Treatment

Patients are usually seen at 3 to 6-month intervals as long as they are experiencing mild symptoms. If heavy and prolonged bleeding occurs, patients should be referred to a specialist for further evaluation and intervention, which may include the following therapies:

- **Drug therapy:** Oral contraceptives may be prescribed to control heavy periods and decrease tumor growth. GnRH agonists such as leuprolide acetate (Lupron, Synarel) suppress the production of estrogen and progesterone and shrink leiomyomas, although patients may complain of menopausal symptoms, such as vaginal dryness, hot flashes, and mood changes. Other medications, such as progesterone acetate (Depo-Provera), danazol (Danocrine), and mifepristone (Mifeprex), may also be prescribed, along with NSAIDs, to relieve discomfort and decrease heavy menses, and oral iron preparations for women whose hemoglobin levels, and hematocrit are low due to blood loss. Women who use GnRH agonists should understand that tumor regrowth occurs once the medication is stopped (Lowdermik & Perry, 2007).

- **Uterine artery embolization (UAE):** This treatment involves the injection of polyvinyl alcohol pellets into selected blood vessels to block the blood supply to the fibroid and cause shrinkage and resolution of symptoms (Society of Obstetricians and Gynaecologists of Canada [SOGC], 2005). This procedure is accomplished under local anesthesia and conscious sedation. An incision is made into the groin, a catheter is threaded through the femoral artery into the uterine artery, and an arteriogram identifies the major blood vessels that supply the fibroid. Most fibroids shrink in size by 50% within 3 months following treatment. However, data are lacking about the long-term effects on fertility and future pregnancies (Lowdermilk & Perry, 2007; SOGC, 2005; Spies et al., 2005).

- **Myomectomy:** Removal of the fibroids (myomectomy) can be accomplished during laparotomy, laparoscopy, or hysteroscopy, depending on the size and number of tumors. Myomectomy can be performed through a laparoscopic or abdominal incision approach or a vaginal (hysteroscopic) approach. The uterus (and therefore childbearing potential) is preserved, although most myomectomy patients require cesarean delivery (Lowdermilk & Perry, 2007).

- **Hysterectomy:** Removal of the uterus (hysterectomy) may be the treatment of choice if bleeding cannot be controlled by other means.

- **Laser surgery or electrocauterization:** These procedures may be used to destroy small fibroids with a vaginal (hysteroscopic) or abdominal (laparoscopic) approach. Laser coagulation may be employed to vaporize the fibroids and produce necrosis. Although the uterus remains intact, scarring inside the uterine cavity may diminish future fertility.

Complications

Depending on their size and location, leiomyomas can interfere with fertility. Excessive bleeding may produce anemia and require surgical intervention.

Patient Counseling and Information

It is important to ensure that, prior to any surgical intervention, women are given information concerning treatment options and the benefits and risks of all procedures. The nurse can direct women to resources such as the Fibroid Treatment Collective (www.fibroid.org) to assist them in their decision-making.

After UAE, patients should be taught these guidelines:

- Take all prescribed medications.

- Contact the physician for symptoms, including bleeding, pain, swelling, or hematoma at the puncture site; fever of 39° C; urinary retention; or abnormal vaginal discharge.

- Eat a normal diet rich in fiber. Include plenty of fluids.

- Do not use tampons, douche, or have intercourse for at least 4 weeks.

- Avoid straining during bowel movements.

(Lowdermilk & Perry, 2007)

After myomectomy or hysterectomy, patients should be taught these guidelines:

- Take all prescribed medications.

- Contact the physician for symptoms, including bleeding, gastrointestinal changes, persistent postoperative symptoms (cramping, distention, change in bowel habits), and signs of wound infection (redness, swelling, heat, or pain at the incision site).

- Eat foods high in protein, iron, and vitamin C to facilitate tissue healing. Include plenty of fluids and fiber.

- Obtain plenty of rest; avoid vigorous activity and heavy lifting for 6 weeks

- Avoid sitting for prolonged periods

- Resume driving when permitted (by the physician) to do so.

- Avoid tub baths, intercourse, and douching until after the postoperative check-up.

(Lowdermilk & Perry, 2007)

ABNORMAL OR EXCESSIVE UTERINE BLEEDING

Heavy bleeding is a common problem for women in the perimenopausal period between the ages of 40 and 50. The abnormal bleeding may be categorized as dysfunctional or structural (Cunningham et al., 2005).

Abnormal bleeding related to dysfunctional causes: Dysfunctional uterine bleeding (DUB) is defined as excessive, prolonged, unpatterned bleeding from the endometrium. It is most commonly caused by hormone imbalances, which account for approximately 75% of cases of excessive bleeding. As ovulation becomes more erratic during the perimenopausal period, progesterone levels decrease. Progesterone stabilizes the uterine lining. In the absence of progesterone, bleeding may become unpredictable, excessive, or prolonged. Anovulation during adolescence may cause abnormal bleeding. Heavy bleeding may also arise from thyroid or adrenal gland disorders, PCOS, clotting disorders, liver or kidney disease, leukemia, herbal preparations such as ginseng, or medications such as anticoagulants (Keehbauch & Nystrom, 2007; Lowdermilk & Perry, 2007; Speroff & Mishell, 2007; Wolfe, 2006).

Abnormal bleeding related to structural causes: Structural causes of excessive bleeding include fibroids, polyps, or infection. As previously discussed, leiomyomas are often asymptomatic. Precancerous or cancerous conditions of the uterus or cervix can also cause abnormal bleeding.

Diagnosis

Diagnostic tests used to evaluate women with abnormal or excessive uterine bleeding may include a pregnancy test to rule out ectopic pregnancy, Pap smear, and complete blood count, as well as endometrial biopsy, transvaginal ultrasound, hysteroscopy, and dilatation and curettage (D&C) (Lowdermilk & Perry, 2007).

Treatment

Current treatment options include drug therapy and surgery:

Drug therapy: Medications used for abnormal or excessive bleeding include low-dose birth control pills, progestins, conjugated estrogen, NSAIDs, and prostaglandin synthetase inhibitors (PGSIs) (Cunningham et al., 2005; Lowdermilk & Perry, 2007).

Surgery: Surgical procedures may be used to treat abnormal or excessive bleeding.

1. *D&C.* Although D&C was once a mainstay of treatment, other options are more effective.

2. *Hysteroscopic endometrial ablation.* With the hysteroscopic endometrial ablation procedure, the uterine lining is viewed through a hysteroscope. An electrosurgical tip or laser is used to burn away the uterine lining. Fertility is not preserved (Song, 2007).

3. *Thermal balloon ablation.* A flexible balloon attached to a thin probe is inserted through the cervix and inflated in the uterus with sterile fluid. The fluid is heated and thereby destroys the uterine lining. Fertility is not preserved (Song, 2007).

HYSTERECTOMY

Hysterectomy was discussed briefly in other chapters. However, it is important to mention here because it is a frequently performed surgery, often at midlife, that can induce an abrupt premature menopause.

After cesarean section, hysterectomy is the second most frequently performed major surgical procedure for women of reproductive age in the United States. Each year in this country, approximately 600,000 hysterectomies are performed, and an estimated 20 million women have had a hysterectomy. The three conditions most commonly associated with hysterectomy are uterine leiomyoma, endometriosis, and uterine prolapse (CDC, 2006b). Prior to the surgery, psychologic assessment is an essential component of care. The nurse should ensure that the woman has an opportunity to consider the personal significance of the loss of her uterus, discuss misconceptions about the effects of the surgery, and ensure that she has an adequate support system for postoperative care and concerns. It is beyond the scope of this course to consider the myriad issues surrounding hysterectomy, but much has been written on the subject. Please refer to the "Resource" at the back of this course book for further information.

OVARIAN TUMORS

Because the ovaries are composed of many different tissue types, growths or tumors involving these structures can also be of various types. In fact, more than 50 different types of ovarian tumors have been identified. Follicular cysts and corpus luteum cysts, which represent two of the most common types of ovarian tumors, are discussed below.

Follicular Cysts

A follicular cyst is the most common growth that occurs on the ovary, and it develops during the first half of the menstrual cycle, the follicular phase. This type of ovarian cyst, termed a "functional" or "simple" cyst, forms when ovulation does not occur. Instead, the developing dominant follicle continues to grow and becomes a large fluid-filled cyst, which contains a high concentration of estrogen. A follicular cyst can also form from one of the smaller follicles that failed to regress after the dominant follicle took over (Lowdermilk & Perry, 2007).

Signs and Symptoms

A follicular cyst is usually asymptomatic, although it may create a heavy, achy feeling in the pelvis. Because of the excessive amounts of estrogen collecting in the cyst, the woman may experience irregular periods (Lowdermilk & Perry, 2007).

Diagnosis

The diagnosis may be made on the basis of symptoms and bimanual examination, then confirmed with an ultrasound. Pregnancy should always be suspected and ruled out.

Treatment

Expectant management, which involves watching and waiting, with another examination performed in 6 to 10 weeks, is the treatment of choice unless symptoms worsen. Most follicular cysts resolve after two or three menstrual cycles without intervention. Oral contraceptive pills may be prescribed to hasten cyst resolution (Lowdermilk & Perry, 2007).

Corpus Luteum Cysts

A corpus luteum cyst forms from the corpus luteum during the second half, or luteal phase, of the menstrual cycle. Menstrual irregularity, especially delayed menstruation, may result. Most often, corpus luteum cysts regress and disappear spontaneously within one or two menstrual cycles. Less commonly, these cysts rupture and can cause severe abdominal pain from the associated bleeding. Surgical removal of the cysts may then be necessary (Lowdermilk & Perry, 2007).

POLYCYSTIC OVARY SYNDROME

PCOS is the most common endocrine disorder in reproductive-age women, affecting approximately 1 in 15 women in the United States (Speroff & Mishell, 2007). The disorder occurs when an endocrine imbalance results in elevated levels of estrogen, testosterone, and LH and a decreased secretion of FSH. Multiple follicular cysts develop on one or both ovaries and produce excessive amounts of estrogen. Clinical findings include obesity, hirsutism (excessive hair growth), acne, and infertility. Menstrual irregularities range from oligomenorrhea (abnormally light or infrequent menstruation) to amenorrhea. Affected individuals typically have insulin resistance and are at high risk for developing type 2 diabetes mellitus (Buggs & Rosenfield, 2005; Speroff & Mishell, 2007; Wolfe, 2006). PCOS is often diagnosed in adolescence and the prevalence of the disorder in Mexican-Americans is twice that of other ethnic groups (Goodarzi et al., 2005; Speroff & Mishell, 2007).

Treatment of patients with PCOS usually depends on the presenting signs and symptoms. In women who are not attempting pregnancy, oral contraceptives are the usual treatment because they inhibit LH and decrease testosterone levels. Oral contraceptives may also lessen acne and hirsutism. If pregnancy is desired, medications to induce ovulation, such as clomiphene citrate (Clomid), are usually prescribed. Insulin medications for type 2 diabetes such as metformin hydrochloride (Glucophage), are used to lower insulin, testosterone, and glucose levels, which in turn can reduce acne, hirsutism, abdominal obesity and other symptoms associated with PCOS (ACOG, 2007; Speroff & Mishell, 2007; Wolfe, 2006).

Nurses can counsel patients with polycystic ovary syndrome about their disorder and the potential long-term effects on their health. Information can be provided about prescribed medications and strategies such as diet and exercise to optimize health. Referrals for resources including counseling regarding body image and self esteem, support groups and nutritional information may be appropriate (Lowdermilk & Perry, 2007; Wolfe, 2006).

ECTOPIC PREGNANCY

A failure of the fertilized egg to implant in the uterus may result in implantation elsewhere in the pelvis (see Figure 11-2). Approximately 95% of ectopic pregnancies occur in the fallopian tubes. Rarely, the egg becomes implanted on an ovary, on the cervix, or in the abdomen outside of the uterus. The implanted fertilized egg, located most often in the tiny fallopian tube, grows until it can no longer be contained in the small space; then it spontaneously ruptures. Without intervention, this event can cause severe bleeding in the abdominal cavity and lead to maternal shock and death (ACOG, 2007; Lowdermilk & Perry, 2007).

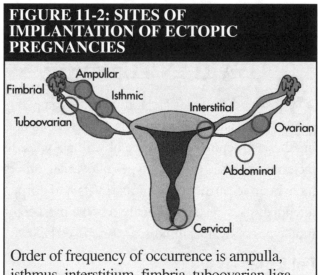

FIGURE 11-2: SITES OF IMPLANTATION OF ECTOPIC PREGNANCIES

Order of frequency of occurrence is ampulla, isthmus, interstitium, fimbria, tuboovarian ligament, ovary, abdominal cavity and cervix (external os).

Note. From *Maternity & Women's Health Care* (9th ed., p. 811), by D. Lowdermilk & S. Perry, 2007, St. Louis: Mosby. Reprinted with permission.

Risk Factors

The single leading predisposing factor in ectopic pregnancy is a history of infection in the fallopian tube (salpingitis or PID), usually caused by an STI, such as *Neisseria gonorrhoeae* or *Chlamydia trachomatis*. Partial obstruction or narrowing and twisting of the tubal canal most often results from infection. The inflammatory process also damages the small hairs (cilia) inside the tube and leaves tiny pockets that can trap the fertilized egg en route to the uterus. The incidence of ectopic pregnancy in the general population is 2% and the frequency is consistent across maternal age ranges and ethnic origins (Murray, Baakdah, Bardell, & Tulandi, 2005). Other risk factors include advanced maternal age, prior treatment for infertility, and previous ectopic pregnancy (ACOG, 2007).

Signs and Symptoms

An unruptured ectopic pregnancy is difficult to diagnose in the early stages because it is often asymptomatic. Signs and symptoms that may be present include lack of menses, lower abdominal pain, slight vaginal bleeding, and a mass in the area of the ovary. A ruptured ectopic pregnancy usually is accompanied by severe abdominal pain, referred shoulder pain as a result of the abdominal bleeding, dizziness, fainting, and shock. Dark red or brown vaginal bleeding occurs in 50% to 80% of women. This event is an emergency situation, and immediate hospitalization is essential for stabilization and surgical intervention (Lowdermilk & Perry, 2007).

Diagnosis

Diagnosis is made on the basis of the history and physical examination, transvaginal ultrasound, and a blood test (quantitative beta hCG) for presence of the pregnancy hormone human chorionic gonadotropin (hCG). A culdocentesis may also be performed to detect intraperitoneal blood, which is present following tubal pregnancy rupture (Cunningham et al., 2005).

Treatment

An unruptured early (a conceptus that measures 4 cm or less on ultrasound examination) ectopic pregnancy may be treated with the drug methotrexate, a therapy traditionally used to treat cancer, psoriasis, and a number of other conditions. Methotrexate is a folic acid analog that halts the growth of rapidly dividing cells. Administered as a single-dose intramuscular injection, methotrexate provides a safe, effective, nonsurgical treatment alternative that is conducted in the outpatient setting (Takacs, Chakhtoura, DeSantis, & Verma, 2005). Surgical intervention (salpingostomy) is usually required with larger ectopic pregnancies and with those that have ruptured (Lowdermilk & Perry, 2007).

Long-Term Complications

A woman who has experienced an ectopic pregnancy has an increased risk for recurrence, although the risk is less with the use of methotrexate (Takacs et al., 2005).

OVARIAN CANCER

Because the pelvis contains major components of the gastrointestinal and urinary tracts in addition to the reproductive organs, determining the cause of any pelvic mass requires careful assessment, including an evaluation for ovarian cancer. Any of the various cell types in the ovaries can give rise to cancerous growth. Although it is beyond the scope of this course to discuss the many different types of ovarian cancer, a brief overview will be presented.

Ovarian cancer is the seventh most common cancer in women in the United States (Ovarian Cancer National Alliance, 2004). It ranks fifth among causes of cancer death in women. According to the National Cancer Institute, it is estimated that 21,560 women will be diagnosed with and 15,520 women will die of cancer of the ovary in 2008 (Ries, Melbert, Krapcho, Stinchcomb, Howlader, Horner, et al., n.d.). About two-thirds of women with ovarian cancer are ages 55 and older, and the disease is slightly more common in white women than in African-American women. A woman's risk of getting ovarian cancer during her lifetime is about 1 in 67; the risk of dying from it is 1 in 95 (ACS, 2006).

Risk Factors

Although the cause is unknown, identified risk factors include nulliparity, pregnancy later in life, presence of BRCA1 and BRCA2 genes, a personal history of breast cancer, and a family history of breast or ovarian cancer. Associative causes include the use of fertility medications, exposure to asbestos, genital exposure to talc, a high-fat diet, and childhood mumps infection. Pregnancy and oral contraceptive use provide some protection against ovarian cancer, and the use of postmenopausal estrogen may increase the risk (ACS, 2006).

Signs and Symptoms

Signs and symptoms are often vague until late in development. Ovarian cancer should be considered in any woman older than 40 years of age who has complaints of vague abdominal or pelvic discomfort or enlargement, back pain, indigestion, lack of appetite, feeling full after eating only a small amount, a sense of bloating, or flatulence. Enlargement of the abdomen due to the accumulation of fluid (ascites) is the most common sign (ACS, 2006; Goff et al., 2007). Because ovarian cancer is a rapidly growing neoplasm, the diagnosis usually is not made until the cancer has metastasized, giving rise to the nickname for ovarian cancer as "the silent killer."

Screening and Evaluation

Ovarian cancer is rarely diagnosed early. Close to 70% of women have already experienced cancer spread outside of the pelvis at the time of the initial diagnosis. Methods for mass screening and early detection have not been successful; currently, an annual bimanual examination is recommended. Several procedures are used to assist in the ovarian cancer evaluation:

1. **Ultrasound:** Transvaginal ultrasound can be used to determine the size, location, and quality (e.g., fluid-filled, solid, complex) of the mass.

2. **Genetic screening:** Alterations in BRCA1 or BRCA2 genes have been noted in women with ovarian cancer. Patients can be screened during genetic counseling and testing to determine whether they carry these genes.

3. **Serum CA-125 antigen levels:** The test to determine the serum CA-125 antigen level was originally used to monitor the course of epithelial ovarian cancer. It is often used currently in preoperative decision-making about managing pelvic masses. False-positive results can be caused by other conditions, including nongynecologic cancers and active endometriosis.

4. **Laparotomy:** Laparotomy is performed for surgical confirmation and clinical staging, which provides direction to the treatment and prognosis of the cancer.

(ACS, 2006; Hordern, 2007; Lowdermilk & Perry, 2007)

Treatment

The treatment is planned according to the stage of the disease at the time of initial diagnosis. Most often, surgical removal of as much of the tumor as possible constitutes the initial step. A TAH with removal of the ovaries and fallopian tubes is frequently performed as well, followed by some combination of chemotherapy. Combination immunotherapy and chemotherapy is also used in some institutions. Radiation therapy is considered a palliative measure, although it is not typically used as a treatment option for ovarian cancer (Goff, Matthews et al., 2007; Hordern, 2007; Lowdermilk & Perry, 2007).

Patient Counseling to Detect Early Disease

Recent research has shown that certain symptoms are more likely to occur in women with ovarian cancer than in the general population. Goff, Mandel, and colleagues (2007) have developed a symptom index, the Goff Symptom Index, for early identification of women with potential ovarian cancer. This tool focuses on symptoms most commonly seen among women who were subsequently diagnosed with ovarian cancer. Although not yet standard of care, the easy-to administer-symptom index has been recommended as a possible tool to aid in screening. Major detection symptoms included in the Goff Symptom Index include bloating, pelvic or abdominal pain, difficulty eating or feeling full quickly, and urinary symptoms (urgency or frequency). Scientists note that the frequency and number of symptoms are correlated with the diagnosis of ovarian cancer, and women who experience any of these symptoms on a daily basis for more than a few weeks should be counseled to contact their women's health care specialist (Fife, 2007; Goff, Mandel, et al., 2007; Hellwig, 2007b).

UTERINE CANCER

Cancer of the endometrium is the most common gynecologic malignancy. The ACS estimates that there will be over 40,000 new cases of uterinc cancer in the United States in 2008. Most uterine malignancies arise within the inner lining of the uterus and are adenocarcinomas that develop from overgrowth of the endometrium. Uterine cancer is rarely found in women under age 45; about 70% of all cases are found in women between the ages of 45 and 74, and the highest number is diagnosed in the 55 to 64 age-group. While the incidence of this type of cancer is higher for Caucasian women than for African-American women, African-American women have mortality rates that are nearly two times higher (ACS, 2006).

Causes

There is an established relationship between unopposed (i.e., absence of progesterone) exogenous estrogen and uterine cancer. Progesterone inhibits the growth of cells stimulated by estrogen and causes them to enter a more mature secretory state. Women who receive estrogen replacement therapy without progesterone have much higher rates of uterine cancer. Progesterone is now added to any hormone replacement therapy for women who have a uterus (see Chapter 13 for additional information). Although the exact cause of uterine cancer is not known, several risk factors have been identified (Lowdermilk & Perry, 2007).

Risk Factors

Risk factors for uterine cancer include those factors that expose the endometrium to estrogen. Unopposed estrogen therapy, nulliparity or low parity, early menarche (before age 12), late menopause (after age 55), therapy with tamoxifen, infertility, diabetes, gallbladder disease, hypertension, a high-fat diet (which increases the levels of circulating estrogen), and obesity are all risk factors for uterine cancer. Factors associated with a lower risk of endometrial cancer include having multiple children, use of combination oral contraceptives, and menopausal estrogen replacement therapy that is combined with progesterone therapy for women who have a uterus. A genetic syndrome known as *hereditary nonpolyposis colon cancer* has been associated with both endometrial and ovarian cancer (ACS, 2006; Lowdermilk & Perry, 2007).

Signs and Symptoms

Endometrial cancer is slow growing and the majority of the neoplasms are adenocarcinomas that develop from endometrial hyperplasia. Most women are symptomatic in the early stages, a factor that leads to early diagnosis and, frequently, successful treatment. For postmenopausal women, the cardinal symptom is vaginal bleeding; perimenopausal women may have heavy or prolonged menstruation or spotting or bleeding between menses. Other symptoms of endometrial cancer include pelvic pain, dyspareunia, and weight loss (Lowdermilk & Perry, 2007; Youngkin & Davis, 2003).

Diagnosis

Pelvic examination may reveal a uterine enlargement or mass. A biopsy of the endometrium is taken to evaluate the uterine lining for diagnosis. Fractional curettage, which involves scraping the endocervix and the endometrium for histologic evaluation may also be performed. Other diagnostic tests that may be conducted include hysteroscopy (examination of the uterus through an endoscope) and vaginal ultrasound. If endometrial cancer is present, staging, which may include a chest X-ray, an abdominal computed tomography scan, liver function tests, renal function tests, bone scans, and serum testing for the presence of cancer antigen 125 (CA-125, released by some endometrial and ovarian cancers) is done to determine the degree of metastasis (Lowdermilk & Perry, 2007). Uterine cancer is staged based on its location and extension into surrounding tissue and distant metastases.

Treatment

Treatment involves TAH along with removal of the ovaries, fallopian tubes, and local lymph nodes. This procedure is followed by radiation, chemotherapy, or both, depending on the individual case. The most common uterine cancer, adenocarcinoma, is slow-growing and usually remains localized for a long time. When diagnosed and treated early, survival rates are good. For all cases of endometrial cancer, the relative 5 year survival rate is 84%; for cancer found at an earlier stage, the survival rate is much higher. The survival rates for Caucasian women are at least 18% better at every stage than for African-American women (ACS, 2006; Lowdermilk & Perry, 2007).

DISEASES OF THE VULVA

The external female genital organs, or vulva, include all visible structures that extend externally from the mons pubis to the perineum. Vulvar tissue is richly supplied with sweat and sebaceous glands. Hair follicles are present in some areas as well. The vulvar region supports a moist environment that contains increased concentrations of skin bacteria.

Symptoms involving the vulva can be caused by a number of different problems that range from benign conditions such as contact dermatitis to malignant growths such as vulvar cancer. Obtaining a careful health history is an essential tool in the patient assessment. The diagnosis of vulvar cancer is almost always delayed because its symptoms are very similar to other conditions. Vulvar itching, or pruritis, is the most common complaint, and women often delay evaluation because they self-treat with readily available vaginal preparations. Other commonly reported symptoms in the vulvar region include a burning sensation, presence of a lump or sore, vaginal discharge, rash, and pain (Youngkin & Davis, 2003).

Five frequently encountered vulvar diseases – vaginal infections, Bartholin's gland abscess, parasites, molluscum contagiosum, and vulvar warts – are described here.

Vaginal Infections

Vaginal infections can produce symptoms on the vulva. Candidiasis, or yeast infection, is the most common infection and often causes intense itching and tissue irritation. Women who are immunocompromised, diabetic, or overweight and those who are receiving long-term antibiotic therapy are particularly susceptible to vulvar yeast infections that may be resistant to treatment. Further testing is indicated because the infection may result from multiple types of yeast or include bacterial organisms (Lowdermilk & Perry, 2007).

Bartholin's Glands Abscesses

The Bartholin's glands are located posteriorly on the sides of the vaginal opening. During sexual arousal, they produce a clear mucus to lubricate the vaginal introitus. Bartholin's cysts are the most common benign lesions of the vulva. Obstruction of the Bartholin duct leads to enlargement and formation of a cyst. The cyst may cause no symptoms, but if it enlarges or becomes infected, the woman often experiences pain, painful intercourse, and an awareness of a mass in the area. When symptomatic, incision and drainage provide temporary relief. Because Bartholin's cysts tend to recur, a permanent opening for drainage may be recommended. Rarely, the abscess is caused by gonorrhea. In postmenopausal women, Bartholin's abscesses are highly unusual and cancer should be suspected (Lowdermilk & Perry, 2007).

Parasites

Lice or mites may infect the vulva. Intense itching of the skin that contains hair follicles is characteristic. With scabies infestation (a dermatitis caused by the mite *Sarcoptes scabiei*), excoriated areas are identified. Scabies is transmitted by person-to-person contact or through infested bedding and clothes. It spreads on the skin by fingernail contamination (Youngkin & Davis, 2003).

Molluscum Contagiosum (Seed Wart)

The lesions of molluscum contagiosum are caused by a pox virus. In adults, transmission is primarily sexual; in children, transmission is nonsexual and occurs via fomites. Infection with molluscum produces a firm, smooth, nontender, dome-shaped papule most commonly located on the lower abdomen, inner thigh, or external genital area. Removal of the central core with a needle is indicated when few lesions are present; multiple lesions may be treated with cryosurgery or electrosurgery (Youngkin & Davis, 2003).

Vulvar Warts

Vulvar warts are caused by certain strains of the human papillomavirus (HPV), different from those that produce cervical lesions. The warts can appear as small, thickened growths or large, cauliflower-like masses on the vulva, along the perineum or in and around the anus. These benign warts can be treated with chemicals, cryosurgery, or laser vaporization. None of these treatments is fully successful, and recurrence is common. Despite removal of the lesions, surrounding tissues continue to harbor HPV. Vulvar warts are not always attributable to sexual contact and can be passed by fomites (Youngkin & Davis, 2003). See Chapters 7 and 10 for further discussion about HPV.

Other Vulvar Diseases

Vulvar disease may also be related to one of the following conditions:

1. **Systemic diseases:** Diseases such as Crohn's disease can cause vulvar symptoms.

2. **Premalignant and malignant lesions:** Vulvar intraepithelial neoplasia is a cancer precursor that is commonly associated with HPV. Women who have a history of genital warts and who smoke have an increased risk of developing vulvar cancer (ACS, 2006). Invasive vulvar cancer, responsible for 5% of all malignancies in women, is the presence of a malignant lesion that breaks through the basement membrane. It occurs most often in older women (ages 60 to 70 years). The most common symptom is persistent itching; the woman may also experience localized burning and pain. Biopsy is needed for diagnosis (Lowdermilk & Perry, 2007; Youngkin & Davis, 2003).

3. **Paget's disease and melanomas:** Paget's disease is a rare neoplasm that is commonly confused with a yeast infection. It occurs more commonly in elderly women, who complain of intense vulvar itching and soreness, usually of long duration. Lesions are red, moist, and elevated. Melanomas appear as bluish black, pigmented or papillary lesions. Melanomas metastasize via the bloodstream and lymphatic system. Diagnosis is made on the basis of biopsy results (Lowdermilk & Perry, 2007; Youngkin & Davis, 2003).

Health Promotion

Nurses can teach women these health-promotion measures to maintain a healthy vulvar environment and decrease the chance of irritation and infection:

- Wear cotton underwear.

- Keep the vulvar area clean and dry.

- Avoid:
  - use of perfumed or colored toilet paper
  - douches.

- Immediately discontinue the use of soaps and laundry detergents that cause an allergic reaction.

- Be aware that:
  - lubricants, spermicides, and barrier birth control methods can provoke allergic reactions
  - food allergies can also cause skin reactions.

- Perform monthly vulvar self-examination (VSE).

(Lowdermilk & Perry, 2007)

Vulvar Self-Examination

Because of the increase in precancerous and cancerous conditions of the vulva in recent years, teaching women about VSE constitutes an important component of their health care. VSE should be performed monthly by all women who are sexually active or are 18 years of age or older. When teaching about VSE, it is helpful to first provide the woman with a simple diagram of the normal anatomy of the vulva and then conduct the examination together, using a mirror. At home, the woman should hold the mirror in one hand and perform the examination in a sitting position. Using the other hand, she should expose the tissues surrounding the vaginal opening. Using her fingers, the woman should gently spread the labia and inspect the vaginal vault. The vaginal walls should be pink and contain small folds or ridges (rugae). Vaginal discharge should be evaluated at this time as well. Normal vaginal discharge is clear to cloudy and white, with a slightly acidic odor. The mons pubis, clitoris, urethra, labia majora, perineum, and perianal areas should also be carefully inspected. The vulva should then palpated, and the woman should be instructed to note and report any changes in appearance or abnormalities, such as ulcers, lumps, warts, or discoloration (Lowdermilk & Perry, 2007).

CONCLUSION

The most common disorders that affect a woman's reproductive system have been highlighted in this chapter. To provide appropriate, personalized care for women, it is important to teach them about the workings of their bodies and help them to discover and implement strategies to maintain and promote good health throughout life.

EXAM QUESTIONS

CHAPTER 11
Questions 85-88

Note: Choose the option that BEST answers each question.

85. Primary dysmenorrhea is related to

    a. prostaglandins.

    b. pregnancy.

    c. perimenopause.

    d. leiomyoma.

86. Patients with uncomplicated lower UTIs usually do *not* report

    a. tenderness above the pubic area.

    b. intense lower back pain.

    c. foul-smelling urine.

    d. urinary urgency and frequency.

87. Uterine thermal balloon ablation is a technique developed to

    a. open blocked fallopian tubes.

    b. treat infertility.

    c. treat excessive uterine bleeding.

    d. treat uterine cancer.

88. Strategies to promote and maintain a healthy vulvar environment include

    a. wearing synthetic underwear.

    b. douching once a week.

    c. using scented toilet paper.

    d. performing monthly vulvar self-exam.

CHAPTER 12

BREAST HEALTH AND DISEASE

CHAPTER OBJECTIVE

After completing this chapter, the reader will be able to describe strategies for promoting breast health.

LEARNING OBJECTIVES

After studying this chapter, the reader will be able to

1. indicate how to teach breast self-examination to women.

2. specify techniques for diagnosing abnormalities of the breast.

3. identify risk factors for breast cancer.

4. describe treatments for breast cancer.

5. recognize diet and lifestyle factors that may decrease breast cancer risk.

KEY WORDS

- Adjuvant
- Fine needle aspiration
- In situ
- Metastasis
- Microcalcifications
- Node negative
- Node positive
- Open biopsy
- Staging

INTRODUCTION

Breast cancer is the most common cancer in women, except for skin cancers, and is the second leading cause of cancer deaths in women (American Cancer Society [ACS], 2007; Smith, E.C., 2007). In 2008, an estimated 182,460 new cases of breast cancer will be diagnosed in the United States (ACS, 2008). The chance of a woman developing invasive breast cancer at some time in a woman's life is about 1 in 8 (12%). Women who live in North America have the highest rate of breast cancer in the world. Presently, there are about 2.5 million breast cancer survivors in this country. Carcinoma in situ is noninvasive and the earliest form of breast cancer. The ACS estimates that more than 62,000 new cases of breast carcinoma in situ will be diagnosed in 2008 (ACS, 2008).

Breast cancer incidence rates increased rapidly in the 1980s, although the rate of increase slowed in the 1990s. In the years from 2000 to 2004, the incidence rates decreased slightly. The chance that a woman will die from breast cancer is about 1 in 35, or 3%. In the year 2008, approximately 40,480 women will die from breast cancer in this country. Death rates from breast cancer have been declining since 1990, with larger decreases in women under 50 years of age. These decreases are believed to be the result of earlier detection through screening and increased awareness, as well as improved methods of treatment (ACS, 2008).

The medical community's approach to breast cancer centers on early detection. It is now widely accepted that breast cancer is not a singular disease. Instead, malignancies of the breast stem from many types of disease, all with distinct histological, biological, and immunological characteristics. It is believed that a multitude of dietary, socioeconomic, and environmental factors may serve as causative or contributing influences in the development of breast cancer. By their very nature, these diverse factors are difficult to isolate and study in human populations; thus, causation is difficult to ascertain. Many of these issues are discussed in more detail later in this chapter.

In response to the likelihood that multiple factors play a role in the development of breast cancer, many health care providers have adopted a holistic approach to care that hinges on health promotion. This strategy involves individualized patient education and counseling concerning diet, lifestyle habits, and environmental exposure – all aspects of health over which individuals have control. Furthermore, the general health benefits of such changes have been proven in terms of improved quality of life. Prevention strategies such as these, when combined with early detection, are clearly the best approach.

NORMAL BREAST ANATOMY

In most women, breast tissue feels somewhat lumpy. Adipose tissue, located just beneath the skin, overlies tissue that is fibrous and glandular. The fatty tissue is thicker in some areas and thinner in others, and there is often a distinct ridge of tissue under the breast. The underlying fibroglandular tissue has ridges and indentations as well (Dillon, 2007).

The breasts are composed of milk-secreting glands and ducts and fatty, connective, and lymphatic tissue. Lobules are the glands that produce milk. Ducts are the small passages that connect the milk-producing lobules to the nipple. When nurses teach women about breast self-examination (BSE), they should show pictures of breast tissue and discuss the normal irregular contours of breasts. Use of breast models is also helpful; these teaching aides often diminish women's fears about checking their breasts (Dillon, 2007; Lowdermilk & Perry 2007).

BREAST SELF-EXAMINATION

Before teaching BSE, the nurse should ascertain the following information from the patient:

- what she knows about BSE
- whether she performs BSE on a regular basis
- which BSE technique she uses
- how she feels about routinely checking her breasts

BSE can be an emotionally charged issue, and women sometimes feel embarrassed confessing that they have not been regularly performing their breast examinations. Nurses can do much to allay women's fears and make BSE a more life-positive, empowering experience. The following tips may facilitate the BSE discussion:

- Try to put the woman at ease.
- Be nonjudgmental and compassionate.
- Remind the woman that the purpose of BSE is to become intimately familiar with her breasts so that she can detect changes.

Obviously, women are not expected to diagnose cancer. But routine BSE help them perfect BSE technique and familiarize them with the contours and tissue characteristics unique to their own breasts. Then, if they detect changes that are worrisome or that persist, they can schedule an evaluation (Smith, E.C., 2007). Nurses can be instrumental in facilitating women's awareness of and comfort with detecting changes in their breasts (Ruhl, 2007).

Components

According to the latest BSE guidelines from the ACS (2007), BSE should include two components: visual inspection and palpation (see Figure 12-1):

1. *Visual inspection:* Visual inspection involves observing for indentations, puckering, or dimpling of the skin (not for lumps protruding from the skin, which would be a very advanced sign). Changes to be alert for during the visual inspection occur subtly, such as minor skin retraction or pulling of the nipple to one side. Breasts that are different sizes are usually not of concern unless the size variation represents a new development.

The visual examination should be performed with the woman facing a mirror, first with arms raised overhead. Then arm, hand, and body movements should progress – and visual examination should take place at each position

---

FIGURE 12-1: HOW TO PERFORM A BREAST SELF-EXAM

- Lie down and place your right arm behind your head. The exam should be done while lying down, not standing up. This is because when lying down the breast tissue spreads evenly over the chest wall and is as thin as possible, making it much easier to feel all the breast tissue.

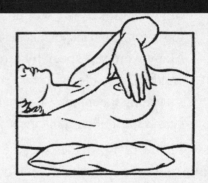

- Use the finger pads of the three middle fingers on your left hand to feel for lumps in the right breast. Use overlapping dime-sized circular motions of the finger pads to feel the breast tissue.

- Use three different levels of pressure to feel all the breast tissue. Light pressure is needed to feel the tissue closest to the skin; medium pressure to feel a little deeper; and firm pressure to feel the tissue closest to the chest and ribs. A firm ridge in the lower curve of each breast is normal. If you're not sure how hard to press, talk with your doctor or nurse. Use each pressure level to feel the breast tissue before moving on to the next spot.

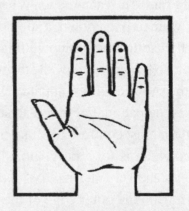

- Move around the breast in an up-and-down pattern, starting at an imaginary line drawn straight down your side from the underarm and moving across the breast to the middle of the chest bone (sternum or breastbone). Be sure to check the entire breast area, going down until you feel only ribs and up to the neck or collarbone (clavicle).

- There is some evidence to suggest that the up-and-down pattern (sometimes called the *vertical pattern*) is the most effective pattern for covering the entire breast without missing any breast tissue.

- Repeat the exam on your left breast, using the finger pads of the right hand.

- While standing in front of a mirror with your hands pressing firmly down on your hips, look at your breasts for any changes of size, shape, contour, and dimpling or redness or scaliness of the nipple or breast skin. (The pressing down on the hips position contracts the chest wall muscles and enhances any breast changes.)

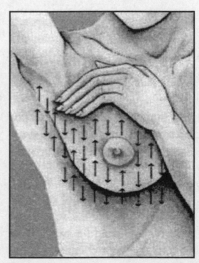

- Examine each underarm while sitting up or standing and with your arm only slightly raised so you can easily feel in this area. Raising your arm straight up tightens the tissue in this area and makes it difficult to examine.

Note. From How to Perform a Breast Self-Exam. Used with the permission of the American Cancer Society, Inc. from www.cancer.org. All rights reserved.

change – to hands squeezing the hips; then body leaning forward; and, finally, arms relaxed at the sides. The nipples should be assessed for symmetry, discharge, and discoloration. The skin should be observed for changes in color and texture.

2. *Palpation:* The entire breast must be palpated, in a section defined by the axillary area, which contains lymph nodes, to the brassiere line and breastbone; and, finally, up to the collarbone. Nipples should be palpated for internal thickening or lumps as the woman simultaneously looks for signs of spontaneous nipple discharge. Many women, especially those who have had children, are able to express some discharge by squeezing the nipples. Discharge that is of concern is most often spontaneous (ACS, 2007).

Figure 12-1 provides specific instructions with illustrations for teaching how to perform a breast self exam. The examination is best conducted with the woman lying down, a supine position is especially useful for women with large breasts. BSE can also be performed while the woman is standing in the shower. Different patterns may be used for breast palpation. Each woman should identify the pattern most comfortable for her. Two commonly used patterns for breast palpation are concentric circles and vertical strips. With concentric circles, start from the outer edge of the breast and spiral inward to the nipple. With vertical strips, begin at the top of the breast, palpate downward and then upward, gradually working over the entire breast. Regardless of the specific technique adopted, it is important to proceed systematically and to include all areas noted (ACS, 2007; Littleton & Engebretson, 2002).

Because menstruating women often have increased discomfort and lumpiness in their breasts during the second half of the menstrual cycle, the ideal time to perform BSE is the week after menstruation. More than 75% of breast cancers are found by women themselves. BSE is a simple yet powerful self-help behavior that can save lives. This procedure for performing BSE is different than previous recommendations. The changes represent an extensive review of the medical literature and input from an expert medical advisory group (ACS, 2007). It should be noted that, according to the latest (2007) statement from the U.S. Preventive Services Task Force (USPSTF), insufficient evidence was found to recommend for or against teaching or performing routine BSE (www.ahrq.gov/clinic/3rduspstf/breastcancer/).

BREAST DISEASE

At some point during their lives, approximately 50% of adult women will experience a breast problem. Many types of breast tumors have been described; fortunately, most are benign.

Benign conditions of the breast are common and include cysts, tumors, masses, nipple discharge, infection, and inflammation of the ducts. Although not cancerous, these conditions may nevertheless have significant effects on women and their families. It is important for health care providers to be sensitive to women's emotional responses to matters concerning breast health, offering supportive, individualized care. Teaching women about early detection and treatment is an essential component of health care for all women. The following discussion describes some of the more commonly encountered benign breast conditions.

Cysts

It is not unusual for a woman to say that she has "cystic breasts." However, she may have mistaken normal breast irregularities for cysts. In many cases, the presence of cysts has never been confirmed by biopsy, mammography, or sonography. There are a number of different types of breast cysts, each with certain defining characteristics:

- **Fluid-filled cysts (fibrocystic changes):** Fluid-filled cysts are often tender and fluctuate in size with the menstrual cycle. Fibrocystic changes are the most common benign breast condition and occur most often in women of childbearing age. They are believed to be exacerbated by caffeine intake.

- **Fibroadenomas:** Fibroadenomas are solid cysts. They are composed of fibrous and glandular tissue, often movable, and usually nontender. Fibroadenomas, the second most common benign breast condition, are usually found in the upper outer quadrant.

- **Lipomas:** Lipomas are fat tumors that are soft with discrete borders. They are mobile and nontender.

- **Intraductal papillomas:** Intraductal papillomas are small, wartlike growths that can occur in the lining of milk ducts near the nipple. They usually produce a clear or bloody discharge from the nipple. Intraductal papillomas are rare.

- **Mammary duct ectasia:** Mammary duct ectasia is an inflammation of the ducts that lie behind the nipple. This condition occurs most often in perimenopausal women and is accompanied by a nipple discharge that is thick, sticky, and green, purple, brown, or white in color.

(Lowdermilk & Perry, 2007)

It is rare for a fluid-filled cyst to be cancerous. It is not known what causes benign breast disease, although an imbalance of estrogen and progesterone may be responsible. The presence of cysts does not necessarily increase a woman's risk for breast cancer. Approximately 70% of fibrocystic changes are *nonproliferative lesions;* 26% are *proliferative lesions* without benign growing cells (atypia), and the remainder are *proliferative lesions with atypical hyperplasia.* The risk of breast cancer is increased when atypical hyperplasia is present. Therapeutic interventions involve differentiating between fibrocystic changes and breast cancer. Screening methods include clinical breast examination (CBE), mammography, and ultrasonography. Contents of

fluid-filled cysts are aspirated and evaluated to determine if malignant cells are present. Although aspiration may eliminate the cysts, they often reform (Lowdermilk & Perry, 2007).

Mastitis

Mastitis is an infection of the breast that occurs when bacteria enter the mammary ducts through a nipple. Bacteria are introduced most often during breast-feeding. Localized pockets of infection appear as tender, warm lumps. Axillary lymph nodes are frequently enlarged and painful. Mastitis is usually treated with antibiotics and warm compresses (Mass, 2004).

Trauma or Injury to the Breast

Trauma or injury to the breast may result in an accumulation of blood at the site (hematoma) or a destruction of the fatty tissue, which can appear as a lump. There is no evidence that injury causes cancer (Lowdermilk & Perry, 2007).

EVALUATION OF BREAST ABNORMALITIES

Over the years, screening methods, especially mammography, have become more precise, allowing for earlier diagnosis. Screening has accounted, in part, for the dramatic increase in the detection of breast cancer and most likely is responsible for the decrease in mortality rates as well (ACS, 2006).

If an area of abnormal breast tissue is found on CBE, unless there is a high index of suspicion, the woman is often asked to return for a second evaluation after her next menses. In many situations, she is also referred for mammography. An ultrasound examination may be performed at the time of mammography to determine whether the lump is solid or fluid-filled (Lowdermilk & Perry, 2007).

If the lump persists after the next menses or if any abnormality is identified on mammography or sonography, further testing is recommended. If the sonogram reveals that the lump is solid, a biopsy is the next step. If the lump is fluid-filled, a needle aspiration biopsy is performed and the woman is monitored on a routine basis for the development of other cysts. If a distinct, palpable lump persists despite normal findings on mammography, immediate follow-up is recommended (Lowdermilk & Perry, 2007).

Mammography, a screening tool, is not diagnostic. A biopsy is also needed to provide a tissue sample for analysis, so that a definitive diagnosis can be made. Although mammography represents the best detection method for early breast cancer, it often is unable to distinguish between benign and malignant tumors. An estimated 60% to 80% of recommended biopsies are for benign abnormalities (Lowdermilk & Perry 2007).

Breast magnetic resonance imaging (MRI) is now being used with increasing frequency to evaluate abnormal breast findings and to screen women at high risk for breast cancer. This modality is especially helpful for breast masses that are not visualized mamographically, for lobular cancers, and for patients at risk for bilateral disease. MRI of the breast has shown an overall sensitivity to breast cancer of 95% (Esserman, Lane, Ewing, & Hwang, 2005; Knutson & Steiner, 2007; Smith, 2007). Recent findings suggest that this diagnostic method can detect cancer in the contralateral breast that was missed by mammography in women with recently diagnosed breast cancer (Lehman et al., 2007; Pomeranz, 2007).

The ACS now recommends both MRI scans and mammograms once per year for women at high risk – those whose chance of developing breast cancer during their lifetimes is 20% or higher – beginning at age 30. Younger women frequently develop more aggressive cancers; they also have more dense breasts, making it harder to see cancer using x-ray mammography alone (Pomeranz, 2007).

Biopsy

In most situations, diagnosis and treatment of breast abnormalities is a two-step procedure: a biopsy is obtained and then decisions are made regarding the treatment based on the biopsy findings. Palpation alone cannot determine whether an abnormal area is cancer. Neither the CBE nor available technology can provide definitive proof that a tissue or structure is cancerous. It can only be said that no evidence of cancer is found. Confirmation of cancer can be made only by examining the suspicious tissue (Smith, E.C., 2007).

Several different biopsy procedures may be used to obtain a sample of breast tissue or fluid within that tissue for evaluation.

Fine Needle Aspiration

The technique of fine needle aspiration (FNA) involves use of a thin needle guided into the suspicious area while the practitioner palpates the lump (see Figure 12-2). FNA is usually performed as an office procedure. If the abnormality is too small to feel, ultrasound or a stereotactic biopsy can be used to help locate and ensure an adequate sampling of the suspect tissue. In the latter technique, the biopsy is conducted with the aid of mammography. The needle is guided to the area by computer-assisted X-ray, which can help the examiner precisely control the needle placement. Suction is applied to the needle. This procedure is used to ascertain whether the lump is a fluid-filled cyst or a solid tumor (Smith, E.C., 2007).

If fluid is aspirated, the FNA procedure may eliminate the lump altogether and provide a preliminary diagnosis. Further testing may be done on the fluid if it is dark in color, if the fluid-filled cyst has recurred several times, or if the sample has been obtained from a postmenopausal woman, who would not be expected to have breast cysts due to low estrogen levels. Clear fluid usually indicates a benign cyst; cloudy or bloody fluid may be present in benign or cancerous tumors (Smith, E.C., 2007).

FIGURE 12-2: DIAGNOSIS

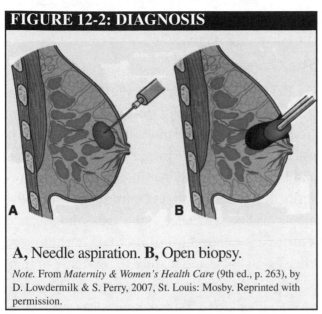

A, Needle aspiration. **B,** Open biopsy.

Note. From *Maternity & Women's Health Care* (9th ed., p. 263), by D. Lowdermilk & S. Perry, 2007, St. Louis: Mosby. Reprinted with permission.

If no fluid is aspirated or if a residual thickened area remains after fluid is aspirated, the next step is a core needle biopsy. The false-positive rate for FNA is almost zero. False-negative results occur more frequently, however, because the needle may have missed the abnormal tissue. If no abnormalities are found with aspiration, a follow-up mammogram or ultrasound is recommended in 2 to 4 months to check for recurrence of the cyst (Smith, E.C., 2007).

Core Needle Biopsy

In core needle biopsy, a large bore needle is used to remove a small cylinder of tissue. The needle placement is often guided as with the FNA procedure. Core needle biopsy can be done as an office procedure with the use of local anesthesia. Although it may be painful, it usually causes little or no scarring. In addition to identifying invasive cancers, core biopsy tissue samples can provide prognostic biomarkers to help direct the course of treatment (Smith, E.C., 2007).

Surgical (Open) Biopsy

Removal of all or a portion of the lump for microscopic analysis may be required. In this case, a number of decisions must be made concerning the amount of tissue needed because the aim is to obtain surgical margins that are free from possibly cancerous tissue. Because these excisions leave a

scar and can disfigure the breast, the incision is made near the areola of the nipple if possible. The surgical, or open, biopsy is considered the most accurate biopsy technique for large masses or large areas of suspicion (Smith, E.C., 2007).

Skin Punch Biopsy

A punch biopsy may be used to confirm a diagnosis of inflammatory breast cancer or Paget's disease of the nipple (Marcus, 2004).

Tests for Estrogen and Progesterone Receptors

Normal breast tissue contains hormone receptors that respond to the stimulatory effects of estrogen and progesterone. A majority of breast cancers retain estrogen receptors, and for these particular tumors, estrogen retains proliferative control over the malignant cells. Thus, an important component in the evaluation of a woman with early breast cancer is to test for the presence of hormone receptors. The estrogen and progesterone receptors are proteins present in the cell cytoplasm and on the surface of some of the breast cancer cells. When the receptors are present, they bind to estrogen or progesterone, and the binding promotes growth of the cancer cells. A malignant tumor in the breast can have estrogen or progesterone receptors or both types. Knowing the patient's hormone receptor status (through biologic testing of the tumor) provides valuable information concerning her predicted response to hormone manipulation therapy. Tumors that lack hormone receptors will not respond to hormonal therapy. Postmenopausal women tend to be estrogen receptor positive; premenopausal women tend to be estrogen receptor negative (Lowdermilk & Perry, 2007; McReady, 2003).

Breast Symptoms

Nipple Discharge

Any spontaneous nipple discharge should be evaluated. Although in most cases discharge from the nipple is physiologic, a small percentage of women who experience this symptom are diagnosed with a serious endocrine disorder or malignancy. There are a number of different causes for nipple discharge (Lowdermilk & Perry, 2007).

Galactorrhea is characterized by a bilaterally spontaneous milky, sticky discharge. While galactorrhea occurs normally during pregnancy, it can also occur in response to increased levels of the hormone prolactin. Elevated prolactin levels may result from a thyroid disorder, pituitary tumor, chest wall surgery, or trauma. In some women, oral contraceptives and certain neuroleptic drugs can also cause galactorrhea. In addition to obtaining a serum prolactin level, other diagnostic tests to assist in the evaluation may include microscopic analysis of the discharge, a thyroid profile, a pregnancy test, and a mammogram (Leung & Pacaud, 2004; Lowdermilk & Perry, 2007).

Nipple discharge can also be caused by an *intraductal papilloma,* which characteristically produces serous or bloody discharge from only one breast. Intraductal papilloma is a rare, benign condition that develops in the terminal nipple ducts; the cause is unknown. *Breast infections* typically are associated with a purulent nipple discharge. Occasionally, *breast cancer* produces a spontaneous unilateral discharge that is bloody, serous, or watery. The bloody discharge associated with breast cancer ranges from bright red to black and the serous discharge is thin, sticky, and yellow to light orange (Lowdermilk & Perry, 2007; Smith, E.C., 2007).

False discharge refers to fluid that appears on the nipple or areolar area but is not secreted by breast tissue. The discharge may be bloody, clear, colored, purulent, serous, or viscous. Conditions that may be associated with false nipple discharge include dermatologic diseases such as eczema and dermatitis as well as nipple trauma and Paget's disease. *Paget's disease* is an inflammatory, malignant neoplasm that originates in the nipple, usually occurs with invasive ductal carcinoma, and can cause bleeding, oozing, and crusting of the nipple (Lowdermilk & Perry, 2007).

Skin Changes

Erythema, or reddening of the skin, may be related to benign or malignant conditions. In young women, infection is the most common cause and is usually associated with increased tissue tenderness and localized warmth. Antibiotic therapy is prescribed. Reddening that occurs at the end of the nipple may be associated with Paget's disease, and a biopsy is needed for diagnosis. A change in breast skin color and texture to resemble orange peel (peau d'orange) is consistent with *inflammatory carcinoma* and warrants immediate evaluation. Other significant findings associated with inflammatory breast cancer include the presence of pink, purplish, or bruised skin; pitting or ridging of the skin; and a nipple newly turning inward (Ruhl, 2007). *Mondor disease* of the breast is a rare, self-limiting condition characterized by thrombophlebitis of the superficial veins. Symptoms include skin redness, edema, and pain in the affected area. Although Mondor disease is usually benign, it may be associated with breast cancer and hypercoagulability (Marcovici, 2007).

Breast Pain

The most common type of breast pain occurs cyclically and is associated with the time period immediately before the onset of menses. Although the exact etiology is unknown, cyclical breast pain is believed to be related to hormone imbalances. Pain can occur in one or both breasts. An association between methylxanthines (a group of chemicals found in coffee, tea, colas, and chocolate) and premenstrual breast pain has been established. Vitamin E and herbal therapies, including bugleweed and evening primrose oil, may be helpful in alleviating this type of cyclic breast pain. Although exceptions do occur, in general, breast cancer is not associated with breast pain; however women with breast cancer may complain of a localized tightening or pulling sensation or a localized burning or itching (Lowdermilk & Perry, 2007).

Mammography

Screening mammography is beneficial for routine breast surveillance for the asymptomatic woman. Clinical detection through use of BSE generally does not occur until the tumor is approximately the size of a walnut. By the time a palpable mass or lump is detected, the tumor has been growing for quite a while. Routine screening mammograms provide a much earlier, high-sensitivity study of developing tumors at the lowest possible cost. Screening mammography also enables the radiologist to detect malignant-appearing calcifications (Lowdermilk & Perry, 2007; Smith, E.C., 2007).

The value of routine screening mammography for women age 50 and older has been well established. In recent times, mammography screening recommendations for women ages 40 to 49 years have met with controversy. Analysis of the major studies of women in this age-group has shown a marginal benefit in decreasing the death rate from breast cancer. However:

- Some of the older studies may be flawed because mammography was much cruder 25 to 30 years ago.

- Breast cancer in women ages 40 to 49 years occurs with less frequency.

- Mammography in premenopausal women has not been as accurate due to the density of breast tissue of women in this age-group. Mammograms may miss as many as 25% of invasive cancers in women ages 40 to 49, compared with 10% in women ages 50 years and older.

- Certain tumors, even when detected early, are not curable. In general, younger women tend to have faster-growing tumors than do older women. Possible explanations include higher levels of estrogens in the blood and tissues of premenopausal women that can stimulate tumor growth or a genetic predisposition that becomes

expressed in this age group (Lowdermilk & Perry, 2007; Smith, E.C., 2007).

In 2002, the USPSTF issued a recommendation that women undergo screening mammography every 1 to 2 years beginning at age 40. Guidelines from the American College of Obstetricians and Gynecologists (ACOG), American Medical Association, and American Academy of Family Physicians are similar, with annual mammography recommended after age 50 (Smith, E.C., 2007). Presently, the ACS recommends that women ages 40 and older receive yearly mammograms in addition to CBEs, and they should continue to perform BSE monthly (ACS, 2006).

Because mammography is considered a less useful screening and diagnostic tool in women younger than age 40, care providers must make the decision to use mammography in this patient population on an individual basis. Compared with film mammography, full-field digital mammography has been demonstrated to be more accurate, especially for women younger than age 50, those with dense breast tissue, and those who are premenopausal or perimenopausal (Pisano et al., 2005; Smith, E.C., 2007).

Educating Women About Mammography

Although most women have heard about mammography, many fail to obtain the screening exam despite their care providers' recommendations. Often, women express fear of mammogram findings and concern about pain believed to be associated with the procedure. Other barriers to breast cancer screening include older age, expense, ignorance, lack of motivation, lack of availability of mammography services, and lack of physician referral (Lowdermilk & Perry, 2007; Yarbrough, 2004). Women with disabilities often face additional barriers, including access to transportation and accessible parking (Mele, Archer, & Pusch, 2005).

With education and individualized counseling, health care professionals can do much to allay their patients' concerns. Women can be informed that the mammography procedure involves the taking of radiographic pictures of the bare breasts while they are compressed between two plastic plates. Many facilities now use a soft pad to cushion the breasts during compression. The procedure takes approximately 10 minutes, and most women find the test to be uncomfortable but not painful. Scheduling the mammogram at a time during the menstrual cycle when the breasts are less tender is one strategy to minimize discomfort for pre-menopausal women. Acetaminophen, ibuprofen, or aspirin may provide relief for tenderness associated with breast compression.

Women should be advised to avoid or remove powder and deodorant prior to the test because these substances can create shadows on the X-rays. Women can be assisted to choose a mammography facility that is accredited by the American College of Radiology and ascertain that the machines used are designed specifically for mammography, that the mammogram is performed by a registered technologist, and that the radiologist is trained to read mammography (Youngkin & Davis, 2003).

Cultural factors may play a role in women's decisions to become involved in breast cancer screening. It has been shown that Hispanic and African-American women are more likely to participate in CBE and mammography screening when these procedures are offered in a mobile van in their neighborhood. Among Chinese women, a perceived lack of confidence in performing BSE may influence their likelihood to practice BSE regularly (Lowdermilk & Perry, 2007).

Factors that increase women's compliance with mammography guidelines have been explored. Reminders such as postcards and direct health care provider referrals can be influential determinants of women's likelihood to seek breast screening activities. Other factors that have been shown to be associated with positive results include adequate insurance coverage and cancer screening interven-

tions provided by trained lay workers (Lowdermilk & Perry 2007).

Mammography, Ultrasonography, and Magnetic Resonance Imaging

Calcifications, which are calcium deposits within the breast tissue, may be detected on mammography. There are two types of calcifications: macrocalcifications and microcalcifications. *Macrocalcifications* are usually degenerative changes within the breast tissue that result from old injuries, inflammations, or aging of the breast arteries and are usually not related to malignancy. They occur in approximately one half of women in the U.S. who are over 50 and usually do not require a biopsy.

Microcalcifications are specks of calcium that may be found in areas of rapidly dividing cells. The residue left by the rapidly dividing cells may appear as microcalcifications. When many micro-calcifications are present in a cluster, they may indicate a small cancer; approximately one half of the cancers detected appear as these clusters.

A limitation to mammography concerns the inability to differentiate between solid and cystic masses. Ultrasound, a diagnostic tool that is most effective for differentiating between solid and cystic masses, may also be used to guide a small needle into the mass for aspiration of its contents.

MRI is most effective for identifying tissue with increased blood flow, such as tumors. However, the expense, limited specificity, and false-positive results are limitations associated with this imaging modality (Aliotta & Schaeffer, 2006; Kuhl et al., 2005; Smith, E.C., 2007).

Radiation Risks Associated with Mammography

The radiation exposure associated with mammography has been greatly reduced in the past 25 years as more rigorous criteria have been established. As previously discussed, women should ensure that the facility they use for screening has been fully accredited by the American College of Radiology. A call to a state or local chapter of the ACS or the NCI can provide them with accurate information about accredited screening facilities in their area (Lowdermilk & Perry, 2007).

Although the dose of radiation received with mammography through an accredited facility is generally considered safe, it is important that health care providers remember that much remains unknown regarding the long-term effects of radiation exposure from mammograms. In general, breast tissue in young women is more sensitive to radiation than is the tissue of postmenopausal women. Although radiation doses with mammography have been greatly reduced, the risks of radiation exposure are cumulative. In addition, no minimum dose has been proven to be safe.

Confounding the problem is the fact that many women have a history of radiation exposure from past injury or disease that must be taken into account. Radiation may also interact with hormones or other factors. In addition, a certain subset of women have a genetic sensitivity to radiation, and exposure can increase their risk more so than in the general population. There is no way to test for this genetic sensitivity. These concerns must all be weighed against the benefits afforded by early detection with mammography. Furthermore, there is no other part of the body in which radiation is recommended on a yearly basis for a large population of healthy individuals. If a woman begins yearly mammograms at age 40, by the time she is 80 years old, she will have had 40 mammograms. Many health care practitioners are concerned about the unknown risks of such prolonged exposure, and this is an area that warrants continued investigation (Lowdermilk & Perry, 2007; Youngkin & Davis, 2003).

Diagnostic Mammography

A diagnostic mammogram is performed when the patient reports specific symptoms or when suspicious clinical findings have been detected. Diagnostic mammography is also appropriate following the detection of an abnormality on a screening mammogram. Research has shown that, although screening mammography provides the best detection of early breast cancer, this tool cannot distinguish between benign and malignant tumors. Between 60% and 80% of recommended biopsies are for benign breast changes (ACS, 2006).

Digital Mammography

Full-field digital mammography is a newer technology for breast cancer screening. This specialized method of mammography records the radiographic image in a digital format that can be stored in a computer. It uses digital code to distinguish a range of subtle differences in tissue density. As with X-ray, digital mammography takes advantage of the fact that tissues of different densities absorb different amounts of radiation. Traditional X-ray films show only gross variations; digital imaging provides more resolution. In addition, these images can be transmitted easily between computers, enabling consultation over long distances. Problems associated with this technique include an inability to adequately compare previous breast X-rays with the digital images and the higher costs associated with this technology.

Other Tools for Breast Cancer Detection

The Oncor INFORM HER-2/neu gene detection system is used to detect the HER-2/neu gene in human breast tissue. This test measures the number of HER-2/neu genes per cell. It is believed that this gene prompts the production of a protein that helps cancer cells reproduce. Amplification of this oncogene occurs in about 20% to 30% of breast cancers. The test can be used to predict breast cancer recurrence as well as to determine the types of treatments that would be most effective. Further information about this test is available at http://www.centerwatch.com/patient/drugs/dru385.html.

BREAST CANCER

The possibility of breast cancer evokes fear in most women. All women have one or more risk factors for breast cancer. Interestingly, most risks occur at such a low level that they do not explain the high frequency of this disease among women.

Statistics

The following statistics provide a foundation for understanding the pervasiveness of breast cancer in women's lives and American culture:

- Every 3 minutes, a woman in the United States is diagnosed with breast cancer.

- Breast cancer is the second leading cause of cancer death in women, exceeded only by lung cancer. It is the leading cause of cancer death among women ages 40 to 55.

- In 2006, estimates were that
  - 212,920 new cases of invasive breast cancer and 61,890 cases of noninvasive breast cancer would be diagnosed among American women.
  - 40,970 women in the United States would die of breast cancer.

- Most breast cancers occur in women older than age 50; women over age 60 are at the highest risk.

- Young women ages 20 to 29 account for 0.3% of breast cancer cases.

- One in eight women will develop invasive breast cancer in her lifetime.

(ACS, 2007; Breastcancer.org, 2008)

The last statistic in the preceding list is somewhat misleading. Women of different ages have different risks of breast cancer. Risk increases with age until menopause; it then increases more slowly with advancing years.

Risk Factors

Known risk factors for breast cancer can be divided into four broad categories: factors related to demographics, history, or lifestyle and those classified as uncertain, controversial, or associated with unproven effects on the actual risk. Risk factors are cumulative – the more risk factors present, the greater the likelihood of developing breast cancer (ACS, 2006; Lowdermilk & Perry, 2007; Smith, E.C., 2007).

1. *Demographics and history*

   - *Age.* Advancing age is the single most important risk factor. Each woman's risk of breast cancer increases as her age increases. About one out of eight invasive breast cancer diagnoses are among women younger than age 45; about two out of three women with invasive breast cancer are age 55 or older when they are diagnosed (ACS, 2007; Lowdermilk & Perry, 2007; Smith, E.C., 2007).

   - *Gender.* Breast cancer is more prevalent in women than in men. Although men do get breast cancer, the disease is about 100 times more common among women than men. Male breast cancer accounts for only 0.7% of all breast cancer diagnoses (ACS, 2007; Smith, E.C., 2007).

   - *Race.* Caucasian women are slightly more likely to develop breast cancer than are African-American women. However, African-American women are more likely to die of breast cancer and to be diagnosed with higher grade tumors that have a poorer prognosis. This may be due, in part, to the fact that they are less likely to receive adequate screening mammography, but also because higher grade tumors may occur more often in African-American women, even in those who are screened regularly (Smith-Bindman et al., 2006). Asian, Hispanic, and Native-American women have a lower risk of developing and dying of breast cancer (ACS, 2007).

   - *Personal history.* Women who currently have

or have been previously diagnosed with cancer in one breast have three to four times the risk of developing new cancer in the same or other breast than do their counterparts who have never had breast cancer (ACS, 2007).

- *Family history.* A history of breast cancer in the family, especially a mother or sister, increases risk; this is particularly significant if the cancer occurred prior to menopause. However, 70% to 80% of women who get breast cancer do not have a family history of this disease (ACS, 2007). Other family risk factors include a combination of breast and ovarian cancer among first- and second-degree relatives, a first- or second-degree relative with breast and ovarian cancer, and a combination of two or more first- or second-degree relatives with ovarian cancer. Also, breast cancer in a male relative increases risk (Ruhl, 2007; USPSTF, 2005b).

- *Previous breast biopsy results* showing benign proliferative breast disease. Nonproliferative lesions such as cysts and simple fibroadenomas do not increase breast cancer risk (ACS, 2007).

- *Breast tissue density.* Dense breast tissue increases breast cancer risk four to six times if such tissue makes up 75% or more of the breast; it is also more difficult to assess by mammography (Boyd et al., 2007).

- *Menstrual periods.* Women who started menstruating at an early age (before age 12) or who went through menopause at a late age (after age 55) have a slightly higher risk of breast cancer. This is believed to be due to the higher lifetime exposure to estrogen and progesterone (ACS, 2007).

- *Chest radiation.* Women who as children or young adults had radiation to the chest area as treatment for another cancer, such as Hodgkin's disease, are at significantly increased risk. Previous radiation to the chest wall can increase breast cancer risk up to 12 times, depending on the age of the patient at the time of the radiation, with a higher risk for those receiving radiation during puberty (ACS, 2007).

- *Diethylstilbestrol (DES) exposure.* Women who were exposed in utero to DES have a slightly increased risk of developing breast cancer (ACS, 2007).

2. *Lifestyle*

- *Alcohol.* Alcohol use increases risk, especially for women who drink more than one alcoholic beverage per day. For those who have two to five drinks daily, the risk is increased one and a half times, compared with the risk of a nondrinker (ACS, 2007).

- *Postmenopausal hormonal therapy (PHT).* Long-term use (several years or more) of combined (e.g., estrogen and progesterone) PHT increases the risk of breast cancer and may also increase the chances of dying of breast cancer. However, the increased risk from combined PHT appears to apply only to current and recent users. A woman's breast cancer risk seems to return to that of the general population within 5 years of stopping combined PHT (ACS, 2007). The risk increase with estrogen-only use is unclear (NCI, 2006).

- *Overweight and obesity.* Being overweight or obese increases breast cancer risk, especially for women after menopause and especially if the extra weight has been gained in adulthood and is accumulated at the waist (ACS, 2007). Because ovarian hormone production declines after menopause, adipose tissue serves as the primary source of estrogen for postmenopausal women. Postmenopausal weight loss lowers circulating estrogen levels, and because these hormones are directly related to the risk of breast cancer, it is believed that weight loss may decrease the risk (Eliassen, Colditz, Rosner, 2006; Hellwig, Willett, & Hankinson, 2007a; Theroux, 2007).

- *Physical activity.* Although the exact amount of physical activity needed is unknown, regular exercise appears to reduce breast cancer risk. The ACS recommends that women engage in 45 to 60 minutes of intentional physical activity five or more days a week (ACS, 2007).

- *Not having children or having them later in life.* Women who have had no children or who had their first child after age 30 have a slightly higher breast cancer risk. Having multiple pregnancies and becoming pregnant at an early age reduces breast cancer risk (ACS, 2007).

- *Breast-feeding.* Breast-feeding may slightly lower breast cancer risk, especially if it is continued for 1.5 to 2 years (ACS, 2007).

3. ***Factors with uncertain, controversial, or an unproven effect on breast cancer risk***

- *High-fat diets.* Studies of fat in the diet have not clearly shown this to be a breast cancer risk factor. However, because a high-fat diet does influence the risk of developing several other types of cancer, the ACS (2007) recommends eating a healthy diet with an emphasis on plant sources.

- *Antiperspirants.* Despite rumors that chemicals in underarm antiperspirants are absorbed through the skin, interfere with lymph circulation, cause toxins to build up in the breast, and eventually lead to breast cancer, there is little laboratory or population-based evidence to support this theory (ACS, 2007).

- *Bras.* Despite rumors that bras cause breast cancer by obstructing lymph flow, there is

no good scientific or clinical basis for this claim (ACS, 2007).

- *Environmental pollution.* Current research is exploring various environmental influences, such as compounds with estrogen-like properties, on breast cancer risk. Presently, research does not show a clear link between breast cancer risk and exposure to environmental pollutants such as the pesticide DDE (chemically related to DDT) and polychlorinated biphenyls (ACS, 2007).

- *Breast implants.* Studies have shown that breast implants do not increase breast cancer risk. However, the formation of scar tissue associated with silicone breast implants can make it more difficult to see breast tissue on standard mammograms (ACS, 2007).

- *Tobacco smoke.* Most studies have found no link between cigarette smoking and breast cancer. The evidence regarding secondhand smoke and breast cancer risk is controversial (ACS, 2007).

- *Night work.* Several studies have suggested that women who work at night (i.e., nurses on a night shift) may have an increased risk of developing breast cancer. Some researchers believe the effect may be due to a disruption in the hormone melatonin (ACS, 2007).

Most known risk factors for breast cancer are generally not under a woman's control. However, it is important to note that the great majority (70% to 80%) of women who develop breast cancer have none of the known risk factors. This fact supports the theory that health promotion measures, which have been shown to be generally preventive for other cancers, can decrease women's risk for breast cancer as well (ACS, 2007; Smith, E.C., 2007).

Genetic Risk Factors: BRCA1, BRCA2, and others

Most breast cancers are not related to genetic factors. Approximately 5% to 10% of breast cancer cases are believed to be hereditary and result from gene changes (mutations) inherited from a parent. The identification of BRCA1 and BRCA2 has clearly demonstrated the role of heredity and genetic mutations in this disease (ACS, 2007; Lessick, 2007).

BRCA1 and BRCA2 genes are the most common inherited mutations. Under normal circumstances, these genes help to prevent cancer by making proteins that prevent cells from growing abnormally. However, individuals who have inherited a mutated copy of either gene from a parent are at increased risk for breast cancer (ACS, 2007).

Women with an inherited BRCA1 or BRCA2 mutation have up to an 80% chance of developing breast cancer during their lifetimes. When breast cancer occurs, it is often at a younger age than in women who are not born with one of the gene mutations. Women with inherited BRCA1 and BRCA2 mutations also have an increased risk of developing ovarian cancer. Although BRCA mutations are found most often in Jewish women of Ashkenazi (Eastern Europe) origin, they also occur in African-American women and Hispanic women and can occur in any racial or ethnic group (ACS, 2007). BRC1 and BRCA2 mutations may also be associated with a risk of other cancers, including pancreatic cancer, colon cancer, and prostate cancer (for male carriers), but to a smaller degree than breast and ovarian cancer risk (Thull & Vogel, 2004).

Other genes have also been discovered that may lead to inherited breast cancers. However, these genes do not impart the same level of breast cancer risk as the BRCA genes, and they are not frequent causes of familial breast cancer. These genes include ATM, CHEK2, p53, and PTEN (ACS, 2007):

- **ATM:** This gene normally helps to repair damaged deoxyribonucleic acid (DNA). Certain families with a high rate of breast cancer have been found to have mutations of this gene (ACS, 2007).

- **CHEK2:** This gene increases breast cancer risk about twofold when it is mutated. In women who carry the CHEK2 mutation and have a strong family history of breast cancer, the risk is greatly increased (ACS, 2007).

- **p53:** Inherited mutations of the p53 tumor suppressor gene can also increase the risk of developing breast cancer as well as other cancers, including leukemia, brain tumors, and sarcomas (cancer of the bones and connective tissue) (ACS, 2007).

- **PTEN:** This gene normally helps to regulate cell growth. Inherited mutations in this gene cause Cowden syndrom, a rare disorder in which affected individuals are at increased risk for both benign and malignant breast tumors as well as growths in the digestive tract, thyroid, uterus, and ovaries (ACS, 2007).

The American Society of Clinical Oncology has identified factors that place a woman at high risk for genetically transmitted breast cancer. These include a family with more than two breast cancer cases and one or more ovarian cancer cases diagnosed at any age; a family with more than three breast cancer cases diagnosed before 50 years of age; and sister pairs that have been diagnosed before age 50 with two breast cancers, or two ovarian cancers, or a breast and ovarian cancer (Lowdermilk & Perry, 2007; Sakorafas, 2003).

Determining Personal Risk

Information about one's personal breast cancer risk can be confusing and women may overestimate or underestimate their risk. The NCI has developed an interactive computer-based tool, The Breast Cancer Risk Assessment Tool, to assist women and health care professionals in calculating risk. The tool can predict a woman's risk of breast cancer in 5 years and over the lifetime (to age 90 years). The risk factors used include present age, number of first-degree relatives affected, age at menarche, age at first live birth, the number of breast biopsies, and a history of abnormal hyperplasia in breast biopsy specimens. The tool is available at the website www.cancer.gov/bcrisktool (Lowdermilk & Perry, 2007).

Another resource for women is the *Strength in Knowing: The Facts and Fiction of Breast Cancer Risk* educational campaign designed to help women separate the facts from fiction regarding breast health. This resource is available on the Internet at www.strength inknowing.com (Newell, 2007).

Breast Cancer Types

Many different kinds of breast cancer can arise in the various tissue types of the breast. It is beyond the scope of this course to discuss these variations in detail. The majority of breast cancers represent a type of adenocarcinoma, a cancer of the glandular tissue. Four subtypes account for most breast cancers. Each is briefly reviewed here.

Ductal Carcinoma In Situ and Lobular Carcinoma In Situ

Ductal carcinoma in situ (DCIS) is a noninvasive cancer of the milk ducts that has not spread through the walls of the ducts into the fatty tissue or lymph nodes. This type of cancer can rarely be detected by clinical examination. Instead, it is usually identified by a finding of microcalcifications on mammography. Nearly 100% of women diagnosed at this early stage can be cured (Smith, E.C., 2007).

Sometimes called *lobular neoplasia,* lobular carcinoma in situ (LCIS) is a rare lesion characterized by a disorderly proliferation of epithelial cells confined to the terminal ductal-lobular units of breast tissue. Diagnosis is most often made on core needle biopsy triggered by an abnormal mammogram. Because the presence of LCIS confers an elevated lifetime risk of breast cancer, patients are offered chemoprophylaxis with tamoxifen (Nolvadex) (Macdonald & Arias, 2007).

Invasive or Infiltrating Ductal Carcinoma

Invasive or infiltrating ductal carcinoma (IDC) breaks through the duct wall and invades the surrounding fatty tissue, where it can also metastasize to other parts of the body by way of the lymphatic or circulatory systems (see Figure 12-3). IDC is the most common breast malignancy; 85% to 90% of invasive carcinomas originate in the milk ducts. Women with this type of tumor usually present with a discrete, solid breast mass (Smith, E.C., 2007).

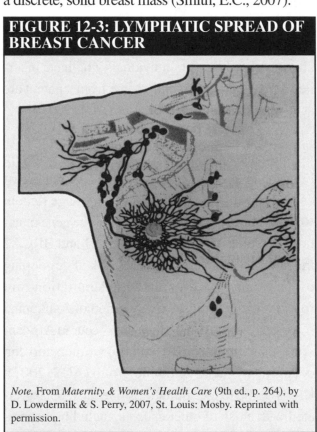

FIGURE 12-3: LYMPHATIC SPREAD OF BREAST CANCER

Note. From *Maternity & Women's Health Care* (9th ed., p. 264), by D. Lowdermilk & S. Perry, 2007, St. Louis: Mosby. Reprinted with permission.

Infiltrating (Invasive) Lobular Carcinoma

Infiltrating, or invasive, lobular carcinoma (ILC) arises in the lobules (milk-producing glands). It has spread into the fatty tissue and can metastasize. ILC accounts for 10% of all breast cancers. Women with ILC are more likely than those with other cancers to have bilateral disease. This cancer type is difficult to detect by examination or mammography; breast MRI is often helpful in the diagnosis of ILC (Cocquyt & Van Belle, 2005; Capobianco et al., 2007; Smith, E.C., 2007).

Inflammatory Breast Cancer

Only 1% to 6% of all breast cancers are of the inflammatory type. Inflammatory breast cancer (IBC) is usually aggressive and metastasizes rapidly. It often makes the skin over the breast appear inflamed, red, warm, thickened, and resembling an orange peel (peau d'orange) (Smith, E.C., 2007).

Indicators Associated with Disease Prognosis

Many variables are associated with the likelihood of breast cancer recurrence. Identifying these factors is helpful in determining the best course of treatment for each woman. Most women who have negative lymph nodes (approximately 60% of women diagnosed with breast cancer today) are cured by surgery alone. Approximately 30% develop recurrent disease within 10 years of the initial treatment (ACS, 2007). In addition to identifying hormone receptor status and histological tumor type, information concerning the status of the axillary lymph nodes and tumor size is useful in determining the disease prognosis.

Axillary Nodes

It has long been recognized that tumor involvement of the axillary nodes is an important indicator for breast cancer prognosis. Clinical assessment of the axillary nodes is associated with a 30% false-positive and false-negative rate. Thus, pathological staging of the patient's lymph nodes is essential. Seventy percent of women with negative nodes survive 10 years following their breast cancer treatment. The disease prognosis worsens as the number of positive lymph nodes increases. Recurrence of breast cancer is seen in approximately 75% of women who have many positive nodes (Smith, E.C., 2007).

Sentinel node biopsy, a technique that targets selected lymph nodes during biopsy, is used in many diagnostic settings. During the procedure, a radioactive tracer is injected into the region of the tumor. The dye travels via the lymphatic system to a lymph node. This node, called the *sentinel node,* is the first node that receives lymphatic drainage from the tumor. If no cancer is found in this node, the patient is able to avoid more extensive lymph node surgery and its accompanying side effects, such as lymphedema (swelling of the arm) (ACS, 2007).

Tumor Size

There is a definite relationship between the size of the tumor and the risk of recurrence. Before the widespread use of mammography, fewer than 8% of women with node-negative breast cancer had tumors that were less than 1 cm in diameter, which has a relative 5-year survival of nearly 99%. Women whose tumors measure 1 to 3 cm have a relative 5-year survival of approximately 91%, whereas those with tumors measuring more than 3 cm have a 5-year survival of 85%. However, the recurrence rates for patients with tumors greater than 3 cm is more than 50% (Smith, E.C., 2007).

Staging

The American Joint Committee on Cancer (2002) uses the TNM classification system to categorize breast cancer:

*   T = size of the largest primary tumor
*   N = lymph node involvement
*   M = the presence of distant metastasis.

Treatment decisions are based largely on staging (Singletary et al., 2002). The cancer is further staged according to the following system:

Stage 0: DCIS. This is the earliest stage of diagnosis. Cancer cells are in the milk duct but have not escaped into surrounding tissue. Cure for this stage is nearly 100%. Mammograms can detect cancer at this early stage. With the increased use of mammograms, this diagnosis is becoming more common.

Stage I: The tumor measures 2 cm (about 0.75 inch) in diameter or less and there is no nodal involvement or distant metastasis.

Stage II: Tumor measures between 2 cm and 5 cm or with ipsilateral movable axillary node involvement and no distant metastasis.

Stage III (A): The tumor is larger than 5 cm (greater than 2 inches) in diameter or involves multiple lymph nodes that are fixed or matted together; distant metastasis is not identified at this stage.

Stage III (B): Includes IBC and cancer that has spread to the skin or chest wall or that involves internal mammary lymph nodes.

Stage IV: Metastases have occurred to distant organs.

Cancer staging has a strong correlation with survivorship. Women with stage 0 breast cancer have a 5-year survival rate of 98%, compared with 26.7% among those with stage IV breast cancer (NCI, 2007).

Treatment

Much progress has been made in the treatment of breast cancer since the days of the Halstead radical mastectomy, which was the standard of care for many years. Currently, breast-conserving surgical procedures (which involve removal of the malignant tissue and a clear margin of normal tissue) are frequently performed. Surgery may also involve removal of lymph nodes, with a goal of preserving as much of the breast as possible. Some form of adjuvant therapy is usually recommended, depending on the individual case.

Surgical strategies include excisional biopsy/lumpectomy, incisional biopsy (rarely performed), and mastectomy. The option of mastectomy depends on many factors, such as tumor size in relation to the breast size, the extent of lymph node involvement, and other factors that must be considered on an individual basis. An encouraging note in the treatment equation is that the earliest forms of breast cancer are almost 100% curable.

It is beyond the scope of this course to discuss in detail the treatment options for each stage of breast cancer. Combinations of surgery followed by radiation, chemotherapy, or hormone therapy, are advised, depending on the stage of the cancer and its characteristics.

It was once believed that metastases could be controlled by extensive surgery at the primary site of cancer. Today it is generally accepted that cells may break away from the primary tumor and begin to spread through the bloodstream even in the early stages of the disease. The stray cancerous cells cannot be detected by any of the diagnostic tools available, and they cause no symptoms. The goal of adjuvant therapy is to use systemic therapy to kill such hidden cells that may have gained access to other parts of the body. Not everyone needs systemic therapy, especially if the cancer was detected at an early stage and is considered to be a slow-growing or localized type (ACS, 2007; Lowdermilk & Perry, 2007; Smith, E.C., 2007).

Adjuvant Treatment Options

Several adjuvant treatment options are currently available for women with breast cancer, including chemotherapy, radiation therapy, and hormone therapy.

Chemotherapy

When administered before surgery, chemotherapy is referred to as *neoadjuvant therapy;* when administered after surgery, chemotherapy is referred to as *adjuvant chemotherapy.* Combinations of drugs have been shown to be more effective than single drugs. Standard protocols are ever changing. Present chemotherapy regimens include the following medications given in combination or as sequential single agents: cyclophosphamide (Cytoxan), methotrexate (Mexate), fluorouracil (5-FU), doxorubicin (Adriamycin), paclitaxel (Taxol), docetaxel (Taxotere), capecitabine (Xeloda), vinorelbine (Navelbine), mitomycin (Mutamycin), and vinblastine (Velban). Chemotherapy is usually administered in an ambulatory setting once or twice per month. New medications are highly effective in reducing nausea and vomiting, symptoms traditionally associated with chemotherapy. Other side effects include change in appetite, loss of hair, mouth or vaginal sores, suppression of the immune system that leads to increased chance of infection, anemia, fatigue, menstrual cycle changes, and infertility. With the exception of infertility, most of the side effects are temporary (Lowdermilk & Perry, 2007; Smith, E.C., 2007).

Trastuzumab (Herceptin), a monoclonal antibody, is used with chemotherapeutic agents to treat women with HER2-positive breast cancer. Monoclonal antibodies are large protein molecules that recognize and bind to certain antigens on the surfaces of tumor cell walls or in the blood. Once attached, monoclonal antibodies attack the HER2 protein or direct the body's natural killer cells and macrophages to destroy the tumor cells. Other medications used for patients with advanced, metastatic breast cancer that is HER2-positive include lapatinib (Tykerb) used in combination with capecitabine (Xeloda). These agents are indicated for women who have received prior therapy with other cancer drugs, including trastuzumab. Unlike monoclonal antibodies, lapatinib is a small molecule that is able to enter the cell and blocks the function of the HER2 protein and other proteins inside of the cells (Smith, E.C., 2007).

Radiation Therapy

Radiation uses X-rays to kill cancerous cells locally around the affected area. It may be used preoperatively or postoperatively to reduce the size of the tumor, but it is usually an adjuvant treatment option following lumpectomy or mastectomy. Treatments are usually given daily for 5 to 6 weeks. Palliative radiation therapy can be used to relieve symptoms associated with bone or brain metastasis. Common side effects of this therapy include fatigue, heaviness or swelling in the breast, and reddening like sunburn of the affected skin (Smith, E.C., 2007).

Hormonal Therapy

Hormonal therapy is usually prescribed after chemotherapy has been completed. Women with estrogen or progesterone receptor–positive breast cancers may be treated with hormone-blockers such as tamoxifen (Nolvadex), which is an antiestrogen. Tamoxifen attaches to the hormone receptors on the cancer cells, preventing natural hormones from attaching to them. Once tamoxifen fits into the receptors, the cell is unable to grow. The use of hormonal therapy for 5 years in premenopausal women with breast cancer significantly reduces recurrence and mortality rates (Kwan, Geller, & Chlebowski, 2007; Lowdermilk & Perry, 2007; Smith, E.C., 2007).

Other hormonal agents that have been used to treat metastatic breast cancer include aromatase inhibitors such as anastozole (Arimidex), letrozole (Femara), and exemestane (Aromasin). Aromatase inhibitors suppress estrogen synthesis in postmenopausal women by inhibiting the peripheral conversion of androgens to estrogens. These agents are indicated in the treatment of hormonally sensitive breast cancer occurring in postmenopausal women or in oophorectomized premenopausal women. Side effects associated with these medications include vaginal dryness, bone pain, hot flashes, and headaches (Kwan et al., 2007; Smith & Dowsett, 2003).

Antiangiogenesis Agents

Angiogenesis is the formation of new blood vessels that supply tumors. The antiangiogenesis agents are a group of compounds that rely on the principle that halting a tumor's blood supply will stop its growth and proliferation. New antiangiogenesis drugs that may prove useful in the treatment of breast cancer are currently under development and investigation (ACS, 2007).

Resources for Information About Treatment Options and Patient Support

Two helpful Internet sources are available to provide patients with information about breast cancer treatment options. The National Comprehensive Cancer Network (NCCN, www.nccn.org) and the ACS (www.cancer.org) offer specific, up-to-date recommendations on breast cancer treatments. These resources help women to learn about scientifically tested protocols for each stage of breast cancer (ACS, 2006). Women with metastatic breast cancer can communicate with those with a similar diagnosis by contacting the Metastatic Breast Cancer Information and Support Group (www.bcmets.org). My Cancer Place (www.mycancerplace.com) is a website similar to MySpace, where patients and their loved ones can connect and network with others online. The Reach to Recovery Program sponsored by the ACS (www.cancer.org) matches trained volunteers who have survived breast cancer with newly diagnosed patients (ACS, 2007).

Follow-Up Care After Treatment

Because breast cancer can recur several years after the initial treatment, meticulous follow-up care is essential. Guidelines from the NCCN (2008) suggest that women treated for invasive breast cancer should undergo a history and CBE every 4 to 6 months for 5 years. After 5 years, a history, CBE and mammography should be performed annually, with the exception of patients who have received breast conservation therapy. These women should have their first posttreatment mammogram 6 months after radiation treatment has been completed. Women who are at risk for bilateral disease (e.g., those with BRCA1 and BRCA2 mutations) should be considered candidates for dedicated breast MRI (NCCN, 2008; Smith, E.C., 2007).

Following treatment for DCIS, the women should undergo a CBE every 6 months for 5 years, then annually; mammography should also be performed annually. The routine use of tumor mark-

ers, computed tomography (CT), MRI, ultrasonography, and positron emission tomography (PET) is not recommended unless the patient is symptomatic (NCCN, 2008; Smith, E.C., 2007).

Metastatic disease can occur long after the initial treatment has been completed. The most common sites of breast cancer metastasis are the bones, lungs, brain, and liver. Health care providers should routinely inquire about the presence of bone or abdominal pain, weight loss, persistent fatigue, neurologic symptoms, headaches, and cough during each assessment (NCCN, 2008). Nearly one-third of breast cancer survivors experience unexplained fatigue that can persist for years following completion of treatment. Although the etiology of persistent fatigue is uncertain, researchers have theorized that immune changes created by the cancer therapy may persist after the treatment and cause long-term inflammatory activity (Collado-Hidalgo, Bower, Ganz, Coe, & Irwin, 2006; Guthrie, 2006). If distant metastasis is suspected, the diagnostic workup may include liver tests, tumor marker levels, chest imaging, abdominal CT or MRI, or PET (NCCN, 2008; Smith, E.C., 2007).

Complementary Therapies

Many believe that holistic medicine has much to offer as a healing strategy in assisting the body, mind, and spirit throughout the process of breast cancer treatment. The immune system can be supported and enhanced naturally through dietary and safe herbal remedies, along with practices that reduce stress and help restore balance to the body. These techniques include visualization, meditation, journal writing, Qi-Gong, and tai chi (oriental movement exercises). Acupuncture, Chinese medicine, and homeopathy may be beneficial in relieving unpleasant symptoms and in supporting the body and spirit during its healing process (Lowdermilk & Perry, 2007).

BREAST RECONSTRUCTION AFTER MASTECTOMY

The decision to have, or not to have, breast reconstruction is a very personal one, shaped by many influences and emotions. Breast reconstruction usually involves additional surgery and pain as well as other dangers associated with major surgical procedures. Breast reconstruction also offers the potential benefit of much less alteration in appearance and body image.

There are several different procedures; all are intended to achieve symmetry and preserve body image. More than one surgery is usually required. Surgical reconstruction can be done at the time of the mastectomy or at a later date. It has been shown that immediate reconstruction during mastectomy does not change survival rates or interfere with therapy or the later treatment of recurrent disease (Osuch, 2002).

Many emotional and lifestyle factors make the decision for reconstruction one that must be considered thoroughly and carefully by each woman. Talking with other women who have experienced breast cancer surgery and reconstruction can be very beneficial. There are a number of organizations to help women identify and contact other women who have been through a similar experience. The nurse can assist women in locating local support groups and other breast cancer resources.

Psychosocial Aspects of Breast Disease and Cancer

Only someone who has experienced breast cancer can truly understand the full impact associated with the diagnosis. At every stage of the process, from the first discovery of a lump during BSE or during a routine physical examination, a woman's life is forever changed. All of her resources are important as she works her way through the diagnostic process, the necessary decision-making concerning treatment and possible breast reconstruction, the surgery and adjuvant therapies, and the future with its uncertainties. Women who are confronted with breast cancer often must find a depth in themselves that they may have never reached before. With this discovery can come a well of strength and self-acceptance.

Nurses can be a tremendous source of support and advocacy for women who are diagnosed with breast cancer. Women should be encouraged to take the time they need to come to clarity about their decisions. They should also be encouraged to seek other opinions or other providers if they do not feel comfortable with recommendations. There are a number of excellent books available, written by women who have shared similar experiences. Many organizations exist nationwide that serve as clearinghouses for information and contact sources for individuals as well as groups. The Internet also serves as a rich source of information.

BREAST CANCER PREVENTION

Ongoing research concerning the role of various modifiable lifestyle factors in the development of breast cancer provides direction for preventive measures for this disease. Women's health care providers must remain up-to-date on the latest information so that they can share accurate information and teach their patients strategies to promote breast health and, hopefully, to lessen their risk of breast cancer.

Suggested Areas to Address

Estrogen and the Hormone Equation

Breast cancer occurs when there are genetic alterations in the DNA of the epithelial cells in the breast. Breast cancer most likely has multiple causes and may follow the classic model of tumor growth that has been defined for cancer in general. This model suggests that an initial genetic change or injury to the DNA at the cellular level occurs at some point in a woman's life. This alteration may occur years before the development of cancer, perhaps through an environmental exposure. At some point, factors that promote the growth of these damaged cells begin a slow process of tumor formation (Lowdermilk & Perry, 2007).

It is not known whether estrogen and other hormonally related growth factors play an indisputable role in breast cancer growth. The majority of breast cancers have estrogen receptors. Efforts at chemoprevention have been directed at changing the body's hormonal environment by decreasing circulating estrogens or by blocking their activity (Lowdermilk & Perry 2007; Smith, E.C., 2007).

Chemoprevention

The National Cancer Institute and other organizations continue to investigate the roles of tamoxifen (Nolvadex), raloxifene (Evista), and anastrazole (Arimidex) in the prevention of breast cancer (NCI, 2006). In postmenopausal women, raloxifene prevents osteoporosis without the possible increased cancer risks of estrogen therapy. This agent may be well-suited for women at high risk for both osteoporosis and breast cancer. Tamoxifen has already been demonstrated to reduce the recurrence of breast cancer in women with prior malignancies. Ongoing studies are attempting to pinpoint which women would gain the most benefits from the administration of these chemopreventive drugs (Lowdermilk & Perry, 2007; Sakorafas, 2003).

Diet

Studies investigating the possibility of a link between a high-fat diet and the development of breast cancer are ongoing. It is not known if a lower-fat diet, fruits, and vegetables can lower one's risk of breast cancer. However, cutting back on saturated and trans fats lowers the risk of heart disease, and eating more fruits and vegetables may lower the risk of heart disease, stroke, and other cancers (ACS, 2007).

CASE STUDY

*M*arlene is a 54-year-old postmenopausal Caucasian woman who underwent a lumpectomy 8 months ago followed by radiation therapy for early stage breast cancer. Marlene experienced no complications related to the surgery or radiation therapy and, according to her physicians, has an excellent chance for cure.

Today at the woman's health center, Marlene confides to the nurse that she feels "down." She states that she knows she has no reason to be depressed, but she just doesn't feel that her body "looks like it did before." Marlene has experienced a decrease in breast size in the affected breast, which is a complication of the surgery and radiation therapy, and this change in breast appearance is concerning her.

Questions

1. What is a priority nursing intervention for Marlene at this time?

2. What information should the nurse provide to Marlene?

3. What other actions should the nurse take?

Discussion

Using therapeutic communication, the nurse should provide ample opportunity for Marlene to express her feelings about her body image changes. This action both clarifies and validates Marlene's feelings. If time constraints prohibit a lengthy discussion during this visit, the nurse should reschedule a return visit within a few days.

The nurse can provide information about breast protheses and other cosmetic devices to assist in promoting and maintaining a positive body image.

If appropriate, Marlene should be encouraged to speak with her physician about the possibility of breast reconstruction surgery to provide additional resources for enhancement of her body image. Also, the nurse can refer Marlene to support groups that will allow her to verbalize her feelings and concerns with other women who have similar concerns.

CONCLUSION

Breast cancer, a problem worldwide, has reached epidemic proportions in both developed countries and developing nations. Nurses can encourage women to practice early detection by performing routine BSE, obtaining regular CBEs, and choosing judicious use of mammography and other diagnostic techniques. Patients can be educated to and supported as they make changes in dietary and exercise habits and lifestyle patterns that can have cancer-preventive effects. Nurses are in a unique position to provide informed, compassionate care for women who are diagnosed with breast cancer.

EXAM QUESTIONS

CHAPTER 12
Questions 89-94

Note: Choose the option that BEST answers each question.

89. When teaching BSE, proper technique includes

    a. avoiding the axillary areas.

    b. refraining from squeezing the nipples.

    c. using the finger pads to apply light, medium, and firm pressure.

    d. placing the arm adjacent to the breast being examined in a relaxed position alongside the thigh.

90. Ultrasound can reveal whether a breast lump is

    a. benign.

    b. malignant.

    c. fluid-filled or solid.

    d. potentially malignant.

91. Breast MRI is useful in screening

    a. patients at risk for bilateral disease.

    b. all women.

    c. postmenopausal women.

    d. women whose screening mammograms are satisfactory.

92. Known risk factors for breast cancer include

    a. pregnancy before the age of 20.

    b. age greater than 50.

    c. menopause before the age of 50.

    d. slender body type.

93. Treatment for breast cancer may include

    a. estrogens.

    b. lactation suppressants.

    c. monoclonal antibodies.

    d. oral contraceptives.

94. When counseling a patient about lifestyle practices to reduce cancer risk, the health professional should include

    a. adhering to a low-fiber, high-fat diet.

    b. consuming a diet rich in fruits and vegetables.

    c. engaging in physical activity every other week.

    d. consuming one to two glasses of wine each day.

CHAPTER 13

CELEBRATING MENOPAUSE AND THE LATER YEARS

"The most creative force in the world is the post-menopausal woman with zest."
—*Margaret Mead*

CHAPTER OBJECTIVE

After completing this chapter, the reader will be able to discuss the special health care needs of women as they enter the menopausal years and beyond.

LEARNING OBJECTIVES

After studying this chapter, the reader will be able to

1. identify the physiologic changes that occur during menopause.

2. identify self-care measures to promote health during menopause.

3. recognize risk factors for osteoporosis.

KEY WORDS

- Bone remodeling
- Climacteric
- Estrogen therapy (ET)
- Hormone replacement therapy (HRT)
- Kegel exercises
- Menopause
- Perimenopause
- Progesterone therapy (PT)
- Osteoporosis

INTRODUCTION

Today, menopause is an important issue in women's health, as growing numbers of women enter the perimenopausal and postmenopausal age-groups. This population of women is increasingly more educated and sophisticated than in the past, and they seek information to help them make informed choices to facilitate a healthy transition into the later years. In this country, women, on average, can expect to live to be 80 years old and spend close to one-third of their lives as postmenopausal women. With a healthy lifestyle, many women are living productive, enriched lives well into the ninth decade. Proper nutrition, exercise, and mental and social stimulation are critical to keeping the body and mind healthy and active into old age. Menopause marks a time to evaluate, take stock, and prepare for many, many healthy years ahead (Lowdermilk & Perry, 2007; Minkin & Wright, 2005).

Research about menopausal physiology continues to constitute a major investigative area in women's health care. Mounting evidence underscores the complex interplay between the female sex hormones and numerous body and brain functions. Some women's organizations and health care providers have expressed concern over the medicalization of menopause and the fear that this biological transitional event will come to be viewed as a disease process rather than as a natural part of aging. Women are wise to seek evidence-based, factual information about menopause and the natural aging process so that they can actively partner with their health care provider in the decision-making process. It is important for nurses to help demystify the process of menopause and provide education and counseling so that women can make fully informed choices (Lowdermilk & Perry, 2007).

THE CLIMACTERIC, MENOPAUSE, PERIMENOPAUSE, AND POSTMENOPAUSE

In the discussion about adolescence (Chapter 4), a natural process was described concerning how a young woman's body matures to achieve child-bearing potential. In a similar manner, menopause is also a natural process that occurs over a number of years and marks the completion of childbearing potential. The ovaries, depleted of most of their supply of oocytes, become progressively less sensitive to signals from the brain that stimulate the menstrual cycle and ovulation. Over time, the complex coordination and synchronization between the brain and the ovaries progressively diminishes (Cunningham et al., 2005).

As with adolescence, this natural process is not fully understood. The initiation of the peri-menopausal period varies among individuals and is somewhat influenced by genetics. For most women, the transition usually begins during the early to mid-forties. In American women, menstrual periods cease around the age of 50 years. By age 52 years, approximately 80% of women are no longer menstruating. It is known that several factors, such as disease, cigarette smoking, and surgical intervention, can influence the timing of menopause and produce an early or premature menopause (Speroff & Fritz, 2005).

Several terms describe various time frames associated with the transitional period, and it is helpful to differentiate among them. The *climacteric* is a phase characterized by declining ovarian function and decreased hormone production. It begins at the onset of ovarian decline and ends during the postmenopausal period, when symptoms stop. *Menopause,* which refers to the last menstrual period, can only be dated with certainty 1 year after menstruation ceases. Thus, menopause is a single physiologic event that can only be quantified in retrospect. The transition to menopause is usually complete by age 55 (Speroff & Fritz, 2005).

Perimenopause is the period of time preceding menopause. Most women begin the perimenopausal transition at around age 46; 95% of women begin perimenopause between ages 39 and 51. Although perimenopause may be as few as 2 or as many as 10 years, on average, perimenopause lasts about 4 years. During this time of transition, levels of estrogen and progesterone increase and decrease at uneven intervals, causing the menstrual cycle to become longer, shorter, and eventually absent. Ovulation is sporadic. Symptoms of perimenopause, including irregular menses, hot flashes, vaginal dryness, dyspareunia, and mood changes are associated with the fluctuation and decline in hormone levels (Cunningham et al., 2005; Speroff & Fritz, 2005).

As this natural transition occurs, luteinizing hormone and follicle-stimulating hormone continue to be produced, but the ovaries become less responsive and decrease the production of estrogen and progesterone. These physiologic changes are responsible for the menstrual cycle irregularity that most women experience during this time. During *postmenopause,* the time after menopause, estrogen is produced solely by the adrenal glands (Cunningham et al., 2005; Speroff & Fritz, 2005).

The entire menopausal transition period produces changes at both the physiological and emotional levels. Hormone levels shift, readjust, and reach new balances, and the tissues and organs whose function is influenced by these hormones also change structurally and functionally. Changes take place at the mental and emotional levels as well. While some of the alterations are physiologic, others involve self-perception and self-concept as women deal with their menopausal passage into a new phase of life (Lowdermilk & Perry, 2007).

Cross-cultural studies have shown that the menopausal experience is very much influenced by the attitudes of the culture and community in which women reside. In this country, due in part to the graying of the baby-boomer generation, attitudes toward menopause and aging are beginning to change. For many traditional cultures throughout the world, menopause represents a time for women to assume leadership roles in the community and a time for honor and recognition as one of the tribal members with an accumulation of wisdom. American women are embracing this broad cultural perspective as an opportunity to shift self-perceptions and create a positive cultural image of women during this stage of life. In fact, the majority of North American women do not believe that menopause interferes with their quality of life (Lowdermilk & Perry, 2005; National Institutes of Health, 2005).

Although menopause is a natural, inevitable process, women do have control over how they pass through this period of life. They can use many strategies to ease uncomfortable symptoms and minimize their risk of chronic disease. Decreasing or stopping smoking, maintaining appropriate weight through exercise and diet, limiting alcohol intake, reducing stress, finding events to look forward to, and recognizing that happiness and long-term health come about through a number of personalized approaches are all valuable tools to help women enjoy maximal health during and beyond menopause. As a noted author explains, "the wise woman achieves menopause, it does not overcome her" (Weed, 2002). During this time in their lives, many women describe an enhanced sense of well-being, hard-won individuality, and a positive attitude toward life, reflective of what Margaret Mead termed "post-menopausal zest!" (Lowdermilk & Perry, 2007).

In 1900, the average age of menopause was 46 years and the average life expectancy was 51 years, although many women lived well beyond this age. In modern times, menopause does not mark the end of life, but rather a transition into another phase, with a potential life span of another 30 to 50 years. Because most women will spend one-third of their lifetimes after menopause, it is important that research continues to be focused on the natural process of aging, hormonal changes that accompany menopause, and the influences of diet and lifestyle on the aging process and the menopausal transition. Much can be learned by studying other cultures, whose levels of osteoporosis and heart disease are significantly lower than those in the American culture and whose women often transition through menopause with fewer uncomfortable symptoms (Lowdermilk & Perry, 2007).

SIGNS AND SYMPTOMS OF MENOPAUSE

Various signs and symptoms typically accompany the physical changes associated with the menopausal transition. Women can embrace a variety of natural and life-enhancing strategies to maintain and promote good mental and physical well-being.

Changes in the Menstrual Cycle

It is rare for a woman to simply stop menstruating. More commonly, menstrual periods become progressively irregular. The volume of blood flow varies as well and may be accompanied by midcycle spotting. Changes in bleeding patterns are largely due to a lack of ovulation. Absence of ovulation interrupts the production of progesterone, the hormone that stabilizes the endometrium, or uterine lining. Instead, the endometrium continues to proliferate due to the influence of estrogen, but in the absence of ovulation, no progesterone is produced. In this situation, the uterine lining is often sloughed off irregularly. Also, when ovulation does not occur, a longer-than-usual release of estrogen may result and cause overstimulation of endometrial growth. When bleeding does occur, it may be heavier or more prolonged. The endometrial lining may also grow with irregular or thickened areas and may not slough off completely or evenly; these events cause the menses to stop and start again (Speroff & Fritz, 2005).

Although irregular menses are usually a normal part of the perimenopausal process, any heavy bleeding should be investigated. Uterine fibroids, a frequent cause of increased bleeding, are common in women who are perimenopausal. Cervical or uterine cancer should also be considered as a possible cause of this symptom. If heavy bleeding is an ongoing problem and cancer has been ruled out, hormonal intervention in the form of low-dose oral contraceptives, progesterone alone, or another form of hormone replacement therapy (HRT) may be suggested. If fibroids are the cause of heavy bleeding, surgical intervention may be advised. It is important to remember that, although fertility declines during this transitional period, it does not disappear until menopause is complete. Menopause is signaled by the passage of 1 full year without menstruation. For most women, birth control remains an important consideration during the perimenopausal period (Alexander, 2007; Secor & Simon, 2006).

Shifts in Hormone Levels

During the perimenopausal period, hormone levels are frequently erratic, with highs and lows occurring without the usual synchronicity. A common hormonal pattern that occurs when ovulation becomes unpredictable is an elevated estrogen level throughout the cycle with low progesterone levels during the second half of the cycle, when progesterone is normally at its peak. Some women develop very low levels of estrogen as well. At this time,

ovarian function declines and the ovaries lose their ability to manufacture large amounts of sex hormones. The physiologic feedback loops between the ovaries, hypothalamus, and pituitary glands also lose their synchronized pattern. Progesterone undergoes the most dramatic drop during menopause because its production depends on ovulation and the development of the corpus luteum (Cunningham et al., 2005; Speroff & Fritz, 2005).

Small amounts of estrogen continue to be produced by the ovaries for up to 10 years following cessation of menses. The body has other means of estrogen production. The woman's fat cells convert androgens produced by the adrenal glands to estrogens. Androgens are female forms of male-type hormones that are produced by the ovaries and the adrenal glands. Androgens are responsible for the maintenance of muscle strength and sex drive. As estrogen and progesterone levels fall, the effects of androgens often become relatively more pronounced. For example, these hormones can produce an increase in facial hair often noticed after menopause. For some women, androgen levels (including testosterone) fall as well, producing symptoms of low libido or decreased muscle mass with a relative increase in the amount of fat tissue (Cunningham et al., 2005; Speroff & Fritz, 2005).

Changes in Skin and Hair

Diminished levels of estrogen affect many tissues. The skin and mucous membranes in various parts of the body become more dry. The fatty layer beneath the skin tends to shrink, and this change is associated with an overall decrease in elasticity and moisture. The skin feels rougher, and the outer skin may be looser than the deeper layers, which results in wrinkling. The skin produces less melanin, and it can burn more easily. The increasing predominance of androgens often causes a darker, thicker, more wiry hair to appear on the symphysis pubis, underarms, chest, lower abdomen, and back. Some women report the appearance of facial hair during this time.

The hair on the head may become drier, and pubic and axillary hair may thin (Speroff & Fritz, 2005).

Breast Changes

Glandular tissues in the breasts shrink during the process of menopause. In addition, the breasts may lose their fullness, flatten, and drop. Nipples may become smaller and flatter (Speroff & Fritz, 2005).

Vaginal Dryness

Vaginal changes may accompany perimenopause, or they may not occur until 5 to 10 years following menopause. The mucous membranes, previously supported by estrogen stimulation, become thinner, drier, and more fragile. The vagina loses its rough texture and dark pink coloration and instead becomes smooth and pale. The vagina also shortens and narrows. Women may complain of vaginal itching, burning, bleeding, spotting, or soreness. The vagina also lubricates more slowly, and less cervical mucus is produced. Due to these changes, intercourse may become painful. There is also an alteration in the normal vaginal flora, which results in a decrease in the normal protective mechanisms of the vagina. Some women experience an increase in urinary tract infections (UTIs) (Alexander, 2007; Cunningham et al., 2005; Speroff & Fritz, 2005).

Nurses can suggest several strategies to improve the symptoms associated with vaginal dryness:

- **Remain sexually active.** Sexual activity increases blood flow to the vagina, increases elasticity and lubrication of the vaginal tissues, and maintains muscle tone.

- **Experience orgasm.** It has been demonstrated that perimenopausal women who experience orgasm by any means three or more times a month are less likely to experience vaginal atrophy than those who have intercourse less than 10 times per year.

- **Consume phytoestrogen-containing foods and herbs.** Phytoestrogens are discussed later in this chapter.

- **Apply vitamin E topically to the vagina.**

- **Take vitamin E supplements orally.** Supplementation can have an estrogenic effect. Women who have hypertension should not supplement the diet with vitamin E.

- **Take vitamin C and bioflavonoids.** These substances increase estrogen levels.
(Lowdermilk & Perry, 2007)

If natural remedies and interventions do not alleviate the discomfort associated with vaginal dryness, various water-based lubricants, such as KY Jelly, KY Liquibeads, and Astroglide, may be applied during sexual activity. Vaseline and other petroleum-based products are not recommended because they increase the risk of infection. Replens is an over-the-counter vaginal moisturizer that is applied at regular intervals, independent of sexual activity (Alexander, 2007).

Almost all hormone therapy regimens help to decrease vaginal atrophy and associated symptoms. Estring, a hormonal vaginal ring, and Vagifem vaginal tablets are products that deliver very-low-dose estrogen (estradiol) directly to the vagina. Neither is systemically absorbed and both appear to be safe for women who have had breast cancer. Estrogen containing creams, such as Premarin, Estrace, and Ogen, are also available by prescription. The estrogen creams appear to have a higher absorption than the Estring and Vagifem products. Because systemic absorption of the hormones may occur with estrogen creams, the woman should be counseled about estrogen replacement therapy and careful dosage recommendations. Presently, U.S. Food and Drug Administration (FDA) guidelines recommend the use of a vaginal hormonal preparation for menopausal women whose only symptom is vaginal atrophy (Alexander, 2007).

Hot Flushes, Hot Flashes, and Night Sweats

One of the hallmarks of menopause is the occurrence of the vasomotor symptoms *hot flushes, hot flashes,* and *night sweats.* A hot flush is a visible red flush of skin and perspiration; a hot flash is a sudden warm sensation in the neck, head, and chest. Night sweats are characterized by profuse perspiration and heat radiating from the body during the night. The woman's sleep may be interrupted each night because her nightclothes and bed linens become soaked. Hot flashes constitute the most common symptom reported by women experiencing menopause and are present in 50% to 75% of women. They can occur often throughout the day and create anxiety and a significantly decreased quality of life (Lowdermilk & Perry, 2007). For some, hot flashes are only a problem for 1 to 2 years; others experience vasomotor symptoms that can last for up to 15 years. Approximately 10% to 15% of women characterize their hot flashes as debilitating. In many non-Westernized cultures, hot flashes either do not occur or are so minimal that they are barely noticed. In this country, hot flashes cause women to seek medical advice more than any other symptom of menopause (Alexander, 2007; Secor & Simon, 2006).

The cause of the alternating vasodilation and vasoconstriction associated with hot flashes is not well understood, but it is known that this symptom is related to hormonal changes that affect the temperature-regulating centers in the hypothalamus. Low levels of estrogen alone are not responsible. It is believed that the presence of estrogen, followed by its withdrawal, triggers an imbalance in the body's temperature control center, which subsequently decreases the core body temperature. The body then attempts to activate heat centers to readjust the body's thermostat (Alexander, 2007). Other problems that may be associated with vasomotor instability include dizziness, numbness or tingling in the fingers and toes, and headaches. Environmental and lifestyle factors – such as being in a crowded or warm room; consuming hot drinks, alcohol, or spicy foods; and stress – can precipitate or aggravate an episode of vasomotor symptoms (Lowdermilk & Perry, 2007).

The experience of a hot flash is very distinct. It may begin with a feeling of pressure in the head, followed by a warm feeling rising from the chest to the neck and face. The heat for some may be a very intense, hot, burning sensation. This sensation is followed by sweating that can be profuse. The frequency of hot flashes can vary from one to two per week to one to two per hour. The average length for each flush is 4 minutes. Also, hot flashes may be accompanied by palpitations, weakness, fatigue, faintness, or dizziness. Hot flashes and hot flushes can cause sleep disruptions, and exacerbation of symptoms such as mood swings, fatigue, lack of concentration, and memory loss. Changes in sleep patterns, common during menopause, are frequently related to vasomotor instability.

Other symptoms that can occur during the menopausal transition include joint pain, loss of libido, migraine headaches, dry mouth, and gastrointestinal disturbances (Lowdermilk & Perry, 2007).

COPING WITH MENOPAUSAL SYMPTOMS

Nonhormonal Therapies

Many women use nonhormonal treatments such as stress management, guided imagery, massage therapy, yoga, chiropractic care, acupuncture, and dietary supplements, to relieve menopausal symptoms. Other nonmedicinal interventions for the relief of mild vasomotor symptoms include engaging in regular exercise; consuming cool, refreshing foods such as cabbage, cucumbers, and pineapple; minimizing the intake of alcohol, fatty foods, sugar, and caffeine; and dressing in layers to keep cool. Nurses can also counsel women to drink 8 to 10 glasses of water each day and perform deep-breathing or paced-respiration exercises at the beginning of a hot flash to diminish its effects (Nachtigall et al., 2006; Nelson et al., 2006).

For women who experience debilitating vasomotor symptoms and wish to avoid traditional HRT, intervention with selective serotonin reuptake inhibitors (SSRIs) or other preparations may be appropriate. The following agents may be somewhat useful in relieving menopausal vasomotor symptoms:

- **SSRIs** (e.g., venlafaxine, paroxetine, sertraline): These antidepressants may reduce hot flashes. However, recent studies that compared the efficacy of venlafaxine with that of medroxyprogesterone acetate (MPA), a progestational agent, found that a single dose of MPA alleviated hot flashes more effectively than did daily use of the antidepressant (Alexander, 2007; Loprinzi et al., 2006).

- **Belladona alkaloid preparation** (a combination of phenobarbital, caffeine, and belladonna): This medication may be useful for certain women with sleep-related vasomotor symptoms. However, this agent is contraindicated with a number of other medications and may interact with many other substances, including acetaminophen, alcohol, antacids, certain antibiotics, digoxin, metronidazole, and warfarin (Alexander, 2007).

- **Clonidine** (Catapres): This antihypertensive medication acts at the central nervous system level to reduce or eliminate hot flashes.

(ACOG, 2007; Alexander, 2007)

Other women seek options that they perceive to be safer or more natural than hormonal and non-hormonal medications. These substances include food supplements that contain plant hormones such as phytoestrogens (sometimes called "dietary estrogens"), often found in herbal remedies for relief of menopausal symptoms. Phytoestrogens are a diverse group of naturally occurring nonsteroidal plant compounds that have a structural similarity with estradiol. Because herbal compounds contain-

ing phytoestrogens are not FDA-regulated, there is no proof of the efficacy, safety, or overall quality of the products. Until such information becomes available, these remedies should be considered to have the same issues as traditional hormone therapy (see later discussion) (Alexander, 2006, 2007; Lake, 2007; McKee & Warber, 2005).

Herbal Therapies for Menopausal Symptoms

Many women use herbal therapies to treat menopausal discomforts. Herbs may be ingested as teas or tinctures, and many herbal preparations are available in capsule form. Nurses must counsel women to become informed about any herbal preparations they are considering and to consult with their health care providers before using them. It is important to understand each substance's mechanisms of action, contraindications, and potential side effects. Herbs may be useful in resolving physical symptoms, as well as mood swings and depression. Internet sites such as the MedlinePlus Dietary Supplements Database (www. nlm.nih.gov/medlineplus/druginformation.html), ConsumerLab.com (www.consumerlab.com), and U.S. Pharmacopeia (www.usp.org) provide safety tips and information about dietary supplements (Lowdermilk & Perry, 2007).

Oriental herbal teas composed of licorice, ginseng, coptis, red raspberry leaf, and Chinese rhubarb may provide some relief from hot flashes. Dong quai and black cohosh have been used for various menopausal discomforts. Dong quai, the most commonly prescribed Chinese herbal medicine for "female problems," purportedly regulates and balances the menstrual cycle and is said to "strengthen the uterus." It is also purported to exert estrogenic activity. Black cohosh may be helpful in the short-term (less than 2 years) treatment of menopausal symptoms, including hot flashes, sleep disorders, anxiety, and depression. Both Dong quai and black cohosh have been investigated for effectiveness, with varying results. According to the National Center for Complementary and Alternative

Medicine (http://nccam.nih.gov), there is very little high-quality scientific evidence about the effectiveness and long-term safety of complementary and alternative medicine for menopausal symptoms. Black cohosh may be effective in reducing hot flashes; Dong quai was not found to be useful in reducing hot flashes and is not recommended (ACOG, 2001; Lowdermilk & Perry, 2007).

Phytoestrogens (isoflavones) interact with estrogen receptors in the body. Foods that contain phytoestrogens include wild yams, cashews, peanuts, almonds, dandelion greens, apples, cherries, alfalfa sprouts, sage, black beans, and soybeans (Lowdermilk & Perry, 2007). The use of soy-rich foods has also been investigated as an alternative to hormonal therapy for menopausal symptoms. According to the Natural Standard (n.d.) database, there is good evidence for the use of sage and soy for menopause symptom management. Although beneficial effects on reducing menopausal discomforts have been documented, more research is needed to investigate the potential effects of soy intake on preventing osteoporosis and reducing the risks of coronary heart disease (Albertazzi, 2005). For women who wish to add soy to their diets, good sources include tofu, roasted soy nuts, soynut butter, edamame, and calcium-fortified soy milk. Women should be counseled to add the soy-rich foods to their diets gradually to lessen the likelihood of gastrointestinal discomfort that may be related to the high fiber content of these foods. Vitamin E may be useful in relieving hot flushes and leg cramps. Vitamin E – rich foods include spinach, peanuts, wheat germ, and soybeans. This vitamin may also be taken as a supplement (Lowdermilk & Perry, 2007).

St. John's wort and valerian root have been used for mood disturbances during menopause. The flower *Hypericum perforatum,* known as St. John's wort, has been used for centuries to treat mild to moderate depression. Commercial preparations typically contain the generally recommended doses, and one capsule is taken three times a day. Side effects are similar to, but much less than, those associated with standard antidepressant medications and include dry mouth, dizziness, and constipation. Valerian root, the common valerian or garden heliotrope, has traditionally been used as a tranquilizer and soporific. Although it has no demonstrable toxicity, there have been reports of adverse reactions and visual disturbances. Little is known about the actions, effects, or potential interactions of valerian with other medications (ACOG, 2001).

Some practitioners have recommended chasteberry and ginseng for menopausal loss of libido. Chasteberry is also known as Vitex, chaste tree, monk's pepper, agnus castus, Indian spice, sage tree hemp, and tree wild pepper. It has been used to treat vaginal dryness at menopause and depression as well as to enhance libido in menopausal women. Ginseng (*Panax ginseng*) is promoted as an "adaptogen" that helps one cope with stress and boost immunity. Ginseng is also reputed to be an aphrodisiac, although this claim has not been substantiated by medical evidence (ACOG, 2001). According to the Natural Standard (n.d.) database, there is poor evidence to support the use of ginseng and chasteberry for the treatment of menopausal symptoms. However, there is good evidence for both sage and soy for menopause symptom management.

Hormonal Therapies

HRT is a controversial issue. A review of the historical background, recent research, and current guidelines for use of HRT can assist women and their health care providers in making appropriate decisions concerning this therapy. Although an in-depth discussion of HRT is beyond the scope of this course, the following review is intended to summarize the key issues.

Historical Perspective

The widespread prescription of estrogen began in the 1960s. It was touted as a wonder drug that allowed women to age more slowly. By 1975, conjugated equine estrogen, marketed under the name of Premarin, was one of the most often prescribed drugs in this country. Premarin is derived from the urine of pregnant mares. For many years, animal rights activists have promoted public awareness of cruelty to these animals and their offspring involved in the production of Premarin (National Women's Health Network, 2000).

In 1975, two studies were published that showed a two- to eight-fold increase in the rate of uterine cancer among nonhysterectomized women receiving estrogen replacement. The risk was linked to estrogen dosage and duration of treatment. In response to this finding, a number of women's organizations sought to heighten public awareness of the risks associated with estrogen use, claiming that women were not given adequate information to make informed choices. As this information became more widespread, use of estrogen in the United States declined. Later, studies were conducted to investigate combinations of estrogen and a progestin (synthetic form of progesterone). Results of these studies revealed that the estrogen-progestin combination protected against precancerous changes of the uterine lining. Based on these findings, a shift to the use of estrogen-progestin combinations occurred (National Women's Health Network, 2000).

By the late 1980s, results of several studies had shown that women who received estrogen were less likely to have heart attacks than those who did not receive estrogen. Although the FDA refused to grant approval to manufacturers for prescribing estrogen to healthy women as a heart disease preventive, many clinicians were recommending estrogen for this purpose. Without long-term data, the combination of estrogen along with a progestin began to be prescribed for this same purpose, even though the combination had not been in use long enough to evaluate its effect on heart disease. The Postmenopausal Estrogen/Progestin Interventions study was published in 1995. Its results showed that the most com-

monly used progestin, MPA (Provera), greatly interfered with the positive effect of estrogen alone on high-density lipoprotein (HDL) levels. Natural progesterone (i.e., oral micronized progesterone), also used in the study, did not negate the positive effects of estrogen on HDL levels (National Women's Health Network, 2000).

Recent Research

The Heart and Estrogen/Progestin Replacement Study (HERS), the Heart and Estrogen/Progestin Replacement Study Follow-up (HERS II), and the Nurses' Health Study were other major clinical trials designed to assess the relationship between HRT and coronary artery disease events among postmenopausal women. Although findings from the HERS II showed that HRT did not provide cardiac protection in women who had previously been diagnosed with heart disease, reanalysis of data indicated that certain women (e.g., women on statins, medications that lower cholesterol) experienced fewer problems associated with thromboembolic events (Alexander, 2007).

The Women's Health Initiative (WHI) was a primary prevention trial in healthy postmenopausal women. The purpose of this long-term clinical investigation and its multiple arms was to evaluate the safety and effectiveness of estrogen as well as an estrogen-progestin combination given to healthy women. The study involved 25,000 women and was intended to extend for a 9-year period. Participants were enrolled between 1993 and 1998, with a final analysis planned for 2005. The WHI was designed to assess the major benefits and risks of hormone replacement therapy with regard to coronary heart disease (CHD), venous thrombotic events, breast cancer, colon cancer, and fractures. Quality of life issues, such as a reduction in hot flashes and vaginal dryness, were not included (Secor & Simon, 2006).

In May 2002, after approximately 5 years of follow-up, the estrogen and progestin arm of the WHI trial was halted because the predetermined boundary for invasive breast cancer was exceeded. At this time, it was concluded that the risks outweighed the benefits for the indicators that were being studied. The risk of cardiovascular disease (CVD), CHD, stroke, and venous thromboembolism (VTE) was increased as well. There was a 37% and a 24% decrease in colorectal cancer and total fractures, respectively. Of importance, there was no difference in rates of mortality between the two groups (i.e., those who received HRT and those who did not). In 2004, the estrogen-only trial was also halted because the risk with the conjugated equine estrogen (Premarin) for stroke was elevated and the other endpoints were unlikely to change with continuation of the trial (Hsia et al., 2006; Secor & Simon, 2006).

Newer thoughts suggest that timing of HRT use has an effect. Follow-up analysis of WHI data has found that in the age 50 to 59 cohort, CHD was decreased. Based on this information, it is believed to be safest to begin HRT within 10 years of menopause. Another follow-up study of the WHI participants demonstrated that women ages 50 to 59 who were on estrogen therapy had less calcium in their coronary arteries (Alexander, 2007; Dranov, 2007; Secor & Simon, 2006).

Considerations of the WHI Research Findings

Many issues must be considered when assessing findings from the WHI and when counseling women about HRT. These include the following points:

- Quality of life issues, including hot flashes, vaginal dryness, and cognitive issues resulting from estrogen loss, were not studied.

- The HRT arm of the WHI trial was stopped because the rate of breast cancer crossed a predetermined boundary set at the initiation of the trial. However, breast cancer rates had not reached statistical significance when the trial was halted.

- The fact that a slight increase in invasive breast cancer was noted during the fourth year of the study, along with the trend toward a later decrease

in the total number of breast cancer cases, suggests that HRT promotes the growth of existing breast cancer rather than causes breast cancer. No increased risk in breast cancer was seen among women on estrogen therapy for an average of 7.1 years. Estrogen-progesterone therapy (EPT) and to a lesser extent, estrogen therapy (ET), increases breast cell proliferation, breast pain, and mammographic density. HRT may impede the diagnostic interpretation of mammograms.

- For the first time for any therapy, findings from the WHI study indicated that HRT reduces hip fractures and colon cancer.

(ACOG, 2007; Secor & Simon, 2006)

Translating WHI Findings Into Counseling Guidelines

When counseling women about HRT benefits and risks, it is helpful to consider a number of factors, such as cardiac protection, osteoporosis prevention, short- and long-term hormone use, and alternatives to HRT. The following brief summaries address these issues:

- **Cardiovascular protection:** Women who are taking or considering HRT only for the prevention of cardiovascular disease should be counseled about other strategies to lower their risks of heart disease. Postmenopausal women on ET or EPT are at increased risk for VTE. The risk appears during the first 1 to 2 years after starting therapy and then decreases over time. Both ET and EPT appear to increase the risk of ischemic stroke in postmenopausal women, but the absolute risk is lower among women ages 50 to 59 than in older women.

- **Osteoporosis prevention:** Women who are taking HRT only for the prevention of osteoporosis should be assessed for their personal osteoporosis risk and should be advised to consult with their health care providers about continuing with HRT for this purpose. There are many alternatives for the prevention of osteoporosis (i.e., bisphosphonates, calcitonin) that should be considered in women whose only need for HRT is in the prevention of osteoporosis.

- **Short-term relief of menopausal symptoms:** For women who seek short-term (1 to 4 years) relief of menopausal symptoms, the benefits of HRT most likely outweigh the risks.

- **Long-term relief of menopausal symptoms:** Although certain symptoms (e.g., hot flashes, night sweats) tend to be of short duration for most women, other menopausal symptoms (e.g., vaginal dryness) generally continue throughout the postmenopausal period. Also, many women believe that estrogen helps them to feel, think, and sleep better. These women may conclude that for them, the added benefits of fracture prevention and colon cancer reduction associated with HRT outweigh the risks. It is appropriate to discuss alternatives to HRT, such as the use of vaginal lubricants and strategies for relief from sleep disorders. However, the decision to continue with long-term HRT is one that must be made on an individual basis following consideration of each woman's benefits and risks, including those benefits and risks that were not addressed in the WHI.

- **Diabetes mellitus:** Large, randomized, controlled trials, including the WHI, have suggested that HRT reduces the incidence of diabetes among postmenopausal women. The reason for this benefit is unknown, although it may be related to lower weight gain or reduced insulin resistance among women using HRT. However, there is inadequate evidence to recommend HRT solely for diabetes prevention in perimenopausal women.

- **Use of other combination HRT:** It should be noted that because the WHI studied only one preparation of HRT, data generated from that study cannot be applied to all HRT therapies. It is advisable, however, that all women who are initiating or continuing HRT should carefully weigh the risks and benefits discussed above.

(ACOG, 2007; Alexander, 2007; National Osteoporosis Foundation [NOF], 2007; Dranov, 2007; Secor & Simon, 2006)

Risks of HRT in Certain Diseases

The risks with HRT and certain diseases, including endometrial cancer, breast cancer, and Alzheimer's disease, are described briefly below.

Endometrial Cancer

Estrogens do not cause endometrial cancer, as long as an appropriate dosage of progestogen (either as progestin or progesterone) is added to the hormonal regimen. Individual regimens and formulations differ and include both synthetic and natural formulations. Each route and type of progestogen carries different effects, risks, and benefits. Estrogen-progesterone combinations are available in oral and transdermal patch formulations. (See discussion below). It has been shown that women who use combined HRT are no more likely than those who have never used HRT to develop overgrowth of the endometrium (hyperplasia) or endometrial cancer (ACOG, 2007; LaCroix, 2005; Liu, 2007; Secor & Simon, 2006).

When a woman begins using HRT, spotting and unscheduled bleeding often occur as the body adapts to a new hormonal stimulation. It is appropriate to advise women that bleeding and spotting are most likely to occur in the first 3 months after initiation of therapy. Follow-up visits should be scheduled at 1 and 3 months, and improvement in symptoms should be noted at that time. Women should be counseled to report persistent bleeding, bleeding that stops but then starts again, or the presence of blood clots in vaginal discharge so that appropriate referrals can be made (Liu, 2007).

Breast Cancer

As discussed in the preceding section, the results from the WHI revealed an increased risk of invasive breast cancer among women using EPT. Analysis of available data suggests that:

- Estrogen should not be used to prevent breast cancer.

- The short-term use of estrogen-only preparations may not substantially increase breast cancer risk. However, these are general guidelines that do not necessarily apply to all menopausal women. Women with risk factors for breast cancer (i.e., family history, early puberty, late parity) should be individually assessed before initiating hormone therapy for the relief of moderate to severe vasomotor symptoms. (Alexander, 2007)

Depression and Cognitive Decline

Evidence that the risk of depression is higher in early menopause is mixed. Although two small, randomly controlled trials found that short-term ET is effective for the treatment of affected perimenopausal women, another trial found no such benefit for depressed older postmenopausal women. Presently, there is insufficient evidence for using HRT to treat depression in general (Dranov, 2007).

Despite earlier findings, no evidence has been found to support the use of hormone therapy to prevent dementia or cognitive decline. Beginning EPT after age 65 for these reasons may actually increase the risk of dementia within the subsequent 5 years. Studies that investigated whether dementia can be prevented in women who begin hormone therapy during the menopause transition or early postmenopause provided insufficient evidence of help or harm. Estrogen therapy does not appear to have any effect on Alzheimer's disease (Dranov, 2007). The U.S. Preventive Services Task Force (USPSTF) and the American College of Obstetricians and Gynecologists (ACOG) advise against the use of HRT to improve cognition or to prevent or treat dementia (ACOG, 2004b; Alexander, 2007; USPSTF, 2007).

Premature Menopause and Premature Ovarian Failure

Premature menopause and premature ovarian failure are associated with a lower-than-normal risk of breast cancer, but an earlier onset of osteoporosis and CHD. The effects of ET and EPT are unknown. The risk-benefit ratio for women who begin therapy at an early age may be more favorable but is currently unknown (Dranov, 2007).

Hormone Replacement Therapy: Available Options

Types and Delivery Systems

HRT is available in a variety of forms, doses, and delivery systems. Various HRT medications are listed below.

- **Oral estrogen equivalencies:** Dosing of these medications varies from one estrogen agent each calendar day for 25 days, followed by 7 to 12 days of a progestin, to continuous estrogen dosing with intermittent progestin dosing, a regimen which tends to be more convenient for most women.
  – Premarin (conjugated estrogens)
  – Estrace (micronized estradiol)
  – Estratab, Menest (esterified estrogens)
  – Estratest (esterified estrogens with methyl-testosterone)
  – Ortho-Est, Ogen (estropipate)

- **Oral progestin equivalencies**
  – Provera (MPA)
  – Prometrium (progesterone USP)
  – Curretabs (medroxyprogesterone)
  – Aygestin (norethindrone acetate)
  – Micronor (norethindrone)

- **Combination oral estrogen-progestin equivalencies**
  - Prempro (conjugated estrogens + MPA)
  - Activella (estradiol + norethindrone acetate)
  - Femhrt (ethinyl estradiol + norethindrone)
  - Ortho-Prefest (estradiol + norgestimate)
  - Premphase (conjugated estrogens + MPA)
- **Vaginal estrogen creams**
  - Premarin (conjugated estrogens)
  - Ogen (estropipate)
  - Estrace (estradiol)
- **Estrogen gel or emulsion**
  - EstroGel (estradiol gel applied to the skin)
  - Estrasorb (estradiol emulsion applied to the skin)
- **Vaginal rings**
  - Estring (estradiol)
  - Femring (estradiol acetate)
- **Transdermal estrogen (patch)**
  - Estraderm (estradiol)
  - Climara (estradiol)
  - Menostar (estradiol)
  - Esclim (estradiol)
  - Vivelle (estradiol)
  - Alora (estradiol)
- **Transdermal estrogen-progestin (patch)**
  - CombiPatch (estradiol + norethindrone acetate)
  - Climara Pro (estradiol + levonorgestrel)

(adapted from Lowdermilk & Perry, 2007; Secor & Simon, 2006)

Use of Transdermal Hormones

When counseling women about hormone therapy, the method of hormonal administration is an important consideration, whether using unopposed estrogen or a combined estrogen-progestin. In general, transdermal estrogen (estradiol) provides the same relief of menopausal symptoms as do the oral preparations but without the side effects of breast tenderness and fluid retention. Transdermal estra-

diol delivery systems have been shown to be safer than oral administration in reducing certain markers of cardiovascular risk. Because the hormones bypass the liver and are directly absorbed into the bloodstream, transdermal administration is more effective in maintaining stable blood levels of estrogen. Also, because transdermal estradiol is absorbed directly into the body, first-pass metabolism by the gastrointestinal tract and liver is avoided. When given orally, larger doses of estrogen are required to achieve therapeutic levels and to offset metabolism by the liver and inactivation by the gut wall. In addition, when compared with transdermal formulations, oral ET has been shown to increase the risk of VTE disease (Dranov, 2007; Minikin, 2004; Secor & Simon, 2006).

No large studies have compared the advantages and disadvantages of the different transdermal formulations. The patch, applied one or two times a week to a hairless area of the skin, is considerably more irritating to the skin than either the gel or emulsion. Also, the gel and the emulsion arc more discrete than the patch. The patient should be taught to apply the gel or emulsion to clean, dry, intact skin at the same time each day. The emulsion should be applied to the complete surface of both legs once a day; the gel should be applied to one upper arm and shoulder once a day. These products should be used for the shortest possible period of time and require 4 to 12 weeks before relief of symptoms is obtained (Secor & Simon, 2006).

Contraindications to Estrogen

When counseling women about HRT, it is important to discuss contraindications, risks, and side effects so that they can make appropriate, informed decisions. Absolute contraindications to ET include:

- known or suspected estrogen-dependent cancer
- undiagnosed vaginal bleeding
- active thrombophlebitis, thromboembolic disorder, or coronary artery disease

- severe liver disease

- known or suspected pregnancy.

(Altman, 2006)

Risks of Estrogen

In addition to the risks of breast cancer and endometrial cancer, estrogen-related risks include:

- increased risk of stroke

- small increase in the risk of VTE

- a possible small increase in the risk of coronary events

- worsening of hypertriglyceridemia

- possible worsening of gallbladder disease

- deterioration of liver function in women with severe liver disease

- worsening of edema in women with severe cardiac disease

- worsening of pain from benign breast disease.

(Altman, 2006)

Side Effects of Estrogen

Side effects of estrogen include:

- increased risk of gallbladder disease

- worsening of estrogen-dependent conditions, such as fibroids and endometriosis

- increase in fibrocystic breast problems

- vaginal bleeding

- hypertension

- nausea and vomiting

- headaches, jaundice, and fluid retention

- impaired glucose tolerance.

(Altman, 2006)

Side Effects of Progestins

Side effects of progestins include:

- fluid retention

- breast tenderness

- jaundice

- nausea

- insomnia

- depression

- menstrual bleeding.

(Altman, 2006)

Bioidentical Compounds

Compounded bioidentical hormones are plant-derived hormones that are prepared by a pharmacist and can be custom made for a patient according to a physician's specifications. The use of bioidentical compounds has been promoted as a natural approach because these substances claim to replace specific hormones that are naturally present in a woman's body. Many bioidentical replacement hormones are compounded in private laboratories or pharmacies as individualized made-to-order products. Women need to be aware of the limitations and poor results that may be associated with this therapy (ACOG, 2007; Alexander, 2006, 2007; Boothby, Doering, & Kipersztok, 2004; Dranov, 2007; Secor & Simon, 2006).

Certain bioidentical preparations of estrogen or progestin are approved by the FDA for oral, intravaginal, transdermal, or percutaneous application. These particular medications have undergone strenuous testing for safety, efficacy, and quality control (Wysocki & Alexander, 2005). However, compounded bioidentical formulations are not FDA-regulated in the same way. These products are not subject to rigorous testing or quality control standards. Also, the compounded products do not carry a package insert that lists important contraindications, warnings, and precautions – which may make them appear to be safer than traditional hormone therapy medications. These products lack standardization and, in many cases, the specific active ingredients and minimally effective dosages are not known (ACOG, 2007). The ACOG considers bioidentical hormone preparations to have the same safety risks as traditional hormone therapy and asserts that they may carry additional risks associated with the compounding process. In addition, evidence-based data supporting the efficacy of bioidentical compounded preparations are lacking. The risks, benefits, and quality of these products have not been evaluated through rigorous testing, a standard requirement for traditional hormone therapy medications (ACOG, 2005; Alexander, 2007; Secor & Simon, 2006).

Current Trends in Hormone Replacement Therapy

While HRT has been shown to be beneficial in the treatment of postmenopausal symptoms such as hot flashes and vaginal dryness, due to recent research findings, many women are understandably reluctant to initiate or continue with this therapy. Side effects such as breast tenderness and vaginal bleeding are common and often result in discontinuation of therapy. Other women experience problems related to the progestin component of HRT prescribed for women with a uterus (e.g., weight gain, mood changes). Most importantly, the fear of an association between HRT and health problems such as breast cancer and VTE has caused many women to be wary (Altman, 2007).

In a recent (2007) position statement, The North American Menopause Society (NAMS) suggested that ET (for women without a uterus) or the combination EPT (for women with a uterus) offers the greatest benefit and the smallest risk to women who are within 10 years of menopause. NAMS supports the short-term use of HRT for hot flushes, night sweats, and other menopausal symptoms. The updated position statement emphasizes how the benefits and risks of HRT differ with age and provides reassuring data on the incidence of heart attacks among newly menopausal women who may need short-term HRT for the relief of symptoms. NAMS also concluded that:

- Based on the newest WHI reanalysis, for younger women, HRT does not present the risk of CHD seen in the WHI study of older women.

- Patients with prevalent CVD have a high baseline risk of stroke and should avoid HRT.

- Lower hormone doses may preserve bone mineral density and offer relief from hot flushes, night sweats, and vaginal dryness (Dranov, 2007; NAMS, 2007).

The 2007 NAMS Position Statement update may be accessed at www.menopause.org/PSHT07.pdf.

Current recommendations include the initiation of HRT in women with troublesome menopausal symptoms. A nonoral formulation of estrogen is preferable to oral estrogen for a variety of reasons, such as the effects on lipid levels and on the development of VTE disease. Women who have a uterus should also take a progestogen unless they are using a combined hormone therapy product. HRT should be initiated within 5 years of the final menstrual period, rather than during the later postmenopausal years. All women who use HRT should be counseled regarding the dosing regimens, the potential benefits, and the possible dangers associated with the treatment (Altman, 2007; NAMS, 2007).

Sexuality

Sexual responsiveness reaches a peak for women in their late 30s and can remain on a high plateau into the 60s. Some women report an increased sexual desire after menopause. The fear of unwanted pregnancy often frees women to be much more sexually expressive and responsive than they were in their premenopausal years (Lowdermilk & Perry, 2007).

Years ago, researchers Masters and Johnson studied sexuality in menopausal women and found a general reduction in the four phases of the sexual response cycle with increasing years after menopause. However, they also discovered that women who maintained regular sexual activity experienced vaginal lubrication similar to levels expected in women who were premenopausal, and these women continued to be capable of full sexual response and enjoyment. Sexual activity is also beneficial in improving tone and blood flow to the pelvic floor (Lowdermilk & Perry, 2007).

Many women do, however, experience changes in libido (sex drive), reduction in vaginal lubrication, discomfort during intercourse, and changes in orgasmic response during menopause. Use of vaginal lubricants that are specifically formulated for menopausal vaginal discomfort allows many older women to continue to enjoy sexual intercourse. Lengthening the foreplay time may promote enhanced vaginal lubrication as well. For women who experience a significant decrease in sex drive along with vaginal symptoms, the use of ET, delivered in the form of a vaginal cream or tablet or via a silastic device may be helpful.

Low-dose vaginal estrogen cream (Premarin, Estrace) has been shown to significantly improve symptoms associated with vaginal dryness and reduce the incidence of UTIs. Because systemic absorption of estrogen is minimal, most experts do not recommend the concomitant use of progestins (to prevent endometrial hyperplasia [overgrowth of tissue] in women who have a uterus). Typically, the woman is instructed to insert the estrogen cream into her vagina every day for the first 3 weeks, and then twice a week or as needed. A tablet that contains a low dose of estradiol (Vagifem) is also available; it is inserted in the vagina twice a week (Alexander, 2007; Secor & Simon, 2006).

Hormonal vaginal rings, which are silastic devices impregnated with estrogen (estradiol), offer another option. The vaginal rings Estring and Femring are designed to deliver a slow release of estrogen (estradiol) locally to the vagina. The vaginal ring is inserted for a period of 3 months and then replaced by the patient or physician. The Estring is formulated with an ultra low dose of estradiol (7.5 mcg released per day) and is associated with minimal systemic absorption. No concomitant progestin therapy (to prevent endometrial hyperplasia in women who have a uterus) is necessary. The Femring is formulated with a higher dose of estradiol (available to deliver 0.05 mg per day or 0.1 mg per day), and women with an intact uterus who use this product almost always receive a progestin to avoid endometrial hyperplasia (Secor & Simon, 2006; Monthly Prescribing Reference, 2008).

The two most important influences on older women's sexual activity are the strength of the relationship and the health status of each partner. The lack of an available partner can have a negative effect on sexual intimacy for many midlife and older women. Older widowed, divorced, and lesbian women may have fewer opportunities to develop close relationships because they are less sought after. When discussing sexuality issues with older women, it is important for nurses to provide accurate information and offer support and nonjudgmental guidance. The nurse can reassure the woman that the desire for sex into old age is a natural one and the body continues to have the capacity for sexual satisfaction (ACOG, 2007; Lowdermilk & Perry, 2007).

Urinary Incontinence

Menopause-induced changes in the genitourinary tract can produce symptoms that include urinary urgency, increased frequency, stress or urge incontinence, and recurrent UTIs. More than one-third of women over the age of 60 in the United States have some form of urinary incontinence (Alexander, 2007; Mallett, 2005). The prevalence of incontinence appears to increase gradually during young adult life, peak around middle age, and then steadily increase during the later years. The estimated annual direct cost of urinary incontinence in women in this country is around $12.43 billion (ACOG, 2007).

Urinary incontinence has been shown to affect women's social, clinical, and psychological well-being. It is estimated that less than one-half of all incontinent women seek medical assistance, even though urinary incontinence can often be treated (ACOG, 2007). Loss of estrogen supply to the estrogen-dependent tissues of the genitourinary tract results in a decrease in muscle tone and control in the bladder and urethra. Stress urinary incontinence (SUI) is a disturbance in urinary control (i.e., loss of urine) due to sudden increases in intra-abdominal pressure that often occur during sneezing, coughing, or laughing. SUI is more likely to occur in women who have given birth. For most women, pelvic muscle exercises, known as Kegel exercises, can be very effective in strengthening the pelvic floor and improving symptoms associated with SUI (Klausner, 2005). Nurses should instruct women on performing Kegel exercises, including these steps:

- Contract the vaginal opening as if trying to stop the flow of urine.

- Hold to the count of three.

- Relax and repeat these maneuvers.

- Or, alternatively, contract and relax quickly five to ten times.

- Do a total of 30 to 80 Kegel exercises per day.

Electrical stimulation administered while performing Kegel exercises can be used to enhance the stimulation and contraction of the pelvic muscles. This approach, conducted in the health care practitioner's office, may be helpful for women who have difficulty contracting the pelvic muscles voluntarily. With biofeedback, the woman is taught to voluntarily control the pelvic muscles and bladder. Using an electrode attached to the skin, biofeedback machines measure the electrical signals elicited when the pelvic muscles and urinary sphincter are contracted. Through visual cues from a graph shown on the monitor, patients can learn to control these muscles voluntarily (Dwyer & Kreder, 2005; Kielb, 2005; Lowdermilk & Perry, 2007; Miller, 2005).

Vaginal cones and weights offer another strategy for strengthening the vaginal muscles and the pelvic floor. The tampon-shaped plastic cones and weights consist of a set of five reusable nonsterile cones of identical size and shape but increasing weight. Each cone contains stainless steel weights numbered from "1" to "5" on the rounded end. The woman is instructed to insert one cone into her vagina, beginning with the lightest weight. Once the cone is in place, she contracts the pelvic muscles in an effort to hold the cone in place for several minutes. The appropriate weight necessitates the pelvic floor muscles to contract around the cone in order to retain it. Gradually, the patient transitions, one at a time, to the next heaviest cone. The weights are designed to use while performing Kegel exercises. As the pelvic muscles strengthen, women can use the cones while engaging in exercise (Dwyer & Kreder, 2005; Kielb, 2005; Lowdermilk & Perry, 2007).

The use of a device such as a pessary or surgical intervention may be needed if urinary incontinence is severe or due to prolapse of the uterus or bladder. A pessary is a device that supports the uterus and holds it in the correct position. There are various types of pessaries; all must be prescribed and fitted by the woman's health care provider. Pessaries must be removed and cleaned regularly with soap and water to reduce the risk of infection. Surgical intervention for a prolapsed bladder usually involves an anterior repair (colporrhaphy). This procedure involves shortening of the pelvic muscles to provide better support for the bladder (Dwyer & Kreder, 2005; Kielb, 2005; Lowdermilk & Perry, 2007).

Urinary urgency or frequency combined with an involuntary loss of urine is a common sign of an overactive bladder. Pharmacologic management of incontinence is aimed at relaxing the involuntary contractions that occur in the bladder. Medications commonly used include tolterodine (Detrol), oxybutynin (Ditropan), and imipramine (Tofranil). Common side effects associated with these medications include dry mouth, nausea, dizziness, drowsiness, and constipation. Low-dose vaginal estrogen creams, tablets or rings may also be prescribed to provide relief of urinary symptoms (Alexander, 2007; Lowdermilk & Perry, 2007).

CARDIOVASCULAR DISEASE

In the past, many people held the belief that menopause caused heart disease and osteoporosis, two serious illnesses frequently seen in older women. Although these illnesses do tend to occur with advancing age, by no means do all aging women develop either heart disease or osteoporosis.

CVD is the number one killer of older American women. This disease includes CHD, stroke, congestive heart failure (CHF), hypertension, and other diseases of the heart and vascular system. Over the past 20 years, improved prevention and treatment have reduced the annual number of CVD deaths in men but not in women. CVD is a particularly important problem among minority women. The death rate due to CVD is substantially higher in African-American women than in Caucasian women. Despite the heightened public awareness of CVD in women, the majority of women in this country continue to underestimate their risk of dying as a result of CVD (American Heart Association [AHA], 2007b).

CVD is a chronic, degenerative disease. Although the exact mechanisms are not well understood, it is known that there is deterioration in arterial wall elasticity due to the deposition of plaque containing cholesterol and other compounds. The plaque formation may result from attempts by the body to repair damage to the lining of blood vessels. Blood flow is slowed through the narrowed areas, and clots tend to form around the deposits, causing further occlusion of the vessels (AHA, 2007b).

Facts About Women's Risk, Diagnosis, and Treatment

According to the AHA (2007):

- The risk of heart disease and stroke increases with age. In the year 2003, over 45 million affected American women were age 50 and older.

- More women than men die of stroke.

- Low blood levels of "good" (HDL) appear to be a stonger predictor of heart disease death in women than in men in the over-65 age-group. High blood levels of triglycerides (another type of fat) may be a particularly important risk factor in women and the elderly.

- Regular physical activity and a healthy weight reduce the risk of non-insulin-dependent diabetes (type 2 diabetes), which appears to be an even stronger contributing risk factor for heart disease in women than in men.

- The diagnosis of heart disease presents a greater challenge in women than in men.

New AHA Guidelines Focus on Women's Lifetime Heart Risk

The *2007 Guidelines for Preventing Cardiovascular Disease in Women* emphasize that health care professionals should focus on women's lifetime heart disease risk, rather than just the short-term risk. This approach underscores the importance of healthy lifestyles in women of all ages to reduce the long-term risk of heart and blood vessel diseases. The new guidelines for risk assessment include personal risk factors and family history as well as the Framingham risk score, which estimates the risk of developing CHD within 10 years. Expanded recommendations on lifestyle factors such as physical activity, nutrition, and smoking cessation, as well as specific recommendations on drug treatments for blood pressure and cholesterol control, are included (AHA, 2007b; Moska et al., 2007; Wenger, 2007).

The new guidelines state that the use of unregulated dietary supplements is not a method proven to prevent heart disease. Research that has become available since the last guidelines were developed suggests that health care providers should consider the use of aspirin in women over age 65 to prevent stroke. In women younger than age 65, routine use of aspirin is not recommended to prevent myocardial infarction (MI). In addition, health care providers should avoid the use of menopausal therapies, such as HRT and selective estrogen receptor modulators (SERMs) (e.g., raloxifene, tamoxifene), to prevent heart disease because they have been shown to be ineffective in protecting the heart and may, in fact, increase the risk of a stroke (AHA, 2007b; Moska et al., 2007; Wenger, 2007).

Here are some highlights of the changes in the AHA (2007a) guidelines:

- Recommended lifestyle changes to help manage blood pressure include weight control, increased physical activity, alcohol moderation, sodium restriction, and an emphasis on eating fresh fruits, vegetables, and low-fat dairy products.

- Besides advising women to quit smoking, the 2007 guidelines recommend counseling, nicotine replacement, or other forms of smoking cessation therapy.

- Physical activity recommendations for women who need to lose weight or sustain weight loss have been added – a minimum of 60 to 90 minutes of moderate-intensity activity (e.g., brisk walking) on most, and preferably all, days of the week.

- The guidelines now encourage all women to reduce saturated fat intake to less than 7% of calories.

- Specific guidance on omega-3 fatty acid intake and supplementation recommends eating oily fish at least twice a week and considering taking a capsule supplement of 850 to 1,000 mg of eicosapentaenoic acid (EPA) and docosahexaenoic acid (DHA) in women with heart disease, 2 to 4 g for women with high triglycerides.

- HRT and SERMs are not recommended to prevent heart disease in women. Estrogen plus progestin can increase the risk of MI, breast cancer, VTE, stroke, dementia, and ovarian cancer. In women who have undergone hysterectomy, estrogen alone confers a risk of stroke, dementia, and memory loss. Likewise, no cardiovascular benefit has been shown for SERMs.

- Antioxidant supplements such as vitamins E, C, and beta-carotene should not be used for the primary or secondary prevention of CVD.

- Folic acid, with or without vitamin B_6 and B_{12} supplementation, should not be used to prevent CVD.

- Routine low-dose aspirin therapy may be considered in women age 65 or older regardless of CVD risk status, if benefits are likely to outweigh other risks.

- The upper dosage of aspirin for high-risk women increases to 325 mg per day rather than 162 mg (AHA, 2007b; Moska et al., 2007; Wenger, 2007).

Go Red for Women Movement

In 2004, the AHA launched its multitiered marketing Go Red For Women campaign to raise women's awareness of their risk of heart disease and to help them take action to reduce their risk. Nurses and patients can obtain accurate, up-to-date information on heart disease and stroke and the Go Red For Women movement by calling 1-888-MY-HEART or by visiting www.goredforwomen.org. The AHA urged Congress to make the number one killer of women a national priority by passing the HEART for Women Act in 2007. The HEART for Women Act is bipartisan federal legislation that would improve the prevention, diagnosis, and treatment of CVD in women. For more information on this proposed legislation, please visit www.heartforwomen.org (AHA, 2007).

Risk Factors

According to the AHA (2007), women are considered to be at high risk for CVD if they have established CVD or CHD, peripheral artery disease, cerebrovascular disease, chronic renal disease, or diabetes mellitus. Other risk factors for CVD include:

- advanced age – About 83% of people who die of CHD are 65 or older.

- gender – Men have a greater risk of heart attack than women do.

- heredity (including race) – Children of parents with heart disease are more likely to develop it themselves. African Americans have more severe high blood pressure than Caucasians and a higher risk of heart disease. Heart disease is also higher among Mexican Americans, Native Americans, native Hawaiians, and some Asian Americans; this is partly due to higher rates of obesity and diabetes.

- cigarette smoking.

- elevated serum cholesterol levels.

- metabolic syndrome.

- hypertension (often related to use of alcohol, cigarettes, excessive sodium, and obesity).

- obesity and overweight.

- other risk factors, such as high-fat diet or sedentary and stressful lifestyles.

(Mosca et al., 2007)

When counseling women about personal risk for CVD, nurses can inform them about the Reynolds Risk Score, developed by experts at Brigham and Women's hospital in Boston. This test, which calculates the risk of having a heart attack, stroke, or other form of heart disease in the next 10 years, is available at www.reynoldsriskscore.org.

OSTEOPOROSIS

As is the case with CVD, osteoporosis is neither caused by nor brought on by menopause. Osteoporosis does occur most often with advanced age. However, menopausal women are not "doomed" to develop osteoporosis as an accompaniment to aging. Osteoporosis is a preventable condition, one that may occur before, during, or after menopause. Thus, osteoporosis is a process to be viewed across the lifetime of a female, particularly from a preventive standpoint.

Definition

Osteoporosis is defined as thin or porous bone; *osteopenia* is a condition of a diminished amount of bone tissue. Three major types of fractures may occur as a result of osteoporosis:

1. **Spontaneous vertebral crush fracture:** With this type of fracture, the vertebrae become so weak that one vertebra collapses under minimal stress of lifting or due to the weight of the woman's body. This action causes a loss of height and kyphosis or dowager's hump, the curvature of the upper back often present in older people (see Figure 13-1).

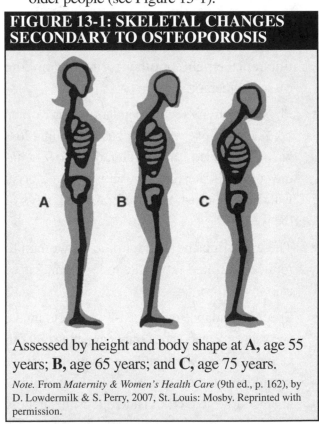

FIGURE 13-1: SKELETAL CHANGES SECONDARY TO OSTEOPOROSIS

Assessed by height and body shape at **A,** age 55 years; **B,** age 65 years; and **C,** age 75 years.

Note. From *Maternity & Women's Health Care* (9th ed., p. 162), by D. Lowdermilk & S. Perry, 2007, St. Louis: Mosby. Reprinted with permission.

2. **Colles' fracture:** Colles' fracture occurs when a person breaks a fall by landing on a hand, causing fracture of the radius.

3. **Osteoporotic hip fracture:** The hip fracture related to osteoporotic processes is the most severe of these three types of fractures.

(ACOG, 2004b)

Tooth loss and periodontal disease represent other aspects of osteoporosis.

In the United States, four to six million women have some degree of osteoporosis; another 15 million are at risk. Osteoporosis varies among ethnic groups. Asian Americans and Caucasians are more often affected by osteoporosis and osteopenia than are African Americans. Among non-Hispanic African-American women who are older than age 50, 5% have osteoporosis and 35% have osteopenia. Among Hispanic women over age 50, 10% have osteoporosis and 49% have osteopenia. And among non-Hispanic white women and Asian American women who are 50 and older, approximately 20% have osteoporosis, while 52% have osteopenia (Lowdermilk & Perry, 2007; Speroff & Fritz, 2005).

Osteoporosis represents a major health threat for women. In this country, the incidence of osteoporosis-related fractures has increased over the past 20 years. Most fractures occur at the femoral neck, the vertebrae, and the distal radius. Postmenopausal women who experience a hip or symptomatic vertebral fracture have a sixfold to eightfold increased risk of death in the year following their fracture (Zizic, 2004). On an annual basis, the associated costs of osteoporosis-related fractures exceed $14 billion, and this figure is expected to increase as the life expectancy increases and the population ages (ACOG, 2004c; Alexander, 2007).

Causes

Simply stated, osteoporosis occurs when the normal balance of bone formation and bone resorption is disrupted. In women and young adults, bone growth and calcium deposition take place continuously throughout young adulthood. Bone mass generally reaches a peak around age 30. As women grow older, net bone loss gradually occurs due to an imbalance in bone tissue and metabolism. A deficiency of estrogen worsens the situation, as does an inefficiency in the calcium and vitamin D assimilation that naturally occur as women age (NOF, 2007; Speroff & Fritz, 2005).

During the first 5 to 6 years following menopause, women lose bone density six times more rapidly than men. By the age of 65, one-third of women have experienced a vertebral fracture; by the age of 81, one-third have suffered a hip fracture. At the age of 80, women have lost approximately 47% of the trabecular bone, which is concentrated in the vertebrae, pelvis, and other flat bones, and the epiphyses. The most well-defined risk factor for the development of osteoporosis is the loss of the protective effects of estrogen, which occurs with declining ovarian function during perimenopause (Lowdermilk & Perry, 2007; NOF, 2007).

Osteoporosis can also result from other causes including rheumatoid arthritis, chronic lung disease, and endocrine diseases such as diabetes, hypogonadism, overactive thyroid, and hyperparathyroidism. Also, certain prescription drugs, including corticosteroids, anticoagulants, and some diuretics, as well as some over-the-counter aluminum-containing antacids, can contribute to bone loss. Excessive caffeine intake increases calcium excretion, and excessive alcohol use interferes with calcium absorption and depresses bone formation (Lowdermilk & Perry, 2007; NOF, 2007).

Risk Factors

There are many risk factors for osteoporosis, including the following genetic and medical factors:

- race – Caucasian women are at the highest risk, followed by Asian-American women; African-American and Latina women have a lower risk.

- advanced age.

- History of:
  - previous fractures that occurred without any major trauma or fracture after the age of 50.
  - poor absorption of calcium and other minerals or nutrients due to celiac disease, chronic diarrhea, low stomach acid (common in older people), and surgical removal of part of the stomach or intestines.

- Family history of female osteoporosis, fractures, or both.

- Body build – Women who are small boned and slim and have small muscle mass are at greater risk than women with other body builds.

- Current osteopenia.

- Early menopause (before age 40 years or if surgically induced).

- Amenorrhea.

- Never having gone through a pregnancy.

- Anorexia nervosa.

- Diabetes, liver disease, kidney disease with dialysis, or daily use of thyroid medication (more than 2 grains).

- Lactose intolerance – Present in 60% of women with osteoporosis and in only 15% of the general population.

- Use of phenytoin sodium (Dilantin), which interferes with the body's ability to absorb calcium; aluminum-containing antacids; steroid medications.

(NOF, 2007)

Risk factors related to lifestyle include smoking; alcohol use; diet low in calcium; diet high in salt, protein, caffeine, phosphates, sugar, or refined flour products; a lack of sun exposure, exercise, or a deficiency in vitamin D (Lowdermilk & Perry, 2007; NOF, 2007).

Hormones and Osteoporosis

Estrogen inhibits bone resorption by binding to estrogen receptors in bone tissue and also by blocking the production of cytokines, substances that increase the number of osteoclasts. Estrogen, however, is not the only hormone that has an important influence on the health of bone. Two other hormones produced by the ovaries, progesterone and dehydroepiandrosterone, influence bone metabolism as well. Testosterone (one of the male hormones also produced by women) may also play a role in bone health (ACOG, 2004c; Lowdermilk & Perry, 2007; NOF, 2007).

Physiology of Bone

Bone is a living tissue. It is involved in a wide range of biochemical processes, which result in the constant breakdown and reformation of new bone. This process of remodeling replaces weakened areas with new, well-formed tissue.

Bone is composed of two types of bone cells, called *osteoblasts* and *osteoclasts,* as well as an intercellular matrix:

Osteoblasts: Osteoblasts are bone cells involved in the laying down of new bone.

Osteoclasts: Osteoclasts are bone cells involved in the breakdown or reabsorption of old or damaged bone tissue.

Intercellular matrix: The intercellular matrix is composed of organic compounds, such as collagen and other proteins, and inorganic components responsible for bone rigidity. Crystals are formed by minerals such as calcium phosphate, calcium carbonate, a small amount of magnesium, fluoride, sulfate, and other trace minerals. These crystalline structures are called *hydroxyapatites.*

(Speroff & Fritz, 2005)

Bone strength is determined by the total bone mass and the integrity of its protein and crystal matrix. Bone strength is also related to the efficiency of bone repair in response to mild trauma, which produces microfractures. Remodeling tends to occur along lines of stress, increasing the strength in those weakened areas (NOF, 2007).

Bone health promotion typically centers on methods to ensure adequate intake of calcium. However, bone health maintenance and the prevention of fractures should encompass other strategies, such as preventing the loss of calcium and other minerals from the bone, maintaining the soft tissue components around the bone, and promoting the efficiency of bone repair (Lowdermilk & Perry, 2007; NOF, 2007; Speroff & Fritz, 2005)

Diagnosis of Osteoporosis: Bone Density Measurement

A clinical diagnosis of osteoporosis is made when a postmenopausal woman suffers a nontraumatic, nonpathologic fracture of the spine. A *radiologic* diagnosis is based on the T score, which is obtained from bone densitometry analysis. The first-line technique for assessing bone mineral density (BMD) (bone densitometry) is the central dual X-ray absorptiometry, or C-DEXA. This test assesses BMD in the spine, hip, and waist. The T score refers to the extent of bone loss and is reflective of the number of standard deviations by which a patient's BMD falls below the expected BMD score for healthy young women. Every decrease of one standard deviation represents approximately a 12% reduction in BMD, which translates into a 1.5- to 3-fold increase in fracture risk (NOF, 2007).

According to the World Health Organization, osteopenia is defined as a T score between –1 and –2.5; osteoporosis is present with a T score of –2.5 or lower. The NOF recommends that a woman begin therapy to prevent fractures when the T score falls below –2 if she has no other risk factors or when her T score falls below –1.5 if she has other risk factors, such as smoking. Bone densitometry is useful in identifying individuals at risk for fracture and in monitoring the effects of therapy (NOF, 2007; USPSTF, 2005c).

As women grow older, routine height assessments should become standard practice during annual examinations. Loss of height may indicate bone loss in asymptomatic women. Identifying height loss in women who are in their 40s or early 50s should signal a need for further testing to determine the cause (NOF, 2007).

According to recommendations established by the USPSTF and the NOF, health care providers should routinely screen all women older than age 65 for osteoporosis. Women with risk factors should be screened beginning at age 60. In this country, women typically reach menopause around age 51, and most bone loss occurs during the first 5 to 7 years after cessation of menses. Thus, it may be prudent to begin screening at an earlier age. In many cases, insurance carriers support BMD measurements in postmenopausal women who are not using HRT or who have other risk factors for bone loss (NOF, 2007; USPSTF, 2007).

In recent years, peripheral densitometry scans of the forearm, heel, and finger have become widely used because they are inexpensive and readily available in many offices and clinics in the outpatient setting. However, C-DEXA remains the standard for the measurement of BMD and the diagnosis of osteopenia and osteoporosis. C-DEXA is also used to monitor treatment progress. It is generally recommended that BMD be reassessed every 3 to 5 years. For certain women, including those who are undergoing treatment for osteoporosis and those who are immobilized, BMD may need to be measured more often, such as every 6 to 24 months (NOF, 2007).

Diet and Bone Health

Although it is impossible to determine the precise effect of diet on bone health, there is at least circumstantial evidence that the standard American diet, which frequently contains excessive sugar, refined grains, and caffeine, promotes the development of osteoporosis. Other dietary factors that affect bone health include alcohol and protein, phosphorus, and sodium (Lowdermilk & Perry, 2007):

Sugar: The average American ingests 139 lb of refined sugar each year. Sugar intake may be associated with large increases in urinary calcium excretion. Because 99% of the body's calcium is stored in bone, and the blood maintains a very narrow concentration range of calcium, when the body loses calcium it is likely to be from bone.

Refined grains: The nutrient-rich portions of grains, including vitamin B complex, calcium, magnesium, and zinc, have been removed through refinement.

Caffeine: Caffeine in coffee, tea, and soft drinks, as well as similar substances in chocolate and some drugs, causes calcium to be excreted in the urine. Increased calcium excretion causes a systemic acidosis that stimulates bone resorption.

Alcohol: Excessive alcohol intake interferes with calcium absorption and depresses bone formation.

Protein, phosphorus, and sodium: The typical American diet contains excessive amounts of protein, phosphorus, and sodium. Calcium is mobilized to neutralize the acidic byproducts and is then excreted in the urine, causing a loss of calcium from the body. Phosphorus is found in many soft drinks, and excess protein results from the high consumption of meat and dairy products in the average American diet.

Prevention of osteoporosis represents an important example of the benefits of a diet that is composed primarily of plant-based, unprocessed, whole foods. Examples of these substances include legumes, fresh fruits and vegetables, whole grains, nuts, and seeds. These foods provide a rich supply of nutrients in the right proportions to enhance absorption and use (Lowdermilk et al., 2007; NOF, 2007).

Nutrients Important in Bone Health

In addition to calcium, many vitamins and minerals play an important role in maintaining bone mass and in preventing osteoporosis. These include:

1. **Vitamin K:** Along with calcium, vitamin K is involved in bone metabolism. This important vitamin attracts calcium into the matrix to form bone – the process of bone mineralization and fracture healing. Vitamin K is made by normal intestinal bacteria, which are destroyed by antibiotic therapy. Vitamin K is found in dark green, leafy vegetables.

2. **Manganese:** The highest concentrations of manganese are located in the bones and endocrine glands. Manganese promotes calcification; deficiencies in manganese levels have been found in individuals with osteoporosis. Sources of manganese include whole grains, nuts, seeds, leafy vegetables, and meat.

3. **Magnesium:** Magnesium is an essential mineral that is involved in more than 50 different reactions in the body. Approximately 50% of the body's magnesium is located in the bones. Magnesium helps the body to use calcium and vitamin D. A magnesium deficiency is associated with abnormal bone formation, which results in decreased bone strength. Emotional stress is associated with increased magnesium excretion. Magnesium is found in whole grains, nuts, seeds, and green vegetables.

4. **Boron:** Boron may play a role in bone health and hormone balance. Boron is believed to enhance the conversion of vitamin D to its biologically active form. Sources of boron include noncitrus fruits (e.g., apples, grapes, pears, cherries), leafy greens (e.g., spinach, parsley, cabbage, broccoli), nuts, and legumes. A diet rich in these foods provides a safe boron intake of 2 to 6 mg per day.

5. **Vitamin B_6:** Vitamin B_6 is believed to be involved in bone matrix formation. Sources of vitamin B_6 include whole grains, fish, chicken, nuts, watermelon, and tomatoes.

6. **Zinc:** Zinc, which enhances the action of vitamin D, is essential for normal bone formation. Zinc is also required for normal deoxyribonucleic acid and protein synthesis in osteoblasts, osteoclasts, and bone matrix. Rich sources of zinc include liver, shellfish, meats, whole grains, and milk.

7. **Vitamin C:** It has been known from the days of widespread scurvy that vitamin C is necessary for normal bone formation. This vitamin

promotes the formation and cross-linking of some of the structural proteins found in bone. Vitamin C is found in citrus fruits, strawberries, melons, broccoli, tomatoes, and raw, deep green, leafy vegetables.

8. **Vitamin D:** Calcium metabolism and absorption depend on the presence of vitamin D. Exposing the skin to ultraviolet rays from the sun causes cholesterol beneath the skin's surface to be converted into vitamin D, which is then stored in the liver until needed. Vitamin D increases the absorption of calcium by the intestines and promotes calcium uptake into the bone. With aging, synthesis of vitamin D by the skin decreases. This problem is exacerbated by the common tendency for older people to decrease their exposure to the sun. Sun exposure consisting of as little as 10 to 15 minutes per day can have a positive impact on bone health by improving calcium absorption and use. Dietary sources of vitamin D include salt-water fish, egg yolks, butter, fortified milk and margarine, liver, and supplements (Dawson-Hughes et al., 2005; Jockers, 2007). The NOF (2007) provides the following recommendations for vitamin D_3:

- adults under age 50: 400 to 800 IU/day
- adults age 50 and older: 800 to 1000 IU/day

Vitamin D_3, also called *cholecalciferol,* is the form of vitamin D that best supports bone health (NOF, 2007).

9. **Calcium:** Calcium deficiency is only one of the predisposing factors for the development of osteoporosis in women, and not everyone with osteoporosis is deficient in calcium. Calcium balance and metabolism in the body are complex and involve a number of factors, including ingestion, absorption, use, and excretion. In addition, calcium balance is modulated by various hormonal systems. Adequate calcium intake for osteoporosis prevention should begin

early in life when bone mass is reaching its peak. This important period for bone health occurs during the late teens to early 20s (Speroff & Fritz, 2005).

The Institute of Medicine (IOM, 2003) has established the following recommendations for daily calcium intake:

- adolescents and young women: 1,300 mg/day,
- women ages 19 to 49: 1,000 mg/day,
- pregnant and lactating women 18 years and younger: 1,300 mg/day,
- pregnant and lactating women 19 years and older: 1,000 mg/day,
- women ages 50 and older: 1,200 mg/day.

In July 2007, the NOF updated its recommendations for daily adequate calcium intake to be consistent with those established by the IOM (NOF, 2007).

When considering dietary sources of calcium, most people are aware that dairy products are rich in calcium, but many do not realize that the animal protein in these products can interfere with the body's ability to absorb the calcium. Other substances that can inhibit calcium absorption are found in wheat bran, raw spinach, salt, caffeine, alcohol, and tobacco, and fructose (present in many soft drinks). Nurses can teach women that good nutritional sources of calcium include sardines, canned salmon, tofu, cheese, collard greens, broccoli, sesame seeds, tahini (a paste made from crushed, toasted sesame seeds), low-fat milk, and molasses. Soy milk, rice, yogurt, cereals, and orange juice, along with many other products, are now available with extra calcium added (Lowdermilk & Perry, 2007; NOF, 2007).

Some people are lactose intolerant, meaning they have difficulty digesting dairy products because they lack the enzyme lactase, which is needed to break down the milk sugar lactose. Lactose intolerance is fairly common in adults, particularly African Americans, Asians, Native

Americans, and Inuits (Alaska Natives). Individuals with lactose intolerance experience abdominal cramping, bloating, and diarrhea following milk consumption, although many can tolerate small amounts of milk without symptoms. Calcium sources such as yogurt, sweet acidophilus milk (fermented with certain bacteria), buttermilk, cheese, chocolate milk, and cocoa may be tolerated even when fresh milk is not. Lactase supplements such as Lactaid are available to consume with milk and lactase-treated milk is also available in many markets. The lactase in these products digests the lactose in the milk so that lactose-intolerant people can drink milk without intestinal symptoms (Lowdermilk & Perry, 2007; NOF, 2007).

Absorption of calcium depends on adequate acidity in the stomach. Low stomach acid is a common problem that becomes more prevalent with increasing age. When counseling women about strategies to optimize the absorption of calcium, nurses can suggest the following actions to improve gastric acidity:

- Eat slowly and chew well.
- Limit fluid intake with meals.
- Consider the use of digestive enzymes.

(Lowdermilk & Perry, 2007)

Many calcium supplements are available today. Patients should be advised that the "best" supplement for them is the one that best meets their needs, based on tolerance, convenience, cost, and availability. Nurses can teach women that, when choosing a calcium supplement, special consideration should be given to the product's purity, absorbability, tolerance, and possibility of interactions with other drugs:

Purity – Patients should only choose supplements that are known brand names and have proven reliability. Product labels should state "purified" or have the United States Pharmacopeia (USP) symbol, although the USP label is voluntary and not all products display this symbol. Avoid calcium from unrefined oyster shells, bone meal, or dolomite without the USP because these products historically have contained higher levels of lead and other toxic metals (NOF, 2007).

Absorbability – Most brand-name calcium products are readily absorbed by the body. If the product label does not state that it is absorbable, it is easy to determine absorbability by placing the tablet in a small amount of warm water for 30 minutes and stirring occasionally. If it hasn't dissolved within this time period, it probably will not dissolve in the stomach. Calcium supplements in chewable and liquid form dissolve well because they are broken down before they enter the stomach. Calcium, whether in the diet or from supplements, is best absorbed when it is taken several times a day in amounts of 500 mg or less. Calcium carbonate is absorbed best when taken with food; calcium citrate can be taken any time (NOF, 2007).

Tolerance – Although calcium supplements are well tolerated by most people, certain preparations can cause side effects, such as gas and constipation, in some individuals. If simple strategies such as increased fluids and fiber intake do not resolve the symptoms, another calcium source should be tried. A combined calcium-magnesium product may be helpful if constipation is a problem. It is best to increase the intake of any calcium supplement gradually, beginning with 500 mg a day for several days, and adding additional calcium slowly (NOF, 2007).

Interactions with other drugs – Before taking calcium supplements, it is important to talk with a physician or pharmacist about possible interactions between prescription or over-the-counter medications and the calcium supplements. For example, calcium supplements may interfere with the absorption of the antibiotic tetracycline. Calcium also interferes with iron absorption and should not be taken at the same time as an iron supplement (unless the iron supplement is taken with vitamin C or calcium citrate). Any medication that is to be taken on an empty stomach should not be taken with calcium supplements (NOF, 2007).

Calcium supplements are available in a vast array of combinations with vitamins and other minerals. Although vitamin D is necessary for the absorption of calcium, it is not necessary that it be in the calcium supplement. While calcium citrate tends to be better tolerated, it is a more expensive form of calcium. Calcium carbonate is adequately absorbed by most people unless they have insufficient stomach acid. Antacids are not the best sources of calcium because they can cause other problems, such as kidney stones, and they may aggravate other medical conditions. Some antacids also contain aluminum, which can cause the body to lose calcium (NOF, 2007).

Exercise and Osteoporosis

Immobilization and bed rest are associated with an increase in bone loss. During travel in space, astronauts have been shown to experience accelerated rates of bone loss. It is known that overall bone mass is directly related to weight-bearing physical exercise. Women who regularly engage in exercise programs that include weight-bearing and muscle-strengthening elements can help prevent postmenopausal bone loss and reduce their risk of falling. The bone-building effect of exercise results mainly from the repetitive physical stress applied to the bones. With weight-bearing exercise, pressure is placed on the bones either by the weight of the body or by the force of muscular contractions. Effective exercises for menopausal women that are generally safe and contribute to cardiovascular health and bone mass are walking, stair climbing, gardening, weight lifting, and low-impact aerobics. An effective program involves regular exercise for at least 30 minutes every day of the week. The 30 minutes do not need to be done all at once; physical activity may be divided into 10 minute segments, if desired (NOF, 2007).

Prevention of Injuries

When counseling older women, it is helpful to include information about fall safety and prevention. Many factors, such as fragility, altered balance, poor vision, and use of certain medications, can contribute to falls. Strategies to minimize falls include lowering the bed, removing throw rugs, illuminating dark areas with nightlights, using safety treads and safety rails in the bathroom, ensuring ready access to a telephone, eliminating exposed electrical cords, and removing all clutter from the floors. Also, older women should be advised to avoid slippery-soled shoes or slippers, because they provide insufficient support, traction, and stability (NOF, 2007).

Early Warning Signs

Nurses should also teach women about the early warning signs of osteoporosis. These include the sudden onset of insomnia and restlessness, leg and foot cramps that commonly occur during the night, persistent lower back pain, gradual loss of height, and the development of gum disease or loose teeth. Women of any age who experience these symptoms should promptly contact their health care provider (NOF, 2007).

Medications for Osteoporosis Prevention and Treatment

Estrogen

Estrogen replacement slows bone loss by inhibiting the activity of osteoclasts (bone breakdown) or resorption of bone, but estrogen does not actually build bone. Trabecular bone in the spine has been shown to be the area most dramatically influenced by estrogen. ET has long been considered the most important strategy in the prevention of osteoporosis in postmenopausal women who have low or normal BMD. An approximate 60% reduction in hip and wrist fractures has been demonstrated in women whose vertebral fracture rate declined following ET. Data from the WHI revealed an overall fracture prevention and reduction in women who were not at high risk for fracture. However, estrogen's influence on bone is short-lived, which necessitates long-term treatment in order to preserve benefits to BMD. Because rapid bone loss and increased fracture risk accompany cessation of hormone therapy, it must be used continually to maintain its benefits on bone (Alexander, 2007).

Presently, the use of HRT for the management of osteoporosis in menopausal women has declined. This is largely due to the introduction of drugs such as the bisphosphonates (discussed below), which do not have the same risks as those associated with HRT (Alexander, 2007).

Progesterone

Progesterone is believed to bind to osteoblasts, and it may also stimulate bone formation. More research is indicated in this area (Liu, 2007).

Raloxifene

Raloxifene (Evista) is approved for the prevention and treatment of osteoporosis in postmenopausal women. Raloxifene is in a class of drugs called *estrogen agonists/antagonists,* also known as SERMs. These medications have been developed to provide the beneficial effects of estrogens without their potential disadvantages. Raloxifene increases BMD and reduces the risk of spine fractures; there are no data indicating that raloxifene reduces the risk of hip and other non-spine fractures. Raloxifene is taken daily as a 60-mg tablet with or without meals. Side effects include hot flashes, leg cramps, and deep vein thrombosis, which is also associated with ET. It should not be given to women at increased risk for stroke (NOF, 2007).

Calcitonin

Calcitonin (Fortical, Miacalcin) is a synthetic version of calcitonin, a hormone secreted from the cells of the thyroid gland. It inhibits the action of osteoclasts (bone breakdown) and decreases bone resorption. Calcitonin has been shown to increase spinal bone mass in postmenopausal women who already have osteoporosis; it is particularly useful for relieving bone pain associated with fractures. It has not been effective in early postmenopausal women; thus, it must be considered more as a treatment than as a preventive agent. It is approved for the treatment of osteoporosis in women who are at least 5 years beyond menopause. Certain women, especially those who cannot use ET or EPT and cannot tolerate bisphosphonates (discussed below) may benefit from calcitonin therapy. Calcitonin is administered intranasally (one puff in one nostril, alternating daily) at a dose of 200 IU; it is also available as an injection (the dosage varies). An oral form of the drug is presently being tested in clinical trials. Side effects are related to local nasal irritation (e.g., nosebleeds, runny nose) and occasional systemic effects such as facial flushing, headache, nausea, and urinary frequency (NOF, 2007).

Teriparatide

Teriparatide (Forteo), a type of parathyroid hormone, is approved for the treatment of osteoporosis in postmenopausal women. This medication rebuilds bone and significantly increases BMD, especially in the spine. Candidates for teriparatide include those who have had an osteoporosis-related fracture and those with a very low BMD; it may also be an option for patients who continue to lose bone during treatment with other osteoporosis medications. Teriparatide is self-administered as a daily injection from a preloaded pen containing a 1-month supply of medication. It can be taken for a maximum of 2 years. At the end of 2 years, treatment with an antiresorptive medication (e.g., bisphosphonates, calcitonin, estrogen, SERMs) is recommended to maintain the benefits of the treatment with teriparatide. Side effects include leg cramps and dizziness (NOF, 2007).

Bisphosphonates

Bisphosphonates are synthetic forms of a class of compounds found in the body. These compounds bind to crystals in the bone matrix and inhibit bone resorption. Alendronate (Fosamax), ibandronate sodium (Boniva), and risedronate (Actonel) are bisphosphonates that have been approved to prevent and treat postmenopausal osteoporosis. Women who cannot or choose not to take estrogen are good candidates for this therapy. Bisphosphonates inhibit normal physiological bone resorption as well as abnormal bone resorption, thereby halting bone loss, increasing BMD, and reducing the risk of fractures. To date, these medications are the only therapy that has been shown to reduce fractures occurring outside of the spine (NOF, 2007).

Because bisphosphonates are associated with esophageal irritation, it is important to provide detailed dosing information when counseling women about the use of these medications. Alendronate should be taken early in the morning with a large glass of water, at least 1 hour before ingesting other foods or liquids. During this time, women should remain in an upright position. For osteoporosis prevention, 35 mg per week (5 mg per day) of alendronate is given; for osteoporosis treatment, the dose is 70 mg per week (10 mg per day). Alendronate is also available in an oral solution taken weekly. The same dosing instructions given with the tablet form apply (NOF, 2007).

Ibandronate sodium is taken once monthly as a 150 mg tablet or every 3 months as an intravenous dose of 3 mg. Oral ibandronate must be taken on the same day each month, first thing in the morning after waking up and on an empty stomach. Again, patients are instructed to remain upright and refrain from having anything to eat or drink for 1 hour after swallowing the tablet with 6 to 8 ounces of plain water. A health care professional administers the intravenous dose in an outpatient setting; it takes less than 1 minute to infuse. A serum creatinine level is obtained prior to the infusion to confirm that kidney function is normal. Risedronate, given 35 mg per week (5 mg per day) for prevention or treatment, affords more flexibility in use. It

may be taken at any time of the day, so long as 1 hour has passed between dosing and food intake. Also, risedronate, which is a third-generation bisphosphonate, has been shown to cause fewer gastrointestinal side effects (NOF, 2007).

Zoledronic acid (Reclast) is approved for the treatment of osteoporosis in postmenopausal women. It is the first and only once-a-year osteoporosis medication. Zoledronic acid increases bone strength and reduces fractures in the hip, spine, and nonspine areas such as the wrists and arms. This medication is administered by a health care professional as an intravenous dose of 5 mg in an outpatient setting. Prior to administration, patients must have two blood tests: one for creatinine to confirm that kidney function is normal and the other for calcium to confirm that the blood calcium level is normal (NOF, 2007).

Possible side effects for all of the bisphosphonates include abdominal, bone, joint, or muscle pain. Side effects associated with the oral tablets include nausea, difficulty swallowing, heartburn, esophageal irritation, and gastric ulcers. Side effects associated with intravenous administration of bisphosphonates include flulike symptoms: fever, pain in the muscles or joints, and headache. Eye inflammation (uveitis) is a rare side effect. There have been rare reports of osteonecrosis (death of the bone cells or tissue) of the jaw with bisphosphonate medications. Nearly all of these cases occurred in cancer patients receiving an intravenous bisphosphonate, pamidronate (Aredia) or zoledronate (Zometa), medications typically administered every 3 or 4 weeks. Although unusual, patients being treated with the bisphosphonate pills alendronate (Fosamax), ibandronate (Boniva) and risedronate (Actonel) for osteoporosis prevention or treatment have also been reported to have developed osteonecrosis of the jaw. An essential component of health teaching for women who take oral bisphosphonate tablets includes the warning that side effects such as chest pain, new or worsening heartburn, and difficult or painful swallowing must be immediately reported to a health care provider (NOF, 2007).

Resources for Clinicians

Several clinical and governmental organizations have published guidelines to assist clinicians in informing and guiding women toward appropriate treatments that can help to relieve their menopausal symptoms without placing their health in undue jeopardy. These organizations include the ACOG, NAMS, American Society of Reproductive Medicine (ASRM), National Association of Nurse Practitioners in Women's Health (NPWH), FDA and USPSTF. Nurses can use these recommendations to discuss options with their patients and provide evidence-based care (Alexander, 2007).

CONCLUSION

It is evident from this discussion that an ever-expanding array of drug therapies is becoming available to women entering menopause. New combinations and dosage recommendations of hormones are being tested, as are nonhormonal drugs that have benefits for heart and bone health. The important roles played by diet, exercise, and lifestyle and the beneficial pharmaceutic properties of specific foods and herbs are being more widely recognized and more rigorously researched.

With the growing menopausal population in the United States today, it is critical that the issues surrounding menopause and aging be well studied and clarified, so that women can have clear guidelines for therapeutic intervention if it is needed. At the same time, women and health care providers alike can learn from the experiences of other cultures where women frequently have a lower incidence of heart disease and breast cancer and experience fewer of the symptoms that have come to be recognized as hallmarks of menopause.

Menopause is not a disease but a natural, inevitable, life-positive transition. The experience of this generation of menopausal women, as well as the research that has been generated from their collective interest and need for information, will inform women in years to come. In the meantime, women and their health care providers can stay well informed and carefully consider the benefits, risks, and long-term effects of available therapeutic options, as together they create individualized plans for care that are minimally invasive and provide protection and enhancement of each woman's health as she ages.

EXAM QUESTIONS

CHAPTER 13
Questions 95-97

Note: Choose the option that BEST answers each question.

95. Normal physiological changes that accompany menopause include

    a. increased levels of estrogen and progesterone.
    b. an increase in muscle mass.
    c. less-elastic skin with decreased melanin.
    d. vaginal lengthening with an increased production of cervical mucus.

96. A self-care strategy that can reduce menopausal symptoms is

    a. dressing in layers.
    b. dietary consumption of foods and beverages that contain caffeine.
    c. decreased physical activity.
    d. increased dietary intake of spicy foods.

97. Risk factors for osteoporosis include

    a. Caucasian ethnicity.
    b. excessive sun exposure.
    c. large body build.
    d. late menopause.

CHAPTER 14

COMPLEMENTARY AND ALTERNATIVE THERAPIES

CHAPTER OBJECTIVE

After completing this chapter, the reader will be able to identify various complementary and alternative therapies to promote women's health across the life span.

LEARNING OBJECTIVES

After studying this chapter, the reader will be able to

1. discuss how complementary and alternative medicine (CAM) differs from traditional Western medicine.

2. identify techniques to promote healing of the mind and body.

3. specify components of the yoga lifestyle approach to health.

KEY WORDS

• Alternative medicine

• Complementary medicine

• Holism

• Homeopathy

• Integrative medicine

INTRODUCTION

This chapter concludes the consideration of various health issues for women. Beginning with Chapter 1's discussion of the present status of the health care system and the Healthy People 2010 national initiative, many personal and societal issues that impact women's health have been highlighted. This final chapter explores various complementary and alternative strategies for promoting women's health across the life span.

In the past several decades, great progress has been made in the field of women's health. Today's women have become empowered to assume control over their health and to actively partner in all aspects of decision-making for their families and children. Women's birth control choices have broadened, their pregnancy options have expanded, and they have achieved greater self-determination and equality in other areas of their lives. Health research that addresses the special needs of women is underway in major centers throughout the country. Complementary and alternative health therapies have proliferated along with myriad health promotion strategies as individuals assume more active roles in their health and happiness. Models of self-care have created an increased awareness of the importance of education as women seek to make informed, appropriate decisions concerning all aspects of their health (Young & Hayes, 2002).

233

INSIGHTS INTO COMPLEMENTARY AND ALTERNATIVE THERAPIES

Concerned about the growing depersonalization of health care and the mounting reliance on hi-tech, low-touch treatment modalities, consumers began to seek alternatives to standard Western medicine. Today, many individuals embrace an approach that values health and nurtures the mind, body, and spirit. Spirituality, ethics, and partnership with health care are valued components of the holistic approach to healing. Holistic healing, which includes alternative and complementary therapies, focuses on the correction of disharmony to bring balance to the interaction of the body, mind, and spirit. This philosophy of care, which views the patient as a whole, unique individual, represents a shift from the traditional emphasis on the clinical signs and symptoms of illness.

CAM is a group of diverse medical and health care systems, practices, and products that presently are not considered to be a part of conventional medicine as practiced in the United States. It is estimated that Americans spent more than $27 billion on CAM in 2005 (Lucey, 2006). According to the National Center for Complementary and Alternative Medicine (NCCAM), conventional medicine is that which is practiced by holders of M.D. or D.O. degrees and by their allied health professionals, including registered nurses, physical therapists, and psychologists. Some health care providers practice both CAM and conventional medicine. *Complementary medicine* is used together with conventional medicine. *Alternative medicine* is used in place of conventional medicine. *Integrative medicine* combines treatments from conventional medicine and CAM for which there is some high-quality evidence of safety and effectiveness (NCCAM, 2007).

Many of the popular alternative healing modalities offer human-centered care. This philosophy recognizes the value of the individual's input and honors and respects personal beliefs, values, and desires. The various modalities focus on the whole person rather than on the disease complex. Patients commonly find that alternative therapies are more consistent with their belief systems and empower them to actively participate in health care decisions (Ferguson, 1980; Gordon, 2004).

Although there are many alternative health care options that focus on a diversity of health and healing modalities, several concepts are common to them. For example, all place emphasis on the patient as a whole being, one who is capable of decision-making and who participates as a valued member of the health care team. Patients are encouraged and, when possible, empowered to take responsibility for their health and healing. This philosophy views each person as a unique individual and the approach to treatment is tailored to that specific person (Dossey, Keegan, & Guzzetta, 2008).

Another commonality concerns the importance of adequate nutrition, rest, relaxation, exercise, and a healthy mind as essential components of the healing approach. Although various modalities advocate a variety of diet and nutritional regimens, all are in agreement that nutrition is a cornerstone of health promotion and must be included in the healing approach. Contemporary society often overlooks the importance of creating time for rest, relaxation, and spiritual renewal (Dossey et al., 2008; Weil, 2004).

Finally, clinical signs and symptoms of disease are considered to be reflective of deeper processes, including those on the spiritual and emotional levels. An alternative healing approach attempts to treat the deeper levels and underlying causes, rather than just the physical expression of symptoms. The physical symptoms are viewed as a signal from the mind and spirit that change is needed (Ferguson, 1980; Gerber, Tiller, & Cousens, 2001; Weil, 2004).

"Nurses' Tool Box"

In 1998, an advanced practice nurse established a "Nurses' Tool Box" of CAM nursing interventions found to be effective in establishing patient and family autonomy, relieving various illness symptoms, controlling pain, improving immune function, decreasing anxiety and depression, improving circulation, excreting toxins, and enhancing healing (Ward, 2002). Presently, the plethora of CAM interventions includes guided imagery, aromatherapy, creating art, writing, prayer, chanting, meditation and channeling, imagining, therapeutic touch, stroking and cuddling, acupressure, tai chi, magnetic forces, massage, music, singing, tonal vibrations, water therapies, storytelling, joking, and humor (Helms, 2006).

Providing Integrative Health Care

The health care community is a fluid and dynamic system that consists of many clinicians, including nurses, physicians, nutritionists, social workers, physical therapists, massage therapists, herbalists, energy healers, and acupuncturists. Various philosophies and approaches to treatment and healing exist. It is essential that health care become an integrative, cooperative venture in which traditional mainstream medicine and alternative medicine can be readily accessed and used. As the present-day health paradigm shifts toward an integrative approach, more and more models of integrative health care are being developed and utilized by medical schools, hospitals, and other health care institutions (Lowdermilk & Perry, 2007).

Congressional support for CAM dates back to 1992, when the National Institutes of Health (NIH) developed the Office of Alternative Medicine (OAM). The OAM was designed to support research and evaluation of various alternative and complementary therapies and to provide information to health care consumers about the various approaches. In 1998, Congress instituted the NCCAM, which incorporates the work of the OAM in its mission and function. To date, funding has been granted to researchers investigating biofeedback, prayer, guided imagery, movement (dance, qi gong, tai chi, yoga), music, acupuncture, chiropractic, massage, herbs, homeopathy and a number of other CAM therapies for health problems and concerns (NCCAM, 2007). The NIH has established seven categories of alternative and complementary healing (see Table 14-1). Although some overlap exists with several of the therapies and categories, this list serves as a starting point for guiding research and data collection (Lowdermilk & Perry, 2007; NCCAM, 2007).

HOLISTIC NURSING

Holism is a philosophy of care that is built upon a framework that values the human relationship and focuses on meeting the physical, emotional, spiritual, and social needs of a person. To practice holistic nursing is to blend technology with healing while providing care that encompasses the interrelated relationships between the patient, the patient's family and other support persons, the providers and the community. The practice of holistic nursing encompasses approaches and interventions that address the needs of the whole person: mind, body, and spirit. Florence Nightingale recognized the value of caring for the whole person and encouraged the use of touch, light, aromatics, empathetic listening, music, quiet reflection, and other methods to empower the individual's ability to draw upon inner strengths to promote healing (American Holistic Nurses Association [AHNA], 2005).

According to the AHNA (2005), holistic nursing embraces all nursing, which has as its goal the enhancement of healing the whole person from birth to death. Holistic nursing recognizes that there are two views regarding holism: 1) that holism involves identifying the interrelationships of the bio-psycho-social-spiritual dimensions of the

TABLE 14-1: NATIONAL INSTITUTES OF HEALTH CATEGORIES OF ALTERNATIVE HEALING MODALITIES

Category	Examples
Alternative systems of medical practice	• Acupuncture • Ayurveda • Environmental medicine • Homeopathy • Native American healing • Naturopathic medicine • Shamanism • Traditional Chinese medicine (TCM)
Bioelectromagnetic applications	• Electroacupuncture • Neuromagnetic stimulation
Diet, nutrition, and lifestyle changes	• Changes in lifestyle • Diet • Macrobiotics • Megavitamins and other nutritional supplements
Herbal medicine	• Herbal approaches from various cultures, including the Americas, Europe, and the Far East
Manual healing	• Acupressure • Chiropractic • Massage therapy • Osteopathy • Reflexology • Therapeutic touch (TT) • Healing touch (HT) • Trager method
Mind-body control	• Art therapy • Biofeedback • Counseling • Dance therapy • Guided imagery and hypnosis • Humor therapy • Meditation • Music therapy • Prayer • Psychotherapy • Relaxation • Support and self-help groups • Yoga
Pharmacologic and biologic treatments	• Antioxidizing agents • Chelation therapy • Oxidizing agents • Vaccines (not currently accepted by mainstream medicine)

(National Center for Complementary and Alternative Medicine, 2007b)

person, recognizing that the whole is greater than the sum of its parts; and 2) that holism involves understanding the individual as a unitary whole in mutual process with the environment. Holistic nursing responds to both views, believing that the goals of nursing can be achieved within either framework (AHNA, 2005).

The holistic nurse is an instrument of healing and a facilitator in the healing process. Holistic nurses honor each individual's subjective experience about health, health beliefs and values. To become therapeutic partners with individuals, families, and communities, holistic nursing practice draws on nursing knowledge, theories, research, expertise, intuition, and creativity. Holistic nursing practice encourages peer review of professional practice in various clinical settings and integrates knowledge of current professional standards, laws, and regulations governing nursing practice (AHNA, 2005).

Practicing holistic nursing requires nurses to integrate self-care, self-responsibility, spirituality, and reflection in their lives, which may lead to a greater awareness of an interconnectedness with self, others, nature, and one's personal concept of God or deity. This awareness may further enhance the nurses' understanding of all individuals and their relationships to the human and global community, and permits nurses to use this awareness to facilitate the healing process (AHNA, 2005).

The AHNA was founded in 1981 by a group of nurses dedicated to bringing the concepts of holism into every arena of nursing practice (www.ahna.org). To date, the AHNA has established basic and advanced certification in holistic nursing practice; a core curriculum of holistic nursing has also been developed (AHNA, 2005; Dossey, Keegan, & Guzzetta, 2008). Many schools of nursing now incorporate various components of the holistic nursing philosophy into their curricula by providing educational offerings that include holistic nursing concepts, herbal healing, energy modalities, environmental concerns, and body work. A number of universities throughout the country also offer graduate-level degrees with a focus in holistic nursing (Richardson, 2004).

HEALING OF THE MIND AND BODY

The use of the mind to promote healing is an approach that dates back centuries. Ancient civilizations recognized the value of the mind as a powerful healing tool and incorporated the innate human qualities of imagination, meditation, reflection, and prayer to facilitate healing of the mind, body, and spirit.

Guided imagery is the purposeful development of mental images while in a deep state of relaxation (Heinschel, 2002). It is used to promote relaxation, manage stress, and enhance immune function (www.academyforguidedimagery.com). Imagery guides the normal flow of thoughts within the imagination and uses the power of the mind to bring about positive images of healing, improve performance, and reduce anxiety. The mind then influences the body to meet the positive image (Heinschel, 2002; Snyder & Lindquist, 2006).

Those who practice imagery believe that a relaxed body and focused mind can foster changes in perception and solutions to problems and heal emotional trauma. Imagery has been successfully used as a healing modality for individuals with musculoskeletal pain, allergies, and acute injuries and during preoperative and postoperative periods. Patients with cancer have used imagery to help them cope with the experience of therapeutic interventions and to decrease the side effects of treatment. Nurses have used guided imagery with patients in inpatient and outpatient clinical settings. Imagery has value in enhancing relaxation, reducing anxiety, decreasing the need for pain medications, and increasing the patient's ability to focus (Dossey et al., 2008; Heinschel, 2002; Snyder & Lindquist, 2006). Nurses can learn about how to incorporate integrative imagery into their practice at www.integrativeimagery.com.

Meditation, reflection, prayer, and *relaxation* are similar healing modalities that focus on creating an environment of peacefulness and inner quiet. With these approaches, one turns inward to examine the self within and connect with inner wisdom and intuition. Some religious traditions view prayer as direct communication with God; others view prayer as a special form of connection with a divine or absolute power that is found in all beings. Prayer is considered to be a form of "speaking out," whereas meditation is a "quiet listening." Reflection is the ability to evaluate and synthesize the experience (Dossey et al., 2008; Henry & Henry, 2004; Snyder & Lindquist, 2006).

Through meditation, reflection, and prayer, relaxation is enhanced. As heart rate and blood pressure are reduced, stress is decreased, one's perception of pain is diminished, and an increased level of self-understanding is achieved. These processes are believed to intensify insights, a cognitive awareness of body functioning and an intuitive understanding of what is needed to foster personal healing (Dossey et al., 2008; Snyder & Lindquist, 2006).

Biofeedback has been used for many years to enhance relaxation and help patients gain control over their pain. It is based on the concept that the mind controls the body: if one can recognize physical signals, certain internal physiologic events can be changed. Biofeedback combines relaxation with learning how to consciously regulate body functions to enhance health and to decrease pain, blood pressure, and heart rate. During the childbirth experience, couples who have practiced how to recognize and respond to painful stimuli during the prenatal period can use biofeedback to achieve and enhance relaxation.

Formal biofeedback, which involves the use of a recording device to measure physiologic responses, requires special training by a skilled biofeedback therapist. Specially designed equipment is used to monitor the heart rate, muscle tension, skin temperature, and moisture. Patients are taught how to reduce tension, induce relaxation, and isolate and exercise certain muscle groups. Because the recording equipment provides immediate information, the therapist is able to show the patient what progress has been made and reinforce desirable responses that brought about the changes (Goldberg, Anderson, & Trivieri, 2002; Snyder & Lindquist, 2006).

Biofeedback can be used to enhance training of specific muscle groups. After several sessions of practice and reinforcement, patients can usually isolate and exercise desired muscle groups, even without the biofeedback equipment. This technique has been successfully used with continence training, pain control, and stress reduction (Lowdermilk & Perry, 2007).

HEALING THROUGH ENERGY AND TOUCH

The use of touch to promote healing dates back over 5,000 years, when Asian healers developed techniques to provide comfort, convey caring, and enhance recovery. As a method for healing, touch can be conveyed in many forms. *Massage* may include rubbing, stroking, and various manipulative techniques of the muscle groups and other connective tissue to reduce tension and pain and increase blood flow to the area. Different methods of massage therapy are believed to relieve muscle tension, promote lymphatic drainage, increase circulation, decrease edema, enhance healing of certain musculoskeletal injuries, and improve the function of certain body systems. Simple massage, long used by nurses in clinical practice, is included in the nursing intervention categories. However, therapeutic massage requires additional formal training and national certification in this area is available. Massage therapists are subject to individ-

ual state laws and regulation (Goldberg et al., 2002; Peck, 2008; Reilly, 2005).

Physical touch and energy theory form the basis of other methods of touch in healing. Many alternative and complementary therapies use an energy-based philosophy that recognizes the presence of an energy field around and inside the human body. The energy field can be modulated and changed to facilitate healing. Energy-based healing focuses on improving the health, balance, and restoration of the energy field so that the body can then heal. Any physical, emotional, or spiritual illness is believed to be detectable in the field and also healed with the field (Hover-Kramer, Mentgen, & Scandrett-Hibdon, 2001; Oschman, 2003).

Energy healing dates back to the writings of the ancient Hindus who spoke of "prana"; the Asians referred to "chi" or "qi." Early Christians and Greeks used various forms of energy healing as well. Considered to be an important component of the spiritual pathway, healing was routinely practiced by both clergy members and laypersons within the context of their religious practices. During the 12th century, Pope Alexander mandated a halt to the healing mission of the church. Although this action removed healing from the domain of the church, many talented healers continued to use energy techniques (Dossey et al., 2008; Gerber et al, 2001; Hover-Kramer et al., 2001). Healing Touch International (www.healingtouch.net) is a professional organization that sets standards for practice, administers certification for practitioners, coordinates research and health care integration, and provides educational opportunities for healing touch.

Acupressure, sometimes called "Chinese massage," involves the application of pressure or heat or cold to identified acupuncture points to decrease the sensation of pain. A variation on massage and touch, acupressure has its origins in traditional chinese medicine (TCM). TCM asserts that chi, or qi, is the body's energy, the vital force of life. If that energy stagnates or becomes blocked, illness, pain, or other dysfunction can occur. Energy travels on specific pathways, called *meridians,* throughout the body. A series of points located on each meridian corresponds to body function and various organs. Those who practice TCM believe that by massaging or compressing a given point, the body energy to that corresponding organ or system can be altered or restored. Once the energy flow is restored, healing can occur (Flaws, 2004; Gerber et al., 2001; Goldberg et al., 2002; Oschman, 2003).

Therapeutic Touch was designed by Dolores Krieger, PhD, RN, a nursing professor at New York University. To perform Therapeutic Touch, the practitioner begins in a calm and centered state of mind (called "centering") and holds thoughts of desiring to help or heal (called "intention"). Therapeutic Touch involves a series of steps in which the practitioner perceives the recipient's energy field and notes areas of uneven activity, deficit, or excess. After observing and feeling the recipient's energy field, the practitioner uses various techniques to modulate the energy and correct the abnormal areas. Therapeutic Touch has been widely researched and used in nursing to reduce anxiety, alleviate pain, and facilitate wound healing (Krieger, 2002; Kunz & Krieger, 2004; Lowdermilk & Perry, 2007; Snyder & Lindquist, 2002; Ventegodt, Morad, & Merrick, 2004).

Healing Touch is an energy-based modality that combines a variety of techniques from several disciplines. This approach provides practitioners with an array of "tools" to facilitate the restoration of alignment and balance to the human energy field. Once alignment and balance have been achieved, the body is better able to heal itself. Healing Touch is believed to be beneficial for a variety of physical, mental, emotional, and spiritual disorders (Hover-Kramer et al., 2001).

ALTERNATIVES TO DRUG THERAPY

Pharmacologic Alternatives

For many American consumers, herbal products and alternatives to medications are the complementary therapies of choice. Safe use of these substances requires an understanding of the actions, side effects, and contraindications associated with each. Nurses should ensure that patients understand that herbs are medicine, that can interact with other drugs and counteract or intensify pharmaceutical effects. When taken in doses that exceed the recommended amounts, they can be dangerous (Simpkins, Thurston, Colyer, & Talbot, 2005). Also, because herbal preparations can vary in concentration, patients should be warned to carefully read all labels to determine the actual herbal component of the selected preparation (Skidmore-Roth, 2005).

Homeopathy is a system of healing founded by a German physician in the 1700s who wished to find a more humane, sensible approach to care than the popular treatments of the day (e.g., bloodletting with leeches, toxic laxatives). Experimentation with various botanic agents confirmed the earlier findings of Hippocrates that small doses of the same agent that caused a disease would also cure it. This basic observation forms the foundation for modern immunologic medicine: exposure to a small amount of a toxin, allergen, or virus prompts the body to create immunity to the substance (Goldberg et al., 2002; Lansky, 2003).

Practitioners of homeopathy believe that each patient is a unique individual and care is tailored to create and prescribe a remedy specific for that person. While many standard remedies are available, homeopathic practitioners frequently blend individual remedies according to the patient's specific needs. Homeopathic philosophy holds that illness, expressed on the physical level, is evidence of disturbances on other, deeper levels. Homeopathic remedies are believed to work through the other levels, beginning with the most recent level and working to the oldest level until full healing has occurred (Goldberg et al., 2002; Lansky, 2003).

TCM, which combines herbal and energy medicine, has become increasingly more popular in recent times. TCM, which has been practiced for over 3,000 years, incorporates theories of energetic healing. Energy flow is often described as being in excess or as deficient. The goal of TCM is to restore total harmony on the spiritual, the emotional, and physical levels. Acupressure is a discipline within TCM. Acupuncture is a TCM therapy used for healing and comfort. Based on the theory that illness results from an imbalance of energy, acupuncure involves the stimulation of specific points on the body with needles, herbs, or heat and herbal treatments. Tai chi and qi gong are examples of movement forms that can be integrated into a program of TCM (Flaws, 2004; Goldberg et al., 2002; Helms, 2006).

Acupuncture is practiced widely throughout the country. With acupuncture, many have found relief from discomforts associated with dental procedures, fibromyalgia and myofascial pain and a variety of other painful conditions. Acupuncture has also shown promise in reducing or eliminating nausea associated with pregnancy and chemotherapy. Research is presently underway to explore its efficacy in other areas (NCCAM, 2007).

Exercise and Nutrition

Current guidelines recommend 60 minutes of daily physical activity as an important strategy in promoting cardiovascular health, decreasing body fat, preventing disease, and improving one's sense of well-being. As a component of health teaching, nurses should assist patients in developing individualized exercise programs that best suit their needs and are most likely to be continued. Women especially benefit from weight-bearing exercise, such as walking, to prevent osteoporosis. Women may also choose to engage in many other forms of exercise,

such as aerobics, weight and endurance training, martial arts, and yoga.

Yoga

Dating back over 5,000 years, *yoga* is the oldest defined practice of self-development. Deriving its name from the root Sanskrit word *yony,* meaning "union," yoga brings together the mind, body, and spirit. As a lifestyle approach to health, the practice of yoga offers benefits in the biological, psychological, social, and spiritual domains.

Biological Domain

Yoga offers structured exercises designed to increase strength, flexibility, and endurance. *Asanas,* postures that focus on various body systems, increase endorphin release and are believed to be corrective for certain disease states. Yoga is practiced in many different forms such as *hatha yoga, astanga yoga,* and *vinyasa yoga.*

Hatha yoga focuses on slowly and deliberately stretching within the asanas to lengthen and strengthen the various muscle groups. Astanga yoga incorporates more difficult and athletic poses and stretches to promote endurance. Vinyasa yoga adds an aerobic component with more rapid progression with the asanas. The postures are thought to affect many body functions, such as balance, muscle tone and coordination (Iyengar, 2007; Martin & Jung, 2002; Mehta, 2006; Mehta, Mehta, & Mehta, 2001).

Yoga also incorporates *pranayama,* which is controlled deep breathing. Pranayama is believed to energize and stimulate the body, enhance cardiovascular functioning, stimulate blood flow, and reduce stress. Yoga proponents believe that there are many other physical benefits, such as relief from symptoms associated with allergy and asthma, lowered blood pressure and heart rate, and reduced cortisol levels. Practitioners of yoga believe that the yoga lifestyle helps them to make healthy choices for enhanced living and, although not required, many choose to adopt a vegetarian life style

(Iyengar, 2006; Martin & Jung, 2002; Mehta, 2006; Mehta et al., 2001).

Psychological Domain

Yoga seeks to provide stress relief through the quieting of the mind and focused concentration. The meditative state one achieves is believed to raise the level of consciousness beyond the day-to-day mundane thought processes and bring inner peace. This is a path to increased awareness (Iyengar, 2006; Martin & Jung, 2002; Mehta, 2006; Mehta et al., 2001).

Exercise is known to increase the release of endorphins. Endorphins are neurochemicals that can affect mood and mental state in a positive way. As endorphins are released, one experiences an increased sense of well-being, enhanced energy, and mental focus for other tasks (Iyengar, 2006; Martin & Jung, 2002; Mehta, 2006; Mehta et al., 2001).

Social Domain

Yoga provides a community structure of other practitioners for the sharing of common goals and experiences. The practice of yoga seeks to bring the practitioner from a fragmented state to one of unity: unity of the body, mind, and spirit. Yoga promotes a lifestyle of balance, harmony, unity, ethics, morals, and personal conduct (Iyengar, 2006; Martin & Jung, 2002; Mehta, 2006; Mehta et al., 2001).

Spiritual Domain

Yoga promotes a form of meditation, focuses the flow of body energy and connects the practitioner to the divine. This is believed to promote inner peace and harmony. Meditation is thought to lead to spiritual experience and profound understanding or insight into the nature of existence. Although intimately connected to the religious beliefs and practices of other Indian religions, yoga is not promoted as a religion (Iyengar, 2006; Martin & Jung, 2002; Mehta, 2006; Mehta et al., 2001).

CONCLUSION

In contemporary society, more questions than answers exist for many women's health issues. Throughout history, health-promotion measures have had a powerful impact on women's health. Thousands of women's lives have been saved by basic actions such as washing the hands and maintaining a clean, safe environment. Women have always been instrumental in ensuring family health; today's women are empowered to actively engage in strategies designed to ensure optimal personal health.

Efforts to purify the water supply and establish proper sewage disposal were primarily responsible for the major community-wide health improvements in the past. Today, citizens are challenged to consolidate efforts to clean up the environment, improve economic conditions, and make health care readily available to all. At the same time, health improvement must occur on a personal level as individuals are challenged to adopt healthy eating, exercise, and work habits. By providing education, counseling, and support, health care providers share an important role in this process toward improved health.

It has been the intention of this course to provide current information about women's health issues, spark your interest, raise questions for your consideration, and encourage you to continue to educate yourself and others.

EXAM QUESTIONS

CHAPTER 14
Questions 98-100

Note: Choose the option that BEST answers each question.

98. CAM is an approach that

   a. focuses only on physical symptoms.

   b. places all responsibility for healing on the care provider.

   c. views medications as an essential component of healing.

   d. places emphasis on the patient as a whole being.

99. The use of the mind to promote healing

   a. includes techniques such as imagery, meditation, and reflection.

   b. is a method developed within the past decade.

   c. is rarely used by nurses in clinical practice.

   d. results in a decreased understanding of body functioning and intuitive insights.

100. As a lifestyle approach to health, yoga

   a. requires one to adopt a vegetarian lifestyle.

   b. requires an ability to perform aerobic exercises.

   c. offers benefits in the biological, psychological, social, and spiritual domains.

   d. attempts to create a state of mental stimulation that decreases the ability to concentrate.

This concludes the final examination.

Please answer the evaluation questions found on page v of this course book.

RESOURCES

BIRTH CONTROL/SEXUALLY TRANSMITTED INFECTIONS/ABNORMAL PAP SMEAR FINDINGS

AIDS Clinical Trials Information Service
1-800-874-2572
P.O. Box 6421, Rockville, MD 20849-6421
http://www.actis.org

The Alan Guttmacher Institute
Research, policy analysis, and public education
(212) 248-1111
120 Wall Street
New York, NY 10005
http://www.guttmacher.org

American Foundation for AIDS Research (AmFAR)
(212) 682-7440
733 Third Avenue, 12th Floor
New York, NY 10017
http://www.amfar.org

American Liver Foundation
1-800-GO LIVER (1-800-465-4837)
1425 Pompton Avenue
Cedar Grove, NJ 07009
http://www.liverfoundation.org

American Social Health Association (ASHA)
Hotline 1-800-230-6039
P.O. Box 13827
Research Triangle Park, NC 27709-3827
http://www.ashastd.org

Centers for Disease Control and Prevention (CDC) National AIDS Hotline
1-800-342-AIDS (1-800-342-2437) (English)
1-800-344-SIDA (1-800-344-7432) (Spanish)
P.O. Box 13827
Research Triangle Park, NC 27709-3827

CDC National Sexually Transmitted Diseases (STD) Hotline
1-800-227-8922

Hepatitis Foundation International
1-800-891-0707
Sunrise Terrace, Cedar Grove, NJ 07009-1423
http://www.hepfi.org

National Cervical Cancer Coalition (NCCC)
(818) 909-3849
16501 Sherman Way, Suite 110
Van Nuys, CA 91406
http://www.nccc-online.org

National Network of Libraries of Medicine
Access to online databases on HIV and other topics
1-800-338-7657
http://nnlm.gov

Project Inform
Information, inspiration, and advocacy for people living with HIV/AIDS
1-800-822-7422
205 13th Street, No. 2001
San Francisco, CA 94103
http://www.projinf.org

EATING DISORDERS

National Center for Overcoming Overeating
(212) 875-0442
P. O. Box 1257, Old Chelsea Station
New York, NY 10113-0920
http://www.overcomingovereating.com

BREAST CANCER

American Cancer Society
1-800-ACS-2345 (1-800-227-2345)
P.O. Box 22538
Oklahoma City, OK 73123
http://www.cancer.org

Breast Cancer Action
1-877-278-6722, (415) 243-9301
55 New Montgomery Street, Suite 323
San Francisco, CA 94105
http://www.bcaction.org

Cancer Information Service, National Cancer Institute
1-800-4-CANCER (1-800-422-6237)
31 Center Drive, MSC 2580
Building 31, Room 10A16
Bethesda, MD 20892-2580
http://www.cancer.gov

MammaCare
Breast models and teaching tools
1-800-626-2273
930 NW 8th Avenue
Gainesville, FL 32601
P.O. Box 15748
Gainesville, FL 32602
http://www.mammacare.com

National Alliance of Breast Cancer Organizations (NABCO)
1-800-80NABCO (1-800-806-2226)
9 East 37th Street, 10th Floor
New York, NY 10016
http://www.nabco.org

National Breast Cancer Coalition (NBCC)
(202) 296-7477
1707 L Street, NW, Suite 1060
Washington, DC 20036
http://www.natlbcc.org

National Cancer Institute
See Cancer Information Service, National
Cancer Institute

National Coalition for Cancer Survivorship
1-888-650-9127
1010 Wayne Avenue, Suite 505
Silver Spring, MD 20910-5600
http://www.canceradvocacy.org

Susan G. Komen Breast Cancer Foundation
1-800-462-9273
5005 LBJ Freeway, Suite 370
Dallas, TX 75244
http://www.komen.org

Y-ME National Breast Cancer Organization
Hotline: 1-800-221-2141 (English)
1-800-986-9505 (Spanish)
212 West Van Buren, 5th Floor
Chicago, IL 60607-3907
http://www.y-me.org

DIET AND NUTRITIONAL GUIDELINES

MyPyramid
http://mypyramid.gov/

Dietary Guidelines for Americans
http://www.healthierus.gov/dietaryguidelines

Office of Dietary Supplements (ODS), NIH
http://ods.od.nih.gov

U.S. Food and Drug Administration (FDA), Center for Food Safety and Applied Nutrition
1-999-723-3366
http://www.cfsan.fda.gov

GENERAL INFORMATION ON WOMEN'S HEALTH ISSUES

Alzheimer's Disease Education and Referral (ADEAR) Center
1-800-438-4380
P.O. Box 8250, Silver Spring, MD 20907-8250
http://www.alzheimers.org

Center for Women Policy Studies

* *National Resource Center for Women and AIDS*
* *Women Health Decision Making Project*
* *The Law and Pregnancy – Women's Reproductive Rights*
(202) 872-1770
1211 Connecticut Avenue, NW, Suite 312
Washington, DC 20036
http://www.centerwomenpolicy.org

Endometriosis Association, Inc.
1-800-426-2END (1-800-426-2363)
(414) 355-2200
8585 North 76th Place
Milwaukee, WI 53223
http://www.endometriosisassn.org

Hysterectomy Educational Resources and Services Foundation
(610) 667-7757
422 Bryn Mawr Avenue
Bala Cynwyd, PA 19004
http://www.hersfoundation.com

National Women's Health Network
(202) 347-1140
514 10th Street, NW, Suite 400
Washington, DC 20004
http://www.womenshealthnetwork.org

National Women's Health Resource Center
(202) 537-4015
5255 Loughboro Road, NW
Washington, DC 20016
htttp://www.healthywomen.org

North American Menopause Society (NAMS)
(440) 442-7550
5900 Landerbrook Drive, Suite 390
Mayfield Heights, OH 44124
http://www.menopause.org
mail to: info@menopause.org

Office on Women's Health
(800) 944-woman
8550 Arlington Boulevard, Suite 300
Fairfax, VA 22031
http://www.4woman.gov/healthpro.index.htm

Ovarian Cancer National Alliance
(202) 452-5910
P.O. Box 33107
Washington DC 20033-0107
http://www.ovariancancer.org

Women's Health Interactive
(970) 282-9437
P.O. Box 271276
Fort Collins, CO 80527-1276
http://www.womens-health.com

INFERTILITY/ ENDOMETRIOSIS

American Society for Reproductive Medicine (ASRM)
(205) 978-5000
1209 Montgomery Highway
Birmingham, AL 3521
http://www.asrm.org

Behavioral Medicine Infertility Program

One of a series of special programs sponsored by the Behavioral Medicine Medical Department at Beth Israel Deaconess Medical Center

> (617) 632-9529
> W/Lowry Medical Office Bldg. 1-A
> http://www.bidmc.harvard.edu/infertility
>   -program.asp
> Also contact:
> Beth Israel Deaconess Medical Center
> (617) 667-7000
> 330 Brookline Avenue
> Boston MA 02215

The Endometriosis Association

> www.ivf.com/endohtml.html

Internet Health Resources Company

> (925) 284-9362
> 1133 Garden Lane
> Lafayette, CA 94549
> http://www.ihr.com/

RESOLVE: The National Infertility Association

> (703) 556-7172
> 8405 Greensboro Drive, Suite 800
> McLean, VA 22102
> http://www.resolve.org

INTEGRATIVE/ COMPLEMENTARY MEDICINE

National Acupuncture and Oriental Medicine Alliance

> (253) 851-6896
> 14637 Starr Road, SE, Olalla, WA 98359
> http://www.aomalliance.org

National Certification Commission for Acupuncture and Oriental Medicine (NCCAOM)

> (703) 548-9004
> 11 Canal Center Plaza, Suite 300
> Alexandria, VA 22314
> http://www.nccaom.org

News from the Herbal Village

> 1-800-437-2257
> Nature's Herbs
> 600 E. Quality Drive
> American Fork, UT 84003
> http://www.naturesherbs.com

NCCAM Clearinghouse

> 1-888-644-6226
> P.O. Box 7923
> Gaithersburg, MD 20898
> http://info@nccam.nih.gov/

Therapeutic Touch NH-PAI, Inc. Nurse Healers – Professional Associates International

> (518) 325-1185
> 1-877-32NHPAI
> P.O. Box 419
> Craryville, NY 12521
> http://www.therapeutic-touch.org

OSTEOPOROSIS

Foundation for Osteoporosis Research and Education (FORE)

> 1-888-266-3015
> 300 27th Street, Suite 103, Oakland, CA 94612
> http://www.fore.org

National Osteoporosis Foundation (NOF)

> 1150 17th Street, NW, Suite 500
> Washington, DC 20036-4603

SEXUALITY

The Women's Sexual Health Foundation
http://www.twshf.org

National Vulvodynia Association
(301) 299-0775
P.O. Box 4491
Silver Spring, MD 20914
http://www.nva.org

Nurture Your Nature: Inspiring Women's Sexual Wellness
http:www.nurtureyournature.org

Sexuality Information and Education Council of the United States (SIECUS)
130 West 42nd Street, Suite 350
New York, NY 10036
(219) 819-9770
http://www.siecus.org

WOMEN WITH DISABILITIES

Center for Research on Women with Physical Disabilities
(713) 798-6539
Baylor College of Medicine
One Baylor Plaza
Houston, TX 77030
http://www.bcm.edu/crowd

Health Promotion for Women with Disabilities
(610) 519-6828
Villanova University College of Nursing
800 Lancaster Avenue
Villanova, PA 19085
http://nurseweb.villanova.edu/womenwith disabilities

Initiative for Women with Disabilities
(212) 263-7300
NYU Langone Medical Center
550 First Avenue
New York, NY 10016
http://www.med.nyu.edu/hjd/iwd

TRAVEL HEALTH INFORMATION

CDC Online Health Information for International Travel (The Yellow Book)
(800) CDC-INFO
1600 Clifton Road
Atlanta, GA 30333
www.cdc.gov/travel/contentYellowBook.aspx

Epidemiology and Prevention of Vaccine-Preventable Diseases (The CDC Pink Book)
www.cdc.gov/nip/publications/pink

GeoSentinel (The Global Surveillance Network of the International Society of Travel Medicine and the CDC)
(770) 736-7060
2386 Clower Street, Suite A-102
Snellville, GA 30078
www.istm.org/geosentinel/main.html

Infectious Diseases Society of America
(703) 299-0200
1300 Wilson Blulevard, Suite 300
Arlington, VA 22209
www.idsociety.org

International Association for Medical Assistance to Travelers
(716) 754-4884
1623 Military Road #279
Niagara Falls, NY 14304
www.iamat.org

World Health Organization (WHO) Online
   International Travel and Health (The Green
   Book)
   Avenue Appia 20
   1211 Geneva 27
   Switzerland
   www.who.int/ith/en

TIPS ON INTERNET RESOURCES

- Check the date of information or data you find on the Internet. Some may be outdated, especially for fast-changing research topics, such as human papillomavirus, hormone replacement therapy, or abnormal Pap smear findings.

- Be aware that some sites have more reliable information than others. Some sites are juried, or reviewed by organizations to control content; others are not.

- Surf at your own risk. Be discriminating about the information you receive, and confirm it with a health practitioner. Look at other sites for confirmation as well.

In addition to the Internet sites previously listed in this guide are the following:

U.S. National Library of Medicine
   8600 Rockville Pike
   Bethesda, MD 20894
   http://www.nlm.nih.gov/

Mayo Clinic Health Oasis
   (507) 284-2511
   200 1st Street SW
   Rochester, MN 55905
   http://www.mayohealth.org

Division of STD Prevention, Centers for Disease
   Control and Prevention (CDC)
   http://www.cdc.gov/nchstp/dstd/dstdp.html

GLOSSARY

adjuvant: Cancer treatment that is not the primary form of treatment for removal of cancerous tissue. It is instead a systemic treatment that is initiated after surgery to prevent return of the cancer by killing cells that may have traveled elsewhere in the body.

agglutination: Clumping together. An abnormal sign in evaluation of sperm function that could indicate an immune response.

alternative and complementary therapies: Nontraditional approaches to healing and health care. Frequently, these therapies are philosophically different from Western medicine. They often involve interventions believed to induce healing from within to allow the body, mind, and spirit to heal.

Alternative therapy: Modalities used in place of conventional health care.

Complementary therapy: Modalities used in conjunction with conventional health care.

amenorrhea: Absence of menstruation.

anovulatory cycle: Menstrual cycle in which no egg is released from the ovary.

artificial menopause: A condition brought on by surgical removal of the ovaries or radiation or chemotherapy treatment that renders the ovaries nonfunctional.

aspiration: Withdrawal by gentle suction.

assisted hatching: A micromanipulation technique used in assisted reproductive technology interventions in which a hole is made in the outer covering of the egg to assist the sperm to penetrate and fertilize it.

assisted reproductive technologies (ARTs): The various new technologies for assisting infertile couples to conceive.

asymptomatic: Absence of symptoms in the presence of a disease.

atherosclerosis: Build up of fatty plaque on the walls of an artery, stiffening the artery and reducing blood flow.

basal body temperature (BBT) charting: Method to determine when ovulation has occurred; used in natural family planning and fertility.

Purpose: To verify ovulation and determine adequacy of the luteal phase of the menstrual cycle.

Procedure: BBT must be taken before arising and at the same time every morning. It is best to use a special BBT thermometer that has the appropriate range for easy reading. Also to be recorded are days of menstrual flow, discharge, mucus, illness, nights up late or with less than 6 hours of sleep, and sexual intercourse. Recordings are made for 2 to 6 months.

Results: Charting reveals whether the couple's timing of sexual intercourse is optimal for conception. Standard recommendation for fertility is intercourse 2 days before ovulation is expected and then every 2 days, until 2 to 4 days have passed after the increase in BBT.

basal thermometer: Specially calibrated instrument to measure body temperature in relation to ovulation.

benign: Noncancerous.

bimanual examination: Part of the standard examination of the female pelvic organs in which the examiner inserts two fingers into the vagina, pressing with the opposing hand on the abdomen. In this way, the ovaries and uterus are palpated for abnormalities.

biofeedback: A technique that teaches the patient to consciously control certain body functions that are usually thought of as unconscious, such as heart rate and breathing.

biopsy: A procedure to remove a small piece of tissue for microscopic analysis by a specialist.

bisphosphonates: Synthetic forms of a class of compounds found in the body that inhibit the process of bone resorption; used to prevent and treat postmenopausal osteoporosis.

bone density screening: Measurement of bone mass by using low-dose X-ray procedures.

breast self-examination (BSE): Monthly examination advised for all adult women in which women examine their breasts for any changes by using both visual inspection and palpation.

carcinoma: Cancer of the tissue that covers body surfaces, both internal and external.

carcinoma in situ (CIS): Carcinoma that has not yet invaded surrounding tissue.

cervicitis: Inflammation of the cervix caused by infection, injury, or irritation.

cervicography: Diagnostic technique in which photographs are taken of the cervix.

cholesterol: A substance that is manufactured by the liver as well as derived from animal fat. Hormones such as estrogen and progesterone are made from cholesterol. It is also a part of cell membranes. Cholesterol is transported through the bloodstream attached to lipoproteins.

chronic fatigue syndrome: A constellation of symptoms characterized by debilitating fatigue and flulike symptoms. The cause is not well understood but is thought to be multifactorial.

climacteric: The period, which can last from months to years, when the menstrual cycle of women becomes irregular, hormone levels fluctuate and eventually decrease, and periods cease altogether. During this time, the woman passes from a reproductive to a nonreproductive state.

clinical breast examination (CBE): A breast examination performed by a licensed professional trained to do breast examinations.

clitoris: A small, pea-sized, hooded, erectile structure located on the vulva above the vagina. It is the anatomic homologue of the penis in the male and is highly responsive to sexual stimulation.

Colles' fracture: A fracture of the radius that occurs when a person extends a hand to break a fall.

colposcopy: Technique for viewing the cervix under magnification, making it possible to see structures not visible to the naked eye. Used to evaluate the cervix and vagina.

columnar epithelium: Glandular tissue of the cervix that is composed of tall, narrow cells.

congenital: Existing at or dating from birth, but not due to heredity.

conization of the cervix: A surgical procedure in which a part of the cervix surrounding the cervical canal is removed.

corpus luteum: A structure formed after ovulation by the remaining tissue of the follicle. Its main function is secretion of progesterone, which prepares the uterine lining for implantation by a fertilized embryo. The corpus luteum helps support the developing embryo, or it disintegrates if fertilization has not occurred.

cryopreservation: Use of a medium, usually liquid nitrogen, to store something in a frozen state. Refers to preservation of embryos in assisted reproductive technology.

cryosurgery: Use of a cold source to freeze abnormal tissue.

cryotherapy: A treatment that involves freezing of abnormal tissue and is commonly used to remove abnormal cervical cells as well as genital warts from the vagina and external genitalia.

Depo-Provera: A synthetic progesterone (medroxyprogesterone acetate) used as an injectable method of birth control.

diethylstilbestrol (DES): A synthetic estrogen that was once given to women early in pregnancy to prevent miscarriage. It was taken off the market because of its multiple effects on the offspring of women who took it, including increased risk of a rare type of vaginal cancer and increased rates of infertility in male and female offspring.

dilatation and curettage (D&C): A vaginal procedure in which the cervical canal is stretched enough to permit the passage of a sharp instrument (a curette). The curette is used to scrape the endometrium to empty the uterine contents or to obtain tissue for examination.

dysmenorrhea: Painful menstrual cramps.

dyspareunia: Pain with sexual intercourse.

dysplasia: Abnormal cell growth that can be a precancerous condition.

dysuria: Painful urination.

ectopic pregnancy: A pregnancy that implants and develops outside the uterus, most often in the fallopian tube. This can be life-threatening and requires immediate intervention.

embryo: Fertilized egg. The developing human organism is an embryo from approximately week 1 of development through week 8.

emergency contraception pill (ECP): Also known as the *morning after pill,* this type of pill is used to deter pregnancy in case of an accidental method failure or unprotected intercourse. Specific birth control pill formulations are used to interrupt fertilization and implantation.

endocervical canal: Canal that runs down the center of the cervix and opens into the vagina on one side and into the uterus on the other.

endometrial biopsy: A test done to sample the uterine lining. Used in infertility evaluation for evidence that ovulation has occurred. Also used to diagnose abnormalities of the uterine lining, such as uterine cancer.

Procedure: Usually done about 10 days after a rise in basal body temperature. A small cannula is inserted through the cervical canal into the uterus, where a sample of the lining is gathered by suction or curettage. Mild to moderate cramping can be expected. Use of a nonsteroidal anti-inflammatory drug beforehand is helpful. A vasovagal response may occur; having the patient elevate the legs and take time to come to an upright position usually abates this response. Nausea and vomiting or fainting may occur if the reaction is more pronounced.

endometrial hyperplasia: Abnormally rapid and extensive growth of the uterine lining.

endometrioma: Implant of endometrial tissue outside the uterus; found in endometriosis.

endometriosis: Tissue that closely resembles the endometrial tissue is located outside of the uterus in the pelvic cavity. Symptoms may include pelvic pain or pressure, dysmenorrhea, dyspareunia, and infertility.

endometrium: Inner lining of the uterus that responds to the cyclic influence of hormones during the menstrual cycle.

endorphins: Hormones found in the brain that give a sensation of well-being and affect pain perception and emotion.

energy healing: A variety of techniques and disciplines that are believed to augment, modulate, stimulate or improve certain deficiencies or blocks, in the human energy system.

enzyme: A protein that is needed for specific chemical reactions in the body but is not changed by the reaction and therefore can be used again.

epithelial cells: Cells that make up the type of tissue that covers the surfaces of the body and its internal organs.

estrogen: Group of similar hormones that stimulate the maturation of egg follicles, leading to ovulation. Three forms of estrogen are found in the human body: estradiol, estriol, and estrone. Synthetic forms are used in formulations of the birth control pill and standard hormone replacement therapy.

estrogen replacement therapy (ERT): Use of a form of the hormone estrogen to create a state of hormone balance in a woman who has stopped menstruating, similar to her hormonal state before menopause. ERT is given to women during and after menopause to prevent hot flashes, mood changes, osteoporosis, and genitourinary symptoms. Use of estrogen alone by a woman who still has a uterus increases the risk of uterine cancer.

false-negative: Failure of a test to detect an existing abnormality.

false-positive: Indication of abnormality when none exists.

fertility awareness methods (FAMs): Birth control methods that identify the beginning and end of the fertile period of the menstrual cycle.

fibroadenoma: A benign tumor that contains glandular and fibrous elements and is commonly found in the breast.

fibrocystic breast disease: Not really a disease but rather a condition in which fluid-filled cysts enlarge in conjunction with the second half of the menstrual cycle, causing discomfort and swelling of the breasts.

fibroid: Fibrous, encapsulated connective tissue tumor, especially of the uterus (leiomyoma).

fine needle aspiration (FNA): Technique for evaluating breast masses thought to be fluid-filled (cysts) by attempting to remove fluid with a fine needle.

folic acid: One of the B vitamins; involved in normal cell growth.

follicle: Group of tissues in the ovary that develop around an immature egg and are responsible for producing hormones and growth-promoting factors. Rupture of the follicle from the ovary is ovulation.

follicle-stimulating hormone (FSH): Hormone produced by the pituitary gland that targets the ovary and promotes growth of ovarian follicles.

fomite: An object, such as clothing or towels, that can provide a location for transmission of infection.

galactorrhea: Spontaneous discharge of milk from the breasts not associated with breast-feeding; may be a symptom of a pituitary tumor.

gamete: A reproductive cell (egg or sperm).

gamete intrafallopian transfer (GIFT): Transfer of a retrieved egg, along with prepared sperm, into the fallopian tube of a woman.

genetic counseling: Education and assessment of heritable risk factors provided by specially trained health professionals in order to help people make informed decisions based on genetic knowledge.

gland: Organized group of cells that secretes substances such as hormones.

gonadotropin: Substance produced by the pituitary gland that stimulates the gonads (ovaries or testes).

gonadotropin-releasing hormone (Gn-RH): Hormone produced by the hypothalamus that stimulates the pituitary gland to release gonadotropins.

gravidity: Total number of a woman's pregnancies.

guided imagery: The use of imagination and thought processes in a purposeful way to change certain physiologic and emotional conditions.

healing touch: The use of energetic healing techniques by nurses and other health care professionals.

health promotion: The motivation to increase well-being and actualize health potential.

high-density lipoprotein (HDL): A protein that carries fats and cholesterol through the blood-stream. Referred to as *good cholesterol* because it transports cholesterol out of tissues and allows it to be excreted.

holism: A philosophy that states that the whole is greater than the sum of its parts. In healing, it refers to consideration and treatment of the whole person as a unified being. It may include alternative and complementary therapies, but it is more a philosophic base than a modality in and of itself.

holistic medicine: Health care treatment with tech-niques not usually taught in U.S. medical schools or widely available in U.S. health care facilities. This approach may include a variety of disciplines that involve diet, exercise, vita-min and nutritional supplements, bodywork, or alternative pharmacologic agents. It is a philos-ophy of medicine that encompasses holism.

holistic nursing: The practice of nursing that stems from the philosophy of holism: one that views the patient as an integrated whole, who is influenced by a variety of internal and exter-nal factors, including the biopsychosocial and spiritual dimensions of that person.

hormone: Glandular secretion that controls the activity of tissues and organs.

hormone replacement therapy (HRT): Use of estrogen and progestin to replace hormones no longer produced after menopause.

hot flash (flush): The transient sensation of warmth, redness, or perspiration experienced by some women during or after menopause. It results from autonomic vasomotor disturbances that accompany the changes that are taking place in the neurohormonal activity of the ovaries, the hypothalamus, and the pituitary gland. A *hot flush* is a visible red flush of the skin and perspiration; a *hot flash* is a sudden warm sensation in the neck, head, and chest.

human chorionic gonadotropin (hCG): Hormone secreted in the urine and into the bloodstream of pregnant women. Its detection is the basis of both urine and serum pregnancy tests.

hyperplasia: An increase in the number of cells.

hypothalamus: Part of the brain that regulates a number of different body processes – including body temperature, appetite, thirst, and hor-monal stimulation to the ovaries, thyroid gland, and adrenal glands – by way of its action on the pituitary gland.

hysterosalpingogram:

Procedure used to indirectly visualize the reproductive tract of a woman and can be used to achieve patency of a blocked tube.

Procedure: A radiopaque iodine-based dye is injected through the cervix and follows the nor-mal pathway into the uterus, fallopian tubes, and abdominal cavity. The procedure should be scheduled for the first half of the menstrual cycle. It can be a very uncomfortable proce-dure, especially if the tubes are blocked. Vasovagal reactions may occur after the dye is injected. This is an outpatient procedure.

Results: It reveals abnormalities of the internal configuration of the uterus, such as fibroids or bicornate uterus. It also determines patency of the tubes, and it can sometimes clear an obstruction.

hysteroscopy: A procedure in which contrast medium, usually iodine-based, is used to distend the uterine cavity. Visualization of the structures is possible by using a hysteroscope, a lighted scope that is inserted through the cervix into the uterus. With hysteroscopy, one can perform a simple biopsy or remove a small polyp in the office setting. It can also be used for more complex operative procedures on the uterine lining, such as electrocautery, laser, and fibroid removal. These procedures would be performed in the operating room. Mild to moderate cramping often accompanies hysteroscopy.

insemination: Introduction of sperm into the female reproductive tract.

in situ: Used in this course in reference to carcinoma in situ, an early stage of cancer that is confined to the immediate area in which it began. In breast cancer, it means that the cancer remains confined to the ducts or lobules and has not invaded the surrounding fatty tissue or spread to other organs.

integrative health care: A general term that refers to the combined use of Western medical therapeutics and other healing modalities, such as traditional Chinese medicine, herbology, and massage.

intracytoplasmic sperm injection (ICSI): A micromanipulation technique used during assisted reproductive technology interventions in which a single sperm is injected into an egg, bypassing the egg's outer coating.

in vitro: *In glass* or outside the human body; usually refers to fertilization of an egg in assisted reproductive technologies.

in vitro fertilization/embryo transfer (IVF/ET): The oldest of the assisted reproductive technologies in which eggs are harvested from the ovary through the vaginal wall, placed in a laboratory environment, and fertilized. Then the fertilized eggs are transferred to the uterus for implantation.

Kegel exercises: Exercises performed to strengthen the muscles of the pelvic floor and control urination.

laparoscopy: Surgical procedure in which a fiber-optic scope and instruments are inserted through a small incision near the umbilicus to view pelvic structures and remove abnormal tissue. It is also used as one method of evaluating the fallopian tubes.

laparotomy: Abdominal surgery.

laser: An electrosurgical instrument in which electricity is converted to light, which is concentrated and thereby produces heat. The light of a laser is ordinary light that has been controlled and organized to emit one wavelength. The light travels through space in a beam, which can be finely focused to intensify its effects. Laser light can be used to cut, vaporize, coagulate, or fulgurate (superficial charring of surface) tissue. Heat is created when the tissue absorbs the radiation.

lesion: Any abnormal tissue.

libido: Sexual drive.

low-density lipoprotein (LDL): A protein that carries cholesterol and tends to promote deposits on arterial walls. Also known as *bad cholesterol.*

luteinizing hormone (LH): One of the hormones secreted by the pituitary gland that is essential to development of the ovarian follicle and ovulation.

lymph nodes: Glands of the lymphatic system that supply white blood cells to the general circulation and filter out bacteria and foreign particles from the lymph fluid.

macrocalcifications: Calcium deposits in the breast tissue detected by mammography; they often result from degenerative changes within the breast tissue following old injuries, inflammations, or aging of the breast arteries and are usually not related to malignancy.

malignant: Cancerous.

medical abortion: Use of drugs to induce abortion, rather than surgical termination of pregnancy.

meditation: Any activity that focuses the attention in the present moment and quiets and relaxes the mind and body in the process.

menarche: Initiation of menstrual cycles with the first menstrual period.

menopausal hormone therapy (MHT): Hormonal therapy, usually estrogen and progestin, prescribed for menopausal symptoms.

menopause: The actual permanent cessation of menstrual cycles, which is diagnosed after 1 year without menses.

menses: Periodic vaginal discharge of bloody fluid from a nonpregnant uterus; occurs from the age of puberty to menopause.

metastasis: Spread of cancer from the original site (referred to as the *primary cancer*) to a lymph node or distant organ.

microcalcifications: Detected by mammography, specks of calcium in the breast tissue that may be found in areas of rapidly dividing cells. When many microcalcifications are present in a cluster, they may indicate a small cancer; approximately one half of the cancers detected appear as these clusters.

micromanipulation: Procedure used to manipulate the tiny sperm or egg to improve chances of fertilization.

minilaparotomy: Female sterilization procedure in which the fallopian tubes are cauterized or blocked through a small abdominal incision.

mittelschmerz: Abdominal pain in the region of an ovary during ovulation that usually occurs midway through the menstrual cycle.

myometrium: Smooth muscle layer of the uterine wall.

natural progesterone: A manufactured form of progesterone derived from plant sources, whose chemical structure is identical to that of the progesterone produced by the female body.

neoplasm: A new and abnormal formation of tissue.

node negative: Results of the biopsy of lymph nodes reveal that the lymph nodes are free of cancer. This is an indication that the cancer is less likely to recur.

node positive: Results of the biopsy of lymph nodes reveal that cancer has spread to the lymph nodes under the arm on the same side as the original tumor.

nullipara: Woman who has never been pregnant.

oophorectomy: Excision of an ovary.

oocyte: Developing ovum or egg.

open biopsy: Surgical removal of all or a portion of an abnormal breast mass, usually with the patient under general anesthesia.

oral micronized progesterone: A specially formulated type of progesterone that has the same structure as the progesterone produced by women's bodies. The particles are very finely ground. This form of progesterone is better absorbed into the bloodstream than other oral forms of progesterone.

os: Opening of the cervical canal.

osteoblasts: Bone cells that are responsible for laying down new bone.

osteoclasts: Bone cells that are responsible for breaking down old bone in a process called *remodeling*.

osteoporosis: A condition in which a large amount of bone mass is lost, leading to brittle, porous bone that can be easily fractured.

ovarian follicle: *See* "follicle."

over-the-counter (OTC) drugs: Medications sold without the need for a prescription.

parity: The number of past pregnancies that have reached viability, regardless of whether the infant or infants were alive or stillborn.

pelvic inflammatory disease (PID): A serious infection of the reproductive organs, often caused by infection with sexual pathogens. Tissue destruction can occur without symptoms. Infertility is a major long-term consequence.

perimenopause: A period of transition of changing ovarian activity before menopause and through the first few years of amenorrhea.

pessary: A device placed inside the vagina to function as a supportive structure for the uterus.

phytoestrogens: Plant-derived compounds that have a weak estrogenic effect in the human body. They are found naturally in whole plant foods and herbs and sometimes used in the management of menopause as an alternative or complement to conventional hormone replacement therapy.

Piaget: A researcher who made major contributions to the field of childhood cognitive development, describing maturation of cognitive abilities by stages from infancy to adulthood.

pituitary desensitization: Medical intervention in which drugs are used during assisted reproductive technology interventions to suppress the release of hormones from the pituitary gland, which would result in ovulation, before all the multiple eggs are matured.

pituitary gland: Structure at the base of the brain that receives instructions by means of hormones from the hypothalamus and sends hormonal messages to a number of glands and organs, including the ovaries.

postcoital test (PCT): Part of infertility workup that is used to evaluate aspects of sperm function and cervical mucus.

Procedure: The test must be timed carefully with the immediate preovulatory phase; basal body temperature should not yet show an increase. Sexual intercourse should have taken place at home either the night before or morning of the examination. A sample of mucus from the exocervix and endocervix is obtained with a small syringe during a pelvic examination. Evaluation under the microscope reveals the type of mucus present and the number and motility of sperm. A normal sperm count is a minimum of 5 to 10 motile sperm per high-power field. Conducive mucus should be present.

Results: If the mucus is favorable and the semen analysis reveals normal findings, more specialized testing is needed to determine sperm-mucus incompatibilities or sperm capacitation problems.

premenstrual dysphoric disorder (PMDD): A severe form of premenstrual syndrome that is characterized by heightened emotional symptoms, such as depression, anxiety, anger, and persistent irritability.

premenstrual syndrome (PMS): Also called *premenstrual tension,* a collection of symptoms that occur during the second phase of the menstrual cycle that improve with the onset of menses. Causes are not well understood.

primary tumor: Original site of a cancer.

prodromal symptom: An early sign of an outbreak of disease. It most typically refers to the itching or skin sensitivity that often precedes an outbreak of herpes.

progestin/progestogen: Synthetic forms of the naturally occurring hormone progesterone, which is produced by the ovaries. Used in hormone replacement therapies and hormonal birth control methods.

proliferation: Rapid and repeated cellular reproduction.

prostaglandin inhibitors: A group of drugs, used to treat inflammatory diseases, that inhibit synthesis and activity of prostaglandins. These drugs have been approved by the U.S. Food and Drug Administration for treatment of menstrual pain. These drugs do have side effects. Although many are over-the-counter drugs, they should be used intelligently and monitored by the patient and health care practitioner. Ibuprofen (Motrin), indomethacin (Indocin), and mefenamic acid (Ponstel) are examples.

prostaglandins: Local substances produced by the tissues and found in many parts of the body. Prostaglandins play an important role in menstrual cramps. They may cause vasodilation and pain in breast tissue. They also play a role in body water content, appetite, and body temperature.

receptor: Part of the molecular structure of a cell. Substances circulating in the bloodstream whose molecular shape fits a receptor's shape can bind to the cell membrane and activate reactions in the cell. This is the process by which hormones produce their effects. Certain tumors also have hormone receptors that recognize estrogen or progesterone. If a tumor has receptor sites for hormones, this information is used in making decisions about treatment options.

recommended dietary allowances (RDAs): Recommended nutrient intakes estimated to meet the needs of almost all of the healthy people in the population.

refractory period: The period after orgasm during which another orgasm cannot occur. This period varies between men and women, and it can change with age and other factors.

relaxation: The absence or alleviation of mental, physical, and emotional tension through purposeful activities that quiet the mind and the body.

rugae: Folds in the vaginal mucosa.

safer sex: A commonly used way of acknowledging that there is no such thing as totally safe sex. Safer sex describes practices designed to minimize transfer of any body fluids (semen, blood, vaginal secretions) between partners.

selective estrogen receptor modulators (SERMs): A classification of drugs that act as estrogen agonists or estrogen antagonists and are commonly used postmenopausally in place of estrogen.

semen evaluation: At least two semen samples are collected on separate days by masturbation. Each sample should be collected after abstaining from ejaculation for a minimum of 48 hours but not longer than 3 to 4 days. The ejaculate should be collected in a sterile container and should be examined within 1 hour of collection. Analysis involves a complex array of tests to evaluate many aspects of sperm health, including count; motility; shape; clumping; presence of bacteria, antibodies, or other elements; and biochemical analysis.

seropositivity: The presence of a certain antibody in a blood sample.

sexual history: Past and present health conditions, lifestyle behaviors, knowledge, and attitudes related to sex and sexuality.

sexually transmitted infection (STI): A newer term that has replaced the term *sexually transmitted disease.* Such infections are spread primarily by intimate contact between partners, through either skin-to-skin or bodily fluid contact.

sexual response cycle: The phases of physical changes that occur in response to sexual stimulation and sexual tension release.

sonogram: Also called *ultrasound,* a procedure that uses sound waves to form an image of internal structures. Hollow or fluid-filled structures appear black, and more solid structures appear white.

sonohysterography: A procedure in which saline solution is inserted into the uterine cavity, distending the cavity. Ultrasound is then used to observe structures such as polyps, submucous myomas, and adhesions.

speculum: Instrument used during a pelvic examination to allow visualization of the cervix and vaginal lining by holding the vaginal walls apart.

sperm penetration assay (SPA): Part of a semen evaluation for male factor infertility that tests the ability of sperm to shed their protein coating and release enzymes that are needed to penetrate the coating of an egg.

spirituality: An individual's connection to her own values, purpose, and meaning of life; may encompass organized religion or belief in a higher power or authority.

squamocolumnar junction: Area on the cervix where the squamous tissue of the outer aspects of the cervix and the glandular tissue arising in the cervical canal meet. Also called the *transformation zone.* This area is characterized by rapid cell turnover and is a common site for development of cancerous or precancerous cells.

squamous epithelium: Flat, platelike epithelial cells that cover the internal and external surfaces of the body. They are one of two types of cells that make up the cervix; there, they cover the outer surface of the cervix.

squamous metaplasia: A normal process of cell growth and replacement in which squamous tissue slowly replaces the glandular tissue that arises in the cervical canal.

squamous tissue: A type of tissue that lines many internal and external body surfaces. It is a smooth, flat, and nonglandular type of tissue.

staging: A system of defining how widespread a cancer is by using information learned through diagnostic techniques. This information is used to determine appropriate treatment.

steroid: A group name for chemicals that have a particular molecular configuration and contain cholesterol as part of their structures. A number of hormones, including the sex hormones, are steroids.

stress urinary incontinence (SUI): A loss of urine that occurs with increased intra-abdominal pressure, such as from sneezing, laughing, or coughing.

surrogate: A substitute.

temporomandibular joint (TMJ) pain dysfunction syndrome: The TMJ is the junction of the jaw and the skull. Usually related to stress, dysfunction of this joint has been linked to headaches and ear pain.

therapeutic touch: A modern interpretation of the traditional laying-on-of-hands for healing, as interpreted by Krieger, a registered nurse, and Kunz, a noted healer.

thromboembolic disease: A disorder in which blood clots can travel to various organs, causing blockage of the circulatory system. Sites of blockage can include the heart (myocardial infarction), the brain (stroke), the lungs (pulmonary embolism), and other organs.

toxic shock syndrome (TSS): A severe, acute disease most often caused by *Staphylococcus aureus* that has been associated with high-absorbency tampon use during menstruation.

traditional Chinese medicine (TCM): Ancient methods of healing that combine herbs, energy healing, and movement as a pathway to health. These modalities seek to heal the person on deeper levels rather than simply treating symptoms.

transformation zone: See "squamocolumnar junction."

transvaginal: Through the vagina, referring to the current methods of retrieving eggs from the ovary. This route is also being used for hysterectomy.

tubal embryo transfer (TET): A variation of the gamete intrafallopian transfer procedure in which the egg is fertilized before being placed in the fallopian tube.

tubal patency: Unobstructed fallopian tubes.

tubal reanastomosis: A surgical procedure in which the cut ends of the fallopian tubes are brought together to reverse a previous sterilization.

ultrasound: Use of high-frequency sound waves to obtain images of internal structures. Used in conjunction with other diagnostic and surgical procedures to guide probes and instruments. Used for diagnosis of breast disease and pelvic reproductive abnormalities and to assist in monitoring women undergoing assisted reproductive technologies. (*See also* "sonogram.")

vacuum aspiration: Removal of tissue by the creation of negative pressure through the removal of air.

vaginal flora: Microorganisms normally found in the vagina, including *Staphylococcus epidermidis*, *Lactobacillus*, *Streptococcus mitis*, and *Corynebacteria.*

vaginismus: Painful, unintentional muscle spasms in the thighs, pelvis, and vagina that lead to constriction of the pelvic muscles, often making sexual intercourse and pelvic examination impossible. Usually occurs when a woman senses that something is about to penetrate the vagina and is typically associated with prior emotional or physical trauma.

vas deferens (ductus deferens): Tube in the male reproductive system through which sperm pass from the testes to the ejaculatory duct and then into the urethra.

vasectomy: Surgical removal or blockage of the vas deferens, resulting in male sterilization.

vulvar self-examination (VSE): A systematic examination of the vulva by the woman.

zygote: Term for an early fertilized egg before implantation.

zygote intrafallopian transfer (ZIFT): An assisted reproductive technology technique in which fertilization of the egg is accomplished before transfer to the fallopian tube. Also called *tubal embryo transfer.*

BIBLIOGRAPHY

Adler, S. (2007). The importance of routine STD screening. *Clinical Advisor, 10(6)*, 35-40.

Advisory Committee on Immunization Practices, *Vaccines for Children Program. Vaccine to prevent papillomavirus (HPV) infection* (Resolution No. 6/06-2). June 29, 2006). Retrieved September 26, 2007, from http://www.cdc.gov/vaccines/programs/vfc/downloads/resolutions/0606hpv.pdf

Aguirre, B., & Smith, B. D. (2007). Handling young patients who cut themselves. *Clinical Advisor, 10(8)*, 64-69.

Albertazzi, P. (2005). Alternatives to estrogen to manage hot flushes. *Gynecological Endocrinology, 20(1)*, 13-21.

Alexander, I. M. (2006). Bioidentical hormones for menopause therapy: Separating the myths from the reality. *Women's Health Care, 5(1)*, 7-17.

Alexander, I. M. (2007). Overview of current HT recommendations using evidence-based decision making. *American Journal for Nurse Practitioners, 11(10)*, 29-41.

Aliotta, H. M., & Schaeffer, N. J. (2006). Breast conditions. In K. D. Schuiling & F. E. Likis (Eds.), *Women's gynecologic health*. Sudbury, MA: Jones & Bartlett Publishers.

Altman, A. M. (2006). Update on hormonal therapy: The variables that matter. *Women's Health Care, 5(6)*, 7-25.

American Academy of Pediatrics and American College of Obstetricians and Gynecologists. (2007). *Guidelines for perinatal care* (6th ed.). Washington, DC: Author.

American Cancer Society. (2006). *Cancer facts & figures 2006*. Atlanta: Author. Accessed May 18, 2008, from http://www.cancer.org

American Cancer Society. (2007). *Cancer reference information: Detailed guide: Breast cancer*. Retrieved November 6, 2007, from http://www.cancer.org/docroot/CRI/content/CRI_2_4_1X_What_are_the_key_statistics_for_breast_cancer_5.asp

American Cancer Society. (2008). *Cancer facts and figures*. Retrieved May 17, 2008, from http://www.cancer.org/docroot/STT/content/STT_1x_Cancer_Facts_and_Figures_2008.asp?from=fast

American College of Obstetricians and Gynecologists. (2000). *Premenstrual syndrome* (ACOG Practice Bulletin No. 15). Washington, DC: Author.

American College of Obstetricians and Gynecologists. (2001). *Use of botanicals for management of menopausal symptoms* (Practice Bulletin Number 28). Washington, DC: Author.

American College of Obstetricians and Gynecologists. (2002). *Diagnosis and treatment of cervical carcinomas* (ACOG Practice Bulletin No. 35). Washington, DC: Author.

American College of Obstetricians and Gynecologists. (2003). *Cervical cytology screening* (ACOG Practice Bulletin No. 45). Washington, DC: Author.

American College of Obstetricians and Gynecologists. (2004a). Chronic pelvic pain (Clinical Management Guidelines for Obstetrician–Gynecologists No. 51). *Obstetrics and Gynecology, 103(3),* 589-605.

American College of Obstetricians and Gynecologists. (2004b). Hormone therapy: Cognition and dementia. *Obstetrics and Gynecology, 104*(Suppl.), 25S-40S.

American College of Obstetricians and Gynecologists. (2004c). Hormone therapy: Osteoporosis. *Obstetrics and Gynecology, 104*(Suppl.): 66S-76S.

American College of Obstetricians and Gynecologists. (2005a). Human papillomavirus (ACOG Practice Bulletin No. 61). *Obstetrics and Gynecology, 105*(4), 905-918.

American College of Obstetricians and Gynecologists. (2005b). Management of abnormal cervical cytology and histology (ACOG Practice Bulletin No. 66). *Obstetrics and Gynecology, 106*(3), 645-664.

American College of Obstetricians and Gynecologists. (2005c). Intrauterine device (ACOG Practice Bulletin No. 59). *Obstetrics and Gynecology, 105*(1), 223-32.

American College of Obstetricians and Gynecologists, Committee on Gynecologic Practice. (2005). Compounded bioidentical hormones (ACOG Committee Opinion No. 322). *Obstetrics and Gynecology, 106,* 1139-1140.

American College of Obstetricians and Gynecologists. (2007). *Women's health care: A resource manual* (3rd ed.). Washington, DC: Author.

American Heart Association. (2007a). *Exercise and fitness.* Retrieved October 26, 2007, from http://www.americanheart.org

American Heart Association. (2007b). *Facts about women and cardiovascular diseases.* Retrieved November 10, 2007, from http://www.americanheart.org/presenter.jhtml?identifier=2876

American Holistic Nurses Association. (2005). *About us.* Retrieved November 15, 2007, from http://www.ahna.org/AboutUs/tabid/1158/Default.aspx

American Psychiatric Association. (2000). *Diagnostic and statistical manual of mental disorders* (4th ed., text revision). Washington, DC: American Psychiatric Association Press.

American Society for Colposcopy and Cervical Pathology. (n.d.). *Medical FAQs on the natural history of HPV.* Retrieved October 30, 2007, from http://cme.asccp.org/faq/histHPV.cfm

American Society for Reproductive Medicine. (n.d.). *Frequently asked questions about infertility.* Retrieved September 21, 2007, from http://www.asrm.org/Patients/faqs.html

Anderson, G. L., Limacher, M., Assaf, A. R., Bassford, T., Beresford, S. A., Black, H., et al. (2004). Effects of conjugated equine estrogen in postmenopausal women with hysterectomy: The Women's Health Initiative randomized controlled trial. *Journal of the American Medical Association, 291*(14), 1701-1712.

Andolsek, K. M., & Rapkin, A. J. (2006). Contraceptive use in women with premenstrual disorders. *Dialogues in Contraception, 10*(4), 4-7.

Annon, J. S. (1976). The PLISSIT Model: A proposed conceptual scheme for behavioral treatment of sexual problems. *Journal of Sex Education and Therapy, 2,* 1-15.

Appel, S. J., & Bannon, J. M. (2007). Hazardous waist: How body shape puts health at risk. *Nursing for Women's Health, 11*(1), 44-53.

Arias, R. D., Kaunitz, A. M., & McClung, M. R. (2007). Depot medroxyprogesterone acetate and bone density. *Dialogues in Contraception, 11*(1), 1-4.

Arrowsmith, F. M. (2007). Preventing the cycle of migraine: A review of patient issues for NPs. *American Journal for Nurse Practitioners, 11*(8), 42-54.

Bachmann, G. A. (2007, April). Preventing pregnancy without hormones. *Clinical Advisor,* (10), 76-79.

Bennett, S. M., Litz, B. T., Lee, B. S., & Maguen, S. (2005). The scope and impact of perinatal loss: Current status and future directions. *Professional Psychology: Research and Practice, 36*(2), 180-187.

Berman, A., Snyder, S. J., Kozier, B., & Erb, G. (2008). *Fundamentals of nursing: Concepts, process, and practice* (8th ed.). Upper Saddle River, NJ: Prentice-Hall.

Bickley, L. S., & Szilagyi, P. G. (2007). *Bates' guide to physical examination and history taking* (9th ed.). Philadelphia: Lippincott Williams and Wilkins.

Boothby, L. A., Doering, P. L., & Kipersztok, S. (2004). Bioidentical hormone therapy: A review. *Menopause, 11*(3), 356-367.

Boston Women's Health Book Collective. (2005). *Our bodies, ourselves: A new edition for a new era.* New York: Simon & Schuster.

Boyd, N. F., Guo, H., Martin, L. J., Sun, L., Stone, J., Fishell, E., et al. (2007). Mammographic density and the risk and detection of breast cancer. *New England Journal of Medicine, 356*(3), 227-236.

Breastcancer.org. (2008). *Who gets breast cancer?* Retrieved May 17, 2008, from http://www.breastcancer.org/symptoms/understand_bc/who_gets/index.jsp

Brown, K. M. (2004). *Management guidelines for nurse practitioners working with women* (2nd ed.). Philadelphia: F.A. Davis.

Brucker, M. C. (2005). Body weight & contraceptives: Exploring the relationship & dosage risks. *AWHONN Lifelines, 9*(3), 252-253.

Buggs, C., & Rosenfield, R. L. (2005). Polycystic ovary syndrome in adolescence. *Endocrinology and Metabolism Clinics of North America, 34*(3), 677-705.

Burki, R. E. (2005, May). Reversible hormonal contraceptives: Update. *Clinical Advisor, 9*(5), 34-38.

Burkman, R. T. (2002 December). Patterns in contraception. *The Female Patient Supplement,* 8-11.

Burkman, R. T., Grimes, D. A., Mishell, D. R., Jr., & Westhoff, C. L. (2006). Benefits of contraception to women's health: An evidence-based perspective. *Dialogues in Contraception, 10*(3), 1-4.

Capobianco, G., Spaliviero, B., Dessole, S., Rocca, P. C., Cherchi, P. L., Ambrosini, G., et al. (2007). Lymph node axillary metastasis from occult contralateral infiltrating lobular carcinoma arising in accessory breast: MRI diagnosis. *Breast Journal, 13*(3), 305-307.

Castle, P. E., Solomon, D., Schiffman, M., & Wheeler, C. M. (2005). Human papillomavirus type 16 infections and 2-year absolute risk of cervical precancer in women with equivocal or mild cytologic abnormalities. *Journal of the National Cancer Institute, 97*(14), 1066-1071.

Cates, W., Jr. (2006). Estimates of the incidence and prevalence of sexually transmitted diseases in the United States. American Social Health Association Panel. *Sexually Transmitted Diseases, 26*(4 Suppl.), S2-S7.

Cedars, M. I. (2007). Progesterone: Uses in ART and prevention of pregnancy loss. *Journal of Family Practice, 6,* 9-13.

Centers for Disease Control and Prevention. (n.d.). *Human papillomavirus (HPV) infection.* Retrieved October 30, 2007, from http://www.cdc.gov/std/hpv/

Centers for Disease Control and Prevention. (2005). *Trends in reportable sexually transmitted diseases in the United States, 2004.* Retrieved April 10, 2008, from http://www.cdc.gov/std/stats04/trends2004.htm

Centers for Disease Control and Prevention, Workowski, K. A., & Berman, S. M. (2006). Sexually transmitted diseases treatment guidelines, 2006. *Morbidity and Mortality Weekly Report, 55*(RR-11), 1-94.

Centers for Disease Control and Prevention. (2006a). *Human papillomavirus: HPV information for clinicians.* Retrieved October 27, 2007, from http://www.cdc.gov/std/HPV/STDFact-HPV.htm

Centers for Disease Control and Prevention. (2006b). *Women's reproductive health: Hysterectomy.* Retrieved April 10, 2008, from http://www.cdc.gov/reproductivehealth/WomensRH/Hysterectomy.htm

Centers for Disease Control and Prevention. (2007a). *Frequently asked questions about the OraQuick Rapid HIV-1 Antibody Test.* Retrieved September 24, 2007, from http://www.cdc.gov/hiv/PUBS/faq/oraqckfaq.htm

Centers for Disease Control and Prevention. (2007b). *Recommendations and guidelines: Adult immunization schedule, United States, October 2007-September 2008.* Retrieved October 25, 2007, from http://www.cdc.gov/nip/recs/adult-schedule.htm#chart

Centers for Disease Control and Prevention. (2007c). Suicide trends among youths and young adults aged 10-24 years – United States, 1990-2004. *Morbidity and Mortality Weekly Report, 56*(35), 905-908.

Clark, B., & Arias, R. D. (2007). Underuse of intrauterine contraception in the United States. *Female Patient, 32*(5), 57-58.

Clark, B., & Burkman, R. T. (2006). Non-contraceptive health benefits of hormonal contraception. *Female Patient, 31*(10), 42-44.

Clark, B., & Jordan, B. (2006). Increasing use of emergency contraception. *Female Patient, 31*(12), 44-45.

Clark, B., & Marrazzo, J. (2006). Reproductive health and sexually transmitted infections in lesbian women. *Female Patient, 31*(8), 38-40.

Clinical rounds. (2007). *Nursing 2007, 37*(3), 34.

Cocquyt, V., & Van Belle, S. (2005). Lobular carcinoma in situ and invasive lobular cancer of the breast. *Current Opinion in Obstetrics and Gynecology, 17*(1), 55-60.

Collado-Hidalgo, A., Bower, J. E., Ganz, P. A., Cole, S. W., & Irwin, M. R. (2006). Inflammatory biomarkers for persistent fatigue in breast cancer survivors. *Clinical Cancer Research, 12*(9), 2759-2766.

Collins Sharp, B. A., Taylor, D. L., Thomas, K. K., Killeen, M. B., & Dawood, M. Y. (2002). Cyclic perimenstrual pain and discomfort: The scientific basis for practice. *Journal of Obstetric, Gynecologic, and Neonatal Nursing, 31*(6), 637-649.

Cook, J. D., & Walker, C. L. (2004). Treatment strategies for uterine leiomyoma: The role of hormonal modulation. *Seminars in Reproductive Medicine, 22*(2), 105-111.

Cooper, M., Grywalski, M. Lamp, J., Newhouse, L., & Studlien, R. (2007). Enhancing cultural competence: A model for nurses. *Nursing for Women's Health, 11*(2), 148-159.

Coutlée, F., Rouleau, D., Petignat, P., Ghattas, G., Kornegay, J. R., Schlag, P., et al. (2006). Enhanced detection and typing of human papillomavirus (HPV) DNA in anogenital samples with PGMY primers and the Linear Array HPV Genotyping Test. *Journal of Clinical Microbiology, 44*(6), 1998-2006.

Cudé, G., & Winfrey, K. (2007). The hidden barrier: Gender bias: Fact or fiction? *Nursing for Women's Health, 11*(4), 254-265.

Cunningham, F., Leveno, K., Bloom, S., Hauth, J., Gilstrap III, L., & Wenstrom, K. (Eds.). (2005). *Williams Obstetrics* (22nd ed.). McGraw-Hill: New York.

Darney, P. D., & Mishell, D. R., Jr. (2006). Etonogestrel-containing single-rod implant: A new contraceptive option. *Dialogues in Contraception, 10*(4), 6-7.

Dawson-Hughes, B., Heaney, R. P., Holick, M. F., Lips, P., Meunier, P., & Vieth, R. (2005). Estimates of optimal vitamin D status. *Osteoporosis International, 16*(7), 713-716.

Dennis, K. E. (2007). Postmenopausal women and the health consequences of obesity. *Journal of Obstetric, Gynecologic, & Neonatal Nursing, 36*(5), 511-517.

Dickerson, V. M. (2007). Premenstrual syndrome and premenstrual dysphoric disorder: Individualizing therapy. *Female Patient, 32*(1), 38-46.

Dillon, P. M. (2007). *Nursing health assessment: Clinical pocket guide* (2nd ed.). Philadelphia: F.A. Davis.

Dossey, B. M., Keegan, L., & Guzzetta, C. E. (Eds.) (2008). *Holistic nursing: A handbook for practice* (5th ed.). Sudbury, MA: Jones and Bartlett.

Dranov, P. (2007). Hormone therapy is making a comeback. *The Clinical Advisor, 10*(5), 72-83.

Drifmeyer, E., & Batts, K. (2007). Breast abscess after nipple piercing. *Consultant, 47*(5), 481-482.

Dunne, E. F., & Markowitz, L. E. (2006). Genital human papillomavirus infection. *Clinical Infectious Diseases, 43*(1), 624-629.

Dwyer, N. T., & Kreder, K. J. (2005). Conservative strategies for the treatment of stress urinary incontinence. *Current Urology Reports, 6*(5), 371-375.

Eliassen, A. H., Colditz, G. A., Rosner, B., Willett, W. C., & Hankinson, S. C. (2006). Adult weight change and risk of postmenopausal breast cancer. *Journal of the American Medical Association, 296*(2), 193-201.

Esserman, L., Lane, K. T., Ewing, C. A., & Hwang, E. S. (2005). Innovations in breast cancer care. *Advanced Studies in Medicine, 5*(6), 294-305.

Faucher, M. A. (2007). How to lose weight and keep it off: What does the evidence show? *Nursing for Women's Health, 11*(2), 170-179.

Ferguson, M. (1980). *The Aquarian conspiracy: Personal and social transformation in the 1980s.* Los Angeles: J.P. Tarcher.

Fife, A. (2007). Ovarian cancer: This "silent killer" does make noise. *Clinician Reviews, 17*(9), 10-16.

Finer, L. B., & Henshaw, S. K. (2006). Disparities in rates of unintended pregnancy in the United States, 1994 and 2001. *Perspectives on Sexual and Reproductive Health, 38*(2), 90-96.

Fishwick, N., Parker, B., & Campbell, J. (2005). Care of survivors of abuse and violence. In G. Stuart & M. Laraia (Eds.), *Principles and practice of psychiatric nursing* (8th ed.). St. Louis, MO: Mosby.

Flaws, R. (2004). *Chinese medical obstetrics.* Boulder, CO: Blue Poppy.

Forbus, S. (2005). Age-related infertility. Tuning in to the ticking clock. *AWHONN Lifelines, 9*(2), 126-132.

Frazer, I. H., Cox, J. T., Mayeaux, E. J., Jr., Franco, E. L., Moscicki, A. B., Palefsky, J. M., et al. (2006). Advances in prevention of cervical cancer and other human papillomavirus-related diseases. *Pediatric Infectious Disease Journal, 25*(2 Suppl.), S65-S81.

Freeman, S. B. (2007). Emergency contraception: A complete guide to use in women and adolescents. *Women's Health Care, 6*(9), 38-54.

Gardner, J. (2006). What you need to know about genital herpes. *Nursing 2006, 36*(10), 26-27.

Gerber, R., Tiller, W., & Cousens, G. (2001). *Vibrational medicine*. Rochester, VT: Inner Traditions.

Giarratano, G., Bustamante-Forest, R., & Carter, C. (2005). A multicultural and multilingual outreach program for cervical and breast cancer screening. *Journal of Obstetric, Gynecologic, and Neonatal Nursing, 34*(3), 395-402.

Gibson, E. J., & Coupey, S. M. (2007). The female athlete triad. *Female Patient, 32*(4), 34-41.

Goff, B. A., Mandel, L. S., Drescher, C. W., Urban, N., Gough, S., Schurman, K. M., et al. (2007). Development of an ovarian cancer symptom index: Possibilities for earlier detection. *Cancer, 109*(2), 221-227.

Goff, B. A., Matthews, B. J., Larson, E. H., Andrilla, C. H., Wynn, M., Lishner, D. M., et al. (2007). Predictors of comprehensive surgical treatment in patients with ovarian cancer. *Cancer, 109*(10), 2031-2042.

Goldberg, B., Anderson, J., & Trivieri, L. (Eds.). (2002). *Alternative medicine: The definitive guide* (2nd ed.). Berkeley, CA: Ten Speed Press.

Goodarzi, M., Quiñones, M., Azziz, R., Rotter, J. I., Hsueh, W. A., & Yang, H. (2005). Polycystic ovary syndrome in Mexican-Americans: Prevalence and association with the severity of insulin resistance. *Fertility and Sterility, 84*(3), 766-769.

Goodman, P., Herman, J., Murdaugh, C. L., Moneyham, L. D., & Phillips, K. D. (2007). Role of decision-making in women's self-diagnosis and management of vaginitis. *Women's Health Care, 6*(2), 57-63.

Gordon, R. M. (2004). Why more patients are seeking alternative therapies. *Advance for Nurse Practitioners, 12*(5), 45-48.

Gray, J. R. (2007). HPV vaccination: Should it be mandatory for entry into public school? *Nursing for Women's Health, 11*(2), 133-138.

Grow, D. R., & Hsu, A. L. (2006). Endometriosis, part 2: Surgery for symptom relief and infertility. *Female Patient, 31*(12), 54-58.

Guo, S. W., & Wang, Y. (2006). The prevalence of endometriosis in women with chronic pelvic pain. *Gynecologic & Obstetric Investigation, 62*(3), 121-130.

Gupton, N. E. (2007). Are Pap tests in danger of being phased out? *Clinical Advisor, 10*(4), 89-92.

Guthrie, C. (2006). Biomarkers identified for persistent fatigue in breast cancer survivors. *Women's Health in Primary Care, 6*(4), 35-36.

Hatcher, R. A., Trussell, J., Nelson, A., Cates, F., Stewart, F., & Kowal, D. (Eds.). (2008). *Contraceptive technology* (19th ed.). New York: Ardent Media.

Heinschel, J. (2002). A descriptive study of the interactive guided imagery experience. *Journal of Holistic Nursing, 20*(5), 325-346.

Hellwig, J. P. (2006). HPV linked to common skin cancer. *AWHONN Lifelines, 10*(4), 289-294.

Hellwig, J. P. (2007a). Breast cancer: Lower fat intake may reduce recurrence. *Nursing for Women's Health, 11*(2), 121-122; 124-128.

Hellwig, J. P. (2007b). Ovarian cancer: Considering symptoms. *Nursing for Women's Health, 11*(2), 123.

Helms, J. E. (2006). Complementary and alternative therapies: A new frontier for nursing education? *Journal of Nursing Education, 45*(3), 117-123.

Henry, L. G., & Henry, J. D. (2004). *The soul of the caring nurse: Stories and resources for revitalizing professional passion.* Washington, DC: American Nurses Association.

Hicks, K. M. (2004). Women's sexual problems: A guide to integrating the "New View" approach. Retrieved November 25, 2007 from http://www.medscape.com/viewprogram/3437

Holloway, B. W., Moredich, C., & Aduddell, K. (2006). *OB peds women's health notes.* Philadelphia: F.A. Davis Company.

Holloway, M., & D'Acunto, K. (2006). An update on the ABCs of viral hepatitis. *The Clinical Advisor, 9*(6), 26-40.

Hordern, B. (2007). Finding ovarian cancer early: What to look for. *The Clinical Advisor, 10*(5), 99-103.

Hoskins, I. A., & Crockett, S. A. (2006). Over-the-counter emergency contraception. *Female Patient, 31*(10), 47-48.

Hover-Kramer, D., Mentgen, J., & Scandrett-Hibdon, S. (2001). *Healing touch: A resource for health care professionals.* Albany, NY: Delmar.

Hoyert, D. L., Mathews, T. J., Menacker, F., Strobino, D. M., & Guyer, B. (2006). Annual summary of vital statistics: 2004. *Pediatrics, 117*(1), 168-183.

Hsia, J., Langer, R. D., Manson, J. E., Kuller, J., Johnson, K. C., Hendrix, S. L., et al. (2006). Conjugated equine estrogens and coronary heart disease: The Women's Health Initiative. *Archives of Internal Medicine, 166*(3), 357-365.

Institute for Clinical Systems Improvement. (2007, October). *Preventive services in adults.* Bloomington, MN: Author.

Institute of Medicine. (2003). *Dietary reference intakes: Applications in dietary planning.* Washington, DC: National Academies Press.

Insurance Institute for Highway Safety. (2006). *Fatality facts: Teenagers 2006.* Arlington, VA: Author. http://www.iihs.org/research/fatality_facts_2006/teenagers.html

Iyengar, B. (2007). *Yoga: The path to holistic health.* London: Dorling Kindersley.

Jemal, A., Siegel, R., Ward, E., Murray, T., Xu, J., & Thun, M. J. Cancer statistics, 2008. *CA: A Cancer Journal for Clinicians, 58*(1), 71-96.

Jepson, R. G., Mihaljevic, L., & Craig, J. (2004). *Cranberries for preventing urinary tract infections. Cochrane Database of Systematic Reviews,* 2006, Issue 3. Chichester, UK: John Wiley & Sons.

Jockers, B. S. (2007). Vitamin D sufficiency: An approach to disease prevention. *American Journal for Nurse Practitioners, 11*(10), 43-50.

Johnson-Mallard, V., & Lengacher, C. A. (2007). STI health communication intervention. *Women's Health Care, 6*(8), 27-31.

Joint Commission on Accreditation of Healthcare Organizations. (2007). *Comprehensive accreditation manual for hospitals.* Oak Bridge Terrace, IL: Joint Commission Resources.

Katz, A. (2005). Sexuality and hysterectomy: Finding the right words: Responding to patients' concerns about the potential effects of surgery. *American Journal of Nursing, 105*(12), 65-68.

Katz, A. (2006). Emergency contraception: Controversy remains. *AWHONN Lifelines, 10*(4), 287-288.

Katz, A., Davis, B., Fogel, C., Johnson, B., Kellogg-Spadt, S., Loe, M., et al. (2007). Sexuality and women: The experts speak, *Nursing for Women's Health, 11*(1), 38-43.

Keehbauch, J. A., & Nystrom, J. (2007). Diagnosis and management of abnormal uterine bleeding. *Female Patient, 32*(7), 38-40.

Kellogg-Spadt, S. (2007). Coping with impediments to sexual expression: Women with multiple sclerosis. *Women's Health Care, 6*(9), 58-59.

Kellog-Spadt, S., & McKay, E. (2006). PT-141: A drug in development for female sexual dysfunction. *Women's Health Care, 5*(3), 16-18.

Kendig, S. (2006). Word power: The effect of literacy on health outcomes. *AWHONN Lifelines, 10*(4), 327-331.

Kielb, S. J. (2005). Stress incontinence: Alternatives to surgery. *International Journal of Fertility and Women's Medicine, 50*(1), 24-29.

Klausner, T. I. (2005). The best kept secret. Pelvic floor muscle therapy for urinary incontinence. *Advance for Nurse Practitioners, 13*(7), 43-48.

Knutson, D., & Steiner, E. (2007). Screening for breast cancer: Current recommendations and future directions. *American Family Physician, 75*(11), 1660-1666.

Krieger, D. (2002). *Therapeutic touch as transpersonal healing.* New York: Lantern Books.

Krychman, M. L., & Goldrich, A. (2007). Fertility and the female cancer patient. *Female Patient, 32*(6), 50-54.

Kuhl, C. K., Schrading, S., Leutner, C. C., Morakkabati-Spitz, N., Wardelmann, E., Fimmers, R., et al. (2005). Mammography, breast ultrasound, and magnetic resonance imaging for surveillance of women at high familial risk for breast cancer. *Journal of Clinical Oncology, 23*(33), 8469-8476.

Kulczycki, A., Bosarge, P. M., Qu, H., & Shewchuk, R. M. (2007). New purpose, old method: NP's perceptions of the diaphragm. *Women's Health Care, 6*(9), 64-70.

Kunz, D., & Kreiger, D. (2004). *The spiritual dimension of therapeutic touch.* Rochester, VT: Bear & Co.

Kwan, K., Geller, M. L., & Chlebowski, R. T. (2007). Chemoprophylaxis for breast cancer. *Female Patient, 32*(6), 13-22.

LaCroix, A. Z. (2005). Estrogen with and without progestin: Benefits and risks of short-term use. *American Journal of Medicine, 118*(12 Suppl. 2), 79-87.

Lake, K. (2007). Beware of bioidentical hormones! *The Clinical Advisor, 10*(9), 121.

Lansky, A. (2003). *Impossible cure: The promise of homeopathy.* Portola Valley, CA: R.L. Ranch Press.

Lauver, D., Nelles, K. K., & Hanson, K. (2005). The health effects of diethylstilbestrol revisited. *Journal of Obstetric, Gynecologic, and Neonatal Nursing, 34*(4), 494-499.

Lazarus, C. J., & Brown, S. (2007). Reproductive health care: Teaching future providers. *Female Patient, 32*(2), 44-45.

Lehman, C. D., Gatsonis, C., Kuhl, C., Hendrick, R. E., Pisano, E. D., Hanna, L., et al. (2007). MRI evaluation of the contralateral breast in women with recently diagnosed breast cancer. *New England Journal of Medicine, 356*(13), 1295-1303.

Lemaire, G. S. (2004). More than just menstrual cramps: Symptoms and uncertainty among women with endometriosis. *Journal of Obstetric, Gynecologic, and Neonatal Nursing, 33*(1), 71-79.

Lessick, M. (2007). Genetic testing for breast and ovarian cancer: Ethical, legal, and psychosocial considerations. *Nursing for Women's Health, 11*(4), 390-401.

Leung, A. K., & Pacaud, D. (2004). Diagnosis and management of galactorrhea. *American Family Physician, 70*(3), 543-550.

Lever, K. A. (2005). Emergency contraception. *AWHONN Lifelines, 9*(3), 218-227.

Littleton, L.Y. , & Engebretson, J.C. (2002). *Maternal, neonatal, and women's health nursing.* Albany, NY: Delmar.

Liu, J. H. (2007). Progestins in hormone therapy: What are the options? *Female Patient, 32*(2), 33-39.

Loprinzi, C. L., Levitt, R., Barton, D., Sloan, J. A., Dakhil, S. R., Nikcevich, D. A., et al. (2006). Phase III comparison of depomedroxyprogesterone acetate to venlafaxine for managing hot flashes: North Central Cancer Treat Group Trial N99C7. *Journal of Clinical Oncology, 24*(9), 1409-1414.

Lowdermilk, D., & Perry, S. (2007). *Maternity & women's health care* (9th ed.). St Louis, MO: Mosby.

Lucey, J. F. (2006). When trust in doctors erodes, other treatments fill the void. *Pediatrics, 117*(4), 1242.

Macdonald, H. R., & Arias, R. D. (2007). Ductal and lobular carcinoma in situ of the breast: Histopathology and significance. *Female Patient, 32*(10), 53-58.

Mahoney, M. C., Cox, J. T., & Kimmel, S. R. (2006). New options in HPV prevention. *Journal of Family Practice, 55*(Suppl), 2-22.

Mallett, V. (2005). Female urinary incontinence: What the epidemiologic data tell us. *International Journal of Fertility and Women's Medicine, 50*(1), 12-17.

Marcovici, I. (2007). Mondor disease of the breast. *Female Patient, 32*(7), 51-52.

Marcus, E. (2004). The management of Paget's disease of the breast. *Current Treatment Options in Oncology, 5*(2), 153-160.

Marrazzo, J. M. (2004). Barriers to infectious disease care among lesbians. Retrieved November 16, 2007 from http://www.cdc.gov/ncidod/EID/vol10no11/04-0467.htm

Martin, L., & Jung, P. (2002). *Taking charge of the change: A holistic approach to the three phases of menopause.* Albany, NY: Delmar.

Martin-Hirsch, P., Jarvis, G., Kitchener, H., & Lilford, R. (2000). *Collection devices for obtaining cervical cytology samples.* In The Cochrane Library Database of Systematic Reviews, 2006, Issue 3. Chichester, UK: John Wiley & Sons.

Martinez, L. (2007). Effective communication: Overcoming the embarrassment. *Female Patient, 32*(2), 33-35.

Mass, S. (2004). Breast pain: Engorgement, nipple pain, and mastitis. *Clinical Obstetrics and Gynecology, 47*(3), 676-682.

Mayeaux, E. J., Jr. (2007). External genital warts: An update. *Female Patient, 32*(12), 38-44.

McKee, J., & Warber, S.L. (2005). Integrative therapies for menopause. *Southern Medical Journal, 98*(3), 319-326.

McReady, T. (2003). Management of patients with breast cancer. *Nursing Standard, 17*(41), 45-53.

Mehta, M. (2006). *How to use yoga.* London: Anness.

Mehta, S., Mehta, M., & Mehta, S. (2001). *Yoga: The Iyengar way.* New York: Alfred A. Knopf.

Mele, N., Archer, J., & Pusch, B. D. (2005). Access to breast cancer screening services for women with disabilities. *Journal of Obstetric, Gynecologic, & Neonatal Nursing, 34*(4), 453-464.

Menon, S., Burgis, J., & Bacon, J. (2007). The college-aged examination: A comprehensive approach to preventive medicine. *Female Patient, 32*(7), 32-36.

Michigan Quality Improvement Consortium. (2006a). *Adult preventive services* (ages 18-49). Southfield, MI: Author.

Michigan Quality Improvement Consortium. (2006b). *Adult preventive services* (ages 50-65+). Southfield, MI: Author.

Mick, J., Hughes, M., & Cohen, M. Z. (2004). Using the BETTER Model to assess sexuality. *Clinical Journal of Oncology Nursing, 8*(1), 84-86.

Miller, E. H., & Wysocki, S. (2007). Vaccines in women. *Forum, 5*(2), 9-14.

Miller, K. L. (2005). Stress urinary incontinence in women: Review and update on neurological control. *Journal of Women's Health, 14*(7), 595-608.

Minkin, M. J. (2004). Considerations in the choice of oral vs. transdermal hormone therapy: A review. *Journal of Reproductive Medicine, 49*(4), 311-320.

Minkin, M. J., & Wright, C. V. (2005). *A woman's guide to menopause and perimenopause.* New Haven, CT: Yale University Press.

Monthly Prescribing Reference. (2008). Menopause and HRT. Retrieved June 6, 2008, from http://formulary.prescribingreference.com/ob_gyn/menopause_and_hrt

Moore, A. (2007). Early assessment of fertility: A new home-based screening method. Women's *Health Care: A Practical Journal for Nurse Practitioners, 6*(9), 61-62.

Moore, S. L., & Seybold, V. K. (2007). HPV Vaccine. *Clinician Reviews, 17*(1), 36-42.

Moracco, K. E., Brown, C. L., Martin, S. L., Chang, J. C., Dulli, L., Loucks-Sorrell, M. B., et al. (2004). Mental health issues among female clients of domestic violence programs in North Carolina. *Psychiatric Services, 55*(9), 1036-1040.

Morin, K. H. (2007). The challenge of obesity. *Journal of Obstetric, Gynecologic, & Neonatal Nursing, 36*(5), 481.

Mosher, W. D., Martinez, G. M., Chandra, A., Abma, J. C., & Willson, S. J. (2004). Use of contraception and use of family planning services in the United States: 1982-2002. *Advance Data, 350*(12), 1-36.

Moska, L., Banka, C. L., Benjamin, E. J., Berra, K., Bushnell, C., Dolor, R. J., et al. (2007). Evidence-based guidelines for cardiovascular disease prevention in women: 2007 update. *Circulation, 115*(11), 1481-1501.

Murphy, P. A., & Schwarz, E. B. (2007). NPs' cervical cancer screening practices. *Women's Health Care: A Practical Journal for Nurse Practitioners, 6*(9), 10-21.

Murray, H., Baakdah, H., Bardell, T., & Tulandi, T. (2005). Diagnosis and treatment of ectopic pregnancy. *Canadian Medical Association Journal, 173*(8), 905-912.

Muthusami, K. R., & Chinnaswamy, P. (2005). Effect of chronic alcoholism on male fertility hormones and semen quality. *Fertility and Sterility, 84*(4), 919-924.

Nachtigall, L. E., Baber, R. J., Barentsen, R., Durand, N., Panay, N., Pitkin, J., et al. (2006). Complementary and hormonal therapy for vasomotor symptom relief: A conservative clinical approach. *Journal of Obstetrics and Gynaecology Canada, 28*(4), 279-289.

National Association of Nurse Practitioners in Women's Health. (2007). Guidelines for screening and management of cervical disease. *Women's Health Care: A Practical Journal for Nurse Practitioners, 6*(1), 24-32.

National Campaign to Prevent Teen and Unplanned Pregnancy. (2007). *Teen birth rate increase 2006.* Retrieved January 7, 2008, from http://www.thenationalcampaign.org/resources/pdf/NCHS_statement1.pdf

National Cancer Institute. (2006). *Breast cancer risk assessment tool.* Retrieved November 10, 2007, from http://www.cancer.gov/bcrisktool/Default.aspx

National Cancer Institute, Surveillance Epidemiology and End Results. (2007). *Cancer of the breast.* Retrieved November 6, 2007, from http://seer.cancer.gov/statfacts/html/breast.html

National Center for Complementary and Alternative Medicine. (2007a). *An Introduction to Acupuncture.* Retrieved May 13, 2007, from http://nccam.nih.gov/health/acupuncture

National Center for Complementary and Alternative Medicine. (2007b). *What is CAM?* Retrieved November 14, 2007, from http://nccam.nih.gov/health/whatiscam

National Comprehensive Cancer Network. (2008). *NCCN clinical practice guidelines in oncology: Breast cancer* (V.2.2008). Retrieved May 13, 2008, from http://www.nccn.org/professionals/physician_gls/PDF/breast.pdf

National Institutes of Health. (2005). National Institutes of Health state-of-the-science conference statement: Management of menopause-related symptoms. *Annals of Internal Medicine, 142*(12 Part 1), 1003-1013.

National Osteoporosis Foundation. (2007). *Prevention: Who's at risk?* Accessed November 13, 2007, from http://www.nof.org/prevention/risk.htm.

National Women's Health Network. (2000). *Taking hormones and women's health: Choices, risks, and benefits* (5th ed.). Washington, DC: Author.

Natural Standard: The Authority on Integrative Medicine. (n.d.). *Premenstrual syndrome.* Retrieved January 7, 2008, from http://www.naturalstandard.com

Nelson, A. L. (2007). Sexually transmitted diseases treatment guidelines, 2006: An update. *Forum, 5*(1), 2-5.

Nelson, A. L., & Le, M. H. H. (2007). Modern male condoms: Not your father's "rubbers." *Female Patient, 32*(5), 59-64.

Nelson, H. D., Vesco, K. K., Haney, E., Fu, R., Nedrow, A., Miller, J., et al. (2006). Nonhormonal therapies for menopausal hot flashes: Systematic review and meta-analysis. *Journal of the American Medical Association, 295*(17), 2057-2071.

Newell, A. (2007). Breast cancer: Do women know their risks? *Nursing for Women's Health, 11*(4), 420-421.

New Product – Implanon. (2006). *Clinician Reviews, 16*(11), 55.

Ninia, J. G. (2007). Pelvic congestion syndrome. *Female Patient, 32*(8), 41-49.

North American Menopause Society. (2007). Estrogen and progestogen use in peri-and post-menopausal women: March 2007 position statement of The North American Menopause Society. *Menopause, 14*(2), 168-182.

Ogden, C. L., Carroll, M. D., Curtin, L. R., McDowell, M. A., Tabak, C. J., & Flegal, K. M. (2006). Prevalence of overweight and obesity in the United States, 1999-2004. *Journal of the American Medical Association, 295*(13) 1549-1555.

Oschman, J. (2003). *Energy medicine in therapeutics and human performance.* London: Butterworth-Heinemann.

Osuch, J. (2002). Breast health and disease over a lifetime. *Clinical Obstetrics and Gynecology, 45*(4), 1140-1161.

Ovarian Cancer National Alliance. (2004). *Ovarian cancer statistics.* Retrieved June 4, 2008, from http://www.ovariancancer.org/index.cfm?fuseaction=Page.viewPage&pageId=765&parentID=764&nodeID=1

Peck, S. (2008). Integrating CAM therapies into NP practice. *The American Journal for Nurse Practitioners, 12*(5), 10-18.

Piaget, J. (1969). *The mechanisms of perception.* London: Rutledge & Kegan Paul.

Piotrowski, K., & Snell, L. (2007). Health needs of women with disabilities across the lifespan. *Journal of Obstetric, Gynecologic, & Neonatal Nursing, 36*(1), 79-87.

Pisano, E. D., Gatsonis, C., Hendrick, E., Yaffe, M., Baum, J. K., Acharyya, S., et al. (2005). Diagnostic performance of digital versus film mammography for breast-cancer screening. *New England Journal of Medicine, 353*(17), 1773-1783.

Polaneczky, M. (2007). Premenstrual syndrome/premenstrual dysphoric disorder. *Female Patient, 32*(9), 40-45.

Pomeranz, S. J. (2007). Breast MRI scans: What women need to know. *Radiology Today, 8*(10), 8-10.

Potts, R. O., & Lobo, R. A. (2005). Transdermal drug delivery: Clinical considerations for the obstetrician-gynecologist. *Obstetrics and Gynecology, 105*(5 pt 1), 953-961.

Ravin, C. R. (2007). Preventing STIs: Ask the questions. *Nursing for Women's Health, 11*(1), 88-91.

Ray, M. M. (2007). The health care crisis: Understanding President's Bush's proposals. *Nursing for Women's Health, 11*(3), 243-246.

Raz, R., Chazan, B., & Dan, M. (2004). Cranberry juice and urinary tract infection. *Clinical Infectious Diseases, 38*(10), 1413-1419.

Reape, K. Z., & Nelson, A. L. (2007). Endometrial effects from continuous low-dose estrogen oral contraceptives. *Female Patient, Aug*(Suppl), 7-8.

Reilly, A. M. (2005). Massage therapy: Integration with traditional medicine. *Advance for Nurse Practitioners, 13*(5), 37-42.

Reiter, S. (2006). Efficacy, tolerability and cycle control: How do the 24/4 and 21/7 regimens of low-dose COCs compare? *Women's Health Care, 5*(2), 7-12.

RESOLVE: The National Infertility Association. (2006). *Demystifying infertility.* Retrieved September 22, 2007, from http://www.resolve.org

Rice, C., & Thompson, J. (November-December, 2006). Selecting a hormonal contraceptive that suits your patient's needs. *Women's Health Ob-GYN Edition, 12,* 26-34.

Rice, R. W. (2007). Care of the traveling patient. *Clinician Reviews, 17*(8), 36-42.

Richardson, S. F. (2003). Complementary health and healing in nursing education. *Journal of Holistic Nursing, 21*(1), 20-35.

Ries, L.G., Melbert, D., Krapcho, M., Stinchcomb, D.G., Howlader, N., Horrner, M.J., et al. (n.d.). *SEER cancer statistics review, 1975-2005,* National Cancer Institute. Bethesda, MD. Available from http://seer.cancer.gov/csr/1975_2005 (based on November 2007 SEER data submission, posted to the SEER web site, 2008).

Ruhl, C. (2006). How well will we age? Why we need to consider our health in old age now. *AWHONN Lifelines, 10*(4), 284-286.

Ruhl, C. (2007). Breast health screening: What all women should know. *Nursing for Women's Health, 11*(3), 326-330.

Sadovsky, R. (2007). Managing first-time and recurrent UTIs. *The Clinical Advisor, 9*(5), 46-51.

Sakorafas, G. H. (2003). The management of women at high risk for breast cancer: Risk estimation and prevention strategies. *Cancer Treatment Reviews, 29*(2), 79-89.

Saraiya, M., Ahmed, F., Krishnan, S., Richards T. B., Unger E. R., & Lawson H. W. (2007). Cervical cancer incidence in a prevaccine era in the United States, 1998-2002. *Obstetrics and Gynecology, 109*(2), 360-370.

Schmidt, J. V. (2007). HPV vaccine: Implications for nurses and patients. *Nursing for Women's Health, 11*(1), 83-87.

Schnare, S. (2002). Clinician-patient counseling. *Female Patient, Dec*(Suppl), 30-32.

Schnare, S. M. (2006). Long-term reversible contraception. In Clinical Issues in Women's Health, 7-10. Washington, DC: Association of Nurse Practitioners in Women's Health.

Scholes, D., LaCroix, A. Z., Ichikawa, L. E., Barlow, W. E., Ott, S. M. (2005). Change in bone mineral density among adolescent women using and discontinuing depot medroxyprogesterone acetate contraception. *Archives of Pediatrics & Adolescent Medicine, 159*(2), 139-144.

Schulman, L. P. (2007). New paradigms in hormonal contraception. *Forum, 5*(1), 19-22.

Secor, R. M., & Simon, J. A. (2006). New options for treating the symptoms of menopause. *Women's Health in Primary Care, 6*(4), 44-52.

Sego, S. (2007). Alternative meds update: Ginger. *The Clinical Advisor, 10*(4), 159-160.

Seidel, H. M., Ball, J. W., Dains, J. E., & Benedict, G. W. (2006). *Mosby's guide to physical examination* (6th ed.). St Louis, MO: Mosby.

Shay-Zapien, G. (2007). Discussing spirituality and the wisdom of aging. *Nursing for Women's Health, 11*(3), 233-234.

Sheweita, S. A., Tilmisany, A. M., & Al-Sawaf, H. (2005). Mechanisms of male infertility: Role of antioxidants. *Current Drug Metabolism, 6*(5), 495-501.

Shulman, L. P., & Westhoff, C. L. (2006). Contraception and cancer. *Dialogues in Contraception, 10*(3), 5-8.

Simpkins, A., Thurston, D., Colyer, M., & Talbot, S. (2005). Nature's wrath? A closer look at complications with five popular herbs. *Advance for Nurse Practitioners, 13*(6), 55-58.

Singletary, S. E., Allred, C., Ashley, P., Bassett, L. W., Berry, D., Bland, K. I. et al. (2002). Breast. In F.L. Greene, et al (Eds.), *AJCC Cancer Staging Manual* (6th ed., pp. 223-249). New York: Springer.

Skidmore-Roth, L. (2005). *Mosby's handbook of herbs and natural supplements* (3rd ed.). St. Louis, MO: Mosby.

Smith, D. M. (2007). Emergency contraception: An update. *Dialogues in Contraception, 11*(1), 8-9.

Smith, E. C. (2007). Breast cancer fundamentals. *Clinician Reviews, 17*(10), 32-40.

Smith, I. E., & Dowsett, M. (2003). Aromatase inhibitors in breast cancer. *New England Journal of Medicine, 348*(24), 2431-2442.

Smith, R. A., Cokkinides, V., & Eyre, H. J. (2006). American Cancer Society guidelines for the early detection of cancer, 2006. *CA: A Cancer Journal for Clinicians, 56*(1), 11-25.

Smith-Bindman, R., Miglioretti, D. L., Lurie, N., Abraham, L., Barbash, R. B., Strzelczyk, J., et al. (2006). Does utilization of screening mammography explain racial and ethnic differences in breast cancer? *Annals of Internal Medicine, 144*(8), 541-553.

Snow, M. (2007). HPV vaccine: New treatment for an old disease. *Nursing, 37*(3), 67.

Snyder, M., & Lindquist, R. (Eds.). (2006). *Complementary/alternative therapies in nursing* (5th ed.). New York: Springer.

Society of Obstetricians and Gynaecologists of Canada. (2005). SOGC clinical guidelines: Uterine fibroid embolization (UFE). *International Journal of Gynaecology and Obstetrics, 89*(3), 305-318.

Song, A. H. (2007). Global endometrial ablation devices: Minimally invasive surgical alternatives to hysterectomy. *Female Patient, 32*(7), 46-50.

Speroff, L., & Fritz, M. A. (2005). *Clinical gynecologic endocrinology and infertility* (7th ed.). Philadelphia: Lippincott Williams & Wilkins.

Speroff, L., & Mishell, D. R., Jr. (2007). Polycystic ovary syndrome: Management and contraception. *Dialogues in Contraception, 11*(1), 5-7.

Spies, J. B., Myers, E. R., Worthington-Kirsch, R., Mulgund, J., Goodwin, S., & Mauro, M. (2005). The FIBROID Registry: Symptom and quality-of-life status 1 year after therapy. *Obstetrics and Gynecology, 106*(6), 1309-1318.

St. Hill, P. F., Lipson, J. G., & Meleis, A. I. (2003). *Caring for women cross-culturally.* Philadelphia: F.A. Davis.

Stonehouse, A., & Studdiford, J. (2007). Allergic contact dermatitis from tea tree oil. *Consultant, 47*(8), 781.

Strauss, L. T, Herndon, J., Chang, J., Parker, W. Y., Bowens, S. V., & Berg, C. J. (2005). Abortion surveillance – United States, 2002. *Morbidity and Mortality Weekly Report, 54*(7), 1-31.

Sulak, P. J. (2006). Elimination and alteration of the hormone-free interval: Reasons and methods. *Female Patient, Nov*(Suppl), 1-8.

Sulak, P. J. (2007). Preferences in oral contraceptive regimens and menstrual frequency. *Female Patient, Aug*(Suppl), 1-2.

Sulak, P. J., Kaunitz, A. M., London, A. M., Moore, A., & Nelson, A. L. (2007). Practical considerations for extended OC regimens. *Women's Health Care, 6*(2), 41-48.

Takacs, P., Chakhtoura, N., DeSantis, T., & Verma, U. (2005). Evaluation of the relationship between endometrial thickness and failure of single-dose methotrexate in ectopic pregnancy. *Archives of Gynecology and Obstetrics, 272*(4), 269-272.

Taylor, D., Schuiling, K. D., & Sharp, B. A. (2005). Menstrual cycle pain and discomforts. In K. D. Schuiling & F. Liskis (Eds.), *Women's gynecologic health.* Sudbury, MA: Jones & Bartlett.

Theroux, R. (2007). Breast cancer after menopause: Do weight and exercise affect risk? *Nursing for Women's Health, 11*(3), 319-321.

Thull, D. L., & Vogel, V. G. (2004). Recognition and management of hereditary breast cancer syndromes. *Oncologist, 9*(1) 13-24.

U.S. Census Bureau. (2005). United States Census 2000. Available from http://www.census.gov/ main/www/cen2000.html

U.S. Census Bureau. (2007). *Health insurance coverage: 2004* (Revised March 2007). Retrieved September 18, 2007, from http://www.census .gov/hhes/www/hlthins/hlthin04.html

U.S. Department of Health and Human Services. (2000, January). *Healthy people 2010* (Conference Edition, in two volumes). Washington, DC: U.S. Government Printing Office.

U.S. Department of Health and Human Services and U.S. Department of Agriculture. (2005). *Dietary guidelines for Americans* (6th ed.). Washington, DC: U.S. Government Printing Office.

U.S. Department of Health and Human Services, Administration on Children, Youth and Families. (2007). *America's children: How are they doing?* Washington, DC: U.S. Government Printing Office.

U.S. Food and Drug Administration. (2004, March 26). *FDA approves first oral fluid based rapid HIV test kit.* Retrieved April 24, 2008 from http://www.fda.gov/bbs/topics/news/2004/NEW01042.html

U.S. Preventive Services Task Force. (2003). Screening for obesity in adults: Recommendations and rationale. *Annals of Internal Medicine, 139*(11), 930-932.

U.S. Preventive Services Task Force. (2005a). *Genetic risk assessment and BRCA mutation testing for breast and ovarian cancer susceptibility.* Retrieved November 10, 2007, from http://www.ahrq.gov/clinic/uspstf05/brcagen/brcagenrs.pdf

U.S. Preventive Services Task Force. (2005b). *Hormone therapy for the prevention of chronic conditions in postmenopausal women.* Retrieved November 12, 2007, from http://www.ahrq.gov/clinic/uspstf/uspspmho.htm

U.S. Preventive Services Task Force. (2005c). Screening for osteoporosis in postmenopausal women. In *Guide to Clinical Preventive Health Services, 2005.* Rockville, MD: Agency for Healthcare Research and Quality.

U.S. Preventive Services Task Force. (2007). *Guide to Clinical Preventive Services 2007: Recommendations of the US Preventive Services Task Force* (AHRQ Publication No. 07-05100). Available from http://www.ahrq.gov

Van Voorhis, B. (2006). Outcomes from assisted reproductive technology. *Obstetrics and Gynecology, 107*(1), 183-200.

Ventegodt, S., Morad, M., & Merrick, J. (2004). Clinical holistic medicine: Classic art of healing or the therapeutic touch. *TheScientificWorldJOURNAL, 4*(3), 134-147.

Walker-Jenkins, A. (2007). Emergency contraception OTC: The drug, the conflict, the decision. *Nursing for Women's Health, 11*(1), 24-28.

Ward, S. L. (2002). Balancing high-tech nursing with holistic healing. *Journal for Specialists in Pediatric Nursing, 7*(2), 81-83.

Weed, S. (2002). *New menopausal years, the wise woman way: Alternative approaches for women 30–90.* Woodstock, NY: Ash Tree.

Weil, A. (2004). *Natural health, natural medicine: A comprehensive manual for wellness and self-care.* Boston: Houghton Mifflin.

Weiss, B. D., Mays, M. Z., Martz, W., Castro, K. M., DeWalt, D. A., Pignone, M. P., et al. (2005). Quick assessment of literacy in primary care: The newest vital sign. *Annals of Family Medicine, 3*(6), 514-522.

Wenger, N. K. (2007). Cardiovascular risk assessment and intervention strategies in women. *Women's Health in Primary Care, Supplement,* September, 2007, S1-S11.

Whitaker, A., & Kaunitz, A. (2007). Intrauterine devices: Contraception's best kept secret? *Female Patient, Aug*(Suppl), 17-19.

Winer, S., & Richwald, G. A. (2007). Genital HSV update. *Forum, 5*(2), 18-22.

Wolfe, J. (2006). Polycystic ovary syndrome: Case study decision tree. *Women's Health Care, 5*(7), 19-31.

Wood, M. R., Kettinger, C. A., & Lessick, M. (2007). Knowledge is power: How nurses can promote health literacy. *Nursing for Women's Health, 11*(2), 180-188.

Woodson, S. A. (2007). Chronic pelvic pain: Can you guess the cause. *Nursing for Women's Health, 11*(2), 200-204.

Workowski, K. A., & Berman, S. M. (2006). Sexually transmitted diseases treatment guidelines, 2006. *Morbidity and Mortality Weekly Report, 55*(RR-11): 1-94.

World Health Organization. (2004). *Medical eligibility criteria for contraceptive use* (3rd ed.). Retrieved September 18, 2007, from http://www.who.int/reproductivehealth/publications/mec/mec.pdf

World Health Organization. (2006). *Controlling the global obesity epidemic.* Retrieved October 26, 2007, from http://www.who.int/nutrition/topics/obesity/en

Wright, T. C., Massad, L. S., Dunton, C. J., Spitzer, M., Wilkinson, E. J., & Solomon, D. (2007). 2006 consensus guidelines for the management of women with abnormal cervical cancer screening tests. *American Journal of Obstetrics and Gynecology, 197*(4), 346-355.

Wright, V., Schieve, L., Reynolds, M., Jeng, G., & Kissin, D. (2004). Assisted reproductive technology surveillance—United States, 2001. *Morbidity and Mortality Weekly Report, 53*(1), 1-20.

Wysocki, S. (2007). Clinical rationale for continuous oral contraception. *American Journal for Nurse Practitioners, 11*(3), 57-68.

Wysocki, S., & Alexander, I. M. (2005). Bioidentical hormones for menopause hormone therapy: An overview. *Women's Health Care, 4*(10), 9-17.

Wysocki, S., Moore, A., & Ramos, D. (2007, August). Intrauterine contraception: Who, why and how. *Clinical Advisor, Supplement,* S4-17.

Wysocki, S., Reiter, S., & Berman, N. R. (2007). Strategies for preventing cervical cancer and HPV-related disease: The role of vaccination. *Women's Health Care, 6*(1), 6-22.

Xu, F., Sternberg, M. R., Kottiri, B. J., McQuillan, G. M., Lee, F. K., Nahmias, A. J., et al. (2006). Trends in herpes simplex virus type 1 and type 2 seroprevalence in the United States. *Journal of the American Medical Association, 296*(8), 964-973.

Yarbrough, S. (2004). Older women and breast cancer screening: Research synthesis. *Oncology Nursing Forum, 31*(1), E9-E15.

Yonkers, K. (2006). Intimate partner violence. *Women's Health OB-GYN Edition, 12*(11), 35-36.

Young, L. & Hayes, V. (Eds.). (2002). *Transforming health promotion practice: Concepts, issues, and applications.* Philadelphia: F.A. Davis.

Youngkin, E. & Davis, M. (2003). *Women's health: A primary care clinical guide* (3rd ed.). Upper Saddle River, NJ: Prentice Hall.

Zizic, T. (2004). Pharmacologic prevention of osteoporotic fractures. *American Family Physician, 70*(7), 1293-1300.

INDEX

Page references followed by *fig* indicates an illustrated figure; followed by *t* indicates a table.

A

abnormal (or excessive) uterine bleeding, 164
abnormal Pap test results
    Bethesda System guidelines on abnormal, 145
    case study on, 148
    cervical transformation zone and, 140
    cervix/cervical transformation zone and, 140
    guidelines during pregnancy, 147
    HPV infection and, 136, 138
    treatments for, 146–147
    treatment specific to cervical cancer, 147
    See also Pap smear
abortion. *See* pregnancy termination
abstinence
    health issue of, 26
    to prevent STIs, 44
ACHES warning signs, 50
acupressure, 238–239
acupuncture, 194, 240
acyclovir (Zovirax), 101
adjuvant chemotherapy, 192
adolescence
    chlamydial infection rate of female, 97
    health issues in, 33–38
    physical, cognitive, and emotional changes during, 30–33
    puberty during, 30
    vulnerability during, 29
adolescent health issues
    contraception, 36
    incest and family violence, 37
    nutritional deficits and eating disorders, 33–35
    STIs (sexually transmitted infections), 35–36
    substance abuse, 35
    tattooing and body piercing, 35
    traffic accidents, homicides, and suicides, 33, 39–40
    undesired sexual activity and rape, 36–37
    unintended pregnancy, 37–38
adolescents
    age-related irregular bleeding in, 153
    birth control education/counseling for, 65–66
    counseling and educating, 39–40
    first pelvic examination of, 38–39
    self-esteem issues of, 31–33
    sexual maturation of, 30
    sexual/reproductive assessment of, 20
    See also women
adoption, 87
age
    breast cancer and, 186
    cardiovascular disease (CVD) and, 219
    as fertility factor, 75
    irregular bleeding related to, 153
    osteoporosis and, 221
AIDS (acquired immune deficiency syndrome)
    health threat of, 2, 3, 5
    trends and statistics on, 93–94
    See also HIV (human immunodeficiency virus)
alcoholism/alcohol abuse
    adolescent, 35
    bone health and, 224
    breast cancer and, 187
    health issue of, 26
    as infertility factor, 75
Aldara, 99
alendronate, 229
allergies, 122
alternative medicine, 234
    See also CAM (complementary and alternative therapies)
amenorrhea, 152, 222
American Cancer Society (ACS), 125, 126, 142, 145, 169, 177, 180, 194
American College of Obstetricians and Gynecologists (ACOG), 94–95, 112, 123, 125, 142, 145, 183, 214, 230
American Fertility society, 84
American Heart Association (AHA), 219
American Holistic Nurses Association (AHNA), 235, 236
American Joint Committee on Cancer, 191
American Society of Clinical Oncology, 189
American Society of Reproductive Medicine (ASRM), 230
anal sex, 22
androgens, 204
anorexia nervosa, 33–34, 222

PRETEST KEY

Women's Health:
Contemporary Advances and Trends
(3rd ed.)

1.	d	Chapter 1
2.	d	Chapter 2
3.	c	Chapter 2
4.	b	Chapter 3
5.	c	Chapter 4
6.	a	Chapter 5
7.	c	Chapter 5
8.	d	Chapter 6
9.	a	Chapter 6
10.	a	Chapter 7
11.	a	Chapter 7
12.	c	Chapter 8
13.	c	Chapter 8
14.	b	Chapter 9
15.	d	Chapter 10
16.	b	Chapter 11
17.	a	Chapter 12
18.	b	Chapter 12
19.	a	Chapter 13
20.	d	Chapter 14

Western Schools® offers over 2,000 hours to suit all your interests – and requirements!

Cardiovascular

Cardiovascular Nursing: A Comprehensive Overview (2nd ed.)
Cardiovascular Pharmacology (2nd ed.)
A The 12-Lead ECG in Acute Coronary Syndromes (3rd ed.)
Women and Cardiovascular Disease (2nd ed.)

Clinical Conditions/Nursing Practice

A Advanced Assessment (2nd ed.)
Ambulatory Surgical Care (2nd ed.)
Arterial Blood Gases: A Systematic and Easy Approach
Assessment of Pain in Special Populations
Clinical Care of the Diabetic Foot (2nd ed.)
A Complete Nurses Guide to Diabetes Care (2nd ed.)
Chronic Obstructive Lung Disease
Death, Dying, & Bereavement (2nd ed.)
Diabetes Essentials for Nurses (2nd ed.)
Essentials of Patient Education
Fibromyalgia in Women
Genetic & Inherited Disorders of the Pulmonary System
Helping the Obese Patient Find Success
Holistic & Complementary Therapies
Home Health Nursing (3rd ed.)
Humor in Health Care: The Laughter Prescription (2nd ed.)
IV Therapy: Essentials for Safe Practice
Management of Systemic Lupus Erythematosus
Multiple Sclerosis: Nursing Strategies to Improve Patient Outcomes
Orthopedic Nursing: Caring for Patients with Musculoskeletal Disorders (2nd ed.)
Ostomy Management
Pain Management: Principles and Practice
A Palliative Practices: An Interdisciplinary Approach
Pharmacologic Management of Asthma
Pneumonia in Adults
Pulmonary Rehabilitation
Rotator Cuff Injury and Recovery
Seizures: A Basic Overview
Wound Management and Healing (2nd ed.)

Critical Care/ER/OR

Acute Respiratory Distress Syndrome (ARDS)
Adult Acute Respiratory Infections (UPDATED 1st ed.)
Auscultation Skills (4th ed.)
   — Heart Sounds
   — Breath Sounds
Basic Trauma Nursing
Critical Care & Emergency Nursing
Fire Risk Reduction for Operative and Invasive Procedures
Hemodynamic Monitoring
Lung Transplantation
A Practical Guide to Moderate Sedation/Analgesia
Traumatic Brain Injury

Geriatrics

Alzheimer's Disease: A Complete Guide for Nurses
Alzheimer's Disease and Related Disorders
Cognitive Disorders in Aging
Depression in Older Adults
Early-Stage Alzheimer's Disease
Geriatric Assessment
Healthy Aging
Nursing Care of the Older Adult (2nd ed.)
Psychosocial Issues Affecting Older Adults (2nd ed.)
Substance Abuse in Older Adults

Infectious Diseases

Avian (H5N1) Influenza (2nd ed.)
H1N1 Flu (2nd ed.)
Hepatitis C: The Silent Killer (2nd ed.)
HIV/AIDS
Infection Prevention for Healthcare Professionals
Influenza: A Vaccine-Preventable Disease (4th ed.)
MRSA
Pertussis: Diagnosis, Treatment, and Prevention
Tuberculosis Across the Lifespan
West Nile Virus (3rd ed.)

Oncology

Cancer in Women (UPDATED 2nd ed.)
Cancer Nursing
Chemotherapy and Biotherapies
Lung Cancer (UPDATED 2nd ed.)
Skin Cancer

Pediatrics/Maternal-Child/Women's Health

A Assessment and Care of the Well Newborn
Birth Control Methods and Reproductive Choices
Birth Defects Affecting the Respiratory System
Childhood Obesity
Diabetes in Children (2nd ed.)
Effective Counseling Techniques for Perinatal Mood Disorders
Fetal and Neonatal Drug Exposure
Induction of Labor
Manual of School Health (3rd ed.)
Maternal-Newborn Nursing
Menopause: Nursing Care for Women Throughout Mid-Life
A Obstetric and Gynecologic Emergencies (4th ed.)
   — Obstetric Emergencies
   — Gynecologic Emergencies
Pediatric Abusive Head Trauma
Pediatric Health & Physical Assessment
Perinatal Mood Disorders: An Overview
Pregnancy Loss
Respiratory Diseases in the Newborn
Women's Health: Contemporary Advances and Trends (3rd ed.)

Professional Issues/Management/Law

Ethical Issues in Children's Health Care
Ethical Practices with Older Adults
Legal Implications for Nursing Practice
Protecting Patient Safety: Preventing Medical Errors
Management and Leadership in Nursing
Ohio Nursing Law Affecting Daily Practice

Psychiatric/Mental Health

A ADHD in Children and Adults
Adoptive Families: Trends and Therapeutic Interventions
Asperger's Syndrome
Attention Deficit Hyperactivity Disorders Throughout the Lifespan
Behavioral Approaches to Treating Obesity
Best Practices With Lesbian, Gay, and Bisexual Youth and Their Families
A Bipolar Disorder
Bullies, Victims, and Bystanders: From Prevalence to Prevention
Caring for Patients with Mental Health Issues: Strategies for All Nurses
A Child/Adolescent Clinical Psychopharmacology (2nd ed.)
A Childhood Maltreatment
Childhood Trauma
A Clinical Psychopharmacology Made Simple (7th ed.)
Clinical Neuropsychology: Applications in Practice
A Collaborative Therapy with Multi-stressed Families
Counseling Substance Abusing or Dependent Adolescents
Depression: Prevention, Diagnosis, and Treatment
Disaster Mental Health
A Ethnicity and the Dementias
A Evidence-Based Mental Health Practice
Evidence-Based Practice: What Every Nurse Needs to Know
Grief, Bereavement, and Mourning in Children and Adults
A Growing Up with Autism
Identifying and Assessing Suicide Risk in Adults
Identifying and Treating Young and Adult Children of Alcoholics
A Integrative Treatment for Borderline Personality Disorder
Intimate Partner Violence: An Overview
Major Depression in Adults: Signs, Symptoms & Treatment Strategies
A Mental Disorders in Older Adults
A Mindfulness and Psychotherapy
A Multicultural Perspectives in Working with Families
Multidimensional Health Assessment of the Older Adult
A Obsessive Compulsive Disorder
Post-Divorce Parenting: Mental Health Issues and Interventions
Posttraumatic Stress Disorder: An Overview
A Problem and Pathological Gambling
Psychiatric Nursing: Current Trends in Diagnosis (2nd ed.)
Psychopharmacology for Nurses
A Psychosocial Aspects of Disaster
A Schizophrenia
Schizophrenia: Signs, Symptoms, and Treatment Strategies
Serious Mental Illness: Comprehensive Case Management
Sexual Health Counseling
Substance Abuse (UPDATED 1st ed.)
Suicide
A Trauma Therapy
A Treating Explosive Kids
A Treating Substance Use Problems in Psychotherapy Practice
A Treating Victims of Mass Disaster and Terrorism
Understanding Attachment Theory
Understanding Loss & Grief: Implications for Healthcare Professionals

Visit our website at **www.WesternSchools.com**
for course descriptions and additional CE offerings!
REV 12-19-12